Shakespeare's Labored Art

Studies in Shakespeare

Robert F. Willson, Jr.
General Editor

Vol. 3

PETER LANG
New York • Washington, D.C./Baltimore • San Francisco
Bern • Frankfurt am Main • Berlin • Vienna • Paris

Maurice Hunt

Shakespeare's Labored Art

Stir, Work, and the Late Plays

PETER LANG
New York • Washington, D.C./Baltimore • San Francisco
Bern • Frankfurt am Main • Berlin • Vienna • Paris

Library of Congress Cataloging-in-Publication Data

Hunt, Maurice.
   Shakespeare's labored art: stir, work, and the late plays / Maurice Hunt
     p.   cm. — (Studies in Shakespeare; vol. 3)
   Includes bibliographical references and index.
   1. Shakespeare, William, 1564-1616—Criticism and interpretation. 2. Shakespeare, William, 1564-1616—Views on work. 3. Work—Religious aspects—Christianity. 4. Courts and courtiers in literature. 5. Working class in literature. 6. Work in literature. I. Title. II Series.
PR3069. W67H86   822.3'3—dc20   94-45385
ISBN 0-8204-2737-3
ISSN 1067-0823

Die Deutsche Bibliothek-CIP-Einheitsaufnahme

Hunt, Maurice:
Shakespeare's labored art: stir, work, and the late plays / Maurice Hunt.-
New York; Washington, D.C./Baltimore; San Francisco; Bern; Frankfurt
am Main; Berlin; Vienna; Paris: Lang.
   (Studies in Shakespeare; Vol. 3)
   ISBN 0-8204-2737-3
NE: GT

Cover design by James F. Brisson.

The paper in this book meets the guidelines for permanence and durability
of the Committee on Production Guidelines for Book Longevity of the
Council on Library Resources.

© 1995 Peter Lang Publishing, Inc., New York

All rights reserved.
Reprint or reproduction, even partially, in all forms such as microfilm,
xerography, microfiche, microcard, and offset strictly prohibited.

Printed in the United States of America

For Alison and Jeffrey,
Andrew and Thomas

Table of Contents

Preface ix

I. Work and Shakespeare's Age 1

II. From *Hamlet* to *Timon of Athens*:
Work in Shakespeare's Later Plays 27

III. *Pericles* 71

IV. *Cymbeline* 95

V. *The Winter's Tale* 135

VI. *The Tempest* 163

VII. *King Henry VIII* 199

VIII. *The Two Noble Kinsmen* 231

IX. Shakespeare's Labored Art 259

List of Works Cited 279

Index 305

Preface

This book originally saw life in 1982 in the form of an article, "'Stir' and Work in Shakespeare's Last Plays," which was published in *Studies in English Literature*. But it was only after 1990 that the idea of Shakespeare's labored art, extending from the late tragedies through *The Two Noble Kinsmen*, occurred to me. An eight-month 1991 Baylor University sabbatical gave me the opportunity to nurture my infant thought into the present, more robust offspring. Its faults must be surely blamed on its parent. I have distantly alluded to literary birth labor and delivery, chiefly because writing about the various manifestations of work and their consequences in Shakespeare's later plays makes one particularly susceptible to the pervasiveness of labor. Secretly I suspect that a protestant (I hesitate to say puritanical) streak in my temperament led me to choose and develop the topic of Shakespeare's labored art. Whatever strain or laboriousness the reader detects in the following pages should not be attributed to my project's enablers.

To my wife Pamela and our children Alison, Jeffrey, Andrew, and Thomas, I owe any grace of argument apparent in these chapters; repeatedly they drew me away from my labored pursuit of Shakespeare's representation of work into family play and communion. This book is dedicated to my four "only begetter[s]." To Dr. James Barcus and Dr. William Cooper, Chairman of the English Department and Dean of the College of Arts and Sciences at Baylor University, I owe the aforementioned sabbatical and the equally important daily encouragement of my research in Shakespeare and English Renaissance drama. My fellow Baylor Shakespearean, Paul W. White, has been the colleague that we all desire but rarely get to enjoy; this book is a better piece of writing because of his friendship. Finally, I owe more than I can express to Ms. Martha Kalnin, my graduate research assistant, who meticulously and cheerfully processed this manuscript several times, saved me from several outrageous errors, and made several intelligent suggestions for its improvement.

All quotations of Shakespeare's plays are taken from *The Riverside Shakespeare*, ed. G. Blakemore Evans, et al. Parts of this book first appeared as essays: "'Stir' and Work in Shakespeare's Last Plays," reprinted by permission of *Studies in English Literature 1500-1900*, 22, 2 (Spring 1982); "Work, Sloth, and Warfare in *Coriolanus*," *Explorations in Renaissance Culture*, Vol. 20 (1994). Reprinted by permission of South-Central Renaissance Conference.

Chapter 1

Work and Shakespeare's Age

The history of labor in Shakespeare's age begins with the Bible and the impact of religious doctrine on successive generations. As Jacques Le Goff has shown, "Christianity did offer a spiritual approach to labor, a veritable theology of work."[1] Later centuries inherited the ambivalent attitude of medieval Christianity toward work. On the one hand, the punishment for original sin entails labor in the sweat of the worker's brow. On the other, work became the qualifying means for a privileged place in Christian society. Paul's pronouncement—"If any would not work, neither should he eat" (2 Thess. 3:10)—became a foundation of medieval preferment. At the end of the ninth century and continuously thereafter, medieval society divided itself into *oratores* (men of prayer), *bellatores* (men of war), and *laboratores* (men of work). The final class mixed rudimentary artisans with manual laborers of all kinds. During the middle ages, both clerics and warriors tended to regard laborers contemptuously. Le Goff notes that "the Church explained the serf's lowly condition as that of society's scapegoat, invoking man's servitude to sin" (110). Manual laborers in the middle ages performed physical penance for the sins of the upper classes who either worked war or conducted the business of the church.

Beginning with the twelfth century, however, a new theology of labor began to emerge, brought about by the specialization of labor in trade guilds and by the birth of the idea of vocation as a consequence of a more developed personal consciousness within the individual. Previously the choice between the active and contemplative lives, between Martha and Mary, or Rachel and Leah, had been weighted toward the thoughtful existence. But beginning with the twelfth century, "there was a rehabilitation of Martha, and in practice manual labor was restored to a place of honor with the Carthusians. . . . The concept of penitential labor was supplanted by the idea of labor as a positive means to salvation."² The Parable of the Vineyard, which stresses that faithful work gains the laborer admittance to the heavenly kingdom, acquired a fresh importance. Chaucer memorably records the medieval reevaluation of work in many portraits and episodes of *The Canterbury Tales*. Manual labor is obviously preferred in the ironic presentation of the gluttonous monk, Hubert, who lazily claims that he sets no store by Augustine's teaching that monks ought to work physically. Conversely, the plowman, close to the earth, laboring in the furrow, becomes one of the most attractive Canterbury pilgrims.

Labor could be revalued in the later middle ages because Judeo-Christian tradition depicts God as a laborer, a worker who had to (or decided to) rest after taking six days to fabricate a world. According to Genesis 2:15, God had put Adam in the Garden "to dress it and to keep it." "Thus before penitential labor, which was a consequence of sin and the Fall," Le Goff concludes that "there had been joyful labor, blessed by God, and earthly labor had kept about it something of the quality of the paradisiacal labor from before the fall" (115). The happy labor of prelapsarian Adam and Eve mirrored the joyous labor of God the universal craftsman. The positive reevaluation of labor, nevertheless, coexisted with the older view of it as a curse or at best a means of penitence—something to be performed by those whom God had not privileged as clerics and warriors (or, later, merchants and even some higher-ranking craftsmen). Like a thread of somber color, the doctrine of cursed work weaves itself throughout the fabric of medieval culture, running below the surface at times to reemerge conspicuously elsewhere.

This brief description of medieval attitudes toward work indicates that Shakespeare's ambivalent depiction of kinds of labor in his late plays grounds itself in a bifurcated view antedating the culture of sixteenth- and seventeenth-century England. By Tudor times, the tripartite classification of society had long since vanished. In 1577, William Harrison distinguished four degrees of people: "gentlemen, citizens or burgesses, yeomen, and artificers or laborers."³ Concerning the latter two degrees, some definitions prove helpful: yeomen were described as either freeholders of land valued at 40 shillings per annum or as farmers of gentlemen, while the lowest stratum of society included "day labourers, poor husbandmen, artificers and servants," people who had "'neither voice nor authoritie in the common wealthe, but are to be ruled and not to rule other.'"⁴ Sir Thomas Wilson's division in 1600 of the English people into nobles, citizens, yeomen, artisans, and rural laborers reveals the essential lines of Harrison's earlier taxonomy.⁵ Despite the division of Elizabethan society into more numerous categories, certain constants remained. The primary work of the nobility was war (although James I's long peace of 1604-1612 would severely erode that hallowed profession), and manual labor continued to condemn men and women to the bottom of society.

Cutting through sixteenth-century horizontal class lines, especially those below the rank of nobility, were distinctive English protestant attitudes toward work. As valuations, they reproduced the divided spirit if not the content of medieval appraisals of labor. Reformation protestants never tired of insisting that their religion based itself on faith and not works, as they claimed Roman Catholicism corruptly did. An understanding of Shakespeare's staging of kinds of labor in its historical context must grapple with the meaning of this claim. "When protestants criticized the doctrine of justification by works," Christopher Hill has written, "they were not saying that charitable works should not be performed. They were attacking the purely formal routine actions by which Roman Catholic theologians taught that merit could be acquired—telling of beads, saying of paternosters, giving of candles. Luther distinguished between 'two kinds of works: those done for others, which are the right kind . . . and those done for ourselves, which are of smaller value.' 'We wear and consume our bodies with watching, fasting and labor, but we neglect charity, which is the only lady and mistress of works. . . . Paul not only teacheth good works, but also condemneth fantastical and superstitious works.'"⁶ Hill concludes that "these 'extern matters and ceremonial observations, nothing conducing to any spiritual purpose' were what the reformers had most of all in mind when they denounced 'works.' . . . Where 'good works' in the wider sense were concerned—acts of mercy or charity—a protestant thought that *what* a man did was less important than the spirit in which he did it" (83).

The reason for this distinction can be traced to the Calvinism informing Reformation protestantism. Article XVII of the Church of England (1563) endorsed the continental protestant doctrine that a man or woman in this life can do nothing to alter his or her election or reprobation, which was fixed by God before birth. Doctrinal English protestants knew that the performance of good works was important, but they also knew that these works could not save them, even if their number were infinite. "By their doing though not for their doing," the elect are saved wrote Thomas Taylor (1576-1633).[7] Martha Rozett has assembled considerable evidence that the great majority of Elizabethan protestants—not surprisingly—thought of themselves as members of the elect rather than as reprobates.[8] Protestants with a sense of their own election theoretically saved themselves by their doing, by their good works, when deeds of charity became proof of the doer's prior election, both in the eyes of beholders and in the mind of the worker him- or herself. The constant performance of good works became a crucial part of that stage in the protestant paradigm of salvation known as justification.[9]

One of the greatest gifts of Reformation protestants to succeeding generations was their reaffirmation of the dignity and beauty of all forms of labor, especially manual work of the most basic and life-sustaining kind, performed in the conviction that labor offered to God constitutes ennobling human activity. Early protestant churchmen such as Bishop Jewell insisted upon the notion of free craftsmen; their theories took "for granted that property in a man's own labour and person which wage labourers had lost" under Catholic rule. "'A servant with this clause/ Makes drudgery divine,'" George Herbert later wrote, "'Who sweeps a room, as for thy laws,/ Makes that and the action fine.'"[10] "'A cobbler, a smith, a farmer, each has the work and office of his task,'" Luther had written, "'and yet they are all alike consecrated priests and bishops, and every one by means of his own work or office must benefit and serve every other, that in this way many kinds of work be done for the bodily and spiritual welfare of the community.'"[11] Charles and Katherine George, in their analysis of English protestant economic theory, have defined the protestant doctrine of calling as the Christian's divinely ordained life work, performed "'to exercise the gifts He hath bestowed upon us.'"[12] The 1559 Prayer Book catechism contains the following injunction: "'to learn and labour truly to get mine own living, and to do my duty in that state of life unto which it shall please God to call me.'"[13] Laboring "truly" in one's calling often had an almost prelapsarian spiritual loveliness about it for the devout protestant, especially if the labor was manual. Despite a fall from grace, he or she through manual work could recreate those powerful and attractive vignettes of simple labor celebrated in certain parables of the New Testament. "The Roman Catholic tradition as represented by St. Thomas" had "made a sharp and invidious distinction between mental and manual toil or the liberal and servile arts."[14] But as the Georges demonstrate, "the metaphors, the examples, the images in English Protestant discussion of the necessity of work are drawn almost entirely from the terms and tasks associated with labor with the hands. The sheep to be watched, the vineyard or the garden to be cared for, the sweat that drops from the diligent worker's brow—these are the references one meets repeatedly. . . . 'The labour of a Christian,' Thomas Adams remarks, 'is like the labour of an husbandman . . . it is endlesse; they have perpetually somewhat to doe, either plowing, or sowing, or reaping.' It is Adams who, starting again from a metaphor of the husbandman, states precisely and emphatically the essential quality of all Christian toil: 'Every one thinkes himselfe Gods sonne: then heare this voyce, Goe my sonne. You have all your vineyards to goe to. Magistrates Goe to the Temple, to preach, to pray, to doe the workes of Evangelists. People Goe to your callings, that you may eate the labours of your owne hands . . . every man to his profession, according to that station, wherein God hath disposed us. . . . The incitation gives way to the Injunction, worke'" (131-32).

Michael Walzer has chronicled the extent to which godly protestants "tended to set themselves apart from both the idle rich and the men whom the rich supported, ex-soldiers, actors, beggars, and the multitude of the urban poor who sought occasional employment."[15] The Puritan minister Samuel Hieron proclaimed that mankind's work is "'the testimony of his religion.' . . . 'He that hath no honest business about which ordinarily to be employed' . . . 'no settled course to which he may betake himself, cannot please God.'"[16] The word "'business' like 'industry,'" Walzer notes, "had taken on a new meaning in the course of the sixteenth century: to a word which originally meant merely occupation or trade, but which until the 1580's also carried the implication of mischief and impertinence, there had been superadded a sense of diligence and systematic activity" (211-12). Manual work consolingly structured socially isolated godly protestants' personal worlds. Labor sweetly performed not only helped one's fellow man; it also served to discipline the protestant's daily life, becoming the principal bulwark against the temptations of sloth and idleness. Godly protestants' praise of work often sprang not from a belief in the inherent value of labor but from a fear of idleness as the nurse of sin. Granted social dislocation, a fact exacerbated by the traditional English practice of placing children as servants in other people's families, the many parishes without ministers, and a decline in a once vigorous parish social life, many protestants found systematic work to be a substitute organization for lost structures and patterns. Work could calm the disoriented and the anxious amid the underworld of London crowds.

Walzer reveals that Elizabethan preachers often stressed the practical advantages of hard work rather than its spiritual significance. Milton would later focus this deflection of godly protestant teaching by giving prelapsarian Eve the questionable opinion that she and Adam must occupy themselves with lopping and pruning the garden lest its luxuriant growth overwhelm them. St. Ambrose had allegorized the Genesis passage concerning prelapsarian work to signify the exercise of humanity's intellect, a symbolic interpretation that Augustine called "'an honorable pleasure of the mind.'"[17] Francis Bacon in *The Advancement of Learning* tapped an Augustinian tradition when he wrote, "After the creation was finished, it is set down unto us that man was placed in the garden to work therein; which work so appointed to him could be no other than work of contemplation; that is, when the end of work is but for exercise and experiment, not for necessity."[18] Yet necessity is precisely the quality communicated by Milton's Eve as she tells Adam of the quick growth of the garden and their need for additional hands. Milton poignantly captures the unfortunate transformation of the godly protestant attitude that work amounts to a physical kind of joyous prayer into the grim conviction that it must be compulsively, anxiously performed at the command of a taskmaster.[19]

Like medieval Christianity's view of work, that of the Reformation was thus Janus-faced, though in different ways and for different reasons. Shakespeare's dramatization of labor in his late plays ultimately reflects the ambiguous, bifurcated attitudes of different segments of his culture. Usually godly protestants limited the privilege of dignifying labor to the middle class, excluding lords, gentry, and the urban poor from its salutary effects. It was not with love but hostility that many godly protestants greeted courtiers and beggars.[20] In his *Treatise of the Vocations* (publ. 1603), William Perkins "listed four groups of men who possess 'no particular calling to walk in,' who live outside the vocational world. The list included: 1) rogues, beggars and vagabonds; 2) monks and friars; 3) gentlemen who 'spend their days in eating and drinking'; and 4) servants—'for only to wait . . . is not a sufficient calling.' All these were dangerous men thought Perkins, because they were not subject to control and discipline."[21] Protestants founded work houses for beggars and vagabonds and their children. It never seemed to occur to them that debilitating poverty might be a condition involuntarily accepted by wretched men and women. Making poor people incapacitated by disease and malnutrition work was cruel. Sadly, the godly protestant prejudice that idleness was freely chosen by the poor applied to the native populations of the New World. According to Stephen Greenblatt, "that the Indians were idle, that they lacked all work discipline, was proved, to the satisfaction of Europeans, by the demonstrable fact that they made wretched slaves, dying after a few weeks or even days of hard labor."[22] Europeans accused the Indians, if freed from slavery, of "'wandering up and down'" after the fashion of

Elizabethan masterless men and women; thus colonizers renewed their "vast projects undertaken to fix and enclose the native populations in the mines, in ecomiendas, in fortified hamlets, and ultimately, in mass graves."[23] In other words, they imported the equivalent of Reformation work houses to a new land.

Co-existing with protestant attitudes toward work were other English Renaissance perspectives on labor, the most notable of which derived from Bacon's revolution of scientific method. Important for understanding the significance of Bacon's emphasis upon industry and scientific work is the Jacobean belief that the world had decayed from its heroic youth and was in its old age—in fact, near death and dissolution.[24] Corrupt humanity's labor, despite workers' good intentions, seemed to many people to hasten the anticipated cosmic dissolution. "Wee seeme ambitious, Gods whole work t'undoe," Donne wrote in *The First Anniversary*; "Of nothing hee made us, and we strive too,/ To bring our selves to nothing backe" (ll. 155-57).[25] Original sin causes men and women to "unwork" themselves, to undo the results of their prior labors. Humankind, noble in reason, infinite in faculties, Hamlet reminds us, is a piece of God's work who is only a "quintessence of dust." The paradox of God's glorious handiwork manifesting his or her unworked (or nonworked) nature—dust—escaped few writers of the period. Jonathan Dollimore has described the sixteenth- and seventeenth-century English opposition to the theory of a rapidly decaying universe. Believing that subscribing to the theory entails a condition of hopeless sloth, opponents such as George Hakewill "argued that 'there is not so much feare of Innovation from the country boares.... if they be once persuaded that nothing can bee improved by industry but all things by a fatall necessity grow worse and worse.'"[26] The fatal necessity inherent in gloomy views of the cosmos touched even God himself, as Thomas Nash suggests in *Summer's Last Will and Testament*: "'Men die in thousands, and then thousands, yea, many times in hundred thousands, in one battle. If then the best husband be so liberal of his best handiwork, to what end should we ... doubt to spend at a banquet as many pounds as He spends men at a battle.'"[27] The implication that God was a careless workman in making—and destroying—humanity can provide an explanation, although a discomforting one, for the compulsion with which many Elizabethans unworked themselves.

Within the context of these cultural beliefs, Bacon's advocacy of scientific industry and the performance of new works gains added meaning. "Of all signs there is none more certain or more noble than that taken from fruits," Bacon wrote in *The New Organon*: "For fruits and works are as it were sponsors and sureties for the truth of philosophy. . . . They too who have busied themselves with natural magic . . . have but few discoveries to show, and those trifling and imposture-like. Wherefore, as in religion we are warned to show our faith by works, so in philosophy by the same rule the system should be judged by its fruits."[28] We will return to Bacon's comparison of magic to empirical industry when we analyze Shakespeare's suggestion that Prospero regards the practice of magic as his distinctive labor. For now, realizing that Bacon believed that works of a scientific or empirical nature would increase and become easier to perform in the seventeenth century is enough. "For the old age of the world is to be accounted the true antiquity," he judged; if the early seventeenth century "but knew its own strength and chose to essay and exert it, much more might fairly be expected than from the ancient times, inasmuch as it is a more advanced age of the world and stocked with infinite experiments and observations. . . . And as it was said of spiritual things, 'The kingdom of God cometh not with observation,' so it is in all the greater works of Divine Providence; everything glides on smoothly and noiselessly, and the work is fairly going on before men are aware it has begun. Nor should the prophecy of Daniel be forgotten, touching the last ages of the world:—'Many shall go to and fro, and knowledge shall be increased'; clearly intimating that the thorough passage of the world (which now by so many distant voyages seems to be accomplished, or in course of accomplishment), and the advancement of the sciences, are destined by fate, that is, by Divine Providence, to meet in the same age."[29] Granted Bacon's sanguine conviction that the work of providence "glides on smoothly and noiselessly," "fairly going on before men are aware it has begun," readers find ironic his later confession that he himself has produced few works of the new method.[30] Like godly protestants' pragmatic, even self-serving, implementation of supposedly spiritual regimes of labor, Bacon's practice (in this case, his limited practice) of his new philosophy of scientific works appears to qualify its optimism.

Thus far we have been investigating mainly protestant theorizing about the place of work in a life. When we turn to actual Elizabethan and Jacobean work practices, we find labor theory partly confirmed but mainly contradicted or denied. Unfortunately the court of King James and the nobility in general behaved themselves so as to invite godly protestants' stereotypes of the upper classes as idle and addicted to vicious pleasures. In this respect, James, the king under whom Shakespeare most fully explored the question of labor, set the tone for aristocrats and even gentry. Obviously demonstrating that James was less industrious than his predecessor Elizabeth I would prove exceedingly difficult, if not impossible. A poetic passage in *A Midsummer Night's Dream* suggests that on occasion Shakespeare may have been critical of Elizabeth for the disastrous impact of her imagined idleness on her people. In this comedy, the deflected arrow of Cupid changes the pansy into a concept, love-in-idleness, an idle love that maddens the four Athenian youths with its vagaries. This love is created because the "fair vestal, throned by the west"—Elizabeth—diverts the arrow of romantic love originally aimed at her chaste heart. In the play, Titania, another name for the moon goddess Elizabeth, also refuses to love romantically—in this case, her husband Oberon. Humankind's lost labors result from this reluctance. Oberon's and Titania's quarrel disrupts nature's rhythms, becoming responsible for a train of disasters ending in the lost sweat of the ploughman and the rotting of green corn. In commenting on the play, Annabel Patterson has argued that sixteenth-century artisan and laborer riots may have inspired Shakespeare's image of this last effect of the moon queen's idleness.[31]

Nevertheless, Shakespeare's implied criticism of the queen's idleness, if that is what it is in *A Midsummer Night's Dream*, represents an anomaly in his pre-1603 work. Sloth and idleness never publicly attached themselves to Elizabeth to the extent that they characterized King James. James' dislike of the business of running a court, his temperamental indolence, and his compulsive hunting when he should have been managing affairs of state—these facts were widely known and lamented. In a letter dated 26 January 1605 and addressed to Ralph Winwood, John Chamberlain wrote: "The Kinge went to Roiston two dayes after Twelfetide, where and there about he hath continued ever since, and findes such felicitie in that hunting life, that he hath written to the counsaile, that he be not interrupted nor troubled with to much busines."[32] James' reaction to dire news of the degree to which the cost of extravagant royal entertainments and luxuries had depleted his treasury and increased a national deficit was the weak reply that others would have to work for him. "'My only hope that upholds me is my good servants, that will sweat and labour for my relief,'" Samuel Gardiner reports him as saying.[33] In the words of G. P. V. Akrigg, the king "was a good judge of men and affairs, yet because of inherent laziness failed again and again to enforce policies he knew to be necessary and good."[34] Against the indolent figure of the king and the backdrop of a lazy court, the hunchbacked Robert Cecil, James' Secretary of State, stood out through his appetite for incessant labor. "The King sported and jested while his 'little beagle,' as he termed Cecil, ran his errands and tried to keep the finances and the government of the realm in working order."[35]

Taking their lead from the king, Jacobean courtiers assiduously cultivated a corrupt idleness, a vice-ridden uselessness that, according to Albert Tricomi and Leah Marcus, became the subject of satire and criticism in Jacobean plays and masques. In Jonson, Marston, and Chapman's *Eastward Ho* (1605), "Seagull imagines a life free from corruption and work, except for 'a few industrious Scots perhaps'" (a gibe at the caterpillars that James had brought from Scotland with him), while in John Day's *Isle of Gulls* (1606), Basilius indicts those courtiers sharing James' passion for hunting: "'*Dametas*, were thine eares ever at more musicall banquet? how thy houndes mouthes like bells are tuned one under another like a slothfulness, the speed of the cry outran my sence of hearing.'"[36] James' addiction to hunting made this barb particularly transparent. Presumably idlers hanging about court preferred not to think about the antilabor satire they saw and heard, such as that of the crab emblematic of "gluttons, parasites, [and] toadies" in Jonson's *The Vision of Delight*.[37] Margot Heinemann has shown how Thomas Middleton's *The Black Book* and *Father Hubbard's Tales* (both published in 1604) express "a radical city contempt for the rich and idle—for courtiers and lawyers and parasitic gentry at least as much as dishonest merchants and moneylenders—and an unforced sympathy for the hardships of small tenant-farmers and the working poor."[38] James' remedy for courtly idlers did not involve work but simply repastoralization, repeated commands (largely ignored) that persons not having any pressing business at Whitehall return to their country estates and manors, where they could discipline local society and dispense hospitality. James' ineffective policy is not surprising, especially when considered in light of his own essentially unreal works. His wholesale creation of knighthoods, a practice that sharply contrasted with Elizabeth's stinginess in this regard, was designed to raise instant cash for his empty coffers. But the fact that the multitude of knightings involved no real production on either side highlighted the illusory status of manufactured titles in the minds of many critical observers.[39]

One could argue that the idleness of James and his courtiers represents simply a pronounced spectacle of the traditional sloth of the nobility. Lawrence Stone has pointed out that, for lords, "active personal occupation in a trade or profession was generally thought to be humiliating" during Elizabethan and Stuart times; "the man of business was inferior to the gentleman of leisure who lived off his rents, for as Edward Chamberlayne bluntly stated in 1669 'Tradesmen of All Ages and Nations have been reputed ignoble.'"[40] "'In these days,'" a Jacobean wrote, "'he is a gentleman who is commonly taken and reputed. And whosoever studieth in the universities, who professeth the liberall sciences and to be short who can live idly and without manuall labour and will bear the port, charge and countenance of a gentleman, he shall be called master.'"[41] Since the middle ages, war had been the primary work of the nobility, but with the long peace of 1604-1612, the venerable idleness of the aristocracy became even more apparent. Robert Burton, writing in *The Anatomy of Melancholy*, who termed idleness "the bane of body and minde, the nurse of naughtiness, stepmother of discipline, the chiefe author of all mischiefe, one of the seaven deadly sinnes," also labeled it "the badge of gentry."[42] Burton crystallizes an opinion held for centuries: "idlenesse is an appendix to nobility, they count it a disgrace to worke, and spend all their daies in sports, recreations, and pastimes, and will therefore take no paines; be of no vocation: they feed liberally, fare well, want exercise, action, employment, (for to worke, I say they may not abide) and company to their desires, and thence their bodies become full of grosse humors, winde, crudities, their mindes disquieted, dull, heavy" (1:240). In short, idleness was regarded as a major cause of melancholy among the nobility. Shakespeare in *Cymbeline* gives aristocratically trained Posthumus Leonatus a causeless melancholy, which dissipates once his own misdoings compel him to travel and suffer hardships. Ironically, King James anticipates Burton's tracing of the gentry's ills to idleness. Writing in the *Basilikon Doron*, a textbook on royal rule intended for Prince Henry, James insists upon the necessity of physical exercise and industry "for banishing of idlenesse (the mother of all vice)."[43] Physical exercise the king may have gotten from his incessant hunting, but the habit of industry could not be detected in him.

Thus many members of the gentry and aristocracy complied with godly protestants' stereotypes of idle men and women, adverse to honest labor. However, in all fairness to more industriously inclined members of these classes, the difficulty of finding suitable work during the late Elizabethan and early Jacobean periods should be noted here. G. K. Hunter has memorably detailed the bleak prospect in the latter decades of the sixteenth century of employment in traditional occupations awarded university graduates.[44] This bleak prospect drove a number of college-educated men to seek patrons for their poetry and paying audiences for—from a godly protestant viewpoint—their scurvy plays. Mark Curtis has demonstrated that the Tudor universities "unwittingly worked against the peace and tranquility of the realm not because they instilled subversive doctrines but because they prepared too many men for too few places."[45] The result led to the stage portrait of the malcontent, perfected by Webster, Chapman, and Tourneur, whose jaundiced turn to wickedness comes after he has been unable to find meaningful employment.[46] Finally, the physical abuse and hard working and living conditions that apprentices often endured made the practice distasteful to noninheriting younger sons of the gentry and nobility, causing them to break their bond and driving them into the large crowd of their dispossessed peers attending plays, bear-baitings, and other pastimes condemned by godly protestants.[47]

Before describing the actual working—and nonworking—conditions of yeomen, tenant farmers, and the lower classes during Shakespeare's age, we should note a final pejorative judgment on the "labor" of landed gentry and the nobility, in this case a self-administered one. At approximately the time that Shakespeare was writing *The Tempest*, King James was making members of Parliament and the privileged constituencies that they represented feel like dispossessed, involuntary laborers. J. P. Sommerville has remarked that "in 1610 James I warned his subjects not to dispute what a king could do. The lawyer Thomas Wentworth ignored the warning, observing that the subject would lose his liberty if royal actions could not be questioned: 'if we shall once say that we may not dispute the prerogative, let us be sold for slaves.'"[48] English common law had for centuries protected property in lands and goods from royal seizure. "If the king had extra-legal powers to take property," Sommerville concludes, "subjects would be no better off than villeins, or beggarly foreigners. They would have no incentive to work, since they could not call the products of their labour their own" (148-49). The taxed classes' picture of themselves as slaves or at best villeins persisted throughout Shakespeare's final phase of playwriting. When the 1614 Parliament refused to grant spendthrift James his requested subsidies, the king angrily levied a benevolence—a form of tax not requiring mutual consent. Prosecuted in Star Chamber for refusal to pay it, Oliver St. John attempted to defend himself by claiming that his labor in his land was not his own if the king could extort the financial proceeds of it from him.[49] Faced with this threat from their monarch, upper-class Englishmen were prone to cultivate their time-honored idleness.

Those who suffered the most, however, were artisans, wage laborers, and poor farmers. Certain provisions in the Statute of Artificers of 1563 and the Vagrancy Act of 1572 virtually enslaved thousands of poor English men, women, and children. An Elizabethan or Jacobean worker could not freely dispose of his or her labor unless he or she owned property valued at 40 shillings per annum, stood to inherit property worth at least this value, or owned material goods appraised at £10. Exceptions were granted only to members of certain callings, chiefly those of clergy, scholar, collier, and miner. Craft masters might ask for and compel the labor of persons under age thirty who had completed apprenticeship in a trade. Anyone between the ages of twelve and sixty who was neither a bound apprentice nor the practitioner of a craft could be forced to work as a farm laborer, even by a householder with only half a plowland in tillage.[50] Refusal to do so entailed the punishment for vagrancy—whipping. All laborers were required to work from five in the morning to seven or eight at night from mid-March to mid-September (in this case, the Statute of Artificers reaffirmed provisions from the Statute of Laborers of 1495); during the rest of the year, they were to work from daybreak to nightfall. Only two-and-a-half hours a day could be taken for eating, drinking, and rest.[51] While these regulations were usually unenforced or ignored,[52] they reflect the harsh restrictive spirit of the Statute of Artificers. This legislation was calculated to insure an adequate supply of corn and foodstuffs for the nation and to eliminate the evils of idleness and vagrancy, which were thought to be the nurses of social unrest and outright rebellion. It was stipulated that workers could not leave their employment without their employers' written consent. Nevertheless, population increases continued to outstrip the number of acres in tillage, and not everyone eligible for compulsory apprenticeship or husbandry was employed. Sadly, the Statute of 1563 mainly "had the effect of depressing wages and lowering the status of all wage-labourers in town and country."[53]

Throughout the Elizabethan and Jacobean periods, but especially in the decades on either side of the year 1600, population growth outran the food supply, creating galloping inflation, exorbitant food prices, and the seizure of ancient farm lands for the grazing of highly profitable livestock. Despite outbreaks of bubonic plague, England's population rose from approximately two-and-a-half million people in the 1520s to perhaps three-and-a-half million by 1580 and five million by 1680. By 1600, London had grown from a city of 50,000-60,000 souls in the 1520s to 200,000-250,000.[54] Keith Wrightson notes that "the average prices of foodstuffs in southern England, which had remained fairly stable throughout the later fifteenth century, had trebled by the 1570s, and by the early decades of the seventeenth century they had risen sixfold, stabilizing only after 1630 and falling somewhat thereafter."[55] In a burgeoning labor market, wages for workers rose slowly. Real wages bottomed out in the early decades of the seventeenth century, when they were less than the real wages of the early sixteenth century. Susan Amussen has computed that "between 1500 and 1620 the real income of English wage labourers was cut at least in half, as prices multiplied and wages merely tripled."[56] As higher prices for foodstuffs forced farmers of small acreage, say, five to fifty acres, to sell their lands to buy progressively more expensive foodstuffs and necessities for themselves and their families, they joined the increasing pool of vagrant cottagers and wage laborers (who themselves were often forced to sell the acre-or-less plot on which they maintained subsistence gardens). Wrightson has chronicled a tragic story of once self-sufficient men and women and their children made beggars by this process of dispossession.[57] New epidemics swept through the English countryside and towns—vagrancy and social violence.[58]

Landed gentry and nobility strapped for funds to maintain a lavish lifestyle at a sumptuously competitive court took advantage of the market by altering hallowed leases for tenant farmers and even yeomen holding large tracts of land to reflect rapidly changing economic conditions.[59] Outraged that lease-owners now required them to pay much more for their leases than their fathers and grandfathers had paid, farmers of small acreage often could not renew their contracts. They bitterly yielded to the agricultural entrepreneurs capitalizing upon the sudden upward shift in the value of land and became wage laborers and workers in cottage industries. Gentlemen constituted about 2% of the population in the early seventeenth century; yet according to Wrightson, "they owned perhaps 50% of the nation's land, with an additional 15% in the possession of the peerage" (24). As for the most prosperous craftsmen, Wrightson calculates that they "tended to enjoy incomes and living standards comparable to those of lesser yeomen and husbandmen, as is evident from taxation assessments and the evidence of wills and inventories. . . ." Other craftsmen "more sporadically engaged, or plying less well-paid trades, or employed at piece rates in domestic industry, were often more akin to laborers" (35).

In the first decade of the seventeenth century, typical wages had sunk to a shilling for a day's work—hardly enough to feed a family. Only now are social historians beginning to document the appreciably large number of deaths from starvation in the England of Elizabeth and James. A regularly employed man in the south of England in the early seventeenth century might earn a maximum of £10.8s. a year, with £9 the average. The costs of subsistence for an average family for this time period have been estimated at between £11-14 annually, with prices substantially higher in years of special scarcity and high food prices. Christopher Hill records that "in Sir Arthur Ingram's Yorkshire alum works wages in James I's reign were often nine months in arrears. The workers complained that they were grossly overworked, paid in kind, with goods seriously overvalued, and that the contractors were deliberately aiming to ruin their credit locally so as to reduce them to complete economic dependence. In such circumstances men fought desperately to avoid the abyss of wage-labour."[60] By the later seventeenth century, wage laborers would make up half of the English population. For the first time in English history, poverty became an inevitable consequence of wage labor.[61] Often unemployed, the poor from the countryside seeking (usually unavailable) employment swelled London, offsetting the city death rate from plague and disease, living cramped in old houses cut up into tiny apartments outside the city walls.[62]

Alternatively, many uprooted men, women, and children sought refuge in the extensive forests and meadows of preindustrial England. There at least they could eke out a living off wasteland. The poverty and teeming populations of Elizabethan and Jacobean forests contrast with contemporary poets' celebration of the pastoral life. Shakespeare's countrymen generally thought that living off forests and wastes fostered idleness. "Of cottagers in Rockingham Forest an Elizabethan surveyor said 'so long as they may be permitted to live in such idleness upon their stock of cattle, they will bend themselves to no kind of labour.'"[63] Cottagers and squatters in forests and on wastes and commons, however, often worked hard at cottage industries such as blacksmithing, tinkering, nail-making, and basket-making. They toiled in garden plots and in nut and herb gathering.[64] By contemporary accounts, the forest of Arden near Shakespeare's Stratford bustled with life, amounting in parts to an extended village. In many cases, these squatters were better off than servants and wage laborers of arable lands and the cities, for they not only fared better but owing obedience to no lord or leaseholder, also enjoyed a freedom that their counterparts had forfeited. But because they were masterless and considered to be idle drones, in 1610 King James urged the House of Commons to raze the multitude of cottages on waste grounds and in forests. Disafforestation, enclosure, and fen drainage gradually became government policy for dealing with a sizable segment of England's population. Rationalized as the means to drive purported rogues to honest work elsewhere, the policy in fact proved cruel. Masking land owners' greed to enclose even more ground for grazing, it added to the masses of starving beggars in London and throughout the countryside. For James, repastoralization applied only to the lords and gentry in London who pestered him for preferment.

Before we turn to Shakespeare's plays themselves, several important distinctions need to be made. Beginning with the petty gentry and extending to the lowest register of Elizabethan and Jacobean society, women worked alongside men; except for the hardest physical labor (but then many lower-class women performed it), women shared men's work. If a husband cultivated and harvested a crop, his wife might be by his side—or in the kitchen or at the hearth processing the fruit of her husband's labor. Nevertheless, the very name for giving birth to a child—labor—identifies English Renaissance women's special work. This work leveled women of every social class. Elizabeth

Sacks has demonstrated the degree to which the motif and imagery of birth-labor pervades Shakespeare's plays.[65] In her first chapter, she describes Elizabethan and Jacobean male writers' appropriation of the metaphor of childbirth to depict their own creative labors. For Sacks, their depiction becomes a kind of "monosexual literary parenthood" (8). Male writers' application of the motif extended to include the human brain and its thought processes: "Renaissance medical terminology likened the brain to a womb. . . . Medical physicians had followed classical Arabic writers in generally calling the cavities of the brain 'ventricles,' a diminutive term which could mean either 'little belly' or 'little womb'. . . . The two protective membranes sheltering the brain from the cranium were called *pia mater* and *dura mater* ('tender mother' and 'hard mother'), metaphorical names which lead us to a 'womb' reading for the word 'ventricle.' By extension, the brain becomes a locus of conception."[66] If the womb-brain is a place of conception, then the delivery of thought amounts to a kind of labor. "In Iago's declaration, 'My Muse labours,/ And thus she is delivered' (*Othello*, II. i. 128-9)," Sacks asserts that "we can discern a creative process identical with Shakespeare's own: the human mind conceiving a brainchild" (14). This literary topos authorizes Shakespeare's conception of the laboring mind as part of Leontes' and Prospero's characterizations as well as a specified prerequisite for the audience of the play *King Henry VIII*.

In drama, the laboring mind usually becomes most apparent when all stage movement ceases. The intellectual activity usually occurring in the soliloquies of Jacobean dramatic characters is often the most intense of its kind in the play. Montaigne speaks for several contemporary generations when he portrays the natural stir of humanity's mind: "Men misacknowledge the naturall infirmitie of their minde. She doth but quest and firret, and uncessantly goeth turning, winding, building and entangling her selfe in hir worke; as do our silke-worms, and therein stiffleth hir self."[67] It is this busy mind that creates the stasis of meditation. Writing of those who like monks genuinely withdraw from the world's bustle into a solitary place, Robert Burton asserts that "these men are neither solitary nor idle, as the Poet made answere to the husbandman in *AEsop* that objected idleness to him; he was never so idle as in his company: or that *Scipio Africanus* in *Tully, Nunquam minus solus, quam quum solus; nunquam minus, quam quum esset otiosus*: never lesse solitary than when he was alone, never more busie then when he seemed to be most idle."⁶⁸ Shakespeare in his late romances represents this busy mind, incessantly questing and ferreting out, explicitly naming it a "working" mind in *King Henry VIII*. Intellectual activity in fact may so preoccupy the thinker that his body becomes paralyzed. "It is reported by *Plato* in his dialogue *de Amore*," Burton writes, "in that prodigious commendation of *Socrates*, how a deepe meditation coming into *Socrates* mind by change, hee stood still musing, *eodem vestigio cogitabundus*, from morning to noone, and when as then he had not yet finished his meditation, *perstabat cogitans* he so continued till the evening" (1:244). The stir of Socrates' meditative mind attracts all his energy to itself, immobilizing his body, making him as static as a statue. The Socratic example indicates that the possible dynamics of stir and stasis include combinations not easily imagined. Shakespeare's characters labor in their minds often as much (or more) than they do in their bodies.

In summary, protestants may have evoked a doctrine of the dignity of labor during the sixteenth and seventeenth centuries, but the actual work and working conditions of the period generally failed to either illustrate or justify it. On the one hand, the middling sort of gentry, yeomen, and merchants saw a vicious idleness among upper gentry and aristocrats, an indolence based on landed wealth and sanctioned by the attitudes and behavior of King James and Queen Anne. On the other, they viewed with alarm—felt for themselves usually rather than for the victims—a crowded class of poor farmers, wage laborers, servants, and unemployed beggars and vagrants. Jacobean Shakespeare (for reasons to be suggested in the final chapter) memorably responded to his culture's many images of labor nobly performed and unjustly abused by incorporating them in his plays. There, they join other representations of Shakespeare's own creative thinking about work and its place in a life. These images inform *Pericles, Cymbeline, The Winter's Tale, The Tempest, King Henry VIII*, and *The Two Noble Kinsmen* to such an extent that these plays may be regarded as Shakespeare's

Notes

1 Jacques Le Goff, *Time, Work, and Culture in the Middle Ages*, trans. Arthur Goldhammer (Chicago: U of Chicago P, 1980) 110. Le Goff's analysis of Christian attitudes toward labor appears primarily in two chapters of his study: "Labor, Techniques, and Craftsmen in the Value Systems of the Early Middle Ages" (71-86) and "Trades and Professions as Represented in Medieval Confessors' Manuals" (107-21). My summary of medieval attitudes toward work is based upon the information found in these chapters.

2 Le Goff 114, 115.

3 William Harrison, *The Description of England*, ed. Georges Edelen (Ithaca, NY: Cornell UP, 1968) 94.

4 Keith Wrightson, *English Society 1580-1680* (New Brunswick, NJ: Rutgers UP, 1982) 19.

5 Wrightson 21. The known facts of Shakespeare's father's life indicate his rise from class three to class two in Harrison's scheme; his occupation as glover and petty bourgeois separated him from the yeomanry of his father, Richard Shakespeare, and that of the Ardens. The case of his precocious son William, however, is more clouded, with his status as a Stratford property and land owner placing him among the minor gentry, his craft of playwrighting placing him lower among artisans rather than higher among poets, and his profession of acting landing him among servants and those fit "'to be ruled and not to rule other.'"

6 Christopher Hill, "Protestantism and the Rise of Capitalism," *Change and Continuity in Seventeenth-Century England* (Cambridge, MA: Harvard UP, 1975) 81-102, esp. 82-83.

7 Thomas Taylor, *Works* (London: J. Bartlet, 1653) 166.

8 Martha T. Rozett, *The Doctrine of Election and the Emergence of Elizabethan Tragedy* (Princeton, NJ: Princeton UP, 1984) 45-53. Rozett argues that characterizations such as Hieronimo and Richard III gave pleasure to protestant playgoers by strengthening their personal sense of election through the contrary dramatic portrait of a terrible reprobate (3-40).

9 Barbara K. Lewalski, *Protestant Poetics and the Seventeenth-Century Religious Lyric* (Princeton, NJ: Princeton UP, 1979) 16-23.

10 Hill, "Pottage for Freeborn Englishmen: Attitudes to Wage-Labour," *Change and Continuity* 219-38, esp. 234.

labored art. In the next chapter, we will trace the evolution of Shakespeare's dramatic representation of labor from *Hamlet* to *Pericles*, the initial play of the group chosen for special analysis.

11 Hill, *Change and Continuity* 94.

12 Charles H. George and Katherine George, *The Protestant Mind of the English Reformation, 1570-1640* (Princeton, NJ: Princeton UP, 1961) 127-43, esp. 127.

13 Quoted by Susan D. Amussen, *An Ordered Society: Gender and Class in Early Modern England* (Oxford: Basil Blackwell, 1988) 36.

14 George and George 131.

15 Michael Walzer, "The New World of Discipline and Work," *The Revolution of the Saints: A Study in the Origins of Radical Politics* (Cambridge, MA: Harvard UP, 1965) 199-231, esp. 211-12.

16 Walzer 211-12.

17 Peter Lindenbaum, *Changing Landscapes: Anti-Pastoral Sentiment in the English Renaissance* (Athens: U of Georgia P, 1986) 143-44.

18 Francis Bacon, *The Advancement of Learning, Book I*, ed. William A. Armstrong (London: Athlone, 1975) 83.

19 For a contrary reading of Milton's dignifying prelapsarian labor in *Paradise Lost*, see Louis A. Montrose, "Of Gentlemen and Shepherds: The Politics of Elizabethan Pastoral Form," *English Literary History* 50 (1983): 415-59, esp. 426.

20 The hostility is documented by Christopher Hill, *The World Turned Upside Down* (New York: Viking, 1972) 261-63.

21 Walzer 215-16.

22 Stephen Greenblatt, *Renaissance Self-Fashioning: From More to Shakespeare* (Chicago: U of Chicago P, 1980) 183.

23 Greenblatt 183.

24 See Victor Harris, *All Coherence Gone* (Chicago: U of Chicago P, 1949) 86-129.

25 *The Poems of John Donne*, ed. Herbert Grierson (London: Oxford UP, 1964) 212.

26 Jonathan Dollimore, *Radical Tragedy: Religion, Ideology and Power in the Drama of Shakespeare and His Contemporaries* (Chicago: U of Chicago P, 1984) 101.

27 Dollimore 106.

28 Sir Francis Bacon, *The New Organon, The Works of Francis Bacon*, ed. James Spedding, Robert L. Ellis, and Douglas D. Heath (Boston: Taggard & Thompson, 1863) 8:59-350, esp. 104-5.

29 *The New Organon*, Aphorism LXXXIV, 116; Aphorism XCIII, 130.

30 *The New Organon*, Aphorisms CXVII and CXXI, 148-49, 152-53.

31 Annabel Patterson, *Shakespeare and the Popular Voice* (Oxford: Basil Blackwell, 1989) 54-57. The same point is made by Richard Wilson, "'Like the old Robin Hood': *As You Like It* and the Enclosure Riots," *Shakespeare Quarterly* 43 (1992): 1-19, esp. 3-4.

32 *The Letters of John Chamberlain*, ed. Norman E. McClure (Philadelphia: American Philosophical Society, 1939) 1:201. For more on James' sloth and idleness, see *James I by His Contemporaries*, ed. Robert Ashton (London: Hutchinson, 1969) 3, 59; and David M. Bergeron, *Shakespeare's Romances and the Royal Family* (Lawrence: U of Kansas P, 1985) 42.

33 Samuel R. Gardiner, *History of England from the Accession of James I to the Outbreak of the Civil War* (1883-84; rpt. New York: AMS Press, 1965) 1:296.

34 G. P. V. Akrigg, *Jacobean Pageant, or the Court of King James I* (1962; rpt. Atheneum, 1974) 14.

35 Akrigg 105-7.

36 Albert H. Tricomi, *Anticourt Drama in England, 1603-1642* (Charlottesville: U of Virginia P, 1989) 32, 36. Tricomi also notes the corrupt idleness and sloth of the courts depicted in Tourneur's *Revenger's Tragedy* and Webster's *The White Devil* and *The Duchess of Malfi*.

37 Leah S. Marcus, *The Politics of Mirth: Herrick, Milton, Marvell, and the Defense of Old Holiday Pastimes* (Chicago: U of Chicago P, 1986) 72-73.

38 Margot Heinemann, *Puritanism and the Theatre: Thomas Middleton and Opposition Drama under the Early Stuarts* (Cambridge: Cambridge UP, 1980) 52-62, esp. 52-53.

39 Wrightson 20.

40 Lawrence Stone, *The Crisis of the Aristocracy 1558-1641* (Oxford: Clarendon Press, 1965) 39-40. Also see Peter Laslett, *The World We Have Lost: England Before the Industrial Age* (New York: Scribner's, 1971) 27-30.

41 Stone, *Crisis of the Aristocracy* 49-50.

42 Robert Burton, *The Anatomy of Melancholy*, ed. Thomas C. Faulkner, Nicholas K. Kiessling, Rhonda L. Blair (Oxford: Clarendon Press, 1989) 1:238.

43 *The Political Works of James I*, ed. Charles H. McIlwain (Cambridge, MA: Harvard UP, 1918) 48.

44 G. K. Hunter, *John Lyly: The Humanist as Courtier* (London: Routledge & Kegan Paul, 1962) 30-35, 43-88 passim. Also see A. L. Beier, *Masterless Men: The Vagrancy Problem in England 1560-1640* (London: Methuen, 1985) 103. The academic trilogy *The Pilgrimage to Parnassus* (1598-99) and *The Return to Parnassus I and II* (1600, 1603) makes clear that "graduates of the expanded universities were . . . unable to find jobs sufficient for their number" (Paul N. Siegel, *Shakespeare's English and Roman History Plays: A Marxist Approach* [Rutherford, NJ: Fairleigh Dickinson UP, 1986] 87).

45 Mark Curtis, "The Alienated Intellectuals of Early Stuart England," *Past and Present* 23 (1962): 27.

46 See Tricomi 110-20.

47 Roger B. Manning, in *Village Revolts: Social Protest and Popular Disturbances, 1509-1640* (Oxford: Clarendon P, 1988), calculates that "the proportion of gentlemen's sons among the apprentices was increasing in the late sixteenth and early seventeenth centuries to close to one-fifth of those bound"—a fraction of a figure which in 1600 amounted to 30,000 persons in a city of 200,000 people (193).

48 J. P. Sommerville, *Politics and Ideology in England, 1603-1640* (London: Longman, 1986) 101.

49 Sommerville 149.

50 Margaret G. Davies, *The Enforcement of English Apprenticeship, 1563-1642*, Harvard Economic Studies 97 (Cambridge, MA: Harvard UP, 1956) 273.

51 *Tudor Economic Documents*, ed. R. H. Tawney and Eileen Power (London: Longmans, Green, 1924) 1:324.

52 D. C. Colman, "Labour in the English Economy of the Seventeenth Century," *The Economic History Review* 8 (1956): 280-95, esp. 291.

53 Hill, *Change and Continuity* 222.

54 Detailed demographics appear in Peter Clark and Paul Slack, *English Towns in Transition 1500-1700* (London: Oxford UP, 1976) 63-64, 82-84.

55 *English Society 1580-1680* 125. Catharina Lis and Hugo Soly note that in England "between 1500 and 1600 grain prices rose sixfold, while wages

rose only threefold. Not surprisingly, workers and cottars were 'but house beggars' for Francis Bacon." (*Poverty and Capitalism in Pre-Industrial Europe*, trans. James Coonan [Atlantic Highlands, NJ: Humanities P, 1979] 72).

56 *An Ordered Society* 8.

57 *English Society 1580-1680* 24, 32-36, 140-42, 172.

58 See Manning 1-252; Beier 14-48.

59 See Joan Thirsk, "Enclosing and Engrossing," *The Agrarian History of England and Wales, Volume IV, 1500-1700*, ed. Joan Thirsk (Cambridge: Cambridge UP, 1967) 200-55.

60 Hill, *Change and Continuity* 221.

61 Lis and Soly 53-96.

62 "London in 1594 had twelve times as many beggars as in 1517, although the population of the capital had risen scarcely fourfold" (Lis and Soly 78).

63 Hill, *The World Turned Upside Down* 262.

64 On the nature of the labor and suffering in pastoral and sylvan areas of Shakespeare's England, see Manning 255-66.

65 Elizabeth Sacks, *Shakespeare's Images of Pregnancy* (New York: St. Martin's P, 1980).

66 Sacks 4.

67 Michel de Montaigne, *Essays*, trans. John Florio (1910; rpt. London: Dent, 1965) 3:325.

68 *The Anatomy of Melancholy* 1:244.

Chapter 2

From *Hamlet* to *Timon of Athens*: Work in Shakespeare's Later Plays

Shakespeare's major tragedies constitute a watershed for our subject. Before 1604, Shakespeare's most sustained portrayal of labor serves to counterpoint the aristocracy's freedom from work. Elliot Krieger establishes this fact with reference to *A Midsummer Night's Dream*, *1 Henry IV*, and *As You Like It*.[1] *Hamlet* also reflects this emphasis. Confronted like Hercules by two diverging paths, Hamlet chooses the one leading to the contemplative life, leaving the active way to his alter ego Laertes. However, the contemplative life, while it prompts several of the most compelling philosophical meditations in literature, also transforms Hamlet into the slothful man. "Hamlet stands for Sloth," Russell Fraser has recently written, remarking that the typology of the morality plays undergirds the complexity of realistic characterization in Shakespeare's tragedies.[2] "I find thee apt," the Ghost of Hamlet's father pronounces, hearing Hamlet's sanguine commitment to swift revenge. Otherwise, the Prince would be "duller . . . than the fat weed/ That roots itself in ease on Lethe wharf" (I. v. 31-33). But Hamlet proves not apt, unable—or not choosing—to bestir himself to hasty vengeance. Gertrude's judgment, spoken during the play-ending duel, "He's fat, and scant of breath" (V. ii. 287), appears to have been written by Shakespeare solely to provoke recollection of the earlier image of "the fat weed/ That roots itself in ease on Lethe wharf," to provoke, that is, the conclusion that Hamlet and Sloth have become one.[3] After the killing of Polonius, Hamlet drifts, allowing himself to be sent to England and then caught in a duel with Laertes. His dueling with Ophelia's brother, like his fighting the pirates in self-defense, represents not a thought-out commitment to the active life but the automatic response of a passive man believing—perhaps mistakenly—that Providence guides his course.

Among the several related causes of Hamlet's sloth, his negative appraisal of work must be counted. The dehumanizing labor of earthly existence tempts him to consider suicide; "who would fardels bear," he asks auditors, "To grunt and sweat under a weary life?" (III. i. 75-76). This amounts to a dangerous rhetorical question for those groundlings who sought the respite of a few hours in the theater from debilitating wage labor. Vincentio's recreation in *Measure for Measure* of Hamlet's bestial image of work indicates that the negative attitude was more than a passing fancy of Shakespeare's. "If thou art rich, thou'rt poor," the disguised Duke tells Claudio:

> For like an ass, whose back with ingots bows,
> Thou bear'st thy heavy riches but a journey,
> And death unloads thee.
> (III. i. 25-28)

Since Hamlet's sloth partly grows out of his dark view of work, searching the play for its origin becomes appropriate.

That source can be found in the sharp contrast between the image of unproductive Claudius, given to drunkenness and lechery and his murdered brother's traditional aristocratic work: warfare. Indolent, Claudius wrings hard labor from his subjects. "Good now, sit down, and tell me, he that knows," Marcellus asks in the play's opening episode,

> Why this same strict and most observant watch
> So nightly toils the subject of the land,
> And why such daily cast of brazen cannon,
> And foreign mart for implements of war,
> Why such impress of shipwrights, whose sore task
> Does not divide the Sunday from the week,
> What might be toward, that this sweaty haste
> Doth make the night joint-laborer with the day:
> Who is't that can inform me?
> (I. i. 70-79)

The cause of such unnatural, even blasphemous, hard labor involves preparations to defend from young Fortinbras' troops that portion of Norway won by Hamlet Senior. Horatio reports that Hamlet's father in single combat won from the elder Fortinbras what Claudius compels virtually a whole nation to work miserably to protect. The disparity serves to underscore Claudius' timidity, which plunges Hamlet's countrymen into labor that the brave former king never required of his subjects.

Thus Hamlet's awareness of the injustice of a slothful ruler's impressing the labor of his people plays its part in his melancholic belief that all the "uses"—a word which includes all the trades and occupations—of this world seem "stale, flat, and unprofitable" (I. ii. 132-34). Since the world is an "unweeded garden" that "things rank and gross in nature" possess, Hamlet will have no part of its customary work.[4] The imagery of sloth that gets attached to Claudius by play's end will claim Hamlet too. Little escapes the Prince's darkening attitude. Even God's crowning labor, humankind, his "piece of work," in Hamlet's jaundiced view is no more than a "quintessence of dust" (II. ii. 303-8). The mediocre, unrealistic acting of the day leads the Prince to think that the work of humanity's creation was botched. From bad actors' distorted depiction of men and women, Hamlet concludes that "some of Nature's journeymen had made men, and not made them well" (III. ii. 28-35). Granted his belief in God's and Nature's imperfect work, Hamlet in the graveyard not surprisingly dismisses as empty occupations the life work of men who were once perhaps lawyers and courtiers, but now are stinking bones. If Mutability could change the matter that was Alexander the Great into the loam stopping a modern beer barrel and the substance of Julius Caesar into the clay patching a rude wall (V. i. 208-16), its power to convert lesser men and women to dust rarely surprised Elizabethans and Jacobeans. Out of the inert dust turbulent life arises, lecherous, vainly ambitious, at war with itself, only to lapse to silent matter again. Despite the glimmerings of providential light late in the play, events in *Hamlet* never erase the impression that mortal life consists of an essentially valueless cycle—a great stir that may be "full of sound and fury" but which signifies "nothing" (*Macbeth* V. v. 26-28).

With the composition of *Othello* and *King Lear*, Shakespeare begins to diversify his imagery of work. Shakespeare in *Othello* develops the image of the undone work of creation that haunts

Hamlet. Desdemona's handkerchief becomes an objective correlative not simply of her virtue but of the woman herself and her marriage with the Moor. Lynda Boose has explained how the red-spotted handkerchief, analogous to the stained sheets of the bridal bed, becomes synonymous in Othello's imagination with Desdemona's married chastity.[5] Unable to display visibly the handkerchief (or her married chastity) upon demand, Desdemona, Othello believes, is a strumpet. He later tells her that possession of the quasi-magical handkerchief insures constancy between married partners (III. iv. 55-68). In his account, a two-hundred-year-old sibyl "In her prophetic fury sew'd the work" (III. iv. 70-72). It is the strawberry pattern of the handkerchief that admirers wish to remove. Finding the accidentally dropped cloth, Emilia says, "I'll have the work ta'en out,/ And give't Iago" (III. iii. 296-97). "Take me this work out" (III. iv. 180), Cassio, overseen and heard by Othello, commands his whore Bianca once the handkerchief comes into his possession. These determinations to violate the work of something marvellous that has been equated with Desdemona provide the context for evaluating Othello's misguided wish that he might pluck out the supposedly whorish part of Desdemona without harming her lovely alabaster skin or damning her soul. Shakespeare implies that God's or Nature's workmanship is an unviolable piece; so cunningly made is humankind that no part can be extracted or rearranged without the ruin of the whole fabric. And yet that is precisely what Othello bitterly does.

Like *King Lear*, *Othello* includes an elemental tempest (II. i), a great stir accompanying the turmoil of the protagonist's mind. When, on the quay at Cyprus, Othello reunites with Desdemona, he suggests that natural storms cause men and women to labor, and that afterwards quiet values are especially appreciated. "O my soul's joy!" Othello exclaims, seeing Desdemona preserved from drowning:

> If after every tempest come such calms,
> May the winds blow till they have waken'd death!
> And let the laboring bark climb hills of seas
> Olympus-high, and duck again as low
> As hell's from heaven! If it were now to die,
> 'Twere now to be most happy; for I fear

> My soul hath her content so absolute
> That not another comfort like to this
> Succeeds in unknown fate.
> (II. i. 184-93)

Othello's "laboring bark," climbing "hills of seas," becomes a metaphor for experience; the intensity of labor makes calm and ease proportionately delightful. Associated with labor, the sea tempest of *Othello* symbolizes not only sexual stir but the tumult of jealousy about to erupt in the Moor's mind. In the above passage, Othello touches upon not just the relaxation following the assurance that his beloved who was threatened is safe but also the calm—the stasis—produced by the tempest of sexual intercourse. The Jacobean pun on "die" links the two meanings in his speech. Critics have argued that events interrupt Othello's consummating his marriage (thus the intensity of his rage at being summoned by the alarm rung over Cassio's drunken riot). In this reading, Othello and Desdemona never know postcoital relaxation, with the euphoric suspension of all physical activity. The profound turbulence of jealousy takes the place within Othello of the sexual tempest, making him labor to fabricate his own and Desdemona's dooms.

"Look on the tragic loading of this bed," Lodovico commands Iago at play's end; "This is thy work" (V. ii. 363-64). Iago's labor has been to impregnate Othello with vile jealousy, so that the Moor undoes Desdemona and himself. "Work on,/ My medicine, work!" (IV. i. 44-45), Iago exclaims after his corrosive innuendoes have wrought Othello into an epileptic fit. Earlier Iago philosophizes for Roderigo: "Our bodies are our gardens, to the which our wills are gardeners; so that if we will plant nettles or sow lettuce, set hyssop and weed up tine, supply it with one gender of herbs or distract it with many, either to have it sterile with idleness or manur'd with industry—why, the power and corrigible authority of this lies in our wills" (I. iii. 320-26). "Manur'd with industry"—the phrase speaks volumes about Iago's attitude toward physical labor. Iago's will has cultivated a weedy garden within him that reflects his underemployment in Othello's service and his predilection for using fools like Roderigo to do his villainous work. Iago prefers the relatively easy work of slander. His inner garden, if not sterile, approximates the spiritual—and perhaps physical—barrenness of the man himself. In *Othello*, Shakespeare chronicles the disproportionate ruin crafted by a fallen, idle soul.

Like Prince Hamlet (though with a world of difference), King Lear resolves to unburden himself of life's painful fardels, to give up a life of royal sweat and toil, and unencumbered crawl toward his grave (*King Lear* I. i. 37-41). Having purportedly shaken off the royal occupation, Lear illustrates the operation of a self-destructive principle formulated in *Measure for Measure*. Claiming that his imprisonment proceeds from the sexual liberties he has taken with Juliet, Claudio asserts that "every scope by the immoderate use/ Turns to restraint" (I. ii. 127-28). These words describe a dynamic of conversion that explains Isabella's and Angelo's sudden swings of mood and character. In Lear's case, the principle underlies the riot and disorder that he and his hundred knights cause in Goneril's household. "Idle old man," Goneril exclaims, "That still would manage those authorities/ That he hath given away!" (I. iii. 16-18). The cruel daughter's epithet for Lear reminds him (and the audience) of what he in fact should be like if he has thrown over life's burdens, as he says he has. The one-hundred knights that Lear insists upon keeping acquire two symbolic values. In Lear's mind, they represent a face-saving fragment of the royalty and pomp that he cannot completely give up. The king's household riots, however, symbolize the destructive release into which Lear's life of royal work has converted.[6] The riots of Lear's knights are a major cause of his personal tragedy. When Goneril and Regan propose reducing his retinue by first fifty and then seventy-five, ninety, and ninety-five knights, to ask finally "What need one?" (II. iv. 263), Lear erupts in anger, condemning his daughters' malice and rushing headlong into the storm on the heath. Reduced to true idleness by his reaction to Goneril's and Regan's cruel verbal stripping of him, Lear comes to know firsthand the disasters of the unemployed, beggarly life.

Ironically, Kent, in laboring to help his master, underscores the futility of work. Banished by Lear, Kent returns faithfully as disguised Caius to serve Lear. Kent hopes that the old man will find him "full of labors" (I. iv. 6-7). But Kent's labors of service unintentionally abet and hasten Lear's demise. His physical abuse of Oswald, spitefully performed out of imagined loyalty to his master, lands him in the stocks. Kent's disorder lumps him with the wild knights. His humiliating paralysis in the stocks exemplifies the conversion of riotous release into bondage. It predicts the restriction of being that Lear tragically experiences after his rages. The Fool baits stocked Kent: "We'll set thee to school to an ant, to teach thee there's no laboring i'th' winter" (II. iv. 67-68). Mocking Kent's work of counterproductive service, the Fool informs him of the foolishness of serving a winter king—one old, barren, and shunned—by remarking that even such insignificant creatures as ants, known for their industry, do not labor during winter. Yet Kent persists in his labors, aiding outcast Lear on the heath. While his labors provoke the audience's admiration, by his own admission they fail to achieve their end. Kent implies that his reason for delaying his discovery of his true identity involves his finding the moment when Lear will be most receptive to understanding the depth of his love for his master and the extent of his service as Caius. But that time never arrives, and when he tries to force this realization on his master at play's end, Lear, broken by Cordelia's death, in his returning madness pays him no heed. Considered in the light of this failure and his final despair, which he says will be lethal, Kent's labors come to nothing. In this tragedy, there is no laboring in winter.

Disguised as Tom O'Bedlam, Edgar makes the same point in a different way. When Lear asks the pitiable beggar, "What hast thou been?" (III. iv. 84), he replies,

> A servingman! proud in heart and mind; that curl'd my hair; wore gloves in my cap; serv'd the lust of my mistress' heart, and did the act of darkness with her; swore as many oaths as I spake words, and broke them in the sweet face of heaven: one that slept in the contriving of lust, and wak'd to do it. Wine lov'd I deeply, dice dearly; and in woman outparamour'd the Turk. False of heart, light of ear, bloody of hand; hog in sloth, fox in stealth, wolf in greediness, dog in madness, lion in prey.
> (III. iv. 85-94)

Thus described, Tom O'Bedlam resembles Jacobeans about the court and streets of London who, supposedly servingmen, served no one but their savage appetite. Their service produced no meaningful work. Addicted to several vices, they were hogs in sloth. Such viciously idle men, although remunerated for basically unproductive service, as a rule collected the fatal wages of sin and disease. They suffered the terrible demise and premature death associated with bankrupt wage labor. Tom O'Bedlam, maddened most likely by venereal disease, portrays a death-in-life that rarely or never provokes alms or charity. Shakespeare's beggar enforces charity only by symbolically crucifying himself, only by striking pins and nails in his "numb'd and mortified arms" (II. iii. 15). Rather than redemptive crucifixion, however, such an act amounts to desperate self-mutilation that indicts a society that largely believed that work houses rather than free charity best benefit the halt and the lame.[7] Through the powerful poetry of Tom O'Bedlam, Shakespeare, however, suggests the other way, the path walked by the charitable Christ of parable and story.

That Lear rightly responds to this portrait is shown by his taking Tom O'Bedlam into his keeping and by his desire to clothe him by tearing off his own garments. This gesture enacts his insight

> Take physic, pomp,
> Expose thyself to feel what wretches feel,
> That thou mayst shake the superflux to them,
> And show the heavens more just.
> (III. iv. 33-36)

Gloucester, once blinded, also practices a new charity when he gives Tom O'Bedlam his purse, moralizing that almsgiving on a large scale could undo the evils of an unjust distribution of wealth. It could create a society in which each man has enough (IV. i. 64-71). Lear's and Gloucester's new-found charity, however, never diverts their tragic courses. In this play of negatively portrayed labor and idleness, the Captain who accepts Edmund's written instructions for murdering imprisoned Lear and Cordelia without first reading them provides the final, chilling commentary on work: "I cannot draw a cart, nor eat dried oats,/ If it be man's work, I'll do't" (V. iii. 38-39). Since the Captain is able to participate in the hanging of Cordelia, Shakespeare implies that humankind is capable of "work" more savage than the depredations of animals who cannot coldly calculate their self-advantage. Unable by his own admission to perform the physical labor of a horse, the Captain's "work" sinks him below the level of beasts. In the Captain's speech, Shakespeare begs a question about the proper limits of humankind's work that he does not answer in *King Lear*. Nowhere in the play does a character perform a relatively long-lasting, redemptive work. Edgar's saving of his father from suicide might seem to qualify, but Gloucester quickly sinks back into despair after Lear's and Cordelia's forces lose the battle and shortly dies thereafter from the shock of his son's ill-timed revelation of his identity.

An image of long-lasting, redemptive work unequivocally appears in *Macbeth*, however. Late in act IV of this play, a Doctor and Malcolm describe the "most miraculous work" of good King Edward the Confessor, his touching "a crew of wretched souls" and curing their scrofula (IV. iii. 140-59). Malcolm's compelling word picture of King Edward's heavenly work contrasts with the many reports of the tyrant Macbeth's destruction of Scots, their lands, and their goods. The report of Edward's life-giving works serves to highlight the barrenness of Macbeth's deeds. This barrenness of the tyrant occurs in spite of Macbeth's incessant toil. The word "toil" in the witches' repeated incantation, "Double, double, toil and trouble," spoken at the beginning of act IV (IV. i. 10, 20, 35), refers not to their work of hellish brewing but to the troubled labors of Macbeth who, virtually sleepless after the murder of Duncan, strives to consolidate and protect his ill-gotten rule. Like the witches' deeds of black magic (see especially IV. i. 52-60), Macbeth's toil, his labor as king, results in a terrible undoing for his subjects and in a hellish transformation of himself into a spiritually and then a physically "dead butcher" (V. ix. 35). Macbeth finally achieves the sleep, the protracted respite from toil, that he has desired for many months.

Concluding the period of the great tragedies, *Macbeth* extends previous plays' negative portrayal of labor but, unlike them, offers an example of unambiguous redemptive work in the healing cure of Edward the Confessor. This English king's works anticipate the salvatory labors of Cerimon and Prospero, suggesting a bridge from Shakespeare's pre-1606 canon to the late romances and *King Henry VIII*.[8] But before we pass over this bridge, an investigation of the place of work in *Antony and Cleopatra, Coriolanus,* and *Timon of Athens* is in order. Composed apparently just before (or simultaneously with) *Pericles*, these plays include complex representations of our subject not included in the great tragedies which are important for understanding certain emphases given labor and idleness in Shakespeare's last plays.

In *Antony and Cleopatra*, the worlds of imperial Rome and ancient Egypt seem upon first consideration to incorporate respectively the values of labor versus idleness and sloth.[9] As imagined by Cleopatra, Rome is a place of uninterrupted physical activity. She conceives of Octavius Caesar commanding Antony to

> "Do this, or this;
> Take in that kingdom, and enfranchise that;
> Perform't, or else we damn thee."
> (I. i. 22-24)

The verbs of her speech stress the extent and intensity of Cleopatra's image of bustling Rome. Rejecting the kinetic Roman world of his birth, Antony, referring to Egypt, replies, "Here is my space" (I. i. 34). He opposes a metaphysical world, one of space, to the physics of motion that make up Roman life. When he shortly says, "the nobleness of life/ Is to do thus [*embracing*]" (I. i. 36-37), Antony furthermore characterizes Egypt as a land of stasis; "doing" results in a frozen tableau of entwined, motionless lovers. Within the opening forty verses of *Antony and Cleopatra*, Shakespeare presents a set of apparently antagonistic values that he will develop throughout the play. Later, the contrasted values of Rome and Egypt are caught in Antony's call, "Eros, mine armor, Eros!"–the war-working Roman's command, which Cleopatra's drowsy "Sleep a little" neutralizes (IV. iv. 1).

During acts I and II, Shakespeare underscores the idleness and static quality of Egypt. Work is held in low esteem there, as its status as a pejorative adjective indicates. "Prithee tell her but a worky-day fortune" (I. ii. 53-54), Charmian teasingly commands the Soothsayer concerning Iras' future. Learning that in his absence Labienus has taken Roman provinces in Asia, Antony exclaims in self-disgust that in Egypt he has brought forth weeds—the growth of idleness (I. ii. 109-11). The Roman warrior for an instant knows the immobility of the figurative imprisonment that lust imposes. "These strong Egyptian fetters I must break," he resolves to himself, "Or lose myself in dotage" (I. ii. 116-17). "Ten thousand harms, more than the ills I know,/ My idleness doth hatch" (I. ii. 129-30), he judges after learning of Fulvia's death. "But that your royalty/ Holds idleness your subject," Antony tells Cleopatra as he departs for Rome, "I should take you/ For idleness itself" (I. iii. 91-93).

The industrious Roman's aversion to idleness manifests itself in the next scene of the play.[10] "Pompey/ Thrives in our idleness" (I. iv. 75-76), Octavius tells Lepidus, condemning their inaction. In pointed contrast to Caesar's and Lepidus' mutual pledge to perform the "business" of war (I. iv. 76-80), Cleopatra in the following episode calls for the opiate mandragora, "That I might sleep out this great gap of time/ My Antony is away" (I. v. 5-6). Indolent, she imagines the time when

> great Pompey
> Would stand and make his eyes grow in my brow;
> There would he anchor his aspect, and die
> With looking on his life.
> (I. v. 31-34)

The verses accentuate Cleopatra's paralytic effect on Romans.

Great Pompey's heir, Sextus Pompeius, beseeches Cleopatra to immobilize Antony. "Tie up the libertine in a field of feasts," he commands, while he foments civil war,

> Keep his brain fuming; epicurean cooks
> Sharpen with cloyless sauce his appetite,
> That sleep and feeding my prorogue his honor,
> Even till a Lethe'd dullness—
> (II. i. 23-27)

Varrius interrupts Pompey's reverie with news that Antony has bestirred himself and traveled more quickly to Rome than anyone could have imagined. In Rome, Antony excuses his sloth by claiming that "poisoned hours had bound me up"—paralyzed him, in other words—"From mine own knowledge" (II. ii. 90-91). Left alone with his Roman peers, Enobarbus boasts that in Egypt he and Antony "did sleep day out of countenance, and made the night light with drinking" (II. ii. 177-78). Roman denigration of leisure and pleasant relaxation surfaces when Octavius Caesar, shrinking from the festive drinking of Antony's barge party, laments, "It's monstrous labor when I wash my brain/ And it grow fouler" (II. vii. 99-100). Later, just before Caesar's and Antony's first battle, Antony wonders at Caesar's alacrity and dispatch in commanding and at his own "slackness" in preparing to do battle (III. vii. 20-27, 74-75).

The above references and quotations more than adequately portray Egypt and Rome as places respectively of static idleness and stirred work. Nevertheless, each country contains within itself the seeds of the other place.[11] Despite his alacrity in conducting the business of war, Octavius, by Antony's account, was formerly idle, at Philippi keeping "His sword e'en like a dancer" (III. xi. 35-36). Octavius "alone," Antony argues, "Dealt on lieutenantry, and no practice had/ In the brave squares of war" (III. xi. 38-40). Conversely, Cleopatra, stung by Antony's accusation of idleness, paradoxically asserts

> 'Tis sweating labor
> To bear such idleness so near the heart
> As Cleopatra this.
> (I. iii. 93-95)

Cleopatra's reference to her heart indicates that passion, especially of the sexual kind, constitutes her special work.

"Stirr'd by Cleopatra" (I. i. 43), Antony has said that "the nobleness of life/ Is to do thus." The passionate embrace of the lovers signified by the verb "do" alludes to Antony's and Cleopatra's distinctive labor-in-idleness, the "doing" of sexual intercourse.[12] Enobarbus' praise of Cleopatra, "a wonderful piece of work" (I. ii. 153-54), resonates with sexual innuendo. When Antony complains, "The business [Fulvia] hath broached in the state/ Cannot endure my absence," Enobarbus jokes, "And the business you have broach'd here cannot be without you, especially that of Cleopatra's, which wholly depends on your abode" (I. ii. 171-75). The radically different senses of the repeated word "business" reflect the polarity of Roman and Egyptian work. Nevertheless, Antony and Cleopatra conduct their sexual business as vigorously as Romans do their statecraft.

For most of his life, Antony's heroic labor has defined him. "O love,/ That thou couldst see my wars to-day," he boasts to Cleopatra before his only battle on land against Caesar,

> and knew'st
> The royal occupation, thou shouldst see
> A workman in't.
> (IV. iv. 15-18)

For Antony, the "royal occupation" consists of working war, a "business" to which he rises early and goes with delight (IV. iv. 20-21). Usually, however, Antony in Egypt is not so confident either of his vocation or his identity. Antony's troubled, compulsive journeying to and from Rome and Egypt jars loose his fixed identity.[13] The dynamic of the conversion of opposites, the Shakespearean motif articulated in *Measure for Measure* and employed in *King Lear*, informs Antony's journeying.[14] "It hath been taught us from the primal state," Caesar complains early in the play,

> That he which is was wish'd, until he were;
> And the ebb'd man, ne'er lov'd till ne'er worth love,
> Comes dear'd by being lack'd. This common body,
> Like to a vagabond flag upon the stream,
> Goes to and back, lackeying the varying tide,
> To rot itself with motion.
> (I. iv. 41-47)

Becoming endeared "by being lack'd," Antony is pulled from Egypt to Rome partly by the wars that Fulvia makes to bring him back to her. The same process of valuation accounts for Cleopatra's allure once he is in Rome. Like the "common body" in its political allegiances, Antony flows back and forth between Egypt and Rome, rotting with motion his sense of self.

Approaching his death, Antony strives to arrest his disintegration by imploring the spirit of his ancestor Hercules to dwell within him (IV. xii. 42-45). But that spirit, his protective daemon, has abandoned him (IV. iii. 16-17). Comparing himself to

> a cloud that's dragonish,
> A vapor sometime like a bear or lion,
> A tower'd citadel, a pendant rock,
> A forked mountain, or blue promontory
> With trees upon't that nod unto the world,
> And mock our eyes with air....
>   (IV. xiv. 2-7)

Antony concludes that he "cannot hold this visible shape" (IV. xiv. 14)—that of the Roman war worker.[15] Self-dissolution, Roman war work, and Egyptian sloth all combine in his poignant utterance, "Unarm, Eros, the long day's task is done,/ And we must sleep" (IV. xiv. 35-36). Punning on the name of the Roman war god, he judges that

> Now all labor
> Mars what it does; yea, very force entangles
> Itself with strength.
>   (IV. xiv. 47-49)

The pun on Mars suggests that Antony's suicide can be considered a form—perhaps the inevitable consequence—of Roman war work. Falling on his sword but not inflicting an instantly fatal wound, Antony complains, "I have done my work ill, friends" (IV. xiv. 104). Bleeding, hoisted aloft on Cleopatra's monument, Antony attempts at the moment of his death to refix his diffused Roman identity. "Please your thoughts," he tells auditors,

> In feeding them with those my former fortunes
> Wherein I liv'd, the greatest prince o' th' world,
> The noblest; and do now not basely die,
> Not cowardly put off my helmet to
> My countryman—a Roman by a Roman
> Valiantly vanquish'd.
>   (IV. xv. 52-58)

The ultimate irony of Antony's death involves his convincing himself of an untruth. The "greatest prince o' th' world" expired some time ago. The nobility of Roman stoic suicide evaporates in Antony's bungled, almost comic, performance. The Roman vanquishing this Roman is Caesar, with his victorious troops—not Antony.

A character of Roman fixity, Antony never succeeds in reversing or halting the gradual dispersal of his heroic self. A creature of mutability, Cleopatra on the contrary stabilizes a "Roman" identity through suicide.[16] "My resolution's plac'd," she stoically pronounces,

> and I have nothing
> Of woman in me; now from head to foot
> I am marble-constant; now the fleeting moon
> No planet is of mine.
> (V. ii. 238-41)

The Roman guard who discovers Cleopatra's body refers to her suicide as "work" (V. ii. 324). Charmian, however, implies that it amounts to "play" (V. ii. 319), a judgment in keeping with the pleasure that the asp's bite gives Cleopatra. "She looks like sleep," Caesar concludes, viewing her corpse, "As she would catch another Antony/ In her strong toil of grace" (V. ii. 346-48). Editors usually gloss "toil" in Caesar's phrase "strong toil of grace" as "net," the notion being that Cleopatra's physical graces, her charms, weave a fatal web for unwary admirers. But "toil" also connotes "work," a possible meaning that certainly makes the phrase "toil of grace" an oxymoron. The Roman guard's prior reference to Cleopatra's suicide as "work" reinforces this alternate interpretation. Caesar likewise construes Cleopatra in terms of the Roman value of labor. Cleopatra's graces, her essentially idle, static beauty, have worked Antony's and her own ruin, as well as indirectly that of lesser characters such as Enobarbus. Cleopatra's effortless labor, her manifestation of her beauteous graces, has been paid with the wages of death.

More so than either *Hamlet* or *King Lear*, *Coriolanus* dramatizes the unjust distribution of the goods of the commonwealth and the suppression and abuse of the working class. The first fifty lines of the play depict a repeated occurrence of Jacobean England: social revolt by malnourished workers convinced that upper classes are hoarding foodstuffs. Many commentators on *Coriolanus* have remarked that this aspect of the play appears to owe much to the 1607 Midlands Revolt and similar rural insurrections.[17] That the citizens' starvation results from a lack of charity on the part of patricians seems clear from the use of language evocative of Lear's and Gloucester's accusations against the hard-heartedness of an elite class (*King Lear* III. iv. 32-36; IV. i. 65-71). "What authority surfeits on would relieve us" (I. i. 16-17), First Roman Citizen concludes. "If they would yield us but the superfluity while it were wholesome, we might guess they reliev'd us humanely; but they think we are too dear" (I. i. 17-19). Utterances such as this character's "I speak this in hunger for bread, not in thirst for revenge" (I. i. 24-25) predispose auditors to sympathize with the citizens and harshly judge the hoarding patricians. The ironic understanding of Menenius' parable of the belly, intended to quell riot by supposedly illustrating the self-sacrificial generosity of the patricians, confirms playgoers' silent condemnation of the Roman upper class. "There was a time when all the body's members/ Rebell'd against the belly," Menenius begins:

> thus accus'd it:
> That only like a gulf it did remain
> I' th' midst a'th' body, idle and unactive,
> Still cupboarding the viand, never bearing
> Like labor with the rest, where th' other instruments
> Did see and hear, devise, instruct, walk, feel,
> And, mutually participate, did minister
> Unto the appetite and affection common
> Of the whole body.
> (I. i. 96-105)

Menenius goes on to describe the belly's function of digesting and refining food in order to provide nourishment for all members of the body. Insisting that the patricians are analogous to the provident belly in the body politic, Menenius asserts that, having given the flour to the other incorporate members of society, his social class—like the laboring stomach—is left with only bran (I. i. 146). Nevertheless, Roman citizens lack bread; they are starving. In the minds of astute listeners, Menenius' parable backfires.[18] Unlike the healthy, functional belly, the Roman patricians hoard grain, refusing to refine and distribute it to dependent members of the commonwealth. Thus Menenius himself—in his imaginative representation of the original accusation against the belly as "idle and unactive,/ Still cupboarding the viand, never bearing/ Like labor with the rest"—portrays the patricians' sloth and unproductive lives. By his strong ironic weighting of the audience's sympathies, Shakespeare appears to be condemning those Jacobean classes corresponding to the patricians who were commonly thought to enjoy the fruits of agrarian laborers without providing workers with life's bare necessities.

Scornful of the citizens' weak appetite for war, Coriolanus proposes that they be given grain only if they earn it by fighting in battle. Regarded in this light, corn amounts to wages paid for the work of war. "They know the corn/ Was not our recompense," Coriolanus grumbles after the patricians release some grain to the people to avert rebellion (as James I's government did in similar circumstances),[19]

> resting well assur'd
> They ne'er did service for't; being press'd to th' war,
> Even when the navel of the state was touch'd,
> They would not thread the gates. This kind of service
> Did not deserve corn gratis.
> (III. i. 120-25)

Unfortunately Coriolanus cannot conceive of an act of free charity. Shakespeare's contemporaries widely remarked the evils attending military impressment.[20] Falstaff's shameful pressing of his company of troops in *2 Henry IV* illustrates Shakespeare's sensitivity to the abuse. Suggesting that starving, impressed citizens be given corn only as wages for fighting wars against neighboring city states strikes auditors as the harsh imposition of the values of a warrior class upon the people.

In fact, Shakespeare repeatedly implies that warfare is properly the work of Coriolanus and his fellow Roman officers. Bleeding, he pauses in battle to claim "My work hath not yet warm'd me" (I. v. 17). Later, about to fight Aufidius single-handedly, he boasts, "Alone I fought in your Corioles walls,/ And made what work I pleas'd" (I. viii. 8-9). After the Roman victory, Cominius tells wounded Coriolanus, "If I should tell thee o'er this thy day's work,/ Thou't not believe thy deeds" (I. ix. 1-2). In the Capitol Menenius begs Cominius "to report/ A little of the worthy work perform'd by Martius Caius Coriolanus" (II. ii. 44-46). In no other play does Shakespeare stress repeatedly that warfare is the warrior's distinctive work. In the monochromatic character of the hero of his final Roman tragedy, war work becomes not simply a passion but the grand obsession by which he weighs and judges all other activities of life.[21]

This obsession has been nurtured by Coriolanus' mother, Volumnia, who gives the most remarkable account of Coriolanus' work as a warrior. A hater of idleness, Volumnia maintains that, had she twelve sons, she "had rather . . . eleven die nobly for their country than one voluptuously surfeit out of action" (I. iii. 24-25). Imagining Coriolanus' martial deeds at Corioles, Volumnia pictures her son thusly:

> His bloody brow
> With his mail'd hand then wiping, forth he goes,
> Like to a harvest-man that's task'd to mow
> Or all or lose his hire.
> (I. iii. 34-37)

Coriolanus' association of war work and payment most likely derives from an expression of his mother's. By likening the slaughtering warrior to a bloody harvestman, Volumnia conflates the world of agricultural production with that of warfare—the two worlds basically opposed by the hungry citizens and Coriolanus disdainful of their right to bread. As conceived by Volumnia, Coriolanus' pay for war work involves an all-or-nothing proposition: he must mow the whole field of soldiers to receive his pay. If he mows down only nine out of ten, he is paid nothing. The absoluteness of Volumnia's conception reflects both her martial idealism and the extreme demands she makes of her son. It also seems designed by Shakespeare to provoke—by contrast—the fleeting recollection of the Parable of the Vineyard (also known as the Parable of the Laborers and the Hours).[22] That teaching of Christ implies that the spirit in which the agrarian worker performs his task takes precedence over the amount of work that he does; those hired last are paid the same as those first hired who have labored all day in the vineyard. Volumnia, however, posits an inhuman criterion for payment of her son's war work. The absolute standard Coriolanus sets for payment of the citizens' war work appears to have been first set for him.

Repeatedly Coriolanus and other patricians think of the work of war in terms of agrarian husbandry. A senator of Corioles turns Coriolanus and his troops into herders when he asserts, "We'll break our walls/ Rather than they shall pound [pen] us up" (I. iv. 16-17). But the livestock that Coriolanus drives are his own impressed citizen soldiers: "All the contagion of the south light on you,/ You shames of Rome! You herd of—" (I. iv. 30-31). Since his "herd" of men fly the enemy, one could conclude that Coriolanus performs poorly the task of collecting, managing, and driving them. The pastoral context of war thickens when Cominius states, "The shepherd knows not thunder from a tabor/ More than I know the sound of Martius' tongue" (I. vi. 25-26). The incongruity of a "thundering" shepherd's tabor—a small drum—suggests the inappropriateness of imagining war in terms of pastoral husbandry. When Cominius pronounces—

> Of all the horses—
> Whereof we have ta'en good and good store—of all
> The treasure in this field achiev'd and city,
> We render you the tenth, to be ta'en forth,
> Before the common distribution, at
> Your only choice.
> (I. ix. 31-36)

—his proposal that a tithe (tenth) of the war harvest be given to Coriolanus evokes the context of Christian agrarianism primarily to emphasize the pagan deification of Coriolanus, the idolatry of Cominius. Coriolanus, to his credit, vetoes this proposal, insisting only upon his "common part" of the goods (I. ix. 38-40). Nevertheless, his deferral stems neither from a modest self-appraisal nor from generous concern for Roman soldiers. He overrules Cominius' plan because he pridefully regards it as "A bribe to pay my sword" (I. ix. 38). The response is noteworthy. Apparently Coriolanus silently values his war work at such a high rate that no material "hire" constitutes adequate payment.[23]

By conflating Coriolanus' war work with agrarian husbandry, mainly that of harvesting, Shakespeare encourages playgoers to draw a conclusion; unlike the life-sustaining labor of the harvestman and shepherd, Coriolanus' war work neither nurtures creatures nor makes any product essential to life. On the contrary, his work mars creation, as the bloody, disfigured faces of his dead and wounded adversaries testify. Viewed from the abused citizens' viewpoint, Coriolanus is neither herder nor harvestman but a dog who has broken into the pinfold and rages among the sheep. Sicinius, the people's tribune, claims that inflaming Coriolanus to rail against Roman citizens is "as easy/ As to set dogs on sheep" (II. i. 256-57). In this respect, Coriolanus becomes the disrupter of a process of husbandry who spells dearth for the husbandman.

This imagery of Coriolanus' destructive effect on a pastoral staple of life underscores the people's belief that he is their "chief enemy" (I. i. 8), responsible for their exclusion from the cycle of foodstuffs. "Let us kill him," First Citizen proposes, "and we'll have corn at our own price" (I. i. 10-11). Granted this citizen's conception, auditors in retrospect realize that Coriolanus bears responsibility for the citizens' abandoning their customary labor for an unaccustomed kind of work. "What work's, my countrymen, in hand?" Menenius asks the turbulent mob; "where go you/ With bats and clubs?" (I. i. 54-56). In the patrician's opinion, such foreign labor would ruin the people: "Why, masters"—note the irony—"my good friends, mine honest neighbors,/ Will you undo yourselves?" (I. i. 62-63). When the people roar mutinously later in the play, Menenius facetiously judges, "Here's goodly work" (III. i. 260). Disposed to think of warfare as work, Roman patricians anxiously contemplate the prospect of a war in their own streets. "Throng our large temples with the shows of peace," Coriolanus beseeches the rabble, "And not our streets with war" (III. iii. 36-37). At no point, however, does Coriolanus accept responsibility, either wholly or partially, for being a principal cause of the people's abandoning their usual trades to take up reluctantly a kind of destructive work claimed by warriors of the patrician class.

Coriolanus' commitment to his warrior work plays a major role in determining not only the citizens' occupation in the play but also those of Volumnia and his wife Virgilia. Newly exiled from Rome, Coriolanus remembers a time when weeping Volumnia loaded him with fortifying precepts:

> . . . you were wont to say,
> If you had been the wife of Hercules,
> Six of his labors you'ld have done, and sav'd
> Your husband so much sweat.
> (IV. i. 16-19)

Volumnia's reported resolution reveals her intense desire, never voiced in so many words, to perform heroic labor.[24] Deprived as a woman of this wish, she lives vicariously through the war work of her fierce son. After all, Volumnia speaks of Coriolanus as a bloody harvestman "task'd to mow/ Or all or lose his hire." No mention of Coriolanus' father occurs in the course of the play.[25] It is as though the mannish Roman matron has somehow both conceived and borne the son made frightfully in her image. In her speech, imagery of female nurturance proper to herself is mixed with the arresting poetry of the war work she would like to perform, the "harvest" she in fact vicariously performs through her carefully molded son:

> The breasts of Hecuba,
> When she did suckle Hector, look'd not lovelier
> Than Hector's forehead when it spit forth blood
> At Grecian sword, contemning.
> (I. iii. 40-43)

The specification of Hector's forehead as the part of his anatomy receiving Achilles' infamous blow creates a faint allusion to the primary myth of male parturition—Zeus' delivery of his daughter Athena, the original brainchild, through his cleft forehead. The allusion for an instant conflates the war work claimed by men with the traditional labor of women, child delivery. Such a psychologically unconscious conflation on Volumnia's part rings true to her character; her motive force has always been the transformation of the biologically and socially mandated labor of women into the heroic, admired war work of men. Under her tutelage, the son she bore has become the ancient world's premier war worker. Yet the grotesqueness of Volumnia's poetic formulation and the auditor's repulsion on hearing it signal a certain wrongness in her buried desire for the transformation.[26] This will not be the only time that Shakespeare in his late plays weights audience sentiment against a character's appropriation of labor natural to the opposite gender as a vehicle for the fulfillment of fantasies.

Virgilia, however, represents another case. Fearful for her husband's safety, left cold by the ethos of Mars, Virgilia is driven by Coriolanus' work into anxious isolation. When Volumnia and Valeria, who rouse her anxiety by their rough talk of war, ask her to join them in visiting a Roman matron recovering from childbirth, Virgilia protests, "Indeed no, by your patience; I'll not over the threshold till my lord return from the wars" (I. iii. 74-75). "Come, lay aside your stitchery," Valeria urges, "I must have you play the idle huswife with me this afternoon" (I. iii. 69-70). Virgilia avoids the stereotype of the slothful wife by adopting and feverishly fulfilling another cliché—that of worried Penelope, relieving her anxiety for her absent husband's safety by weaving. "You would be another Penelope," Volumnia rebukes her daughter-in-law; "yet they say, all the yarn she spun in Ulysses' absence did but fill Ithaca full of moths" (I. iii. 82-84). The compulsiveness of Virgilia's incessant labor (I. iii. 81, 109-10) duplicates that of Coriolanus engaged in bloody warfare, reminding playgoers that weaving amounts to the means by which Virgilia displaces her mounting fear for his safety. Shakespeare never describes the product of her weaving; her work—like Penelope's—appears to produce nothing. Virgilia pays a heavy compensatory price for Coriolanus' war work.

Coriolanus' tragic downfall and death can be understood as a direct consequence of botched work. The conflation of agrarian work and that of war culminates in Coriolanus' reported reply to Cominius' plea that he save his "private friends" from the threatened sack of Rome:

> His answer to me was,
> He could not stay to pick them in a pile
> Of noisome musty chaff. He said 'twas folly,
> For one poor grain or two, to leave unburnt
> And still to nose th' offense.
> (V. i. 24-28)

Nevertheless, Coriolanus, melting before his mother's pleas, later relents, striking a peace with Rome because he would save a few grains—his family—from the intended conflagration. The compromise that he imagines will please the Volscians, however, does not placate them. They make clear their dissatisfaction with the mower who has failed to perform his agreed-upon labor, for reasons—in terms of the agrarian imagery—that make no sense: failing to burn a field of musty chaff because it includes a few wholesome grains of corn. Regarded in this light, Coriolanus is a foolish, reneging hired worker.

When he joins in league with Aufidius to destroy the city that has banished him, Coriolanus galvanizes the Volscians so strongly that he stirs his adversary's long-nurtured jealousy, making Aufidius feel like his paid subaltern.[27] "He wag'd me with his countenance," Aufidius bitterly tells three conspirators against Coriolanus, "as if/ I had been mercenary" (V. vi. 39-40). Aufidius converts the former, brief friendship of the two warriors, a bond that the Volscian has ecstatically pictured in nuptial imagery (IV. v. 101-18), into a degenerate relationship of taskmaster and paid soldier. That Coriolanus acts as a Volscian mercenary is confirmed by dialogue at the play's conclusion. "But there to end/ Where he was to begin," a Volscian lord complains upon learning of Coriolanus' negotiated settlement with Rome,

> and give away
> The benefit of our levies, answering us
> With our own charge, making a treaty where
> There was a yielding—this admits no excuse.
> (V. vi. 64-68)

Clearly the Volscians have considered Coriolanus their hired agent whose purpose is to offset the cost of sending troops to sack Rome with an abundance of delivered war loot. Choosing to feel like a paid mercenary, Aufidius vindictively insists that Coriolanus' decision to negotiate peace with Rome has made Coriolanus the mercenary who merits no pay because he has failed to perform his contracted war work.

It has been labor for stony Coriolanus to admit the stunted feeling of pity for his family. "It is no little thing to make/ Mine eyes to sweat compassion" (V. iii. 195-96), he tells Aufidius, who is shocked at the exile's sudden loss of martial resolve. "At a few drops of women's rheum," Aufidius later tells his fellow conspirators, "which are/ As cheap as lies, he sold the blood and labor/ Of our great action" (V. vi. 45-47). Aufidius characterizes Coriolanus' negotiated peace, in which the Volscians have received goods worth only one-third the cost of mounting the invasion (V. vi. 76-83), as a fraudulent business transaction, in which Coriolanus has traded the Volscians' expeditionary labor for cheap tears. "Therefore he shall die" (V. vi. 47), he concludes. The conspirators kill Coriolanus because he has failed as a hired worker to perform the terms set forth in the agreement between himself and his Volscian taskmasters.[28] That Coriolanus should die as a direct result of a broken war contract amounts to ironic poetic justice. Coriolanus thought that the Roman citizen soldiers should not be paid. The callousness of this attitude reverts upon Coriolanus' own head in the conspirators' stated motives for killing him. The perceived abuse of contracted labor leads to the wondrous war worker's death.[29] The tears that Coriolanus shed and the compassionate spirit out of which they welled become the worker's redemptive hire only with the advent of Christ and the parables that he taught. The poetic imagery of Shakespeare's final Roman tragedy evokes the distant context of redemptive labor in order to remind playgoers of an ethos that could save Romans and Volscians alike, if only it were a historical possibility.[30]

Commentators on *Coriolanus* have argued that Shakespeare's depiction of the famous Roman warrior to some extent derives from the public images of either Robert Devereux, Earl of Essex, or Sir Walter Ralegh, contemporary soldiers wholly devoted to destroying a national enemy—Spain—whose headstrong, militaristic temperaments led directly to their personal ruin. The model of Ralegh is the more plausible of the two, for his imprisonment as a concession to the Spanish for his unrelenting desire to wage war against them preceded and extended beyond the 1607-8 date usually assigned for the writing and first performances of *Coriolanus*. The Treaty of London, signed in August 1604, began an eight-year period of relative peace with Spain. Displeased with James I's peacemaking, many militant English protestant lords lamented the decay of England's warrior class and the general idleness and sloth of countrymen hardened in previous decades by constant training for war.

Viewed uncritically, *Coriolanus* glorifies the work of war that was no longer highly valued or practiced. From 1604-1612, "the militia in the words of one Lord Lieutenant, underwent a period of 'long vacation and rest.' In 1614, the Earl of Essex [Robert Devereux's son], who mustered the Staffordshire trained bands, reported that they were so out of practice that they could hardly stand up straight, let alone use their weapons properly."[31] Ralegh himself concluded that "'the lords in former times were stronger, more warlike, than now they are.... There were many earls could bring into the field a thousand barbed horses, whereas now very few of them can furnish twenty fit to serve the king.'"[32] In 1614, Fulke Greville, nostalgic for Queen Elizabeth's reign, lamented the "exchanging that active, victorious, enriching and balancing course of her defensive wars for an idle, I fear deceiving, shadow of peace."[33] When county militia under the command of crown officers replaced private retinues under the command of territorial magnates, "England," J. H. Hexter concludes, "advanced with giant strides toward domestic tranquility and military incompetence."[34] Leah Marcus and Lawrence Stone also cite evidence of the widespread rusting of lords who had formerly fought—or whose fathers had fought—Elizabeth's so-called defensive wars.[35] Regarded in this context, the compelling traits of the fiercely martial Coriolanus and the play that bears his name appear designed to appeal to a sizable body of English men and women dissatisfied with James' peace and the evident decline of national prowess.

In the opinion of many of Shakespeare's fellow citizens, physical idleness fostered an inner unrest that corrupted society. As early as 1600 Thomas Wilson (c. 1560-1629), writing on the state of England, argued that "'the long continuance of peace had bred an inward canker and unrest in men's minds, the people doing nothing but jar and wrangle one with another, these lawyers by the ruins of neighbours' contentions are grown so great, so rich and so proud, that no other sort dare meddle with them.'"[36] Granted the currency of views such as

Wilson's, one could regard the following dialogue of *Coriolanus* as Shakespeare's appeal to popular sentiment:

> *1. Serv.* Let me have war, say I, it exceeds peace as far as day does night; it's sprightly, waking, audible, and full of vent. Peace is a very apoplexy, lethargy, mull'd, deaf, sleepy, insensible, a getter of more bastard children than war's a destroyer of men.
> *2. Serv.* 'Tis so, and as wars, in some sort, may be said to be a ravisher, so it cannot be denied but peace is a great maker of cuckolds.
> *1. Serv.* Ay, and it makes men hate one another.
> *3. Serv.* Reason: because they then less need one another. The wars for my money! I hope to see Romans as cheap as Volscians.
> (IV. v. 221-33)

The work of war scours rust from both individuals and society as a whole. Ralegh asserted that "when wars are ended abroad, sedition begins at home, and when men are freed from fighting for necessity, they quarrel through ambition."[37] Paul Jorgensen, remarking that opinions like Wilson's and Ralegh's can be traced to Machiavelli's *Discorsi*, has assembled an impressive collection of passages from the Shakespeare canon wherein either peace is criticized or war glorified.[38] Donatus had made the work of war supersede the work of tillage by establishing Virgil's literary life as a cultural paradigm for later ages. Pastoral *otium* (the bucolics) preceded the georgics and the epic in Virgil's life; the fullest existence grew from adolescent *otium*, into the *negotium* of cultivating the land and then waging war—an activity realizing mankind's heroic potential.[39]

Upon first consideration, the Servants' exchange in act IV of *Coriolanus* constitutes a loud, jingoistic chorus praising the work of war. But a more careful analysis of this Roman play of Shakespeare's reveals the opposite truth.[40] The war-glorifying servants have no sooner departed from the stage than the tribunes Brutus and Sicinius enter and the latter says of exiled Coriolanus,

> We hear not of him, neither need we fear him;
> His remedies are tame—the present peace
> And quietness of the people, which before
> Were in wild hurry. Here do we make his friends
> Blush that the world goes well, who rather had,

> Though they themselves did suffer by't, behold
> Dissentious numbers pest'ring streets, than see
> Our tradesmen singing in their shops, and going
> About their functions friendly.
> (IV. vi. 1-9)

Providing the corrective to the Servants' view, Sicinius celebrates the friendly harmony of Roman society resulting from the expulsion of the war principle incarnated in Coriolanus. The "tradesmen singing in their shops, and going/ About their functions friendly" signify that the performance of domestic labor proceeds ideally once a society banishes the worker of war. Even the tribunes Brutus and Sicinius and the patrician Menenius, formerly at each other's throat, have forged a new friendship (IV. vi. 10-17). This celebration of peace at the expense of war accords with Shakespeare's implicit criticism of Coriolanus' character throughout the play, especially his staging of his hero's tragic death as a result of a flawed understanding of the place of war and military contracts in society. For the less perceptive playgoer, *Coriolanus* endorses heroic warfare; for the more acute analyst, the play becomes an anatomy of the self-destruction accompanying martial labor.[41]

If the war worker develops into a mercenary in *Coriolanus*, the Poet and Painter of *Timon of Athens* from the beginning stigmatize their art as work done solely for material gain. In this perplexing, most likely unfinished play that was perhaps never performed by the King's Men, Shakespeare shifts his focus from the work of the warrior to the artist's labor. In doing so, he anticipates the more comprehensive exploration of art as labor in *Pericles* and the other late romances. "You are rapt, sir, in some work," the Painter tells the Poet, "some dedication/ To the great lord" (I. i. 19-20). "A thing slipp'd id'ely from me," he replies; "Our poesy is as a gum, which oozes/ From whence 'tis nourish'd" (I. i. 20-22). Gary Schmidgall has recently charted both the depth and extent of Elizabethans' and Jacobeans' belief that writing poetry amounts to an idle occupation.[42] "'O, my Lord, you tax me/ In that word poet of much idleness,'" Surrey protests in the play *Sir Thomas More* (c. 1594); "'It is a study that makes poor our fate.'"[43] Shakespeare, in the dedicatory matter of *Venus and Adonis* (1592-93), taps into a cultural stereotype, assuring the Earl of Southampton that "I account my selfe highly praised, and vowe to take advantage of all idle hours, till I have honoured you with some graver labour." In his analysis of the language of dedications to patrons of Elizabethan and Jacobean volumes of poetry, Schmidgall has established the convention of the poet's claiming that his work reflects the triviality and idleness of his life (68-85).

Obviously in most, if not all, cases, the protest constitutes false modesty. Reconsidered within the context of the Poet's and Painter's later conversations, the Poet's terming his work idle at the outset of *Timon of Athens* appears especially hypocritical. The Poet's and Painter's initial talk is foregrounded against the conversation of a Jeweller and a Merchant, which concerns the rare gem that the Jeweller has brought Timon as the catalyst for a shower of riches from the prodigal Athenian. The design of the staging suggests that the Painter and Poet are planning to give their works to Timon as similar bribes. Furthermore, the part of the Poet's dedicatory matter that the audience hears him reading aloud to himself pertains to the material remuneration that he expects from his chosen patron Timon:

> "When we for recompense have prais'd the vild,
> It stains the glory of that happy verse
> Which aptly sings the good."
> (I. i. 15-17)

Hearing these verses read aloud, auditors assume that the Poet has been an artistic mercenary of vile men in the past. Quickly the theater audience adopts a negative view of the play's Poet and his craft.[44]

Calling his poem a "rough work" (I. i. 43), the Poet summarizes his argument for the Painter's benefit:

> I have, in this rough work, shap'd out a man
> Whom this beneath world doth embrace and hug
> With amplest entertainment. My free drift
> Halts not particularly, but moves itself
> In a wide sea of wax; no levell'd malice
> Infects one comma in the course I hold,
> But flies an eagle flight, bold, and forth on,
> Leaving no tract behind.
> (I. i. 43-50)

The Painter's response to this partly opaque speech—"How shall I understand you?" (I. i. 51)—implies that the efforts of generations of editors to make sense of verses 45-47 may be misdirected; Shakespeare appears to have put purposely obscure utterances in the mouth of the Poet.[45] Among the vices of poetry, which he catalogues in *The Arte of English Poesie* (1589), George Puttenham includes "*Periergia*, or Over labour," which occurs when the poet displays "overmuch curiositie and studie to shew himselfe fine in a light matter."[46] Paradoxically, supposedly idle poetizing can produce an overlabored, obscure poetic style that resists comprehension. That Shakespeare in the Poet's and Painter's initial dialogue implies that the labored art of poetry is ineffective is confirmed by the unoriginality and inappropriateness of the subject of the poem which the Poet attempts to clarify (I. i. 51-88).

The Painter responds to the Poet's logorrhetic paraphrase of his matter—Timon favored by Lady Fortune, followed by a press of suitors and supposed friends, but deserted by them when Fortune shifts her mood—by protesting that a painting could communicate better the intent of the Poet's word picture and by judging that the idea of Lady Fortune enthroned on a high hill from which she beckons and rejects mortals is a stale commonplace (I. i. 72-77, 89-92). "A thousand moral paintings I can show," the Painter boasts, "That shall demonstrate these quick blows of Fortune's/ More pregnantly than words" (I. i. 90-92). Ironically, the Poet's mercenary, miscast, and perhaps overlabored work conveys a truth that could save Timon, if he could apply it to himself.[47]

The Poet's disingenuousness in terming his art idle is confirmed when he finally speaks directly to Timon: "Vouchsafe my labor," he begs, "and long live your lordship" (I. i. 152). But Timon ignores the Poet, preferring instead the Painter, whose portrait of Timon magnifies attractively the subject's physical traits.[48] "Painting is welcome," Timon exclaims:

> The painting is almost the natural man;
> For since dishonor traffics with man's nature,
> He is but outside; these pencill'd figures are

> Even such as they give out. I like your work,
> And you shall find I like it.
> (I. i. 156-61)

To value painting because it is a superficial medium appropriate for humanity's superficiality scarcely resembles genuine praise. Timon's reason for preferring painting over poetry reflects a flaw in the patron. Flattering Timon by his enhanced likeness, the portrait instantly engrosses his attention. When Timon asks the cynic Apemantus, "How lik'st thou this picture," the latter quips, "The best, for the innocence" (I. i. 195-96)–for its foolishness, in other words. Faulty labor becomes Shakespeare's focus when Timon in turn asks, "Wrought he not well that painted it," and Apemantus snarls, "He wrought better that made the painter, and yet he's but a filthy piece of work" (I. i. 197-99). At the beginning of this strange play, Shakespeare implies that the work of the flawed artist can never transcend his botched nature.[49] Attacking in this vein, Apemantus also speaks the final word on the poet and his labor. Trapping the Poet into admitting that his profession brands him a liar, Apemantus tells his shaken victim to look in his last work, wherein he "feign'd [Timon] a worthy fellow." When the Poet angrily protests that Timon's worth validates the truth of his feigning, Apemantus agrees: "Yes, he is worthy of thee, and to pay thee for thy labor. He that loves to be flatter'd is worthy o' th' flatterer" (I. i. 222-27). Written for an idle patron and slothful society, the conventionally idle work of the Poet is ironically fitting, as perhaps only Apemantus grasps.

Shakespeare in the course of the play never associates productive work of any kind with Timon or the Athenians who flatter him for his riches. The idleness of their lives is everywhere apparent. Cupid identifies Timon's first banquet as a Banquet of Sense (I. ii. 122-25), the morally dangerous feast depicted in Renaissance art. Ladies disguised as Amazons signify the unnaturalness of its chief entertainment, the masque of Cupid. As a provocation of the senses to sin, the masque befits a banquet described as "idle" by Timon himself (I. ii. 155). Like the visual art of the painter, the masque appeals primarily to the eyes of its audience. Considered in the context of his preference of the Painter over the Poet, Timon's confession that the entertainment is "mine own device" ought not to surprise auditors. The obviously sycophantic, carnal nature of the masque's visually enticing performance may constitute the poet/dramatist Shakespeare's criticism of the masques produced for the idle, wasteful banquets of James I and Queen Anne. Degenerate works perhaps in the playwright's opinion suited indolent lords and ladies.

Nowhere in the play does Shakespeare indicate the manner by which Timon acquired his immense wealth. Timon "is so completely lacking in wisdom," according to Willard Farnham, "that one wonders how he could ever have been useful to Athens in a responsible position."[50] Apparently never earned through productive labor, his riches slip easily through his fingers to parasites, who also are not engaged in any constructive employment. The Athens that Shakespeare portrays appears to be an essentially idle city, the precursor of Cleon's idle Tharsus in *Pericles*.[51] In a soft society, original art of moral integrity rarely, or never, appears. Once Timon's riches vanish and his false friends desert him, he becomes a bitter misanthrope, seeking a hermit life in the woods about Athens. In the forest, Timon enacts a parody of the pastoral Golden Age. Digging for roots to sustain life, he finds, to his disgust, gold instead. As portrayed by Ovid and other classical poets, the original age was golden because gold was absent from pastoral men's and women's idyllic relationships. Never having had to sweat to earn his wealth, Timon—almost comically—does not have to labor to acquire gold in the Athenian woods; it appears below the earth's surface almost as soon as he begins digging for roots. Giving it to the bandits and whores he meets in the woods, Timon proposes using the gold as a weapon of pestilence against the city which deserted him. In the midst of his terrible instructions to the bandits, Timon discovers the work that Athenians perform—if work it can be called. "Like workmen, I'll example you with thievery" (IV. iii. 435), he announces, proceeding to portray the natural processes of the cosmos as myriad stealings of light and energy by one body from another. The strongly transitive verbs that cluster in Timon's catalogue of gold's working of humanity reflect the misanthrope's belief that the dull metal chiefly stirs Athenians to whatever activity they pursue (IV. iii. 25-48, 381-92, 429-49). Gold, in Timon's opinion, moves humanity to perform its defining labor—thievery (IV. iii. 435-49). By their chosen "trade," the Bandits honestly realize human nature. Or so Timon claims.

Shakespeare represents the injustice of Timon's categorizing all humanity as thieving "workers" through the painstakingly honest service of Flavius and Timon's other servants. Never leaving Timon until his master drives them away, the Steward Flavius and his fellow servants present the major images of admirable work in the play.[52] Their performance of their duties in attending to Timon's needs—while he permits them to do so—perhaps amounts to Shakespeare's commentary on the locus of meaningful labor at the Jacobean court and in the great houses of English lords. As the play unfolds, Timon becomes a progressively static, fixed character. Like Malbecco in Book 3 of *The Faerie Queene*, he gradually transforms himself from a relatively three-dimensional character into an allegorical emblem. "I am Misanthropos, and hate mankind" (IV. iii. 54), he informs Alcibiades. This hypostatization of being is a consequence of Timon's narcissistic fixation on self, a long-established trait conclusively identified by Flavius. "It is vain that you would speak with Timon," he tells two senators at the beginning of act V:

> For he is set so only to himself,
> That nothing but himself which looks like man
> Is friendly to him.
> (V. i. 116-19)

Idleness has played a major role in feeding the narcissism that locks Timon in an empty prison of the self. The senators, fearful of Alcibiades' troops, initially suggest that Timon would continue to be idle, were he to accept their invitation to return to Athens. Timon hears that the senators "have thought/ On special dignities, which vacant lie,/ For thy best use and wearing" (V. i. 141-43). The slightness and the hollowness of the occupation—the "using" of "dignities" by simply "wearing" them, dignities that have lain "vacant"—are made apparent by Shakespeare's diction. Afterwards, however, the senators disclose their cowardly motive in trying to draw Timon back to Athens by offering him the captainship of Athens' defense against Alcibiades' imminent attack (V. i. 159-66). Even if he could transcend his misanthropy—which he cannot—to accept the senators' offer, Timon's formerly idle life—his general unpreparedness for any kind of work—disqualifies him from the position.

In act V of the play, Shakespeare brings back the Painter and the Poet. Timon's newly acquired gold, like his original wealth, continues in the fashion of a magnet to draw the greedy to him. In uncharacteristic dramaturgy, Shakespeare reintroduces a pair of opening-scene characters—the Painter and the Poet—at the end of the play to emphasize the issues that they delineated in act I, scene i. In act V, the artists' avarice becomes especially transparent. Attending Timon in the woods, the Painter maintains, will "very likely . . . load our purposes/ With what they travail for" (V. i. 14-15). Unproductive, the Painter and Poet on this occasion can only promise Timon future works as recompense for his patronage. The artists seem to have become absolutely idle. "Promising is the very air o' th' time," the Painter argues lazily:

> It opens the eyes of expectation.
> Performance is ever the duller for his act,
> And but in the plainer and simpler kind of people
> The deed of saying is quite out of use.
> To promise is most courtly and fashionable;
> Performance is a kind of will or testament
> Which argues a great sickness in his judgment
> That makes it.
> (V. i. 22-30)

Coming out of his cave, Timon interrupts the Painter's rationalization of nonperformance, ironically greeting him as "Excellent workman!" (V. i. 31). Forming the blank-verse conclusion of the Painter's speech, Timon's phrase functions by contrast to stress the artist's idleness. Timon's next utterance—"thou canst not paint a man/ So bad as is thyself" (V. i. 31-32)—recalls the earlier notion that the artist in his work can never transcend his own innate corruption, which he shares with fallen humanity. Overhearing the Poet's resolution to promise him a "satire against the softness of prosperity,/ With a discovery of the infinite flatteries/ That follow youth and opulency," Timon in an aside asks, "Must thou needs/ Stand for a villain in thine own work?" (V. i. 35-38). Shakespeare reformulates Duke Senior's victory over Jaques, who protests in *As You Like It* that he can satirize citizens with impunity, in Timon's probing query, "Wilt thou whip thine own faults in other men?" (V. i. 39). If *Timon of Athens* is the unfinished play that it appears to be,[53] Shakespeare may have abandoned its composition because he became convinced that his own mortal faults disqualified him from putting the extreme satire of humankind in Timon's mouth as prescribed by his Plutarchan source material. "I will chide no breather in the world but myself," he had made Orlando say, "against whom I know most faults" (*As You Like It*, III. ii. 280-81). In his work, Shakespeare may have resolved not to project or perpetuate his imagined badness upon audiences already weighed down by the inheritance of cursed Adam.

In Timon's and the Poet's exchange, Shakespeare implies that the most effective, accurate representation of humanity requires an honest artist. Concerning Timon's so-called friends' falling away, the Poet objects, "I am rapt and cannot cover/ The monstrous bulk of this ingratitude/ With any size of words" (V. i. 64-66). "Let it go naked," Timon replies facetiously, "men may see't the better." "You that are honest," he sarcastically asserts, "by being what you are/ Make them best seen and known" (V. i. 67-69). Beneath Timon's irony, Shakespeare suggests that the artist must strive to make himself honest so that the vices of humanity can be known by contrast. Initially, the artist's labor involves self-fashioning—his making of himself a relatively excellent piece of work. Shakespeare in *Timon of Athens* articulates the principle that informs the characterizations of honest artists in the late romances such as Cerimon, Cornelius, and Prospero (though the magician's honesty is somewhat ambiguous). If a certain nakedness typifies the relatively uncomplicated, less dense poetic style of *Pericles*, the honest playwright's desire not to "cover/ The monstrous bulk" of the vices of characters such as Antiochus and Dionyza "with any size [quantity/facing] of words" may be its source. When

Timon tells the Poet, "Why, thy verse swells with stuff so fine and smooth/ That thou art even natural in thine art" (V. i. 84-85), he implies that his pompous artistry necessarily reveals his inner nature, which is proud and vain. When he says, "There's never a one of you but trusts a knave [the self]/ That mightily deceives you" (V. i. 93-94), he indicates that the dishonest artist lacks the self knowledge requisite for meaningful work. Promising to give the dull-witted Poet and Painter gold for killing these slanderous knaves, Timon suggests that the artist must strive to separate himself from his baser nature, which deserves extinction.[54] "Each man apart, all single and alone," he pronounces; "Yet an arch-villain keeps him company" (V. i. 108). Seeing that the artists still do not catch his meaning, Timon ragefully throws gold at the Painter, shouting "You have work for me; there's payment, hence!" (V. i. 113). Timon gives gold, the agent of vice and self-destruction for no-work, the empty promise of labor. In this sense, the wages of the nonproductive corrupt artist worker is death. Throwing a stone at the stunned Poet, he cries, "You are an alcumist, make gold of that" (V. i. 114). Timon's fierce allusion to the alchemist's imagined ability to turn base matter into gold serves to remind auditors that this Poet in his work cannot refine humanity into moral and spiritual gold, as the magician artist Prospero will later do.

Does anyone beside Flavius perform meaningful work in *Timon of Athens*? Delivering his final speech, despairing Timon contends that "Graves only be men's works, and death their gain!" (V. i. 222). Timon's writing of his epitaph, carved into his gravestone at the sea's edge, appears to be the only significant labor of his life. His conceit may be "rich," in making "vast Neptune weep for aye/ On [his] low grave" (V. iv. 78-79), in placing his grave where the tide regularly washes it; yet the epitaph itself consists of only two poetically undistinguished couplets. Not much value inheres in the hateful verses of Timon's grave-work, which simply realizes his immense self-pity (in the "tears" of Neptune shed daily on the grave).

Only Alcibiades promises to perform socially beneficial labor. Banished from Athens by angry senators who resent his challenge to their authority (III. v), Alcibiades returns with his troops, intending to raze his birthplace. At the walls of the "coward and lascivious town" (V. iv. 1), senators convince him not to kill the innocent but only those citizens guilty of crimes against their fellow Athenians. (Conveniently, those guilty of Alcibiades' banishment have already died). "Like a shepherd," First Senator begs, "approach the fold and cull th' infected forth,/ But kill not all together" (V. iv. 42-44). At the conclusion of *Timon of Athens*, Shakespeare reemploys the pastoral imagery of warfare that permeates *Coriolanus*. Alcibiades agrees to become a husbandman whose labor involves the curing of a diseased city.[55] He promises to do the work of the physician-soldier, performing a regenerative task and fulfilling a role that eluded Coriolanus. Alcibiades speaks the play's last words, pledging to

> Make war breed peace, make peace stint war, make each
> Prescribe to other as each other's leech.
> Let our drums strike.
> (V. iv. 83-85)

With these verses, Shakespeare forges a link to *Pericles* and *Cymbeline*. By making war and peace physic each other, the soldier Alcibiades becomes society's master doctor, a laborer like Cerimon and Cornelius for the common good.

Notes

1. Elliot Krieger, *A Marxist Study of Shakespeare's Comedies* (London: Macmillan, 1979) 54-64, 68; 89-96; 131-33, 140-42, 147-53. Also see Paul N. Siegel, *Shakespeare's English and Roman History Plays: A Marxist Approach* (Rutherford, NJ: Fairleigh Dickinson UP, 1986) 25.

2. Russell Fraser, *Young Shakespeare* (New York: Columbia UP, 1988) 38-39.

3. Bert O. States, in *"Hamlet" and the Concept of Character* (Baltimore: The Johns Hopkins UP, 1992), demonstrates that the speech about the "fat weed" and "Lethe wharf" is a "perfect description of the phlegmatic [slothful] condition" (75-76).

4. For an alternative reading of labor in *Hamlet*, one that stresses the work of the scriptive hand, see Jonathan Goldberg, "Hamlet's Hand," *Shakespeare Quarterly* 39 (1988): 307-27.

5. Lynda E. Boose, "Othello's Handkerchief: 'The Recognizance and Pledge of Love,'" *English Literary Renaissance* 5 (1975): 360-74.

6. Cf. Rosalie L. Colie, "Reason and Need: *King Lear* and the 'Crisis' of the Aristocracy," *Some Facets of "King Lear": Essays in Prismatic Criticism*, ed. Rosalie L. Colie and F. T. Flahiff (Toronto: U of Toronto P, 1974) 185-219, esp. 199-202; and Raman Selden, "King Lear and True Need," *Shakespeare Studies* 19 (1987): 143-69, esp. 146, 157-58.

7. William C. Carroll, in "'The Base Shall Top Th'Legitimate': The Bedlam Beggar and the Role of Edgar in *King Lear*," *Shakespeare Quarterly* 38 (1987): 426-41, esp. 431-34, shows from contemporary accounts that Jacobeans generally regarded the bedlam beggar as the fictitious persona of a charlatan, who deserved whipping rather than charity.

8. Alexander Leggatt, "*Macbeth* and the Last Plays," *Mirror Up to Shakespeare: Essays in Honour of G. R. Hibbard*, ed. J. C. Gray (Toronto: U of Toronto P, 1984) 189-207.

9. Evocative descriptions of opposed Roman and Egyptian values appear in Robert Ornstein, "The Ethic of the Imagination: Love and Art in *Antony and Cleopatra*," *Later Shakespeare*, ed. John Russell Brown and Bernard Harris, Stratford-upon-Avon Studies 8 (London: Edward Arnold, 1966) 31-46, esp. 36-38; and in Julian Markels, *The Pillar of the World: "Antony and Cleopatra" in Shakespeare's Development* (Columbus: Ohio State UP, 1968) 36-48.

10. This aversion receives indirect reinforcement in Antony's case from his close association throughout the play with his ancestor Hercules, noted

for his twelve grand labors. Critics who describe the relevance of Hercules' traits for Antony's characterization—notably Eugene M. Waith, *The Herculean Hero in Marlowe, Chapman, Shakespeare, and Dryden* (New York: Columbia UP, 1962) 113-21; Janet Adelman, *The Common Liar: An Essay on "Antony and Cleopatra"* (New Haven: Yale UP, 1973) 134-37; and J. Leeds Barroll, *Shakespearean Tragedy: Genre, Tradition, and Change in "Antony and Cleopatra"* (Washington: Folger Books, 1984) 89-90, 256-57—neglect this linkage.

11 See Ernest Schanzer, *The Problem Plays of Shakespeare: A Study of "Julius Caesar," "Measure for Measure," and "Antony and Cleopatra"* (1963; rpt. New York: Schocken, 1965) 138-41.

12 In Egypt, doing enigmatically produces arrested motion, a phenomenon anticipating the conflation of stir and stasis in late romances such as *Pericles* and especially *The Winter's Tale*. In *Antony and Cleopatra*, the phenomenon usually consists of a simultaneous undoing of what is done, the result producing an impression of stasis at the heart of action. Enobarbus' magnificent description of Cleopatra recumbent on her barge on the Nile captures the essential idleness, the static quality, of the eastern queen:

> she did lie
> In her pavilion—cloth of gold, of tissue—
> O'er-picturing that Venus where we see
> The fancy outwork nature.
> (II. ii. 198-201)

The only motion reported in this tableau comes from the wind of the "divers-color'd fans" of the "pretty dimpled boys" on either side of Cleopatra (II. ii. 201-3). This breeze seemed "To glow the delicate cheeks which they did cool,/ And what they undid did" (II. ii. 204-5). Referring to the sexual attraction resulting from the breeze disturbing the gauzy fabric of Cleopatra's gown to reveal her physical beauty, the paradoxical phrase "undid did" introduces into the play the notion of two contrary movements whose simultaneity suggests arrest—stasis. (G. Wilson Knight, in *The Imperial Theme* [1931; rpt. London: Methuen, 1965], notices, during his suggestive analysis of Enobarbus' memorable speech as a "microcosm of the play's peculiar vision" [256-58], that "there is motion in this description; but, as in a picture, it is a motion within stillness" [257]). The delicate undoing of doing that occurred on Cleopatra's barge occurs within the context of a stronger, grander operation of the dynamic between stir and stasis. Lying motionless on her barge, a golden idol, Cleopatra draws seemingly all nature to herself:

> The city cast
> Her people out upon her; and Antony
> Enthron'd i' th' market-place, did sit alone,
> Whistling to th' air, which, but for vacancy,

> Had gone to gaze on Cleopatra too,
> And made a gap in nature.
>
> (II. ii. 213-18)

Cleopatra's beauty, condensed in the perfume that wafts over the wharf, magnetically draws Egyptians and Romans alike to the riverside. The only person unmoved by Cleopatra's attraction is Antony paradoxically, her soon-to-be lover. Sitting "Enthron'd i' th' market-place," he represents another static idol, the complement of her venereal image. Not only does his immobility prefigure his later, repeated resistance to Cleopatra's allure and his final, tragic isolation from the queen, it also suggests the alternative stasis at the heart of Roman "business," here symbolized by the marketplace. The fixed purposes, the stoic calm highly valued by Romans in the work of war and statecraft, constitute the alternative to the motionless icon of Cleopatra about which Egyptian life whirls.

13 Cf. Markels 139.

14 In *Mighty Opposites: Shakespeare and Renaissance Contrariety* (Berkeley: U of California P, 1979), Robert Grudin details the extent to which "extreme courses lead to their own opposites" in *Antony and Cleopatra* (165-79, esp. 167-71).

15 On the lack of fixity in Antony, see A. P. Riemer, *A Reading of Shakespeare's "Antony and Cleopatra"* (Sydney: Sydney UP, 1968) 111-14. Adelman (esp. 14-52) persuasively demonstrates that Antony's difficulty in unambiguously interpreting his identity mirrors that of the playgoer/reader with regard to a text/performance singularly resistant to certainty of judgment.

16 For Cleopatra's mutability, see Adelman 154. She asserts that "Cleopatra in her death becomes marble-constant, like a work of art" (155).

17 See E. C. Pettet, "*Coriolanus* and the Midlands Insurrection of 1607," *Shakespeare Survey* 3 (1950): 34-42. Recently, however, Richard Wilson, in "Against the Grain: Representing the Market in *Coriolanus*," *The Seventeenth Century* 6 (1991): 111-48, esp. 111-21, has argued that the contemporary matrix for this aspect of *Coriolanus* was the disturbance associated with the 1597-8 hoarding of corn by Stratford maltsters and farmers. For detailed accounts of the frequency and violence of sixteenth- and seventeenth-century English agricultural riots and disorders, see Susan D. Amussen, *An Ordered Society: Gender and Class in Early Modern England* (Oxford: Basil Blackwell, 1988) 154-56; and Keith Wrightson, *English Society 1580-1680* (New Brunswick, NJ: Rutgers UP, 1982) 143-45, 149-50, 173-79.

18 The latest in a long line of critics to make this point are (most originally) Thomas Sorge, "The Failure of Orthodoxy in *Coriolanus*," *Shakespeare Reproduced: The Text in History and Ideology*, ed. Jean E. Howard

and Marion F. O'Connor (New York: Methuen, 1987) 225-41, esp. 233-35; Michael D. Bristol, "Lenten Butchery: Legitimation Crisis in *Coriolanus*," *Shakespeare Reproduced: The Text in History and Ideology* 207-24, esp. 213-14; and Zvi Jagendorf, "*Coriolanus*: Body Politic and Private Parts," *Shakespeare Quarterly* 41 (1990): 455-69, esp. 458-60. The fullest explication of the importance of Menenius' fable of the belly for *Coriolanus* is given by Leonard Barkin, *Nature's Work of Art: The Human Body as Image* (New Haven: Yale UP, 1975) 95-109.

19 On James I's government's empaneling inquiries into the abuses of enclosures and its doling out a little corn to avoid social revolt, see *Dudley Carleton to John Chamberlain 1603-1624: Jacobean Letters*, ed. Maurice Lee, Jr. (New Brunswick: Rutgers UP, 1972) 99.

20 Roger Lockyer, *The Early Stuarts: A Political History of England, 1603-1642* (London: Longman, 1989) 271-72.

21 This emphasis agrees with Coriolanus' virtually non-existent introspection, which has been gauged by Stanley D. McKenzie, "'Unshout the noise that banish'd Martius': Structural Paradox and Dissembling in *Coriolanus*," *Shakespeare Studies* 18 (1986): 189-204, esp. 189-90. Matthew N. Proser, in *The Heroic Image in Five Shakespearean Tragedies* (Princeton, NJ: Princeton UP, 1967), 144-45, 154, argues that Coriolanus never achieves the *anagnorisis* of Shakespeare's major tragic protagonists.

22 The importance of interpreting *Coriolanus* within a Christian context is shown by J. L. Simmons, *Shakespeare's Pagan World: The Roman Tragedies* (Charlottesville, UP of Virginia, 1973) 18-64.

23 In this respect, see Jagendorf 463: "Looked at from an economic point of view, the language of labor and its reward gives us contradictory answers. On the one hand, Coriolanus' labor, his military prowess, is self-rewarding. As the First Citizen says of him in the first scene, 'he pays himself with being proud' (l. 31). This evokes an economic absurdity, though perfect for an aristocrat. It suggests a form of self-employment, a self-supporting activity in which pride is an inexhaustible form of wealth, both capital and wages. On the other hand, in Volumnia's eyes Coriolanus' work is far from self-rewarding. For her, in a shocking image, the intrepid soldier becomes the lowest kind of agricultural laborer, a wage slave. She imagines Coriolanus on the battlefield:

> His bloody brow
> With his mailed hand then wiping, forth he goes,
> Like to a harvest-man that's tasked to mow
> Or all or lose his hire.
> (1.3.36-39)

This soldier-mower is employed by a very hard taskmaster, and he is subjected to the cruelest of wage conditions, which reduce the heroic challenge of all or nothing (victory or death) to a slave's choice between exhaustion and hunger. Volumnia cannot entertain the possibility that her son may fail. The hero's birthright is to take all. But the possibility of 'nothing' may not be ignored, especially when that absurdity, the aristocrat-laborer, must receive his hire and salary from that political oddity, the plebeian employer." For an excellent analysis of *Coriolanus* in terms of the fluctuating valuation of labor as a marketplace commodity of emerging Renaissance capitalism, see Richard Wilson 111-25, 140-44.

24 Harold Bloom, in the Introduction to *William Shakespeare's "Coriolanus"* (New York: Chelsea House, 1988), remarks that Volumnia "would be at home wearing armor in *The Iliad*" (4).

25 Coriolanus' fatherless status has been explored by Phyllis Rackin, "Coriolanus: Shakespeare's Anatomy of *Virtus*," *Modern Language Studies* 13 (1983): 68-79, esp. 74; and by Stanley Cavell, "'Who Does the Wolf Love?': *Coriolanus* and the Interpretations of Politics," *Shakespeare and the Question of Theory*, ed. Patricia Parker and Geoffrey Hartman (New York: Methuen, 1985) 245-72, esp. 255-56.

26 A contrary reading of Volumnia's speech, one stressing her vulnerability, is given by Christina Luckyj, "Volumnia's Silence," *Studies in English Literature* 31 (1991): 327-42, esp. 330-31.

27 In the words of Michael McCanles, appearing in "The Dialectic of Transcendence in Shakespeare's *Coriolanus*," *PMLA* 82 (1967): 44-53, "The very superiority for which Aufidius embraced Coriolanus in envious love has elicited the envious hate for which Aufidius will kill him. Mirroring Coriolanus's implicit relation to the Roman people, Aufidius's pride perversely bends him to his adversary in a posture of subservience which will generate its dialectical opposite in spiteful revenge" (46).

28 This point is also made—in considerable detail—by Richard Wilson 140-42.

29 In other words, Coriolanus' death is not that of a scapegoat in a tragic ritual—the popular interpretation of (among others) John Holloway, *The Story of the Night: Studies in Shakespeare's Major Tragedies* (1961; rpt. Lincoln: U of Nebraska P, 1963) 130-31; Kenneth Burke, "*Coriolanus*—and the Delights of Faction," *Hudson Review* 19 (1966): 185-202, esp. 190; and James Holstun, "Tragic Superfluity in *Coriolanus*," *English Literary History* 50 (1983): 485-507, esp. 489.

30 "Heavenly virtue," Simmons argues, "is beyond Rome's aristocratic apprehension" (19, 20-26, 53-59).

31 Lockyer 270.

32 Qtd. in Lawrence Stone, *Social Change and Revolution in England 1540-1640* (New York: Barnes & Noble, 1965) 130.

33 Fulke Greville, *The Prose Works of Fulke Greville, Lord Brooke*, ed. John Gouws (Oxford: Clarendon Press, 1986) 127.

34 J. H. Hexter, "Storm Over the Gentry," *Reappraisals in History* (Evanston: Northwestern UP, 1962) 117-62, esp. 147.

35 Leah Marcus, *The Politics of Mirth: Herrick, Milton, Marvell, and the Defense of Old Holiday Pastimes* (Chicago: U of Chicago P, 1986) 83, 278; Lawrence Stone, *The Crisis of the Aristocracy 1558-1641* (Oxford: Clarendon Press, 1965) 58-59, 74, 217. Stone notes that "about three-quarters of the peerage . . . had seen service in the wars of the 1540's, but by 1576 only one peer in four had any military experience. In the early seventeenth century only about one in five had seen action" (266).

36 Qtd. in Stone, *Social Change and Revolution* 119.

37 Sir Walter Ralegh, *The Works of Sir Walter Ralegh*, ed. William Oldys and Thomas Birch (Oxford: Oxford UP, 1829) 8:259.

38 Paul A. Jorgensen, *Shakespeare's Military World* (Berkeley: U of California P, 1956) esp. 4-13, 35-38, 170-207.

39 Peter Lindenbaum, *Changing Landscapes: Anti-Pastoral Sentiment in the English Renaissance* (Athens: U of Georgia P, 1986) 13-14.

40 L. C. Knights, in *Some Shakespearean Themes and An Approach to "Hamlet"* (1960, 1961; rpt. Stanford, CA: Stanford UP, 1966), asserts that "the 'comic' talk of the serving men (IV. v) about the superiority of war to peace . . . merely transposes into another key Volumnia's denial of values essential to life" (144).

41 For the self destruction of the war worker, see also *Antony and Cleopatra* IV. xiv. esp. 39-41, 105.

42 Gary Schmidgall, *Shakespeare and the Poet's Life* (Lexington: UP of Kentucky, 1990) esp. 68-91.

43 Schmidgall 5.

44 Concerning the Poet and Painter, Rolf Soellner, in *"Timon of Athens": Shakespeare's Pessimistic Tragedy* (Columbus: Ohio State UP, 1979), judges that they "are not in competition about the first rank of the arts in the imitation of nature; they belong to the society at the base of Fortune's hill that competes for gold" (134).

45 See Anthony D. Nuttall, *"Timon of Athens,"* Twayne's New Critical Introductions to Shakespeare (Boston: Twayne, 1989) 8-13.

46 George Puttenham, *The Arte of English Poesie*, ed. Edward Arber, A Facsimile Reproduction (1906; rpt. Kent, OH: Kent State UP, 1970) 265.

47 Coppélia Kahn, "'Magic of bounty': *Timon of Athens*, Jacobean Patronage, and Maternal Power," *Shakespeare Quarterly*, 38 (1987): 34-57, esp. 35-37; and W. M. Merchant, "*Timon* and the Conceit of Art," *Shakespeare Quarterly* 6 (1955): 249-57, esp. 249-50, 256-57.

48 That the portrait represents a magnification of Timon's physical traits is clear from the Poet's response to it (I. i. 30-34).

49 This implication is also noted by Soellner 131.

50 Willard Farnham, *Shakespeare's Tragic Frontier* (1950; rpt. Berkeley: U of California P, 1963) 46-47. In "The Unmediated World of *Timon of Athens*," *Shakespeare's Mediated World* (Amherst: U of Massachusetts P, 1976) 119-42, Richard Fly shows that Timon "never really seems to be an integral part of [Athenian] society" (126).

51 Frank W. Brownlow, in *Two Shakespearean Sequences: "Henry VI" to "Richard II" and "Pericles" to "Timon of Athens"* (Pittsburgh: U of Pittsburgh P, 1977), remarks that "the Athenians, from what we see of them, only consume. They do not produce" (223).

52 Kenneth Burke, however, in "*Timon of Athens* and Misanthropic Gold," *Language as Symbolic Action* (Berkeley: U of California P, 1966) 115-24, believes that Flavius' "doglike loyalty of service" amounts only to a dramatic technique for getting Shakespeare's audience to admire a basically "problematical hero" (117-19).

53 See Una Ellis-Fermor, "*Timon of Athens*: An Unfinished Play," *Review of English Studies* 18 (1942): 270-83.

54 In "Shakespeare and the Paragone: A Reading of *Timon of Athens*," *Images of Shakespeare*, ed. Werner Habicht, D. J. Palmer, Roger Pringle (Newark: U of Delaware P, 1988) 47-63, John Dixon Hunt argues that Shakespeare stages a paragone between Poet and Painter in *Timon* in order to call attention to the fact that the subtle synchronization of seeing and hearing in his own theatrical art transcends the single capacities of poetry (limited only to words) and painting (limited only to vision).

55 Fly further explains this dimension of Alcibiades' role at the end of *Timon* (141-42).

Chapter 3

Pericles

At the beginning of *Pericles*, when Antiochus likens his Daughter to "this fair Hesperides,/ With golden fruit, but dangerous to be touch'd" (I. i. 27-28), he identifies the myth that the Prince of Tyre has used to express his desire for her:

> You gods that made me man, and sway in love,
> That have inflam'd desire in my breast
> To taste the fruit of yon celestial tree
> (Or die in th' adventure), be my helps,
> As I am son and servant to your will,
> To compass such a boundless happiness!
> (I. i. 19-24)

To win Antiochus' Daughter, suitors must solve a riddle; an incorrect answer condemns them to death. Antiochus focuses the gravity of Pericles' task by comparing it to one of the twelve labors of Hercules. The mythic embellishment suggests that the intellectual exercise of trying to solve the riddle amounts to heroic work. Undertaking the solution of the riddle requires courage of the magnitude that Hercules expressed when he fought and killed the dragons guarding the Hesperidean garden where the golden apples grew. Antiochus extends the myth to cover the impaled skulls of suitors who failed to solve the riddle; they are the "death-like dragons" who ought to "affright" Pericles "hard" (I. i. 29).[1] Secretly committing incest with the Daughter, Antiochus has no intention of releasing her to the successful riddle solver. The ominous skulls almost certainly include some that once contained minds sufficiently shrewd to solve the riddle—it is, after all, rather transparent—but not clever enough to devise a quick defense against Antiochus' knife. Playgoers familiar with the transmitted story of Pericles realize that the Prince is in a no-win situation. The heroic labor of attempting to solve the riddle produces no golden fruit. It represents work bound by design for frustration.

Significantly, the riddle itself underscores the labor involved in seeking a mate. Pericles reads:

> I am no viper, yet I feed
> On mother's flesh which did me breed.
> I sought a husband, in which labor
> I found that kindness in a father.
> He's father, son, and husband mild;
> I mother, wife—and yet his child.
> How they may be, and yet in two,
> As you will live, resolve it you.
> (I. i. 64-71)

Seeking a worthy mate usually requires an often risky venturing abroad, an expense of physical and emotional energy. In this sense, the Daughter has not labored—as Pericles has in traveling to Antiochus' court and risking his life. Father and daughter collapse the family inwardly upon itself; like a black hole, it traps and neutralizes all energy that would escape. Antiochus' and the Daughter's turning sexually to one another amounts to no labor at all but the easiest, sin-ridden kind of solution to the challenge posed by self-fulfillment beyond the family. By thinking of her father/husband as her son, the Daughter reveals that, in her own mind at least, she has already performed the labor associated with womankind. And yet of course the labor is no labor. No son has been—or will be—born.[2] The Daughter's absent, never-mentioned mother performed the only true labor in Antiochus' family when she gave birth to the Daughter. But the fruit of that labor promises barrenness in the sterile incest which the Daughter practices. Her diabolical, so-called labor of incest (I. i. 66-67) cancels Pericles' heroic labor of sailing to Antioch and bravely venturing for her.

Prepared to work to win the Daughter, Pericles finds instead that he must strive to conceal from Antiochus his knowledge of the true import of the riddle. The result is the most fretted poetry in the first half of the play:

> Great King,
> Few love to hear the sins they love to act;
> 'Twould braid yourself too near for me to tell it.

> Who has a book of all that monarchs do,
> He's more secure to keep it shut than shown;
> For vice repeated is like the wand'ring wind,
> Blows dust in others' eyes, to spread itself;
> And yet the end of all is bought thus dear,
> The breath is gone, and the sore eyes see clear
> To stop the air would hurt them. The blind mole casts
> Copp'd hills towards heaven, to tell the earth is throng'd
> By man's oppression, and the poor worm doth die for't.
> Kings are earth's gods; in vice their law's their will;
> And if Jove stray, who dares say Jove doth ill?
> It is enough you know, and it is fit,
> What being more known grows worse, to smother it.
> All love the womb that their first being bred,
> Then give my tongue like leave to love my head.
> (I. i. 91-108)

The sheer energy expended in this laborious circumlocution, packed with tortuous, obscure imagery, represents the vigor that Pericles planned to release in solving the riddle. To the degree that a riddle employs difficult, enigmatic language, Pericles' frustrated response to the simple riddle becomes the real riddle of the play.[3] Moreover, in keeping with Shakespeare's focus upon labor in this episode, Pericles' speech communicates an aborted birth. He toils to say that he will never labor—never deliver the child/secret of Antiochus' and the Daughter's incest. In the concluding couplet of his speech, Pericles likens his head to a womb, with the child his tongue. By saying "Then give my tongue like leave to love my head," he ambiguously states that he will never proclaim Antiochus' secret, thus qualifying as a solver worthy of keeping his head on his shoulders. But by remaining in the "womb," continuing to love the parent head, the child/tongue in Pericles' complex metaphor commits a kind of incest certainly different in kind from that of Antiochus and the Daughter but lethal nevertheless.[4] The image of infanticide contained within Pericles' declaration to smother "what being known grows worse" conveys the moral price he pays for aborting the labor of delivering the truth.

Paradoxically, however, Pericles' toil in uttering the labored circumlocution that he will never labor to deliver Antiochus' secret discovers to Antiochus his knowledge of the incest. In a mangled form, Pericles *has* given birth to the truth, apparently without knowledge of the fact. "Heaven, that I had thy head! He has found the meaning" (I. i. 109), Antiochus exclaims in an aside. "He must not live to trumpet forth my infamy," the guilty king concludes, "Nor tell the world Antiochus doth sin/ In such a loathed manner" (I. i. 145-47). Pericles, given the respite of forty days to come up with a more satisfactory answer to the riddle, nevertheless flees Antioch. Once in Tyre, "dull-ey'd melancholy" afflicts him. By not giving birth to the whole, well-shaped truth, by having his tongue in a sense incestuously make love to his head, Pericles must live with the consciousness of an aborted, bloody thought.

The knowledge of evil freezes him in melancholy idleness. This physical idleness, however, contrasts with the profound stir of his passions. "Then it is thus," he tells Tyrian lords,

> the passions of the mind,
> That have their first conception by misdread,
> Have after-nourishment and life by care;
> And what was first but fear what might be done,
> Grows elder now, and cares it be not done.
> (I. ii. 11-15)

While he has botched truth's birth, Pericles nevertheless has conceived a multitude of offsprings, the passions of his mind which, fed by anxiety and now grown to formidable size, have begun—like the dragonets in Spenser's Cave of Error—to feed on their begetter's flesh. Pericles says that his concern as ruler for his people threatened by Antiochus' homicidal guilt "Makes both my body pine and soul to languish." It also makes him determined to "punish that"—his flesh—"before that he would punish" (I. ii. 32-33). Pericles eats his flesh as effectively and as terribly—at least in his own estimation—as the Daughter ate her mother's flesh when she "changed flesh" (copulated) with her father (into whom marriage and intercourse had assimilated her mother's flesh). Pericles has come to participate in the incest he fled.

The faithful counselor Helicanus dissolves the Prince's physical lassitude with the advice that he "go travel for a while" (I. ii. 106), until Antiochus either forgets his rage or dies. In Helicanus' opinion, this absence will save the lives of both Pericles and his innocent subjects. In his regressive mood, however, Pericles regards this strategy of wandering as a kind of secure withdrawal from the (inevitable) turbulence of living. "But in our orbs we'll live so round and safe," he concludes, "That time of both this truth shall ne'er convince,/ Thou show'dst a subject's shine, I a true prince" (I. ii. 122-24). The resemblance of the image of a self-contained ball in Pericles' phrase "orbs . . . so round and safe" to the round womb and the enclosure of incest suggests the mistaken nature of the Prince's conclusion. When, in the next scene, Helicanus tells a white lie designed to turn Antiochus' assassin, Thaliard, aside from his pursuit of the traveling Prince, the counselor characterizes the kind of activity represented by Pericles' journeying:

> Royal Antiochus, on what cause I know not,
> Took some displeasure at him, at least he judg'd so;
> And doubting lest he had err'd or sinn'd,
> To show his sorrow, he'd correct himself;
> So puts himself unto the shipman's toil,
> With whom each minute threatens life or death.
> (I. iii. 19-24)

Pericles' sea travel in fact amounts to labor, "the shipman's toil," a kind of work not highly prized during Shakespeare's age. His traveling indirectly results from his inability to solve or respond successfully to Antiochus' riddle. In this respect, the heroic labor that he had hoped to display in solving it instead appears as the apparently demeaning toil of a common sailor.[5]

This image of work immediately contrasts with the picture of decadent idleness presented in the next episode, which concerns Pericles' gift of grain to the starving citizens of Tharsus. Shakespeare locates the source of Tharsus' collapse in a supersophistication, an idle epicureanism that saps moral and physical strength. King Cleon exclaims,

> This Tharsus, o'er which I have the government,
> A city on whom plenty held full hand,
> For riches strew'd herself even in her streets;
> Whose towers bore heads so high they kiss'd the clouds,
> And strangers ne'er beheld but wond'red at;
> Whose men and dames so jetted and adorn'd,
> Like one another's glass to trim them by;
> Their tables were stor'd full, to glad the sight,

> And not so much to feed on as delight;
> All poverty was scorn'd, and pride so great,
> The name of help grew odious to repeat.
> (I. iv. 21-31)

The lords and ladies of Tharsus never valued clothing or food rightly—as the necessary means to lives of productive and charitable works. Consequently, in their weakened, listless condition, even their mouths "are now starv'd for want of exercise" (I. iv. 38). The voluptuous idleness of the citizens of Tharsus left granaries empty and the city unable to defend itself from invaders. Through the imagery of cannibalism, Shakespeare links the defect of unheroic sloth to the moral slackness of incest. Even as incestuous desire drove Antiochus' Daughter to eat her mother's flesh, so in Queen Dionyza's words,

> Those mothers who, to nousle up their babes,
> Thought nought too curious, are ready now
> To eat those little darlings whom they lov'd.
> So sharp are hunger's teeth, that man and wife
> Draw lots who first shall die to lengthen life.
> (I. iv. 42-46)

By preventing a kind of incest—cannibalism—Pericles begins atoning for his complicity with sexual incest. His humane gift of corn to these starving people, while not the product of his personal toil, nevertheless stresses the value of provident work.[6] Gower's Chorus to act II, the subsequent scene, accentuates this idea in the portrait of industrious Helicanus:

> Good Helicane, that stay'd at home,
> Not to eat honey like a drone
> From others' labors; for though he strive
> To killen bad, keep good alive....
> (Chorus II, 17-20)

These verses suggest the alternative to the citizens of Tharsus—drones of no socially useful labor.

Shakespeare keeps the stress on productive labor in the following episode of the play: Pericles' encounter with three homely fishermen, who sustain him after shipwreck. Shakespeare consistently portrays the fishermen as exemplary figures of vigorous work. "Look how thou stir'st now!" (II. i. 16), the

Master exclaims to Pilch and Patch-breech; "Come away, or I'll fetch th' with a wanion" (II. i. 16-17). Patch-breech's whimsical remedy for the injustice of whale-like misers, who swallow the poor along with "the whole parish, church, steeple, bells, and all" (II. i. 34), consists of redemptive stirring—"and when I had been in his belly, I would have kept such a jangling of the bells, that he should never have left till he cast bells, steeple, church, and parish up again" (II. i. 40-43). In the next piece of dialogue, Shakespeare immediately associates such a moral stirring, punishing to idle misers, with the fishermen's honest, productive work:

> But if the good King Simonides were of my mind—
> *Per.* [*Aside.*] Simonides?
> *3. Fish.* We would purge the land of these drones, that rob the bee of her honey.[7]
> (II. i. 43-47)

Images of drone-like idleness and redemptive labor closely connect three geographically disparate scenes early in *Pericles*. "All poverty was scorn'd" by the epicurean lords and ladies of Tharsus, who become dependent sponges. Poverty, however, is dignified in the industrious fishermen of Pentapolis, who shrewdly anatomize a social injustice of Jacobean England—one involving idle landlords who disrupted the economies of production and distribution so that poor laborers were deprived of the fruits of their work. Shipwrecked Pericles, who has just relieved the starving citizens of Tharsus with a gift of corn, is given food by the industrious fishermen. If they had not been pursuing their work, casting nets in the sea, his father's armor, essential to his plan for winning Thaisa, would never have been recovered. The fishermen's labor thus indirectly advances Pericles at a crucial moment in his providential quest.

Given the valuation of work in the fishermen's dialogue, the playgoer finds Pericles' greeting especially appropriate: "Peace be at your labor, honest fishermen" (II. i. 52). Within a three-scene sequence (I. iv, Chorus II, II. i), the pronouncement places the fishermen at an apex built upon the opposition of idleness and socially useful labor. However, Pericles himself, at this moment in his pilgrimage, has not attained a full appreciation of the virtue of labor. Stripped by the tempest of all worldly goods, he is reduced to begging aid from the fishermen. "He asks of you," he rather stiffly exclaims, "that never us'd to beg" (II. i. 62). The master fisherman quickly hears the slight tone of aristocratic disdain in Pericles' voice. He responds with a mild rebuke illustrating a social injustice: "No, friend, cannot you beg? Here's them in our country of Greece gets more with begging than we can do with working" (II. i. 63-65). Pericles' lordly ignorance of the practical labor required to provide the necessities of life emerges.

> 2. Fish.   Canst thou catch any fishes then?
> Per.   I never practic'd it.
> 2. Fish.   Nay then thou wilt starve sure; for here's nothing to be got now-a-days unless thou canst fish for't.
> (II. i. 66-70)
>
> 2. Fish.   Hark you, my friend. You said you could not beg?
> Per.   I did but crave.
> 2. Fish.   But crave? Then I'll turn craver too, and so I shall scape whipping.
> Per.   Why, are your beggars whipt then?
> (II. i. 85-90)

This last dialogue casts Pilch as Pericles' superior in mental acumen; he shrewdly catches the aristocratic obtuseness of the Prince's self-serving equivocation of "craver" for "beggar" and turns it into a joke that reveals his tough grasp of society's dynamics, a joke that further incriminates Pericles when Pilch discovers the Prince's ignorance of a whole stratum of life: that of beggars whose whipping was a common sight. Pericles' disadvantage deepens in his failure to grasp the thrust of Pilch's insight into wishing to be beadle if all the beggars are to be whipped (II. i. 91-93). Pericles' patronizing rejoinder, "How well this honest mirth becomes their labor!" (II. i. 94-95), reveals that he regards their keen quips as pastime. The Prince of Tyre does not understand that the life of honest labor itself is the catalyst for the fishermen's social wisdom.[8]

As part of the festivities surrounding the tourney, each knight presents Thaisa with a shield emblematically painted by the bearer. "'Tis now your honor, daughter, to entertain/ The labor of each knight in his device" (II. ii. 14-15), Simonides judges. Pericles' labor consists of "A withered branch, that's only green at top;/ The motto: '*In hac spe vivo*'"—"a pretty moral," in Simonides' opinion. "From the dejected state wherein he is," Simonides interprets, "He hopes by you his fortunes yet may flourish" (II. ii. 43-47). Despite his success in defeating all challengers, Pericles' behavior in Simonides' court continues to manifest the uncomplimentary passivity dating from his traumatic experience in Antioch.[9] It is as though the superficial resemblance of a trial for a royal daughter's hand and Antiochus' test becomes an identity in his melancholy mind, and he resolves upon a strategy of frightened detachment from events. "In framing an artist, art hath thus decreed," Simonides pronounces, "To make some good, but others to exceed,/ And you are her labor'd scholar" (II. iii. 15-17). Pericles' scholarly labors of art, however, never become an onstage image.

When Simonides praises Pericles' playing of music, a skill that playgoers have never witnessed, Pericles demurs: "It is your Grace's pleasure to commend,/ Not my desert" (II. v. 29-30). To Simonides' persistent "Sir, you are music's master," he limply replies, "The worst of all her scholars, my good lord" (II. v. 30-31). Such watery disclaimers work against the establishment of the image of Pericles as labored scholar. Unlike the other knights, Pericles has to be coerced into dancing with Thaisa (II. iii. 100-6), a fact that undercuts Simonides' judgment that the Prince excels in the art (II. iii. 107-8). It is not Pericles' accomplishments in the liberal and courtly arts that win Thaisa but his offstage martial prowess, his good looks (II. iii. 36-37), and—for playgoers at least—his stirring rejection of Simonides' accusation of villainy. Melancholy Pericles finally stirs himself, just at the moment when playgoers' interest in him has almost evaporated; yet the labor of art plays a negligible role in this reclamation. Pericles' scholarly accomplishments recommend his appointment as Thaisa's tutor—her "schoolmaster" (II. v. 40)—but Simonides appoints him only in the scene in which their betrothal occurs, after, that is, they have fallen irrevocably in love.

Simonides' stirring of Pericles represents the faint hope that the Prince may someday act in a way to win playgoers' admiration. As a male aristocrat, Pericles has had few opportunities for either ennobling or productive labor. The work that helps to give the fishermen their insights is beneath him. The creative labor of childbirth into which Thaisa falls is denied him. What remains is the profound agitation—the work—produced within him by the natural tempest of living a star-crossed life. The sea storms that periodically shake Pericles symbolize these figurative tempests. Significantly, a great sea storm induces Thaisa's labor (Chorus III, 46-52). This dramatic fact encourages playgoers to think of the tempest itself as a kind of labor, nature's labor that can move subjected persons to different kinds of work. "The sea works high" (III. i. 47-48), First Sailor proclaims. In the Antioch episode, Pericles fashioned a metaphor of head and tongue expressive of aborted birth and silence. The Prince gives birth to memorable poetic speech at the precise instant that Thaisa gives birth to Marina.[10] Both works represent responses to nature's great labor—the tempest. Battered by the storm, Pericles exclaims,

> The god of this great vast, rebuke these surges,
> Which wash both heaven and hell; and thou that hast
> Upon the winds command, bind them in brass,
> Having call'd them from the deep! O, still
> Thy deaf'ning, dreadful thunders, gently quench
> Thy nimble, sulphurous flashes!—O, how, Lychorida!
> How does my queen?—Thou storm, venomously
> Wilt thou spet all thyself? The seaman's whistle
> Is as a whisper in the ears of death,
> Unheard.—Lychorida!—Lucina, O!
> Divinest patroness, and midwife gentle
> To those that cry by night, convey thy Deity
> Aboard our dancing boat, make swift the pangs
> Of my queen's travails!—Now, Lychorida!
> (III. i. 1-14)

Generations of commentators on *Pericles* have praised this poetry as marking Shakespeare's appearance in another dramatist's composition.[11] By contrast with the mostly puerile expression of Pericles in the first two acts of the play—the intricate "blind mole" speech constitutes a notable exception—these verses possess an attractive energy and eloquence, faintly reminiscent of similar idioms of *King Lear*. The utterance "those that cry by night" resonates beyond the local episode, signalling an inclusive empathy for all those distressed persons who moan to darkness, while the phrase "dancing boat" reflects a relative originality beyond the reach of the Pericles of acts I and II. Nevertheless, this stirred verse, which represents a kind of labor on the speaker's part, paradoxically concerns itself with stasis and quiet. Pericles calls upon Neptune to "rebuke these surges"—to quiet them, that is—and upon Aeolus to bind the roaring winds in brass and "still" the "deaf'ning, dreadful thunders." The same paradox informs the other noteworthy mid-play speech of Pericles'—his moving farewell to the apparent corpse of Thaisa:

> A terrible child-bed hast thou had, my dear,
> No light, no fire. Th' unfriendly elements
> Forgot thee utterly, nor have I time
> To give thee hallow'd to thy grave, but straight
> Must cast thee, scarcely coffin'd, in the ooze,
> Where, for a monument upon thy bones,
> The e'er-remaining lamps, the belching whale
> And humming water must o'erwhelm thy corpse,
> Lying with simple shells.
>
> (III. i. 56-64)

Again, what will be called in later Shakespearean plays a "working" mind produces charged, richly textured poetry expressive of silence and rest. Pericles' meditation concludes in the imaginative vision of Thaisa's embalmed corpse "lying with simple shells" and "humming water" that it cannot hear.[12]

Pericles' grim tribute to the victory of stillness and quiet over the human spirit negates his plea to the gods to save his family. His capitulation to despair reflects his weak faith in the gods' providence for his and Thaisa's lives. He has no way of knowing that the goddess Diana orders the great tempests of life to make elected mortals happier eventually through the refining crosses that they bear. When Pericles first leaves Tyre, Second Lord prays, "keep your mind, till you return to us,/ Peaceful and comfortable!" (I. ii. 35-36). In retrospect, playgoers value Helicanus' harsh labeling this advice as flattery potentially harmful to the Prince. The troubled, working mind refines and develops character. In other words, Diana makes nature labor in the form of events such as tempests in order to provoke a corresponding labor within elected men and women. In the case of aristocratic Pericles, exempt from the labor of the mass of humankind, this strategy is one of the few means for inciting work.

Allied with the tempest is Cerimon, the learned physician who restores Thaisa to life. By his own account, Cerimon "can speak of the disturbances/ That nature works, and of her cures" (III. ii. 37-38). His phrase "her cures" describes not only remedies such as nature's but also the man-made methods for curing the turmoil that nature works in afflicted persons such as Thaisa. The physician Cerimon represents in *Pericles* a kind of learned labor capable of redressing the destructive work of nature.[13] Early in the episode of Thaisa's recovery, Shakespeare clearly identifies Cerimon as a figure of industry. When two storm-beaten lords enter, Cerimon asks, "Gentlemen,/ Why do you stir so early?" (III. ii. 11-12):

> *1. Gent.* Sir,
> Our lodgings, standing bleak upon the sea,
> Shook as the earth did quake;
> The very principals did seem to rend,
> And all to topple. Pure surprise and fear
> Made me to quit the house.
> *2. Gent.* That is the cause we trouble you so early,
> 'Tis not our husbandry.
> (III. ii. 13-20)

By the word "husbandry," Second Gentleman asserts that zeal for work is not the cause of their early rising. The dialogue and the characters exist solely to define by contrast Cerimon's work habits. The first ten verses of the scene have portrayed him as an industrious doctor, who commands that fire and meat be prepared for two men stunned by the tempest. He requests one of these men to give a drug with which he has been experimenting to the apothecary in order to discover "how it works" (III. ii. 10). All this occurs before the indolent, frightened gentlemen make their appearance. In his ignorance of the virtues of painstaking labor, First Gentleman links himself to the epicurean inhabitants of Tharsus:

> But I much marvel that your lordship, having
> Rich tire about you, should at these early hours
> Shake off the golden slumber of repose.
> 'Tis most strange
> Nature should be so conversant with pain,
> Being thereto not compelled.
> (III. ii. 21-26)

Worshipping sleep, taking pains only when compelled, First Gentleman reveals his superficiality when he implies that lords who can afford expensive robes should sleep late. Cerimon's sarcastic "O, you say well" (III. ii. 20), a response to First Gentleman's uncomplimentary explanation of their early visit, indicates that he judges the effete lords as harshly as we do.

First Gentleman refers to Cerimon as "your lordship"; by making the physician a lord—almost certainly an anomaly in Jacobean England—Shakespeare implies that not all aristocrats are lazy or socially useless. Cerimon explains that he has conditioned himself to the pain involved in learning and practicing his art because he believes that "Virtue and cunning [are] endowments greater/ Than nobleness and riches" (III. ii. 27-28). In his opinion, these qualities can confer immortality, "Making a man a god" (III. ii. 30-31). Dwelling and working in Ephesus, a city which later would acquire Christian overtones, Cerimon has "pour'd forth/ [His] charity, and hundreds call themselves/ [His] creatures, who by [him] have been restored" (III. ii. 43-45). In Shakespeare's physician, work and charity are joined.

Servants carrying the chest containing Thaisa appropriately interrupt Second Gentleman's oily adulation of Cerimon; the industrious doctor does not have the leisure to hear windy eulogies. That it is Cerimon's labor that saves Thaisa's life is underscored by the physician's angry rebuke of a servant:

> The rough and woeful music that we have,
> Cause it to sound, beseech you.
> The vial once more. How thou stir'st, thou block!
> The music there!
> (III. ii. 88-91)

By not stirring quickly or intensely enough, the unfortunate assistant contrasts with his animated master, who has applied a "rough and woeful" homeopathic therapy to Thaisa. By his labored art, Cerimon preserves Pericles' queen.[14]

With act IV, Shakespeare shifts his focus to Marina, who is mystically linked to the sea for which she is named. Her reenactment of the moment of her birth appears compulsive:

> Ay me! poor maid,
> Born in a tempest when my mother died,
> This world to me is a lasting storm,
> Whirring me from my friends.
> (IV. i. 17-20)

In her complete ignorance of Marina's existence, Thaisa appears to have lost the fruit of her labor. Associated with the great natural stir of her birth, Marina, however, is a creature of labor—the labored courtly arts that her father possesses but which never, in his case, become a stage reality. And yet physical labor becomes a reality in Marina's vivid portrait of Pericles, which forms part of her recreation of the moment of her birth:

> My father, as nurse says, did never fear,
> But cried, "Good seamen!" to the sailors, galling
> His kingly hands haling ropes,
> And clasping to the mast, endur'd a sea
> That almost burst the deck.
> (IV. i. 52-56)

Her reply to Leonine's question "When was this?" associates the sailors' work with the moment of her birth:

> When I was born.
> Never was waves nor wind more violent,
> And from the ladder-tackle washes off
> A canvas-climber. "Ha!" says one, "wolt out?"
> And with a dropping industry they skip
> From stem to stern.
> (IV. i. 57-63)

This memorable speech closely identifies Marina with the principle of industry.

Leonine's interruption of Marina's narrative with an order that she say her prayers signals his murderous intent. As Dionyza's assassin, Leonine has his own task to perform. "I am sworn," he says, "To do my work with haste" (IV. i. 69-70). His characterization of his bloody task as work recalls the chilling remark of the Captain that Edmund asks to kill Lear and Cordelia. "I cannot draw a cart, nor eat dried oats," he replies, "If it be man's work, I'll do't" (*King Lear*, V. iii. 38-39). The response begs the question of what the proper limits and nature of humanity's work ought to be. This philosophical chord resonates faintly behind Leonine's cold appraisal of his task as work. In the Mytilene brothel scenes, Shakespeare more clearly urges playgoers to consider the question of socially beneficial, proper work.

With "continual action," the Bawd's three remaining whores "are even as good as rotten" (IV. ii. 8-9). The question of whether the occupations of bawd, pander, and whore involve work extends to other unnamed professions through the following dialogue:

>   *Bawd.*   Come, other sorts offend as well as we.
>   *Pand.*   As well as we! ay, and better too; we offend worse. Neither is our profession any trade, it's no calling.
>   (IV. ii. 36-39)

The Pander's punchy rejoinder inadvertently reminds auditors of the noblest kind of labor, a spiritually ordained vocation ("calling"). Neither a profession like Cerimon's medicine nor a trade, the Bawd's and Pander's "business" is a socially destructive activity. By their own account, they are the cause of many bastards, whom they make fatally diseased by the prostitution that they force them to practice at the young age of eleven (IV. ii. 13-16). By speaking of prostitution in capitalist terms, the Pander and Bawd drive home the point that Mytilene, like Jacobean London, accommodates the "business" of pimping and whoring, recognizing it as work by countenancing the marketplace dynamics of buying and selling. The Bawd and Pandar cut the figures of prosperous businesspersons:

>   *Pand.*   Three or four thousand chequins were as pretty a proportion to live quietly, and so give over.
>   *Bawd.*   Why to give over, I pray you? Is it a shame to get when we are old?
>   *Pand.*   O, our credit comes not in like the commodity, nor the commodity wages not with the danger; therefore if in our youths we could pick up some

> pretty estate, 'twere not amiss to keep our door hatch'd.
>
> (IV. ii. 26-33)

By putting the language of commerce into the Bawd's and Pandar's mouths, Shakespeare encourages auditors to regard them as prudent, respectable merchants—an image that playgoers violently reject upon the briefest consideration. Shakespeare's dramatic strategy thus results in playgoers' reactive tendency to condemn the capitalist methodology that permits the sleazy characters to mask their so-called work.[15]

In Boult's opinion, "thunder shall not so awake the beds of eels as my giving out her beauty stirs up the lewdly inclin'd" (IV. ii. 142-44).[16] Marina's physical beauty is so alluring that verbal descriptions of it produce a tempest of libido among carnally inclined listeners. Or so Boult imagines. Actually, the effect of Marina upon the brothel's patrons is otherwise. Preaching divinity in the stews, she spiritually converts gallants, driving them, in the words of one surprised gentleman, "out of the road of rutting for ever" (IV. v. 9). In the Bawd's view, paralysis describes her effect: "Fie, fie upon her, she's able to freeze the god Priapus, and undo a whole generation" (IV. vi. 3-4). Arresting the carnal stir, Marina undoes (renders static) not just the libidos of men but the Bawd and Pander's so-called business. This emphasis upon Marina's undoing of prostitution persists throughout this scene, with Boult exclaiming that her chastity "shall undo a whole household" (IV. vi. 124) and the Bawd complaining that "She's born to undo us" (IV. vi. 149). Whether Marina has a right to undo the institution of whoredom becomes the question posed at the conclusion of the Mytilene segment of the play. When Marina paints a graphic word picture of Boult's occupation, reminding him that "To the choleric fisting of every rogue" his "ear is liable," and that his "food is such/ As hath been belch'd on by infected lungs" (IV. vi. 167-69), he defends his attempt to earn a livelihood by sketching a callous, corrupt society weakened by unemployment: "What would you have me do? Go to the wars, would you? where a man may serve seven years for the loss of a leg, and have not money enough in the end to buy him in a wooden one?" (IV. vi.

170-73). Boult powerfully implies that a society that corrupts one kind of worker cannot without hypocrisy disqualify as labor another kind of corruptible activity.

Nevertheless, Marina vividly reminds Boult that social usefulness rather than corruption ought to be the standard for judging acceptable labor. Even activities as (or more) repulsive than the activity of prostitution can by their social utility dignify the worker. "Do any thing but this thou doest," she pleads:

> Empty
> Old receptacles, or common shores, of filth,
> Serve by indenture to the common hangman:
> Any of these ways are yet better than this;
> For what thou professest, a baboon, could he speak,
> Would own a name too dear.
> (IV. vi. 174-79)

Marina's final utterance suggests that Boult's so-called occupation sinks below the proper limits of humanity's work by imaging the disgust of beasts at being forced to practice it. Her comparison evokes again the question of the proper focus of work that was broached in the Leonine episode. Yet the sheer fact that men and women from the beginning of time have found themselves able to perform the most heinous acts of assassination and prostitution, deeds animals instinctively do not perform, challenges Marina's opinion that Boult's activity has no place in society. Still, his earlier, pregnant remark about wars and wooden legs indicates—in the world of *Pericles*, at least—that his activity can be regarded as work only within the context of an unjust society that has not undertaken the equitable definition, regulation, and reward of various kinds of socially beneficial labor.

One beneficial kind of work involves teaching. Marina proposes to redeem the professors of prostitution by means of her labors in both fine and performance arts. "If that thy master would gain by me," she tells Boult,

> Proclaim that I can sing, weave, sew, and dance,
> With other virtues, which I'll keep from boast,
> And I will undertake all these to teach.
> I doubt not but this populous city will
> Yield many scholars.
> (IV. vi. 182-87)

Boult's acquiescence to her plan reveals the power of her eloquent argument of social utility. That Marina escapes the degradation and early death of a whore is the result of her training to perform life-enhancing work.

When we return to Pericles, we find him catatonic, frozen in despair by the loss of his wife and daughter. Granted the redemptive effects of Marina's skill in the arts, playgoers might suppose that "her sweet harmony,/ And other chosen attractions" (V. i. 45-46) will revive him. But when she sings, Pericles neither looks at her nor marks her music. What first moves him to speak haltingly and turn his face to hers is her intimation that she has suffered as grievously as he has. Marina's words induce a kind of labor in Pericles. "I am great with woe," he exclaims, "and shall deliver weeping" (V. i. 106). According to Stevie Davies, "through Thaisa and Marina the terms of political language are restated, and the second Pericles—ruined and remade in a new image—can 'deliver' this language as if (in his own phrase) he were a woman in labour with an eloquence fitting to his tragic-comic experiences."[17] In the sense that his halting speech and tears will lead to Marina's rebirth, Pericles reprises the childbirth labor of Thaisa. Indeed, Thaisa is not far from his mind, for his first words spoken after his childbirth metaphor are "My dearest wife was like this maid" (V. i. 107). In Pericles' revived vision, Marina "look[s] like Patience gazing on kings' graves, and smiling/ Extremity out of act" (V. i. 138-39). Paradoxically, the stirred Pericles sees a maiden so still and motionless that she resembles a funerary sculpture. Actually, it is Patience's enigmatic smile that immobilizes Extremity—that is to say, Calamity—with all its overtones of frenzy.

John F. Danby has argued that patience in *Pericles* reflects its Latin root, *patiens* (enduring); in the play, patience is an active, performative Christian virtue not to be confused with Stoic apathy.[18] Yet the definition scarcely seems to fit the iconography of Pericles' regeneration. The serene calm that Marina communicates to her father developed within her as she learned to transcend the several life-tempests that assailed her. This paradox underscores the ennobling effect that tempestuous stir can produce in providential lives. The "working pulse" of Marina (V. i. 153), the vital motion of her body that confirms her mortal rather than supernatural being for Pericles, beats stronger as she prepares to tell her story of suffering. Once briefly told (V. i. 170-75), that tale encapsulates the tempest that her life has been, persecuted by "cruel Cleon, with his wicked wife," threatened with death, stolen by pirates and sold to the Bawd and Pander in Mytilene. It is the labor of Diana, represented by the tempests that are her agents, that animates Marina and that, condensed in her story, most fully stirs Pericles into new life. Indirectly the goddess' labor delivers a father and a daughter. "O, come hither," Pericles exclaims, "Thou that beget'st him that did thee beget" (V. i. 194-95). This resonant utterance makes Marina into a supernatural mother—since no earthly daughter can give birth to her father—whose miraculous deed, perhaps evocative of the Virgin Mary's role, draws attention to the deity for whose labor Marina has been the chosen vessel.[19] Shakespeare recollects the crime of Antiochus and his Daughter to stress that such a thing as sanctified incest exists.[20]

And what of the character Gower the poet, whose tale the play *Pericles* supposedly is? How does he illustrate Shakespeare's concern with labor? In his first Chorus, Gower implies that his life coincides with the telling of his tale. "To sing a song that old was sung,/ From ashes ancient Gower is come," he announces, "Assuming man's infirmities,/ To glad your ear and please your eyes" (Chorus I, 1-4):

> If you, born in these latter times,
> When wit's more ripe, accept my rhymes,
> And that to hear an old man sing,
> May to your wishes pleasure bring,
> I life would wish, and that I might
> Waste it for you like taper-light.
> (Chorus I, 11-16)

The notion of wasting life like a taper light, in order to give pleasure through the telling of a tale, clearly suggests that the poet's work provides the rationale for his existence.[21] Shakespeare implies that the writer's life *is* his labor, his art. His work and his existence are coterminous. Just as Shakespeare depicts Gower's stirring to life in the opening verses of the play, he accentuates the poet's diminished flame as the narrative approaches its conclusion. "Now our sands are almost run,"

Gower states at the beginning of act V, scene ii; "More a little," he says, "and then dumb" (V. ii. 1-2). Whether by the accident of collaboration or by design, the dwindling and extinguishing of Gower's life as his artistic labor draws to its end contrast with the vigorous life that the language of the play gains from act III onward to its conclusion. If the life of the writer is coterminous with his work, the labor of creation seems to have energized Shakespeare.[22]

In this respect, the playgoer's experience of the play resembles the playwright's. At first, Gower's narrative and the enacted scenes are sufficiently clear and straightforward that audience reception and interpretation remain relatively passive. But beginning with act II, Gower introduces the first of several cryptic dumb shows, which playgoers must work to interpret. He appeals to their capacities for imagining vividly parts of the story that the stage cannot convey: "In your imagination hold/ This stage the ship, upon whose deck/ The sea-toss'd Pericles appears to speak" (Chorus III, 58-60). These pleas encourage playgoers to work more actively to perceive and interpret not only difficult scenes but also the dialogue and events of the romance as a whole.[23] Shakespeare through Gower demands that his audience work progressively harder to comprehend and evaluate the play in cooperative labor with the playwright. Through this aesthetic strategy, members of the audience appreciate more fully the value given labor in the play. Just as Pericles gains a fuller life from his various labors, spectators feel a more complete theatrical pleasure as Shakespeare and Gower make them work harder as perceivers. By this method, the playwright extends the great labor of *Pericles* beyond the thrust stage of the Globe onto the floor and into the thronged galleries of the theater itself.

Notes

1 For other analyses of the Hercules/Hesperides image cluster of *Pericles*, see G. Wilson Knight, *The Crown of Life: Essays in Interpretation of Shakespeare's Final Plays* (1947; rpt. New York: Barnes & Noble, 1966) 37-38; and John Pitcher, "The Poet and the Taboo: The Riddle of Shakespeare's *Pericles*," *Essays and Studies* 35 (1982): 14-29, esp. 15, 17, 28-29.

2 An extended analysis of the incestuous dimension of Antiochus' riddle is conducted by Ruth Nevo, *Shakespeare's Other Language* (New York: Methuen, 1987) 39-40.

3 Other interpretations of the riddle's place in *Pericles* appear in Pitcher 15-16 and in Phyllis Gorfain, "Puzzle and Artifice: The Riddle as Metapoetry in *Pericles*," *Shakespeare Survey* 29 (1976): 11-20, esp. 13-16.

4 Alternative arguments that Antiochus' and the Daughter's incest radically taints Pericles are given by G. Wilson Knight, *The Crown of Life* 38-40; W. B. Thorne, "*Pericles* and the Incest-Fertility Opposition," *Shakespeare Quarterly* 22 (1971): 43-56, esp. 47, 49-50; Howard Felperin, *Shakespearean Romance* (Princeton, NJ: Princeton UP, 1972) 149; and by Nevo 42-44, 53, 55.

5 In *Last Things and Last Plays: Shakespearean Eschatology* (Carbondale: Southern Illinois UP, 1991), Cynthia Marshall asserts that, "while Pericles is not actually condemned to labor with sweat on his brow, he undergoes a sort of penance, 'punish[ing] that before that [Antiochus] would punish,'" a penance that leads to the expiation of the "shipman's toil" (73).

6 My reading of the dramatic importance of this scene counters those of critics who dismiss it. For examples of their point of view, see Annette C. Flower, "Disguise and Identity in *Pericles, Prince of Tyre*," *Shakespeare Quarterly* 26 (1975): 30-41, esp. 32; and Stephen Dickey, "Language and Role in *Pericles*," *English Literary Renaissance* 16 (1986): 550-66, esp. 556.

7 For a different reading of the mighty fish/little fry image, see Anthony J. Lewis, "'I feed on Mother's Flesh': Incest and Eating in *Pericles*," *Essays in Literature* 15 (1988): 147-63, esp. 156.

8 In the past decade, critics have argued that Pericles' deficiencies of thought and word are calculated quantities. See, for example, Dickey 553-62; and Maurice Hunt, "Pericles and the Emblematic Imagination," *Studies in the Humanities* 17 (1990): 1-20.

9 Pericles' distinctive passivity is analyzed by John Arthos, "*Pericles, Prince of Tyre:* A Study in the Dramatic Use of Romantic Narrative," *Shakespeare*

Quarterly 4 (1953): 257-70, esp. 269; Knight, *Crown of Life* 73-74; Norman Rabkin, *Shakespeare and the Common Understanding* (New York: Macmillan, 1967) 194; Thelma N. Greenfield, "A Re-Examination of the 'Patient' Pericles," *Shakespeare Studies* 3 (1967): 51-61, esp. 55; and Michael Taylor, "'Here is a thing too young for such a place': Innocence in *Pericles*," *Ariel* 13.3 (1982): 3-19, esp. 12-13.

10 In *Time, Tide, and Tempest: A Study of Shakespeare's Romances* (San Marino, CA: Huntington Library, 1972), Douglas L. Peterson judges that Pericles' description of Marina's birth (III. i. 27-37) "is expressed in lines that are among the most moving in the entire play" (92).

11 See, for example, Nevo 33-34. For some critics, the corrupt text and possible joint authorship of *Pericles* will always negatively affect any analysis of the play that discovers aesthetic integrity in certain scenes (or especially in the entire play). In this chapter, I do not speculate about the bearing that the infamous cruxes of *Pericles* might have upon my interpretation. "The whole matter," according to F. D. Hoeniger in the Arden edition of the play (London: Methuen, 1963), "is incapable of being finally decided for the simple reason that external evidence is wholly wanting" (liii). Joan Hartwig, in *Shakespeare's Tragicomic Vision* (Baton Rouge: Louisiana State UP, 1972), cites Hoeniger's judgment with approval as part of her argument that a reading of *Pericles* need not always include references to the textual difficulties (181-83). Quoting Northrop Frye, Hartwig notes that even "collaborated works may create 'a distinct and unified personality' as the artistic control" (182)— an opinion resembling Lascelles Abercrombie's judgment (as quoted by G. Wilson Knight) that "non-authentic material can assume authenticity through incorporation, deriving sustenance from the new organism into which it has been incorporated, as when flesh is grafted onto a living body" (*Crown of Life* 33). The current analysis of the textual problems of *Pericles* appears in Stanley Wells and Gary Taylor, *William Shakespeare: A Textual Companion* (Oxford: Clarendon Press, 1987) 556-92.

12 The most noteworthy analysis of Pericles' farewell speech appears in John F. Danby, *Poets on Fortune's Hill: Studies in Sidney, Shakespeare, Beaumont and Fletcher* (1952; rpt. Port Washington, NY: Kennikat Press, 1966) 94-95; and in Stevie Davies, *The Idea of Woman in Renaissance Literature: The Feminine Reclaimed* (Brighton: Harvester Press, 1986) 137-40. But also see Derek A. Traversi, *Shakespeare: The Last Phase* (1954; rpt. Stanford, CA: Stanford UP, 1965) 27-28; and Robert M. Adams, *Shakespeare: The Four Romances* (New York: Norton, 1989) 36.

13 Maurice Hunt, "'Stir' and Work in Shakespeare's Last Plays," *Studies in English Literature* 22 (1982): 285-304, esp. 287.

14 Davies associates Cerimon's work with birth labor: "He has heard, he says, of 'an Egyptian/ That had nine hours lien dead,/ Who was by good appliances recovered' (III. ii. 86-8). This rumoured individual's

nine hours of death had been in reality a nine hours' gestation from which he emerged into new life" (140-41).

15 For a different analysis of the commercial dynamics of the Mytilene episode, see Steven Mullaney "'All That Monarchs Do': The Obscured Stages of Authority in *Pericles*," *The Place of the Stage: License, Play, and Power in Renaissance England* (Chicago: U of Chicago P, 1988) 135-51, esp. 142-45. Mullaney cites Fredric Jameson's opinion that "the signature of Shakespearean romance" consists of "its efforts to dissociate itself from the 'bustling commercial activity at work all around it'" (140-41), arguing that the Mytilene episode of *Pericles* amounts to the only exception to Jameson's judgment. I claim, on the other hand, that Shakespearean romance widely incorporates the playwright's preoccupation with labor, its inequities, and the place of work in a life.

16 On the commodification of Marina, see Lorraine Helms, "The Saint in the Brothel: Or, Eloquence Rewarded," *Shakespeare Quarterly* 41 (1990): 319-32, esp. 326-27.

17 Davies 132. Later Davies concludes that "the glory of the speech stems from its source in the initiating metaphor of childbirth, which gathers into itself the paradox upon which the whole play has turned. The speaker conceives of himself as a woman in labour. 'His' labour delivers neither the tears nor the 'woe' of the first sentence but rather the words that follow; that is, the speech itself, with its precious ore of memory. Words are his delivered child. . . . The pain, as in childbirth, is evacuated, the word-child delivered. The tragi-comic resolution of the Last Plays depends on emphasis on deliverance, enacted here through recurrent word-play involving conception, pregnancy, labour and delivery of a girl-child" (148).

18 Danby 81-82.

19 Adams has judged that Pericles' resonant lines "can be understood as paralleling the ancient Christian amphibole of Mary the creature of God giving birth in the Christ child to the God himself who was her begetter" (48). For Traversi, Pericles' verses amount to "the symbolic kernel of the whole play" (40).

20 A different formulation of this idea is expressed by C. L. Barber, "'Thou That Beget'st Him That Did Thee Beget': Transformation in *Pericles* and *The Winter's Tale*," *Shakespeare Survey* 22 (1969): 59-67. The idea of this article is developed in C. L. Barber and Richard Wheeler, *The Whole Journey: Shakespeare's Power of Development* (Berkeley: U of California P, 1986) 310-28. Also see R. S. White, *"Let Wonder Seem Familiar": Endings in Shakespeare's Romance Vision* (London: Athlone, 1985) 127-28.

21 In this respect, see Dickey 551-52: Gower's "production . . . takes on the air of a sacrifice of himself to his art" (551). Also see Richard Hillman, "Shakespeare's Gower and Gower's Shakespeare: The Larger Debt of

Pericles," *Shakespeare Quarterly* 36 (1985): 427-37, esp. 436-37; Peterson 73; and Richard P. Knowles, "'Wishes Fall Out as They're Will'd': Artist, Audience, and *Pericles's* Gower," *English Studies in Canada* 9 (1983): 14-24, esp. 17-18.

22 For an alternative negative view of this relationship, see Kirby Farrell, *Shakespeare's Creation: The Language of Magic and Play* (Amherst: U of Massachusetts P, 1975) 193, 210-12—Gower's "condition parodies one consequence of the creative life: the artist's anxiety about isolation and exhaustion after a life given to—wasted on—imagination. Gower would willingly sacrifice himself again to win our praise: he accosts us as an artist-beggar craving renewed connection with life at any cost. In this posture he allows Shakespeare to satirize the servility latent in the artist's relation to his patrons" (193). But this critical judgment turns Gower and *Pericles* into the meretricious Poet/Painter and *Timon of Athens*—an equation which cannot be made.

23 The most recent critic to comment on this phenomenon is Knowles 14-24. Also see Hoeniger, Arden *Pericles* xx, lv.

Chapter 4

Cymbeline

In the early acts of *Cymbeline*, work is espoused by the play's villains—the Queen, Jachimo, and Cloten. Wickedly bent on incapacitating or killing her step-daughter Imogen and making her boorish son Cloten heir to her husband's throne, the Queen has collected potent drugs from the court physician Cornelius. She proposes to test them on "such creatures as/ We count not worth the hanging (but none human)" (I. v. 19-20). Cornelius knows, however, that the Queen's amateurish Baconian science masks as unknown but deadly purpose. "Those she has/ Will stupefy and dull the sense awhile," he tells playgoers in an aside, "Which first (perchance) she'll prove on cats and dogs,/ Then afterward up higher" (I. v. 36-39). The doctor knows, in other words, that the Queen's avocation, her "scientific" work, serves to screen the operation of her malice. Usually this spite expresses itself in Machiavellian policy. "Here comes a flattering rascal," she says when Pisanio—Posthumus' servant—enters; "upon him/ Will I first work" (I. v. 27-28). Working upon Pisanio entails attempting to persuade him to slander Posthumus and recommend Cloten to Imogen. "Do thou work" (I. v. 48), she entreats Pisanio when she tries to persuade him to become Cloten's advocate. It also involves convincing him that the box which she drops and he retrieves contains life-restoring drugs.[1]

For the Queen, work is essentially verbal, taking the form mainly of deceptive—specifically Machiavellian—utterances. Thus her remark, "and every day that comes comes to decay/ A day's work in him" (I. v. 56-57), made as part of her effort to discredit exiled and presumably idle Posthumus in his servant's hearing, seems out of character. The remark implies that the speaker values the kind of labor that fills up and gives meaning to the worker's days. What the Queen's or Posthumus' day's work in Cymbeline's court is (or was) we have no idea. As a personal attendant of King Cymbeline, a servant of the royal bedchamber (I. i. 40-42), Posthumus, like his counterpart in Jacobean Whitehall, has had no taxing duties. Moreover, the extensive learning to which Cymbeline has subjected his ward has been received without effort. According to First Gentleman, Posthumus took instruction "As we do air, fast as 'twas minist'red,/ And in's spring became a harvest" (I. i. 45-46). Pointedly unlike Pericles in Simonides' estimation, Posthumus is not a labored scholar of the arts; for the Briton, learning was as easy as breathing.

Shakespeare puts the positive valuation of work in the Queen's mouth chiefly to stress by contrast her own debased notion of labor. The Queen craftily drops the box of drugs when she becomes aware from silent Pisanio's facial expression that he does not agree to become a slanderer and proxy-wooer. Thinking the drugs lethal, she intends to kill unswayed Pisanio, "unpeopl[ing]" Imogen "Of liegers for her sweet" lover (I. v. 79-80). When Pisanio automatically, in the trained servant's reflexive stooping, bends and picks up the dropped box, the Queen states, "Thou tak'st up/ Thou know'st not what; but take it for thy labor" (I. v. 60-61). Her word "labor" has two functions in this context. By its contrast with the relatively small amount of energy expended in performing the retrieval of the box, it accentuates the privileged Queen's notion of what constitutes work. By the trained nature of Pisanio's act, it reminds viewers of the unproductive nature of so-called work at court. The Queen's initial lie concerning the box focuses the uncreative nature of court work. "It is a thing I made" (I. v. 62), she tells dutiful Pisanio. Ironically, the devaluation connoted by her term for the box—"thing"—seems appropriate, since the projection of value accompanying the labor of making something has not been part of her experience.

Not surprisingly, the Queen's Machiavellian counterpart, Jachimo, shares her degenerate notion of work. As part of his rhetorical effort to persuade Imogen that Posthumus in Rome has sunk to being a whoremonger, he portrays her betrothed as a lecher who now "gripes with hands/ Made hard with hourly falsehood (falsehood, as/ With labor)" (I. vi. 107-8). Jachimo implies that the dregs of society perform hard physical labor. That whores have to labor to supplement their earnings from prostitution indicts a callous society as much as the remark slanders Posthumus. Jachimo's villainous mind links physical labor and falsehood: those persons driven to eke out a living through lying assurances and vicious deeds perform physical labor.[2] In fact, the "gentleman" Jachimo works on Posthumus and Imogen almost exclusively through false utterances, easy for the speaker to make. Shakespeare draws a parallel between the Queen's pretended interests in scientific experimentation and Jachimo's and Posthumus' contrived trial—their testing —of Imogen's "mettle." Jachimo purports to undertake the kind of work that the Queen says she practices. Yet just as she never performs experiments, so Jachimo never truly and disinterestedly tests Imogen's fidelity. Like his counterpart the Queen, he instead works upon his victim through poisonous language. Disposed as he is to slander, Jachimo never legitimately labors.

Finally, Cloten joins his mother and Jachimo in voicing a debased idea of work. Attempting, as the Queen did, to suborn Pisanio, he crudely exclaims, "Sirrah, if thou wouldst not be a villain, but do me true service, undergo those employments wherein I should have cause to use thee with a serious industry, that is, what villainy soe'er I bid thee do, to perform it directly and truly, I would think thee an honest man" (III. v. 108-13). For Cloten, "serious industry" consists of deceptive practices. His aristocratic contempt of physical labor surfaces in his initial use of the term "villain"; if Pisanio does not wish to resemble (or become) a "villein," a peasant condemned to labor miserably for a bare livelihood, then he should become a villain, a conscienceless knave willing to implement Cloten's design of wrenching Imogen's affection from Posthumus to himself. In his stupidity, Cloten does not comprehend that the "true" villainy of his conception would be morally worse than undergoing villeinage. Left alone on the stage, unshakable Pisanio tells the audience, "This fool's speed/ Be cross'd with slowness; labor be his meed" (III. v. 161-62). Even the good servant Pisanio, bred in the court, cannot imagine that labor might be its own reward. Like other, mostly vicious characters in the play, he conceives of work negatively as barren, painful punishment.

What then, besides the practice of verbal policy, makes up Cloten's idea of work? The ill-tempered quarreling to which he is addicted, swordplay that so exercises him that he reeks in the nostrils of several lords (I. ii. 1-4), scarcely qualifies as productive work. Nor does the gambling at bowls to which he is drawn. In Cloten, Shakespeare vividly depicts the kind of destructive activity that idleness often fostered in Jacobean aristocrats. Lechery complements Cloten's other vices. After dressing in Posthumus' clothing to rape Imogen, and so take vengeance upon her for her boast that her lover's garments outvalue him, Cloten nastily puns, "How fit his garments serve me! Why should his mistress, who was made by him that made the tailor, not be fit too? the rather (saving reverence of the word) for 'tis said a woman's fitness comes by fits. Therein I must play the workman" (IV. i. 2-7). Sexual intercourse is work in Cloten's corrupt view. Accustomed as the Queen's son to having his way, Cloten brutishly imagines the male, himself in this case, making a woman obedient by fitting her physically to himself and his carnal desires through forced sex. This obscene work of physical fitting amounts to labor in Cloten's twisted mind, a labor in which women involuntarily but naturally cooperate. The coarse male chauvinism heard in his sexual stereotype, "'tis said a woman's fitness comes by fits," implies that her compelled orgasms—her fits—over time physically fit her to the body of the aggressive male. Such physical fitness in Cloten's distorted view sums up his idea of woman's fitness, her qualification to be admitted to male companionship and society at large. The depravity inherent in playing the workman to achieve these aims needs little further clarification. According to Cloten, Imogen was "made by him that made the tailor" (IV. i. 3-4). She, like all other women, exists mainly to be made, sexually exercised and impregnated by men. Cloten imagines that Posthumus, who has "made" his tailor through the expense of a commissioned, rich wardrobe, has already sexually made Imogen. For Cloten, women are made neither by the gods nor by nature, but by self-serving men. The blasphemy of such a belief in craftsmanship seals Cloten's mistaken idea of work—and his doom.

Jacobean upper gentry and aristocrats, exempted for the most part from the work involved in life support, primarily made warfare and childbearing their principal labors (and rationale for being). Significantly, Shakespeare in *Cymbeline* shows these two kinds of court work to be futile, even self-destructive. In Wales, the old soldier Belarius attempts to instruct Cymbeline's sons in the "toil o' th' war,"

> A pain that only seems to seek out danger
> I' th' name of fame and honor which dies i' th' search,
> And hath as oft a sland'rous epitaph
> As record of fair act; nay, many times
> Doth ill deserve by doing well; what's worse,
> Must curtsy at the censure.
> (III. iii. 49-55)

"O boys," Belarius laments, "this story/ The world may read in me" (III. iii. 55-56). Slandered as a Roman confederate by two villains, Belarius instantly became an exile bereft of the martial reputation honestly earned through the work of war. More grievously, Posthumus' father, Sicilius, upon learning of the deaths of this two sons "in the wars o' th' time" (I. i. 35), in the words of First Gentleman, "took such sorrow/ That he quit being" (I. i. 37-38). Indirectly the "toil o' th' . . . war" kills not only Posthumus' brothers but his father as well, leaving his mother shortly to die in the labor of childbirth (I. i. 38-40). Her nameless character in the play graphically stresses the thoroughness with which her fatal labor stripped her of personal identity. Later, during Posthumus' dream vision, the ghost of his mother stresses in her complaint to Jupiter the seeming fruitlessness of her labor both for herself and her only surviving son:

> Hath my poor boy done aught but well,
>   Whose face I never saw?
> I died whilst in the womb he stay'd
>   Attending nature's law;
> Whose father then (as men report
>   Thou orphans' father art)
> Thou shouldst have been, and shielded him
>   From this earth-vexing smart.
> Lucina lent not me her aid,

> But took me in my throes,
> That from me was Posthumus ripp'd,
> Came crying 'mongst his foes,
> A thing of pity!
>
> (V. iv. 35-47)

Even from the time of his excruciating delivery, Posthumus' life, in the ghost of his mother's opinion, has been a kind of protracted toil: "earth-vexing smart" producing no fruit.

Granted this negative portrayal of work, playgoers wonder whether any productive work is performed at Cymbeline's court. Attempting to convince Imogen to disguise herself as a page and suffer hardships in order to travel to Rome to observe first-hand Posthumus' behavior, Pisanio reveals that he believes that Imogen's troubles spring from her unintentionally having insulted the vain queen of the gods—Juno. In his account, Imogen must "forget/ [her] laborsome and dainty trims, wherein/ [She] made great Juno angry" (III. iv. 163-65). In other words, her wearing the humiliating dress of a male page would amount to penitential behavior that might appease the goddess. Or so Pisanio imagines. While he is generally correct in his opinion that a deity crosses Imogen in order to refine her character, specifically her love for Posthumus, Pisanio errs in identifying the deity and the flaw in Imogen capable of amendment. Nevertheless, the faithful servant strikes close to a truth when he implies that the hardship of traveling as a male page through Wales and across the seas to Rome would rectify a certain softness in Imogen bred by the easy, indolent life of a princess in Cymbeline's court. The term "laborsome" in Pisanio's phrase "Your laborsome and dainty trims" attributes a certain overworked quality to the sumptuous and delicate gowns worn by Imogen—an overworked quality that might be called epicurean, or at least negatively artificial. A character of integrity, Pisanio suggests that the labor involved in producing such "trims" is detrimental to the consumer.

Shakespeare implies that other products of fine artisans in Cymbeline's court are as useless as Imogen's gowns have been for her development of character. In order to convince Posthumus that he has seduced Imogen, Jachimo enumerates in writing the details of the fine art embellishing her bedchamber:

> Such and such pictures; there the window; such
> Th' adornment of her bed; the arras, figures,
> Why, such and such; and the contents o' th' story.
>   (II. ii. 25-27)

The mundaneness of the linguistic marker "such and such," as delivered by the actor playing Jachimo, devalues the features of fine art. Whatever labor went into producing the art is lost in these virtually meaningless words. When, only minutes before, he emerged from the trunk in which he was hiding,[3] Jachimo exclaimed, "The crickets sing, and man's o'erlabor'd sense/ Repairs itself by rest" (II. ii. 11-12). While primarily functioning to time the scene and create a sense of foreboding, Jachimo's words also evoke the image of hard physical labor bathed in deep sleep (a sleep that apparently does not come early or easily to relatively idle Imogen, awake at midnight after three hours of reading practiced partly as a soporific). This image of one kind of labor, while fleeting, contrasts with that involved in the products of art toward which the actor playing Jachimo variously turns a moment later as he studies them in order to record them in his tables.

These artistic details become poetic realities a few scenes later when Jachimo recreates them imaginatively in Posthumus' presence. In Jachimo's words, the

> . . . .tapestry of silk and silver; the story
> Proud Cleopatra, when she met her Roman,
> And Cydnus swell'd above the banks, or for
> The press of boats or pride

amounts to a "piece of work/ So bravely done, so rich, that it did strive/ In workmanship and value" (II. iv. 69-74). So gifted was the artist that, according to Jachimo, "true life" was "exactly wrought" upon the silk. Similarly, he describes the bedchamber's "chimney-piece" of "Chaste Dian bathing" as the work of a cutter who so "outwent" nature in his lively imitation that only "Motion and breath" are missing from the sculpture. Despite Jachimo's praise of these art works, they lack unique significance.[4] Posthumus interrupts Jachimo in the midst of his utterance about the liveliness of the tapestry—

> This is true;
> And this you might have heard of here, by me,
> Or by some other
>
> (II. iv. 76-78)

—and he repeats, concerning the chimney-piece's ravishing effect on beholders,

> This is a thing
> Which you might from relation likewise reap,
> Being, as it is, much spoke of.
>
> (II. iv. 85-87)

While Posthumus admits the truth of the beholders' wonderment at the fine art ("This is true"), he discredits that art's testamentary power when he points out that the artifacts, along with their supposedly essential meanings, can be easily translated into the lesser medium of descriptive speech. Whatever labor went into making the artifacts unique signifiers of the dangers of pride and vanity (in the case of the tapestry) and of chastity (in that of the chimney piece) gets lost when unscrupulous men can reproduce them in the untrustworthy medium of language.

The warning against pride conveyed by the marvelous tapestry never discouraged Imogen from wearing "laborsome and dainty" trims as she dressed in front of it, and the chimney piece of Diana offers no bulwark against Posthumus' predilection to believe in Imogen's lapse in virtue.[5] The vivid description of the art works is inconsequential, bearing not at all upon the outcome of the wager. The bracelet and knowledge of the mole beneath Imogen's breast that Jachimo produces almost instantly destroy Posthumus' faith in his beloved. Considered in retrospect, a detail in Jachimo's description of the ceiling of Imogen's bedchamber may indicate a partial reason for the inconsequential moral effect of the art works on beholders. The ceiling is "fretted" with golden cherubins. While "carved" might be a suitable gloss for the word, the term also has overtones of "teased," "troubled" in the sense of overworked or excessive Mannerist detail. This reading links the art work of the ceiling of Imogen's bedchamber with the "laborsome and dainty trims" that, by Pisanio's account, have made great Juno angry with Imogen. Like her gowns, the art work serves no useful purpose.

Enraged against his beloved, Posthumus adopts Cloten's wicked idea of procreation as a kind of labor—a parallel that has gone unnoticed in criticism of the play.[6] Posthumus begins his terrible indictment of women by misogynistically exclaiming, "Is there no way for men to be, but women/ Must be half-workers?" (II. v. 1-2). Posthumus enjoys a questionable advantage over Cloten in granting part of the work of generation to women. But in the bitter words which follow he betrays a Renaissance sexist notion of woman as the completely passive matter in which the male "stamps" the form of life. "We are all bastards," he tells the men in the Globe and Blackfriars audiences,

> And that most venerable man which I
> Did call my father, was I know not where
> When I was stamp'd. Some coiner with his tools
> Made me a counterfeit.
> (II. v. 2-6)

By imagining an adulterous male worker with his tools—his genitalia—stamping him in the completely passive matter of his supposedly faithless mother, Posthumus adopts a prejudice of Jacobean patriarchy: that women are basically non-entities capable only of being receptive vessels. But by the notion of a counterfeit coiner, he ironically discredits the idea of sex as male work.

Paradoxically, this patriarchal idea of woman as immobile, passive matter contrasts with the male belief that she incarnates inconstancy. During his blamable shifting of all human vices to woman (II. v. 19-35), Posthumus includes mutability among the catalogue of thirteen flaws that he names. "For even to vice/ They are not constant," he declares in a Donne-like spasm of hatred, "but are changing still:/ One vice but of a minute old, for one/ Not half so old as that" (II. v. 29-32). The general resemblance of this sentiment to that expressed in the final verses of John Donne's "The Bait" suggests that unenlightened male members of Shakespeare's audience may have subscribed to Posthumus' portrayal of inconstancy as a female vice. Imogen's loss of faith in Posthumus' trothplight and her change of identity in Wales force the question of whether she—as a woman—embodies chaotic stir—a basic changeableness.[7]

Mutability—the shifting of shape—attaches itself to Imogen when she disguises herself as Fidele and plays several roles. Having recounted the persecutions visited upon Imogen by her father, stepmother, and stepbrother, Second Lord prays,

> The heavens hold firm
> The walls of thy dear honor; keep unshak'd
> That temple, thy fair mind, that thou mayst stand
> T'enjoy thy banish'd lord and this great land!
> (II. i. 62-65)

Shakespeare includes this kind of wish in the last romances mainly as a foil to offset the value of the various tempests that stir characters' minds and bodies to know and enact redemptive truths unavailable to the placid, never-troubled intellect. While admirable as a pious wish, Second Lord's prayer in *Cymbeline* echoes Second Lord's wish in *Pericles* that the Prince of Tyre, leaving his native city on Helicanus' advice, "keep your mind, till you return to us,/ Peaceful and comfortable!" (*Pericles*, I. ii. 35-36). But even as a comfortable, peaceful mind produces no meaningful insights or character development within Pericles, so an "unshak'd" mind does not promote Imogen's eventual happiness. The god Jupiter's profound shaking of that mind and the very roots of her being, in the torments devised by the Queen and Cloten, in the agitation produced by the loss of Posthumus' love and by his homicidal intent toward her, and in the afflictions suffered in the Welsh mountains, results in a steadfastness of love and faith that an untroubled Imogen could never acquire.

Hard work chiefly makes possible Imogen's acquisition in Wales of new virtues. In *Cymbeline*, Shakespeare associates the "hard" pastoral realm of Wales with labor.[8] Belarius and the young princes must labor to make primitive nature yield the bare necessities of life. For them, hunting is important work—not simply idle sport:

> You, Polydore, have prov'd best woodman, and
> Are master of the feast. Cadwal and I

> Will play the cook and servant, 'tis our match.
> The sweat of industry would dry and die,
> But for the end it works to. Come, our stomachs
> Will make what's homely savory; weariness
> Can snore upon the flint, when resty sloth
> Finds the down pillow hard.
> (III. vi. 28-35)

Outside the pampered court of Cymbeline, in Wales, the end that the "sweat of industry" works for is life itself. "Resty sloth" finds no place in the mountains. Productive labor provides the standard for reward and recognition. The sweat of Belarius' and the young princes' industry contrasts with the reeking odor of Cloten, strenuously exercised in his dueling. Because he has on this day excelled in hunting, Guiderius enjoys the distinction of being "master of the feast," with Arviragus and Belarius his dutiful attendants. Since this arrangement of reward for productive labor obviously depends upon a kind of daily game ("'tis our match"), the servant's role shifts, an arrangement that forestalls the abuses that permanent master/servant relationships, usually based on aristocratic privilege rather than productive labor, often foster.[9]

Belarius works Arviragus and Guiderius even in their schooling and his stories of martial deeds. When the old soldier narrates his "warlike feats," Guiderius' spirits fly out into his story, physically bringing it to life:

> ....say, "Thus mine enemy fell,
> And thus I set my foot on's neck," even then
> The princely blood flows in his cheek, he sweats,
> Strains his young nerves, and puts himself in posture
> That acts my words.
> (III. iii. 91-95)

Arviragus likewise labors to mime Belarius' words, both young men learning heroic acts of warfare through rehearsing them and incorporating them into their behavior. Furthermore, they must physically exercise themselves to gain a healthy perspective upon the injustices of the court. Belarius directs them to climb a neighboring hill, from which they can perceive him below, on flat land, as small as a crow. Having gained this viewpoint, they can see an abstract truth—"That it is place which lessens and sets off" (III. iii. 13). Then they would stand in a position to appreciate fully the tales that Belarius has told them "Of courts, of princes, of the tricks in war" and of service that was not rewarded for its intrinsic merit but according to the pleasure of a lord (III. iii. 14-17). While Belarius calls this singular pedagogy "mountain sport" (III. iii. 10), the physical labor involved in his pupils' response to it makes it work of an instructive kind.[10]

Like those of her brothers, Imogen's laborious life in Wales teaches her truths she would most likely never learn in her father's court.[11] Upon her first appearance dressed as Fidele, she remarks, "I see a man's life is a tedious one,/ I have tir'd myself; and for two nights together/ Have made the ground my bed" (III. vi. 1-3). Learning through hardship some aspects of a man's life, she concludes that "Plenty and peace breeds cowards; hardness ever/ Of hardiness is mother" (III. vi. 21-22). Belarius almost immediately elaborates this truth in his recommendation of "the sweat of industry" and accompanying condemnation of sloth that was analyzed above. Like the work of the princes, Imogen's labors educate her, even though a human tutor neither organizes nor directs them. One of the virtues she learns is a bold courage ordinarily identified with men. Sword in hand, famished, she enters the ominous cave of the Welsh exiles. Once Belarius and the princes discover her eating their cold meat and welcome her, she remarks to herself,

>   Great men,
> That had a court no bigger than this cave,
> That did attend themselves and had the virtue
> Which their own conscience seal'd them, laying by
> That nothing-gift of differing multitudes,
> Could not outpeer these twain.
>   (III. vi. 81-86)

In Wales Imogen quickly learns that being forced to attend oneself, perform the work routinely done by a herd of servants, could bring great men—aristocratic lords—to practice the fine courtesy seen in Belarius and the princes. Having to do without the attention of servants has helped her to appreciate the duties they perform. Such remade lords would be peers in a new sense: they could theoretically begin to learn certain humbling truths conferred by their vision of—their "peering at"—a natural landscape that functions as a primitive school. Imogen adumbrates a radical social hierarchy based on men and women's willingness to labor for themselves and endure hardship. If as a version of hard pastoral Wales possesses utopian overtones, they cause it to contrast with Gonzalo's sentimental portrait of the Golden Age, limned in *The Tempest* for shipwrecked Alonso and his court party. Welsh labor replaces primitive humanity's life of sloth and indulgence in Gonzalo's account.

When we next see Imogen, she has put into practice her insight that a basically idle life at court, waited on by servants, stunts character. Despite their industriousness, Belarius and her brothers clearly need the services of a housekeeper. "Poor house, that keep'st thyself!" (III. vi. 36), Belarius laments at the end of his praise of labor. Imogen chooses to become that housekeeper upon Belarius' suggestion (IV. ii. 45-46). She cuts their diet of roots "in characters"—in alphabetical letters and shapes—and sauces their broths "as Juno had been sick/ And [Fidele] her dieter" (IV. ii. 49-51). Imogen's novel characters symbolize the literate culture that she would extend to her primitive hosts. Guiderius' apparently gratuitous comparison of himself, Belarius, and Arviragus to Juno serves to identify the benefit of Imogen's labor. One might think of the goddess Juno as sick in two senses. As the queen traditionally acting to exalt herself in Jupiter's and her own opinion by persecuting mortal women either alluring to or already seduced by her husband, Juno had often been represented in literature as a vain deity. By dieting Juno, attempting to cure her pride, Imogen might be thought of as a princess who has come to recognize the self-destructive dangers inherent in vanity. She may have silently agreed with Pisanio's belief that she suffers hardships and disappointment in love because her "laborsome and dainty trims" angered a jealous female deity, Juno. Her assumption would not have seemed implausible to older members of Shakespeare's audience. Queen Elizabeth's commandeering of an exceptionally gorgeous gown of Lady Mary Howard, her wearing it even though it was too small for her, and her subsequent jealous declaration that it was unfit for anyone to wear ever again composed a widely known anecdote.[12] More to the point,

Juno is also the goddess of marriage. If she is sick, she is so because Imogen and Posthumus' "marriage"—their handfast—has sickened and seemed to die. Imogen diets Juno, cures, that is to say, her own marriage by dutifully working as a huswife. This demeaning role, demeaning at least for a princess, amounts to a kind of penance for her too easy loss of faith in Posthumus. Rather than suspect an Italian intriguer as Pisanio does, she imagines that Posthumus has abandoned her for a Roman whore. While Posthumus himself may be unworthy of her strong faith, her lapse reveals a minor flaw that could stand refining.[13] To the degree that her huswifery represents a Jacobean sexist role, her service appears a rather humiliating penitential experience. Imogen's Welsh huswifery is symbolic of her serviceable deeds as Fidele, all those works that reestablish her faithfulness and qualify her to become the eventually rejuvenated, purified helpmate of Posthumus.[14]

By the conclusion of her Welsh adventure, Imogen has experienced the typically masculine life to the extent that she instructs others in it. "The boy hath taught us manly duties" (IV. ii. 397), Lucius tells his Captains concerning Imogen's resolve to bury the headless corpse that she believes is that of Posthumus. By such brave reverence, Imogen incarnates for Lucius her assumed name Fidele. Hearing this name, Lucius concludes, "Thou dost approve thyself the very same;/ Thy name well fits thy faith; thy faith thy name" (IV. ii. 380-81). Still, Imogen's resolve is not so great that it can fully condition her to the hardships of Wales. They make her ill; and in her apology to Belarius and the princes for troubling them with her disease, she suggests that her formerly soft life in court figures in her malaise. She claims to be "not so citizen a wanton as/ To seem to die ere sick" (IV. ii. 8-9)—not, that is, so city-bred a spoiled child as to seem to die ere sick. And yet so easy has been Imogen's physical life in her father's court that a few moments later she anticipates dying.

Cloten cannot imagine primitive life as the catalyst for vital, productive labor. When he stumbles upon Guiderius, he can conceive of him only as a slave: a creature condemned to endless labor without personal benefit. "A thing/ More slavish did I ne'er than answering/ A slave without a knock" (IV. ii. 72-74),

Guiderius replies. In his vicious ignorance, Cloten can never know the imaginative role playing that constitutes the so-called mountaineers' meaningful reward for successful labor in such an activity as hunting. Addicted to his self-defeating vices of quarreling and gambling, Cloten, as Guiderius indicates, is the play's true slave, since these compulsive pursuits bring him no personal advantage.

Believing that the box that Pisanio has given her contains cordials, heart-sick Imogen takes Cornelius' drugs and appears to die. Grief-stricken, Arviragus and Guiderius speak the memorable dirge of *Cymbeline*. The dirge, "Fear no more the heat o' th' sun," reflects not only skeptical Jacobean attitudes about the existence of an afterlife; it also distills the essence of labor. Work in the dirge is a metaphor for life. "Thou thy worldly task hast done," Guiderius pronounces over the body of drugged Imogen; "Home art gone, and ta'en thy wages" (IV. ii. 260-61). The dirge's message concerns the calm acceptance of the passing away of natural things, and its greatness derives from the poetic inclusiveness of its statement. Guiderius' and Arviragus' judgment of transience appears to cover all cases:

> Golden lads and girls all must,
> As chimney-sweepers, come to dust.
> . . . .
> The sceptre, learning, physic, must
> All follow this and come to dust.
> . . . .
> All lovers young, all lovers must
> Consign to thee and come to dust.
> (IV. ii. 262-63, 268-69, 274-75)

Given these absolute sentiments and the stress of finality conveyed by the triple "must"/"dust" refrain, the listener accepts the metaphor of work and wages as definitive. The emphasis extends back through the play to invigorate previous remarks, such as the Queen's "And every day that comes comes to decay/ A day's work in him" (I. v. 56-57), that have implied that the quantity of performed work—especially in its relationship to relatively short, irrecoverable time periods—matters greatly.[15]

Shakespeare takes pains to suggest that the vision of life as work is inspired. Part of the song is recited by "Cadwal"

(Arviragus), whose bardic name has prophetic overtones, to the accompaniment of Belarius' "ingenious instrument." Yet what, one might ask, are the wages that the supposedly dead Imogen has taken to her long home? And what is the home that the pagan princes imagine? Unaware of Imogen's royal identity, Belarius and the young men have only Imogen's brief chores as their huswife to apply to the idea of wages. And she never received any wages in the conventional sense of money—only cold meat and a little food. The grim connotations of the "must"/"dust" refrain in the dirge underscore a pagan depression, a prospect of unredeemed work where the best rot with the worst without resurrection. Shakespeare powerfully captures the ancient conviction that the value of death lies in its release of a life-long sufferer from the continual fear, slander, and tyranny accompanying earthly existence.

Shakespeare seems to have interjected the notion of wages into the depiction of life as consisting of a prolonged worldly task in order to provoke the audience's recollection of the Parable of the Laborers and the Hours (Matthew 20:1-16):

> For the kingdom of heaven is like unto a man that is a householder, which went out early in the morning to hire laborers into his vineyard. And when he had agreed with the laborers for a penny a day, he sent them into his vineyard. And he went out about the third hour, and saw others standing idle in the market place, And said unto them; "Go ye also into the vineyard, and whatsoever is right I will give you." And they went their way. Again he went out about the sixth and ninth hour, and did likewise. And about the eleventh hour he went out, and found others standing idle, and saith unto them, "Why stand ye here all the day idle?" They say unto him, "Because no man hath hired us." He saith unto them, "Go ye also into the vineyard; and whatsoever is right, that shall ye receive." So when even was come, the lord of the vineyard saith unto his steward, "Call the laborers, and give them their hire, beginning from the last unto the first." And when they came that were hired about the eleventh hour, they received every man a penny. But when the first came, they supposed that they should have received more; and they likewise received every man a penny. And when they had received it, they murmured against the goodman of the house, Saying, "These last have wrought but one hour, and thou hast made them equal unto us, which have borne the burden and heat of the day." But he answered one of them, and said, "Friend, I do thee no

wrong: didst not thou agree with me for a penny? Take that thine is, and go thy way: I will give unto this last, even as unto thee. Is it not lawful for me to do what I will with mine own? Is thine eye evil, because I am good? So the last shall be first, and the first last."[16]

Guiderius' utterance "Fear no more the heat o' th' sun" may be indebted to the biblical laborers' complaint that they have had to bear the scorching heat of the sun in order to earn wages. The Parable depicts a God who condemns idleness and espouses physical work, of which the wine of life is the ultimate product. On his deathbed, the puritan divine Thomas Taylor exclaimed, "we serve such a master who giveth much wages for a little work."[17] The householder's paying all laborers the same wage regardless of time worked or amount of energy expended dequantifies work, clearly implying that he values the quality rather than the duration of labor. In the spirit of protestantism, emphasis falls upon the single task performed in a faithful spirit. In God's scheme, the wages, so important to the worker, are inconsequential; they are all the same, as evidenced by the one penny paid to each worker. Theologians often interpret this coin as the passport to salvation. The evocation in the dirge of the Parable of the Laborers and the Hours thus reminds Shakespeare's audience of a world view in which labor, faithfully performed in the Taskmaster's vineyard, becomes the agent of salvation.

Imogen's labors in Wales as Fidele refine her so that she qualifies for the final blessings of Jupiter's providence. Performed in a humble, devout spirit, her work as Lucius' page and "cave keeper to honest creatures" resembles the brief, eleventh-hour labor that brings the Christian to salvation. Like the God of Matthew, Shakespeare's Jupiter is a deity of work, a deity who makes elect mortals labor to achieve secular salvation. At a dark moment in the play, Pisanio piously asserts that, for the unperplexing of the characters' clouded minds, "The heavens still must work" (IV. iii. 41). Pisanio's utterance directly following his claim that the "heavens still must work" suggests the method of Jupiter's working. "Wherein I am false, I am honest," Pisanio protests; "not true, to be true" (IV. iii. 42). The sentiment represents a version of Jupiter's dictum "Whom best I love, I cross;

to make my gift/ The more delay'd, delighted" (V. iv. 101-2). Jupiter's seeming falsity with regard to Imogen, his crossing of a relatively spotless princess with afflictions and rough trials, works to make her marriage truer for the falsity: his apparently authentic hatred of the lovers. It is possible that Shakespeare intended Jupiter's tortuous dynamic to represent divine intervention before the advent of Christianity; the absence of falsity in Christ's relation to humanity acts as a foil highlighting the questionable method of Jupiter. Or if Jupiter's rough method of operation appeared to Jacobeans to resemble the program of a Calvinist God who causes elect souls to doubt their election, Shakespeare forces into his playgoer's consciousness the falsity latent in such divine treatment. Certainly the Parable of the Laborers and the Hours must have struck some of the more socially sensitive Jacobeans as unintentionally advantageous to perpetrators of social injustice, large landowners and gentry who had reduced poor farmers and laborers to the smallest wages for their endless work. If those laborers who worked longest under the scorching sun were paid the same meager wage as those who worked for a brief period of time, corrupt landowners could twist a biblical text to increase their riches *and* the poverty of wage laborers. The last may be first in the kingdom of heaven, but the poor upon earth were likely to become poorer.

All this is to say that a minority of Jacobeans who saw *Cymbeline* must have had conflicting reactions to Shakespeare's presentation of Jupiter's false way of treating elect mortals and his imposition upon Imogen of labor for little or no wages. Through one of Imogen's remarks, Shakespeare reveals his awareness of the ethically ambiguous issues that his play raises regarding treatment of the poor and laboring classes. Initially lost in the Welsh mountains, Imogen complains that

> Two beggars told me
> I could not miss my way. Will poor folks lie,
> That have afflictions on them, knowing 'tis
> A punishment or trial? Yes; no wonder,
> When rich ones scarce tell true. To lapse in fullness
> Is sorer than to lie for need; and falsehood
> Is worse in kings than beggars.
> (III. vi. 8-14)

Not understanding that the hordes of beggars who swarmed over London and the English countryside were chiefly victims of exploding population growth coupled with limited employment opportunities, Jacobeans generally regarded them as vicious exemplars of sloth and the host of sins that laziness breeds. (Sloth does precede the six other deadly sins in Book I of Spenser's *Faerie Queene*). Considered as slothful avoiders of labor, beggars often found themselves in cruel work houses that compounded their physical and mental diseases. Thus Imogen's excusing of two beggars who lie to her constitutes a generous, startlingly humane attitude toward the plight of the dispossessed. If rich men lie to their tenant farmers and laborers, no one should be surprised that beggars lie. But if Jupiter himself lies to mortals, no one should be surprised that rich men lie—or that any man or woman lies. Shakespeare catches out the potentially destructive effect of a protestant belief in a lying God, one who harshly misleads and deceives his elect in order to refine their souls and prepare them for ultimate happiness. Imogen reveals that she knows that beggars usually interpret their afflictions as a spiritual punishment or trial; and yet, possessing the knowledge to rationalize their suffering, they continue to lie. Once persons believe that a deity treats them falsely, they often practice personally gratuitous falsehood. The beggars' lying to Imogen, while it may be part of Jupiter's providence (to get her lost in Wales), is of no conceivable advantage to the liars.

Nevertheless, Imogen reveals early in her suffering that she comprehends a possibly divine rationale for pain; but, like the beggars whom she excuses, she lies like the god who has lied (and is lying) to her. When Lucius asks Fidele the name of the man over whose headless corpse she weeps, she replies "Richard du Champ," adding in an aside, "If I do lie and do/ No harm by it, though the gods hear, I hope/ They'll pardon it" (IV. ii. 377-79). A god who regularly lies to mortals according to a program has no choice but to pardon Imogen's lie. While no harm is done by her lie, it serves no positive purpose either. Imogen's lie may tell the theater audience that suffering Posthumus' seeming death has helped recreate him as a hero—a chivalric champion—in her mind, but she is not aware of an audience watching her in a playhouse. Her lie in the world of *Cymbeline* appears personally gratuitous. She lies because she correctly intuits that the gods lie (have lied) to her.

While one could argue that Imogen's lie is not gratuitous because it makes Lucius disposed to take into his service a page who has served a knight, this reason does not dissolve the ambiguity of divine falsehood. If lying is a means for creating a master/servant hierarchy, one extending from Lucius and Fidele through Posthumus and Imogen to Cymbeline's obedience to Roman masters and ultimately their servitude to the Christian religion born in their midst, it simply reifies the landowner's or hirer's inclination to lie to poor laborers. Even though the householder in the Parable said he would pay the laborers first hired a single penny for a day's work, they implied that he treated them falsely when he paid the same amount to workers last hired who worked only a brief time. If salvation can be won by a few works of faithful service, and if salvation is something that one cannot add to once one attains it (the pay is a *single* penny for a day's work), then the grumbling laborers of the Parable have no complaint. But if they are wage laborers in Jacobean England, lied to by wealthy men and perhaps even by a protestant God who often damns the reprobate by making him think that he is elect, then workers may have a complaint. Richard Wilson has shown that "for a landowner like Fulke Greville," deaf to the complaints of Shakespeare's hungry, disenfranchised Stratford neighbors, "the parable of the labourers is the perfect text of economic mastery, since it presents the god of the hiring fair as an employer who fixes pay on his own terms: 'for many be called, but few chosen' (Matthew 20:16)."[18]

As it does for Imogen, work provides Posthumus with the means for spiritual refinement, in his case repentance and atonement for supposedly killing Imogen. "Therefore, good heavens,/ Hear patiently my purpose," he exclaims, having joined the Roman troops and Italian gentry invading Britain:

> I'll disrobe me
> Of these Italian weeds and suit myself

> As does a Britain peasant; so I'll fight
> Against the part I come with; so I'll die
> For thee, O Imogen, even for whom my life
> Is every breath a death.
>
> (V. i. 21-27)

That warfare is heroic mankind's work is a sentiment that reverberates throughout the Shakespeare canon, especially prominent in plays such as *Troilus and Cressida* and *Coriolanus*. Idle Elizabethan and Jacobean aristocrats considered warfare their reason for being, the reason for God's having made them. When Posthumus, disguised as a poor Briton, turns the tide of battle against the Romans, Lucius asserts that "the disorder's such/ As war were hoodwink'd" (V. ii. 15-16). The traditional disorder of war can be heard in both the violent content and fractured form of Posthumus' narration of the battle:[19]

> ... the King himself
> Of his wings destitute, the army broken,
> And but the backs of Britains seen, all flying
> Through a strait lane; the enemy full-hearted,
> Lolling the tongue with slaught'ring—having work
> More plentiful than tools to do't—strook down
> Some mortally, some slightly touch'd, some falling
> Merely through fear, that the strait pass was damm'd
> With dead men hurt behind, and cowards living
> To die with length'ned shame.
>
> (V. iii. 4-13)

In Posthumus' words, the enemy at first was "Lolling the tongue with slaught'ring—having work/ More plentiful than tools to do't." The work metaphor communicates war's savagery. An idle lord, who cannot comprehend such brutality, drives Posthumus into a rage by concluding, "This was a strange chance./ A narrow lane, an old man, and two boys!" (V. iii. 51-52). In reply, Posthumus snarls,

> Nay, do not wonder at it; you are made
> Rather to wonder at the things you hear
> Than to work any. Will you rhyme upon't,
> And vent it for a mock'ry? Here is one:
> "Two boys, an old man (twice a boy), a lane,
> Preserv'd the Britains, was the Romans' bane."
>
> (V. iii. 53-58)

War is portrayed as a kind of work in *Cymbeline* that strongly defines virtuous character. Those things that are worked, Posthumus suggests, are not wondered at; wonder derives from a degree of ignorance, while work involves the understanding that comes from direct experience. While the work of war does not provide Posthumus with the atonement he seeks, it does heroically define him, especially by contrast with the cowardly, slothful lord. Posthumus implies that the gods have made the lord in the image of a sapless coward. The old man and two boys, however, are the products of divine craftsmen designed magnificently to work war.

Work is opposed not only to naive wonder but also to facile art, represented in the passage by Posthumus' facetious rhyme and identified with the idle lord. He twice mentions Posthumus' mounting anger (V. iii. 59-63), which at last causes him to exit fearfully. Posthumus' doggerel verse—"Two boys, an old man (twice a boy), a lane,/ Preserv'd the Britains, was the Romans' bane"—is spoken contemptuously. "You have put me into rhyme" (V. iii. 63), he complains. Posthumus attempts to caricature a superficial, pretty poetry, a kind of expression that he associates with wonder and sloth. The idle lord expresses in a form of verse that some might call charming a wonder that work would dissolve. Posthumus' vigorous, muscular verse of the moment, his narrative of the battle, represents the antithesis of the mocked pretty poetry. Unrhymed, elliptical, writhing with the violence of the battle itself, Posthumus' working language accurately mirrors the labor of war. The poetry attributed to the lord is unworked in the sense that it is the characteristically naive expression of a speaker who has never worked through—experienced—the subject of the verse. Shakespeare reprises the war worker Hotspur's dislike of effete aristocrats and the pretty poetry he associates with them. The tempest in Posthumus' mind, aroused by the battle and exacerbated by the irritating lord, causes both speaker and auditor alike to work to process meaning.

Shakespeare appears to weight this episode in favor of Posthumus' fitful expression and against the limpid speech of the lord. A passage appearing early in *Cymbeline* predicts the dynamics of the late episode just analyzed. Lamenting Posthumus' forced exile, Imogen states,

> I did not take my leave of him, but had
> Most pretty things to say. Ere I could tell him
> How I would think on him at certain hours
> Such thoughts and such; or I could make him swear
> The shes of Italy should not betray
> Mine interest and his honor; or have charg'd him,
> At the sixt hour of morn, at noon, at midnight,
> T'encounter me with orisons, for then
> I am in heaven for him; or ere I could
> Give him that parting kiss which I had set
> Betwixt two charming words, comes in my father,
> And like the tyrannous breathing of the north
> Shakes all our buds from growing.
> (I. iii. 25-37)

The tempest of Cymbeline's rage stifles Imogen's "charming words"; the "pretty things" that she had to say remain unsaid. As is the case in act IV, a fitful, stirred mind is inimical to pretty, charming poetry. Pisanio has formulated—condensed actually—this antagonism just prior to Imogen's lament in act I, scene iii. The good servant reports that Posthumus, his figure rapidly diminishing on the out-bound ship,

> did keep
> The deck, with glove or hat or handkerchief
> Still waving, as the fits and stirs of's mind
> Could best express how slow his soul sail'd on,
> How swift his ship.
> (I. iii. 10-14)

In Pisanio's expression, the "fits and stirs" of Posthumus' working mind translate into the relatively pretty sentiment of the neatly balanced, alliterated final verses.

The implicit antagonism between "working" expression, the fits and stirs of a tempestuous mind, and a relatively untroubled pretty or sweet kind of poetic expression provides another way of appreciating Shakespeare's strong valuation of labor in *Cymbeline*. Imogen never voices the "pretty things" and "charming words" she meant to utter on the occasion of her beloved's sailing; as reported by her, they remain "Such thoughts and such" (I. iii. 28). The virtual nonmeaning of terms like "things" and "such" testifies to the destructive force of Cymbeline's tempestuous rage upon pretty poetry. Yet, as David Frost remarks, if we do not hear the charming things that Imogen planned to say, "she and Pisanio make up for it by some thirty-seven lines of 'pretty things' on the circumstances of Posthumus' departure."[20] Frost does not specify which verses of act I, scene iii he has in mind, but one assumes that they include such sentiments of Imogen's as the following:

> If he should write
> And I not have it, 'twere a paper lost
> As offer'd mercy is.
>
> I would have broke mine eye-strings, crack'd them, but
> To look upon him, till the diminution
> Of space had pointed him sharp as my needle;
> Nay, followed him till he had melted from
> The smallness of a gnat to air, and then
> Have turn'd mine eye and wept.
> (I. iii. 2-4, 17-22)

Frost concludes that often Imogen "is given to ornamenting with 'pretty things,' with sentimental or sententious utterances: opening a letter from Posthumus, she will apologize to the wax" (31). "Good wax, thy leave," she politely asks,

> Blest be
> You bees that make these locks of counsel! Lovers
> And men in dangerous bonds pray not alike;
> Though forfeiters you cast in prison, yet
> You clasp young Cupid's tables.
> (III. ii. 35-39)

Victorian admirers of *Cymbeline* such as Swinburne praised Imogen's pretty speech, which went a long way toward fashioning the charming heroine of their commentaries. Yet Shakespeare himself appears critical of pretty verse in the play. It is not surprising that Imogen utters fewer charming speeches once she is in Wales. As she suffers adversity and labors in the Welsh mountains, her language becomes comparatively less "poetic" in a charming sense. Instead, its rhythms and diction become more supple and barer, more prosaic when hard experience works itself into her speech.

When anger stirs Imogen's mind and speech, playgoers also hear less studied, sententious poetic expression. Cloten's slander of Posthumus provokes her to tell him—

> Wert thou the son of Jupiter, and no more
> But what thou art besides, thou wert too base
> To be his groom. Thou wert dignified enough,
> Even to the point of envy, if 'twere made
> Comparative for your virtues, to be styl'd
> The under-hangman of his kingdom, and hated
> For being preferr'd so well

—and that

> His mean'st garment
> That ever hath but clipt his body, is dearer
> In my respect than all the hairs above thee,
> Were they all made such men.
> (II. iii. 125-31, 133-36)

The stirred, the fitful mind—in short, the vigorously working mind—preempts the calculated prettiness of sententious verse.

Posthumus criticizes the unmartial lord of act V for a slothful attitude and a naive wonder, the result of a lack of experience, which voices itself in noticeably artificial poetic conceits. Auditors have heard such conceits throughout the play, most obviously in Jachimo's response to the beauty of sleeping Imogen and in Arviragus' flower elegy for supposedly dead Fidele. "Cytherea,/ How bravely thou becom'st thy bed!" Jachimo exclaims:

> fresh lily,
> And whiter than the sheets! That I might touch!
> But kiss, one kiss! Rubies unparagon'd,
> How dearly they do't! 'Tis her breathing that
> Perfumes the chamber thus. The flame o' th' taper
> Bows toward her, and would under-peep her lids,
> To see th' enclosed lights, now canopied
> Under these windows, white and azure lac'd
> With blue of heaven's own tinct. But my design!
> (II. ii. 14-23)

Jachimo's sexual excitement, evident in his exclamations, abruptly freezes, and wonder expresses itself over a rarity never seen before. This expression takes the form of a relatively static, highly conceited poetry of a pretty, sweet nature.[21] The delicate artificiality of Jachimo's conceits of taper flame and "enclosed lights" and of "windows, white and azure lac'd/ With blue of heaven's own tinct" contrasts sharply with his recovered excitement—"But my design!" Wonder over Imogen's apparent death likewise compels Arviragus to a similarly sweet, conceited, and static mode of expression:

> With fairest flowers
> Whilst summer lasts and I live here, Fidele,
> I'll sweeten thy sad grave. Thou shalt not lack
> The flower that's like thy face, pale primrose, nor
> The azur'd harebell, like thy veins; no, nor
> The leaf of eglantine, whom not to slander,
> Outsweet'ned not thy breath. The raddock would,
> With charitable bill (O bill, sore shaming
> Those rich-left heirs that let their fathers lie
> Without a monument!), bring thee all this,
> Yea, and furr'd moss besides. When flow'rs are none,
> To winter-ground thy corse—
> (IV. ii. 218-29)

Arviragus' pretty conceits and sweet verse are enameled, "poetic" in a stereotypically feminine sense. The lack of ellipses, the absence of syntactic convolution, the relative stasis of the verse reveal a mind gripped by wonder, deprived for the moment of the fits and stirs of grief.

Guiderius rudely interrupts this wondrous art, portraying himself as opposed to it:

> Prithee have done,
> And do not play in wench-like words with that
> Which is so serious. Let us bury him,
> And not protract with admiration what
> Is now due debt. To th' grave!
> (IV. ii. 229-33)

By the phrase "wench-like words," Guiderius characterizes Arviragus' charming poetry as unvigorous, nonconforming to a stereotypically rougher, less sweet masculine idiom. Like Perdita in *The Winter's Tale*, Guiderius is ultra-decorous; he judges that Arviragus' sweet, pretty words do not suit the solemn occasion and sadness of death. Unmeditated deeds and work seem to be Guiderius' distinguishing traits. As noted, he is the best hunter of the day, and he is the brother who immediately and remorselessly kills Cloten. Moreover, he is the brother who sweats and strains his sinews to enact Belarius' tales of war work, while Arviragus shows much more his own conception of the story. Evidently Arviragus labors less in mimesis. The relatively sweet nature, which produces sugared art, and the rough, angry nature, which instinctively expresses itself in work, are brought into focus in *Cymbeline*; but they remain in conflict in Guiderius' interruption of Arviragus' elegy. A resolution or compromise of a kind occurs in the famous dirge, whose rhymes and couplets frame conceits about the worldly work called life.

Deprived during battle of a death of atonement for his sins, Posthumus, reassuming his Italian garments and captured by Cymbeline's victorious troops, prays in prison that the gods will accept his anticipated execution as a delayed deed of penance (V. iv. 9-29). Instead, he has a dream vision of the ghosts of his family and Jupiter's descent upon an eagle. During his ugly diatribe against women, Posthumus lamented that men must depend upon women for the creation of families. He gets his wish in his dream, wherein he autonomously creates (actually recreates) his father, mother, and brothers. But they are shades, not the warm flesh and blood—capable of physical embraces—that only women can create in conjunction with men. The ghost of his mother's wrenching account of her death in birth labor—

> That from me was Posthumus ripp'd,
> Came crying 'mongst his foes,
> A thing of pity!
> (V. iv. 45-47)

—serves to remind him of both the self-sacrificial love and necessity of women for the making of children. The pain that dreaming Posthumus presumably feels upon hearing these words constitutes a just punishment for his hateful, self-centered wish that men could be the authors of themselves.

Dreaming Posthumus' imagined pain suggests that, in certain respects, the dream vision itself may act as a vehicle for redemption.[22] The ghosts of the Leonati certainly think so. The shade of Sicilius angrily asks Jupiter, "Hath my poor boy done aught but well,/ Whose face I never saw?" (V. iv. 35-36). By suggesting that Posthumus' good deeds in battle merit salvation, he evokes the terms of a contemporary religious controversy. Can (or should) Posthumus' good works save him? The issue is complicated by the fact that the principal works of Posthumus' mother's and father's lives—the labors of battle and childbearing—led to their premature deaths. Nevertheless, the ghosts of Posthumus' brothers imply that the shades of Posthumus' family have in some pagan sense been saved by their noble deeds, and that this precedent ought to allow Posthumus' good works to save his life:

> 2. Bro.   For this from stiller seats we came,
>   Our parents and us twain,
> That striking in our country's cause
>   Fell bravely and were slain,
> Our fealty and Tenantius' right
>   With honor to maintain.
> 1. Bro.   Like hardiment Posthumus hath
>   To Cymbeline perform'd.
> Then, Jupiter, thou king of gods,
>   Why hast thou thus adjourn'd
> The graces for his merits due,
>   Being all to dolors turn'd?
>   (V. iv. 69-80)

Since Posthumus has performed "hardiment" (valorous works) like those of his brothers, their shades believe that Jupiter's "graces" should be reinstated upon him. Moreover, the ghost of First Brother assumes that Posthumus' "merits," his good deeds, obligate Jupiter to bestow the god's graces on the worker without delay (without adjournment). The brother's word "due" reflects his belief in a covenant between Jupiter and Posthumus that requires the god promptly to reward good deeds.[23]

But rather than enjoying a covenant relationship with Jupiter, Posthumus and Imogen appear to have been elected—in the protestant sense of the term—by a god who painfully probes and tests those whom best he loves. The Reformation difference between Catholic and protestant is often superficially thought of as one between works and faith, with Luther and Calvin rejecting the ritualized deeds of Catholic penance and piety in favor of salvation by faith alone. But Elizabethan and Jacobean protestants in sermons and diaries emphasized the importance of a life of good works, not because good works could save the doer (only election and faith could do that), but because they were a primary means for justification and sanctification—for proving to oneself, the world, even God, that one had been elected before the beginning of time and saved (see Chapter 1, 3-4). Thus the ghosts of the Leonati voice a popular misconception about the spiritual efficacy of good works, a misconception that descended Jupiter quickly and harshly corrects.

Jupiter's explanation of his practice of crossing those he best loves, making their ultimate delight more joyful for the delay, presupposes the afflicted mortals' divine election. "Your low-laid son our godhead will uplift," Jupiter asserts, *because* "Our Jovial star reign'd at his birth" (V. iv. 103-5). Significantly, the god suggests that a cause and effect relationship exists between the pagan equivalent of protestant election and Posthumus' final blessedness. In this Calvinistic scheme, Posthumus' good works serve to refine his character, as those of Imogen do hers; but they do not save the characters or even qualify them for salvation. More forms of the word "election" appear in *Cymbeline* than in any other Shakespeare play except *Titus Andronicus* (where the word basically is used in a governmental sense). In each case, they are applied to Imogen and Posthumus. According to First Gentleman, Posthumus' "virtue" may be "read" in Imogen's "election" of him as husband (I. i. 52-54). In a sarcastic remark, spoken aside, on Cloten's bewilderment over Imogen's preferring Posthumus, Second Lord asserts, "If it be a sin to make a true election, she is damn'd" (I. ii. 27-28). And Jachimo acknowledges Imogen's "great judgment/ In the election of a sir so rare" (I. vi. 174-75). Finally, when she realizes that Posthumus has ordered Pisanio to kill her, Imogen asks the servant,

> Why hast thou gone so far,
> To be unbent when thou hast ta'en thy stand,
> Th' elected deer before thee?
> (III. iv. 107-9)

Because she is Jupiter's elected dear (his agent), Imogen's election of Posthumus reflects the god's election of him. Both lover and beloved unknowingly enjoy the spiritual election of a god who roughly refines their characters through trials and afflictions. By this process, he reveals their chosenness to those who have faithful eyes to see and hearts to know his divine ways.

Jupiter's election of Posthumus manifests itself in the tablet and inscribed riddle that he orders the chastened ghosts to place on sleeping Posthumus' breast. The god's rejection of good works as by themselves deserving of salvation gets reinforced in awakened Posthumus' humble response to finding the tablet:

> Many dream not to find, neither deserve,
> And yet are steep'd in favors; so am I,
> That have this golden chance and know not why.
> (V. iv. 130-32)

In protestant fashion, Posthumus knows that some are elected whose life reveals few or no good works (they do not "deserve" to be "steep'd in favors," and yet they are). Contritely, Posthumus lumps himself with these persons, revealing that he does not think that the legitimate good deeds that he has performed and that the ghosts have cited manifest his salvation.

Nevertheless, work precipitates secular salvation in *Cymbeline*. Earlier, the labored syntax of Posthumus' description of the battle between Romans and Britons was noted. His difficult ellipses, constant parentheses, sudden stops and starts, and headlong rush of words mirror the work of war. *Poesis* and *mimesis* coincide. Auditors must literally work to understand heroic effort. Likewise, Jachimo spasmodically delivers his turgid story at play's end. His listeners must work through digressions, obscure coinages, rephrasings, linguistic compressions and inversions—verbal thickets of several kinds—in order to understand the Italian's plots. Communication and understanding are special labors in the world of a god who values painful striving. Specifically, Jupiter makes characters labor through lengthy narratives of discovery that then must be gradually pieced together in order to forestall the sudden, potentially fatal kind of painful revelation. Sicilius Leonatus, in First Gentleman's words, "took such sorrow" upon abruptly learning of Posthumus' brothers' deaths "That he quit being" (I. i. 37-38). At one point during Jachimo's lengthy, digressive narration of his plots, Cymbeline protests, "I stand on fire:/ Come to the matter" (V. v. 168-69). "All too soon I shall," Jachimo replies, "Unless thou wouldst grieve quickly" (V. v. 169-70). Humanely, Jupiter protracts discoveries and narratives so that auditors *slowly* work for their knowledge, in the process feeling grief in nonlethal increments.

During the final scene of revelations, Imogen says, when Lucius believes that she will plead on behalf of his life,

> No, no, alack,
> There's other work in hand. I see a thing
> Bitter to me as death; your life, good master,
> Must shuffle for itself.
> (V. v. 102-5)

Imogen alludes to her ring, which she sees on Jachimo's finger. In the process she implies that the unfolding of the plot and the discovery of meaning involve work. During the wager scenes, Shakespeare, through Posthumus' dismissal of Jachimo's verbal description of the art objects in Imogen's bedchamber, makes his audience realize that art must be directly experienced if its virtues and testamentary powers are to be known. In *Cymbeline*, experience itself assumes the form of a wondrous labor, which appears to be a highly unconventional artifact. Jachimo's work of narration proves so inspiring that disguised Posthumus reveals his identity at the moment that the story calls for his appearance. So vivid has Jachimo's tale become that even the narrator believes that the approaching Posthumus might be a figment of his stirred imagination. "Whereupon—/ Methinks I see him now—" (V. v. 208-9), the Italian exclaims. "Ay, so thou dost,/ Italian fiend!" (V. v. 209-10), Posthumus snarls. Throughout *Cymbeline*, Shakespeare has presented images of humanity as a decaying building needing repair. The Queen, for example, has likened Posthumus to "a thing that leans" . . . that "cannot be new built, nor has no friends/ So much as but to prop him" (I. v. 58-60). And Lucius speaks of Cloten's bloody trunk as a "ruin . . . that sometime . . . was a worthy building" (IV. ii. 354-55). Along with these images appear allusions to the divine creation of humanity, references that on occasion possess Christian overtones. Penitent Posthumus in prison begs the gods,

> For Imogen's dear life take mine, and though
> 'Tis not so dear, yet 'tis a life; you coin'd it.
> 'Tween man and man they weigh not every stamp;
> Though light, take pieces for the figure's sake;
> You rather, mine being yours . . . [24]
> (V. iv. 22-26)

Posthumus' complex metaphor of the gods as coiners of humanity, stamping a figure (a face) upon each creation, makes them workers and their acts of creation a form of labor. In this respect, men and women imitate the gods. "And that most venerable man which I/ Did call my father," Posthumus grieves in act II, "was I know not where/ When I was stamp'd. Some coiner with his tools/ Made me a counterfeit" (II. v. 3-6). When Posthumus argues that some pieces of workmanship, although materially deficient (as he at the moment feels himself to be), are accepted because of the authorizing figure stamped upon them, he alludes to the idea that humanity, made in the image of God, is accepted through the sacrifice of the figure that it bears and in whose image it has been made. The prerequisite that peace reign at the end of *Cymbeline* so that Christ might be born invests the play's Christian overtones with strength.[25] In the present case, a new, redemptive idea of the deity as creative laborer and humanity as his work rectifies the falling building that pagan humanity has become.

This true workmanship, this true creation, receives emphasis from the foil offered by Jachimo's semi-comic creation of a man: Posthumus himself, suddenly emerging from his alien "Italian weeds" (V. i. 23). In his sense of unfulfilled penance and inadequate atonement, Posthumus strains to enact what only Christ can do; "it is I," he exclaims, "That all th' abhorred things o' th' earth amend/ By being worse than they" (V. v. 215-

17). "Spit, and throw stones, cast mire upon me" (V. v. 222), he commands. Providential time, however, is not ripe for the act of ultimate martyrdom. It will be so only when the Christian God eclipses Jupiter and the panoply of classical deities. Until that moment, the pagan gods unknowingly labor to set the stage for Christ's advent.

In this divine scheme, the artistic works of mortals complement the gods' labors of preparation. Belarius explains that Arviragus' royal identity can be confirmed by "a most curious mantle" in which he was wrapped, a mantle in the old soldier's possession and one "wrought by th' hand/ Of his queen mother" (V. v. 361-63). Through its testamentary power, this artistic work of the dead queen partly compensates for the fatal labor of childbirth. Even the possibly overworked product of an effete culture (the mantle is "curious"—exquisitely made) finds its place in a benign providential design. This work of revelation leads to Cymbeline's own labor. Like Pericles at a comparable moment in his story, Cymbeline experiences the birth pangs of creation:

> O, what, am I
> A mother to the birth of three? Ne'er mother
> Rejoic'd deliverance more.
> (V. v. 368-70)

Cymbeline's words, rather than unjustly relegating women to the inferior role in making the family, turn the complaint of the ghost of Posthumus' mother into a joyous statement. Cymbeline's joy and his words redeem her apparently lost labor, celebrating it in the happy tones she would use had she lived to participate in this moment. In other words, Cymbeline finally becomes his wife's co-worker in creating a royal family, empathetically assuming her birthing role as an equal rather than as a superior. No sense of personal shame or diminished stature attaches itself to his expansive willingness to become a mother.

Posthumus also shares in Cymbeline's revaluation of mankind's role as creative worker. Rather than ending in dust, Posthumus' and Imogen's labors culminate in the memorable image of fruit and tree by which Posthumus expresses his renewed married love. "Hang there like fruit, my soul," he exclaims, embracing Imogen, "Till the tree die!" (V. v. 263-64). This organic symbol, in its reversal of sinful experience as described in Genesis, suggests that paradise in which the curse of work is not known.[26] By making the preservation of the fruit as important as the creating tree, Posthumus reveals his new humility, refined in the fire of Jupiter's afflictions. In the sense that fruit represents the tree's creative labor, Posthumus imagines his wife Imogen as his fulfilling work. Yet this is not the proud, solipsistic notion of creation heard voiced at different moments in *Cymbeline*; instead, it signals Posthumus' self-sacrificial desire to nurture Imogen to ripeness, to as long a life as his own. In the words of Peggy Muñoz Simonds, "Shakespeare seems to have arrived here at a poetic criticism of the hidden agricultural metaphor in the term 'husband' itself as applied to human life and has substituted the notion of mutually supportive friendship as a superior ideal for matrimony. Only God has the rights of a gardener or husbandman over human affairs."[27]

Only when heaven's work has reached a stage of near-completion can the Soothsayer's work of interpretation accurately be performed. Only after the characters have worked through their multiple discoveries and reunions can the Roman seer correctly read Jupiter's enigmatic tablet, left on sleeping Posthumus' breast. Posthumus proves to be the "lion's whelp," embraced by "a piece of tender air," Imogen—his wife (*"mulier"*/*"mollis aer"*); and Arviragus and Guiderius become Cymbeline's "branches," formerly "lopp'd" but now "jointed" to "the old stock" of the king—a "stately cedar" (V. v. 435-58). In *Cymbeline*, the interpretation of meaning self-consciously occurs retrospectively, after dramatic action has provided the key for unlocking the significance of obscure or convoluted and elliptical dialogue. And even then the gathering of meaning proves to be hard work.[28] In this respect, Shakespeare as dramatic craftsman resembles his god Jupiter. Both make auditors labor to interpret clouded messages. Critics have noted that the poetic style of *Cymbeline* is especially fretted, troubled by turgid expression and strange condensations of utterance when the demands of neither characterization nor scene call for such a style.[29] Analysis of this dense, tortuous talk raises a perplexing question. Why did Shakespeare make it so when it often serves simply to provide background information?[30] At this phase of his career, the playwright may have thought that he ought to work as programmatically as the characters who labor in the plays he created. Whatever the case, such a "working" style befits a dramatic taskmaster, a craftsman whose design reveals itself as finally benign in the providence of the working god Jupiter.

Notes

1. An excellent account of the character dynamics of this short, eighty-seven line scene (I. v) is given by Barbara A. Mowat, *The Dramaturgy of Shakespeare's Romances* (Athens: U of Georgia P, 1976) 37-42.

2. Concerning Jachimo's utterance, Ann Thompson and John O. Thompson have written that "the simile may seem strange in that labor seems so much worthier a thing than falsehood—but would it have seemed so to Shakespeare? (It was a Victorian commentator, Staunton, who suggested we should amend to 'falsehood, *not* With labour,' thus saving the work ethic from dishonor)." Jachimo's simile could "be taken to mean 'as hardened by hourly falsehood as they also are by labour,' thus suggesting that Posthumus is having an affair in Rome with a woman of low social status.... The context of 'joining gripes' implies that the hands could literally have become hardened by the number of times they have been clasped." ("The Syntax of Metaphor in *Cymbeline*," *Images of Shakespeare*, ed. Werner Habicht, D. J. Palmer, Roger Pringle [Newark: U of Delaware P, 1988] 80-97, esp. 91).

3. Cynthia Lewis, in "'With Simular Proof Enough': Modes of Misperception in *Cymbeline*," *Studies in English Literature* 31 (1991): 341-64, interprets Jachimo's emergence from the trunk as a "black parody of birth" (348)—a "cruelly teasing, subversive" image (of labor, I would claim).

4. Derek Traversi, in *Shakespeare: The Last Phase* (1954; rpt. Stanford, CA: Stanford UP, 1965) 60-61, characterizes Jachimo's account of the bedchamber's art as deliberately artificial and counterfeit so as to focus the lifeless sophistication and opulence of Cymbeline's court. According to Traversi, Imogen "needs to discover her true moral being, and the full implications of her love for Posthumus, by being taken from her court surroundings to another world [that of nature] in which the social artifices are not so prominent" (66).

5. This predilection is described by Coburn Freer, *The Poetics of Jacobean Drama* (Baltimore: The Johns Hopkins UP, 1981) 110-13; and by Ruth Nevo, *Shakespeare's Other Language* (New York: Methuen, 1987) 69-75.

6. Commentators on *Cymbeline* have regularly drawn parallels between Shakespeare's characterizations of Posthumus and Cloten, roles most likely doubled in original performances of the play. Dressed in Posthumus' garments, Cloten's headless body so resembles that of Posthumus that Imogen thinks that it is her lover's. Typical expressions of this view are given by Joan Hartwig, "Cloten and Caliban: Parodic Villains," *Shakespeare's Analogical Scene* (Lincoln: U of Nebraska P, 1983) 171-90,

esp. 172-75; Freer 116-17, 238 n21; and Stephen Booth, "Speculations on Doubling in Shakespeare's Plays," *Shakespeare: The Theatrical Dimension*, ed. Philip C. McGuire and David A. Samuelson (New York: AMS Press, 1979) 103-31, esp. 121-25.

7 Cloten, however, is the true figure of changeableness in *Cymbeline*. Recognizing him after twenty years even in his severed head, Belarius tells the princes,

> Though his humor
> Was nothing but mutation, ay, and that
> From one bad thing to worse, not frenzy, not
> Absolute madness could so far have rav'd
> To bring him here alone.
> (IV. ii. 132-36)

Frenzy and the absolute madness of sexual jealousy, however, have driven Cloten foolishly into the wilds of Wales. The play's avatar of mutation, he gives vent to a destructive stir in his frenzied alternation between quarreling and gambling. The fact that the play's exemplar of mutability is the male Cloten nicely reveals the ignorance of Posthumus' female stereotyping.

8 For the realm of Wales in *Cymbeline* as "hard" rather than "soft" pastoral, see Rosalie L. Colie, *Shakespeare's Living Art* (Princeton, NJ: Princeton UP, 1974) 292-302. Cf., however, Peggy Muñoz Simonds, "The Iconography of Primitivism in *Cymbeline*," *Renaissance Drama* 16 (1985): 95-120, esp. 95-98, who argues that Wales represents the values of emblematic primitivism rather than those of pastoral.

9 Concerning Belarius, Arviragus, and Guiderius, G. Wilson Knight, in *The Crown of Life: Essays in Interpretation of Shakespeare's Final Plays* (1947; rpt. New York: Barnes & Noble, 1966), argues that "the tiny community has its own rough aristocracy to be daily reasserted and rewon" (158).

10 See Maurice Hunt, "Perspectivism in *King Lear* and *Cymbeline*," *Studies in the Humanities* 14 (1987): 18-29, esp. 26-27.

11 Simonds, "The Iconography of Primitivism in *Cymbeline*" 111-12, provides an excellent alternative catalogue of the lessons that Imogen learns in Wales.

12 See Jasper Ridley, *Elizabeth I: The Shrewdness of Virtue* (New York: Viking, 1988) 324-25.

13 Several inadequacies in Imogen's love of Posthumus have been described by R. A. Foakes, *Shakespeare: The Dark Comedies to the Last Plays–From Satire to Celebration* (Charlottesville: UP of Virginia, 1971) 109-12.

14 This achievement represents a reversal of the attitude expressed in *Troilus and Cressida* (1601). According to Agamemnon, the god Jupiter weighs humankind's labors in the scales of steadfastness. "Why then, you princes,/ Do you with cheeks abash'd behold our works,/ And call them shames which are indeed nought else/ But the protractive trials of great Jove/ To find persistive constancy in men?" (I. iii. 17-21). Agamemnon, however, has just explained that a basic discontinuity between human intention and execution inevitably entails the failure of mortal works and the radical inconstancy of humankind. Agamemnon's Jove tests for a virtue incapable of realization in the world of this play. The Jupiter of *Cymbeline*, on the other hand, shows characters' works successfully precipitating the virtue of constancy, chiefly because Shakespeare has reconceived humankind as capable of eventually attaining and practicing relative steadfastness.

15 A detailed analysis of the dirge and its relevance for major motifs of *Cymbeline* appears in Derick R. C. Marsh, *The Recurring Miracle: A Study of "Cymbeline" and the Last Plays* (Pietrmaritzburg: U of Natal P, 1962) 81-85.

16 *The Dartmouth Bible*, ed. Roy B. Chamberlin and Herman Feldman (Boston: Houghton Mifflin, 1961) 926-27.

17 Thomas Fuller, *The History of the Worthies of England* (1840; rpt. New York: AMS Press, 1965) 3:432

18 Richard Wilson, "Against the Grain: Representing the Market in *Coriolanus*," *The Seventeenth Century* 6 (1991): 111-48, esp. 135.

19 The stylistic difficulty of Posthumus' battle-speech has been described by F. R. Leavis, "The Criticism of Shakespeare's Late Plays," *The Common Pursuit* (London: Chatto & Windus, 1958) 173-81, esp. 177-78; G. Wilson Knight, *The Crown of Life* 138-39; and by Hallett Smith, *Shakespeare's Romances: A Study of Some Ways of the Imagination* (San Marino, CA: Huntington Library, 1972) 180-82.

20 David L. Frost, "'Mouldy Tales': The Context of Shakespeare's *Cymbeline*," *Essays and Studies* 39 (1986): 19-38, esp. 26-27.

21 Jachimo's "Elizabethan" style and manner in this speech are described in detail by Freer 106-9.

22 For a psychoanalytic reading of Posthumus' vision, see Meredith Skura, "Interpreting Posthumus' Dream from Above and Below," *Representing Shakespeare: New Psychoanalytic Essays*, ed. Murray Schwartz and Coppélia Kahn (Baltimore: The Johns Hopkins UP, 1980) 203-16, esp. 210-13.

23 See Lila Geller, "*Cymbeline* and the Imagery of Covenant Theology," *Studies in English Literature* 20 (1980): 241-55.

24 Peggy Muñoz Simonds, in "'No More . . . Offend Our Hearing': Aural Imagery in *Cymbeline*," *Texas Studies in Literature and Language* 24 (1982): 137-54, argues that this penitent speech of Posthumus' "reaches the divine ears and evokes the appearance of Jupiter on his eagle" (148).

25 This aspect of *Cymbeline* has been explored by, among others, Emyrs Jones, "Stuart *Cymbeline*," *Essays in Criticism* 11 (1961): 84-99; Robin Moffet, "*Cymbeline* and the Nativity," *Shakespeare Quarterly* 13 (1962): 207-18; Bernard Harris, "'What's past is prologue': *Cymbeline* and *Henry VIII*," *Later Shakespeare*, ed. John Russell Brown and Bernard Harris, Stratford-Upon-Avon Studies 8 (London: Edward Arnold, 1966) 203-33, esp. 207-9; and by Howard Felperin, *Shakespearean Romance* (Princeton, NJ: Princeton UP, 1972) 180-88.

26 For an exhaustive analysis of this symbol, especially within Renaissance emblematic contexts, see Peggy Muñoz Simonds, "The Marriage Topos in *Cymbeline*: Shakespeare's Variations on a Classical Theme," *English Literary Renaissance* 19 (1989): 94-117.

27 "The Marriage Topos in *Cymbeline*" 115-16.

28 This point is made by Judiana Lawrence, "Natural Bonds and Artistic Coherence in the Ending of *Cymbeline*," *Shakespeare Quarterly* 35 (1984): 440-60, esp. 449.

29 Consult, for example, *Johnson on Shakespeare*, vols. 7 and 8 of the *Yale Edition of the Works of Samuel Johnson*, ed. Arthur Sherbo (New Haven: Yale UP, 1968) 7:73-74, 8:874; Traversi 44-46; James Sutherland, "The Language of the Last Plays," *More Talking of Shakespeare*, ed. John Garrett (New York: Theatre Arts Books, 1959) 144-51; Michael Taylor, "The Pastoral Reckoning of *Cymbeline*," *Shakespeare Survey* 36 (1983): 97-106, esp. 100; and Maurice Hunt, *Shakespeare's Romance of the Word* (Lewisburg, PA: Bucknell UP, 1990) 43-73.

30 See, for example, First and Second Gentleman's play-opening talk (I. i. 1-27).

Chapter 5

The Winter's Tale

In *Cymbeline*, Shakespeare depicts the breeding of children as a kind of work. That continues to be the case in *The Winter's Tale*. "This has been some stair-work," the Old Shepherd judges when he finds the abandoned babe Perdita—"some trunk-work, some behind-door-work" (III. iii. 73-75). Grown into a lovely maiden, Perdita poses a question for her disguised lover Florizel concerning his father's reaction to his masking: "O, the Fates!/ How would he look to see his work, so noble,/ Vildly bound up?" (IV. iv. 20-22). Posthumus in his hatred of women wishes that men could beget children without the participation of their co-workers, women. In *The Winter's Tale*, Leontes, suspecting his wife's adultery, works by himself to conceive an issue. The labor takes place wholly in his mind.

Doubting Hermione's married faith, Leontes seeks to reassure himself that Mamillius is no bastard by reading his own features in the boy's face:

> Come, sir page,
> Look on me with your welkin eye. Sweet villain!
> Most dear'st! my collop! Can thy dam?—may't be?—
> Affection! thy intention stabs the centre.
> Thou dost make possible things not so held,
> Communicat'st with dreams (how can this be?),
> With what's unreal thou co-active art,
> And fellow'st nothing. Then 'tis very credent
> Thou mayst co-join with something, and thou dost
> (And that beyond commission), and I find it
> (And that to the infection of my brains
> And hard'ning of my brows).
> (I. ii. 135-46)

Leontes' words "Most dear'st! my collop!"—my portion of my own flesh—indicate that he has found the assurance of paternity that he has been seeking. Yet the conviction is only momentary; his next words establish Hermione's adultery and the illegitimacy of the child in her womb. If affection, love, can couple with dreams to breed art, if it can join with what is unreal in the artist to create an illusion, then certainly love can join with something in reality.[1] In Leontes' jaundiced mind, this something is Polixenes' and Hermione's supposed scheme to breed "beyond commission" a bastard child. Leontes' thoughts about breeding between themselves work a kind of birth, ironically an illegitimate one. A passage in Shakespeare's *Richard II* provides a gloss on the process.

Stripped of his earthly power and influence, imprisoned Richard, now more than ever richly imaginative, studies how he may compare his prison to the world:

> And for because the world is populous,
> And here is not a creature but myself,
> I cannot do it; yet I'll hammer it out.
> My brain I'll prove the female to my soul,
> My soul the father, and these two beget
> A generation of still-breeding thoughts;
> And these same thoughts people this little world,
> In humors like the people of this world. . . .
> (V. v. 3-10)

Even as Richard's "male soul" begets upon the "female" of his brain "A generation of still-breeding thoughts" (the phrase "still breeding" suggests that the thoughts are still-born), so Leontes' "intention"—his imagining of love—cojoins with something in his mind to conceive a bastard thought, a "brainchild": the belief that the child in the womb is not his own. The stirred quality of Leontes' poetic speech mirrors the work of conception. In tracing the supposed coupling of Hermione and Polixenes, Leontes' thoughts themselves couple to mold a grotesque child, a monstrous issue. The masculine sexual connotations inherent in the utterance "thy intention stabs the centre" identify Leontes' pornographic imaginings as the male working on a passive female something in his brain.

Leontes competes with Hermione to produce a child, an offspring that he is absolutely sure is his own (because self-created).[2] His competition with his wife, his twisted desire alone to breed and deliver a son or daughter, makes him unjustifiably mystify the reality of female parturition. "As by strange fortune/It came to us" (II. iii. 179-80), he later says of Perdita's birth, so he commands Antigonus to leave the child in a foreign land. But all that Leontes succeeds in producing is a bastard issue. His labor contrasts with the benign, naturally endorsed labor of his wife. Shakespeare conveys the rightness of Hermione's labor of conception and childbearing through such sanctifying commentary as First Lady's "The Queen your mother rounds apace" (II. i. 16) and Second Lady's "She is spread of late/Into a goodly bulk. Good time encounter her!" (II. i. 19-20). Yet Leontes, bearing his monstrous birth in his brain, denies the goodness of her pregnancy be remarking "let her sport herself/With that she's big with, for 'tis Polixenes/Has made [her] swell thus" (II. i. 60-62). The wholesome remarks of the ladies in waiting suggest that Perdita's conception and Hermione's pregnancy, in their naturalness, are relatively painless, existing in sharp contrast to Leontes' tortured labor and delivery.

Nevertheless, because of her husband's harsh treatment of her, Hermione labors painfully to deliver Perdita:

> On her frights and griefs
> (Which never tender lady hath borne greater)
> She is, something before her time, deliver'd.
> (II. ii. 21-23)

Hermione's delivered "something" invites comparison with the imagined "something" of Leontes' affection/conception speech (I. ii. 143). Hers is a live miracle, whereas his is an empty wraith. The tempest that Leontes creates about Hermione causes her child's premature birth, even as the sea storm in *Pericles* compels Thaisa to deliver early her burden, Marina. The "something" that Leontes' thought has bred "beyond commission" finally appears in the "something" that Hermione delivers before her time. Contrary to Paulina's belief that the child, formerly "prisoner to the womb," is "By law and process of great Nature thence/Freed and enfranchis'd" (II. ii. 57-59), Leontes identifies Perdita with the bastard child of his brain, condemning her to suffering and isolation. His work of generation cancels Hermione's labor; at least it does so for sixteen years.

When enraged Leontes, physically menacing his new-born daughter, exclaims "The bastard brains with these my proper hands/Shall I dash out" (II. iii. 140-41), his words refer ironically and unconsciously to the bastard birth of his own mind. He would ease by delivery the painful presence of his self-created child, if he could. Shakespeare keeps this desire of Leontes before playgoers through repeated puns upon the words "issue" ("child"/"event") and "burthen" ("load"/"child"). First Lord begs Leontes to change his paranoid purpose, "Which being so horrible, so bloody, must/Lead on to some foul issue" (II. iii. 152-53). While Hermione lives, Leontes proclaims, "My heart will be a burthen to me" (II. iii. 206). Like the bastard of his brain, Leontes conceives of his heart as a heavy burden, a child, that he must labor to deliver. At the opening of Hermione's so-called trial for adultery, he announces, "This sessions (to our great grief we pronounce)/ Even pushes 'gainst our heart" (III. ii. 1-2). While Leontes says that the trial grieves him, at some preconscious level he believes that the "sessions" will induce labor, push against his heart, deliver his child of grief and so end his pain. However, that delivery, that labor, never occurs; and rather than acting as an easeful drug, the trial produces its own issue—that of Apollo.

Concerning Apollo's sealed-up oracle on the matter of Hermione's married fidelity, Dion judges that, when the contents are discovered,

> something rare
> Even then will rush to knowledge. Go; fresh horses!
> And gracious be the issue!
> (III. i. 20-22)

The seal broken, Apollo's "issue"—the god's "something"—rushes forth, a quick delivery but an enigmatic one (in the obscurity of the riddle). This obscurity allows Leontes to proclaim Apollo's issue a bastard. "There is no truth at all i' th' oracle," he blasphemously asserts, "The sessions shall proceed; this is mere falsehood" (III. ii. 140-41). Almost immediately, Mamillius, the son who Leontes believes is no bastard, dies.

Ironically Shakespeare suggests that the son in whose making Hermione was co-worker in some sense is wholly Leontes' child, for his existence depends upon Leontes' religious faith or blasphemy. Even though he insists otherwise, working Zeus-like to give birth in his male mind, Leontes has had a child of his body. Although Leontes realizes that Hermione has helped to make Mamillius ("I am glad you did not nurse him," he tells her; "Though he does bear some signs of me, yet you/Have too much blood in him" [II. i. 56-58]), Mamillius' life appears to be virtually identical with his father's spiritual existence. Tortured by the burden of his mind and heart, sleepless Leontes believes that Mamillius' sickness results from the boy's conception of his mother's dishonor (II. iii. 12-17). Instead, Mamillius' insomnia, illness, and eventual death record the withering of the soul of the father to whom he is so closely bound. By the play's mid-point, both Leontes and Hermione appear to have lost the fruit of their physical labors—Mamillius and Perdita.

In Paulina's opinion, "Fancies too weak for boys, too green and idle/For girls of nine" (III. ii. 181-82) agitate Leontes. But these purportedly idle fancies have wrought the most profound suffering and devastation in the royal family. When his son Mamillius dies, Leontes becomes completely isolated in a dead world, having banished those with whom he had affectionate bonds. A terrible stasis fixes the king; the wintry half of the play concludes with Paulina's powerful image of a frozen realm:

> O thou tyrant!
> Do not repent these things, for they are heavier
> Than all thy woes can stir; therefore betake thee
> To nothing but despair. A thousand knees,
> Ten thousand years together, naked, fasting,
> Upon a barren mountain, and still winter
> In storm perpetual, could not move the gods
> To look that way thou wert.
> (III. ii. 207-14)

A highly-wrought energy has shot through several of Leontes' early speeches. His frantic words about the relationship between affection and dreams whipped and snapped until their syntax became almost incomprehensible. But this agitation lessens as the king's affections congeal, harden, and cease altogether. Paulina's image locates the paralyzed, barren center of the play, occurring in the second scene of act III. It contains several suggestions of tragic stasis. The gods will never turn their faces toward Leontes. They will never enact the literal meaning of "repent"—to turn redemptively in a new direction, as Hermione will at play's end when Paulina commands "Turn, good lady,/Our Perdita is found" (V. iii. 120-21). Leontes' woes can never stir his crimes to repentant life. Cold and numb within him, they remain a heavy burden from whose pain labor never delivers him. Leontes' "child" dies still within him. What motion there is in Paulina's remarkable image remains trapped, fixed; the juxtaposition of the terms "still" and "perpetual" in her phrase "still winter in storm perpetual" conveys a Yeatsian impression of frozen motion, in this case motion so perpetual that it appears "still"—no longer motion at all.

Stir soon releases itself, however, from paralysis in the great sea tempest that buffets Antigonus' ship, that accompanies Perdita's abandonment on the Bohemian shore, and that drowns the sailors as they attempt to sail clear of land. The storm of *The Winter's Tale* symbolizes the stirred anger of the play's governing deity Apollo, who applies it not so much as a refiner of character (the goddess Diana's use of storms in *Pericles*) as a punishment for those who, like Antigonus and the sailors, willingly perform evil commands. Critics such as Ernest Schanzer and David Young have likened the structural design of *The Winter's Tale* to the shape of the hourglass.[3] They have taken their cue from the stage prop that Time, the Chorus, manipulates when he says, "I turn my glass, and give my scene such growing/As you had slept between" (IV. i. 16-17). Certainly the leisureliness of the great pastoral scene's growth to almost eight-hundred-and-fifty lines of poetry and prose reflects the gradual accumulation of figurative sand in the expansive lower half of the hourglass. Granted this structural metaphor, playgoers realize that turbulent act III, scene iii represents the narrow waist of the hourglass, where Time turns (as the hourglass and its sand do), running in a direction away from tragedy toward comic fulfillment.[4] In this imaginative conception, Time gives birth to Perdita. Torn from her mother, despised by her father, she is Time's issue, Time's burden, his Daughter in fact.[5]

*Veritas filia temporis.*⁶ "Now bless thyself," the Old Shepherd who finds the babe Perdita says; "thou met'st with things dying, I with things new-born" (III. iii. 113-14). The storm accompanying Time's delivery of Perdita represents Time's labor, and the narrow waist of the hourglass—the symbol for Time itself—replicates the constricted uterine passage through which Perdita, like humankind, passes tempestuously into life. "Look thee," the Old Shepherd tells his son, pointing to the rich cloth in which Perdita is wrapped, "a bearing-cloth for a squire's child" (III. iii. 115-16). Perdita's new-born status is signaled by the "bearing-cloth"—the rich cloth in which Jacobean children were carried to baptism. The rain accompanying Apollo's tempest has baptized the child Perdita into a world of crosses and afflictions—the lasting storm of the world of late Shakespearean romance.

Yet when we next see Perdita grown to a pretty country girl, she neither speaks nor acts as though suffering has been her lot in the house of her "father"—the Old Shepherd. In fact, in comparison with other characters at the sheepshearing festival, she appears passive, idle, both in her role as the Old Shepherd's daughter and as Flora, the mistress of the feast. A large segment of Shakespeare's audience would have considered this inclination of idleness and passivity to be not so much the result of the Old Shepherd's kindly pampering the source of his secret riches, the gold found alongside the abandoned babe, but the ambiguous mark of Perdita's aristocratic nature. They had heard covert and not-so-hidden satire on the idle aristocracy in plays by Shakespeare (such as *Cymbeline*) and by other Jacobean dramatists such as Chapman and Tourneur. Thus the Old Shepherd's goading passive Perdita to labor as the hostess of the festival would have struck them as less noteworthy than it does some modern commentators on the play. By nature, she is not disposed to strenuous work. "Fie, daughter," the Old Shepherd complains,

> when my old wife liv'd, upon
> This day she was both pantler, butler, cook,
> Both dame and servant; welcom'd all, serv'd all;
> Would sing her song, and dance her turn; now here,
> At the upper end o' th' table, now i' th' middle;

> On his shoulder, and his; her face o' fire
> With labor, and the thing she took to quench it
> She would to each one sip. You are retired,
> As if you were a feasted one and not
> The hostess of the meeting. Pray you bid
> These unknown friends to's welcome, for it is
> A way to make us better friends, more known.
> Come, quench your blushes, and present yourself
> That which you are, mistress o' th' feast. Come on,
> And bid us welcome to your sheep-shearing,
> As your good flock shall prosper.
> (IV. iv. 55-70)

It is not simply a maiden's shyness or a constitutional aversion to feigning, to role playing, that urges Perdita to forgo the duties involved in hosting the festival. Her inbred aristocratic antipathy to menial labor and to mingling with rustic folk also comes into play. Perdita's reluctance to perform the work of horticultural grafting strengthens this impression. She later admits to Polixenes that she abhors to labor at gardening to produce grafted flowers of late summer. It is as though this girl stigmatised as a bastard carries within herself a sensitivity to and an aversion toward anything that might be termed adulterated, even when it is only a streaked gillyvor.

Paradoxically, the Old Shepherd terms his deceased wife's former duties as the feast's hostess labor—"her face o' fire/ With labor."[7] The Shepherd's portrayal is remarkable when considered in the context of the literary conventions of English Renaissance pastoral. Following Virgil's lead, English Renaissance pastoralists regularly depicted the shepherd's life as one of *otium*—ease—that gained value from being set against *negotium*, the debilitating business of the city and court. Certainly the Shepherd's striking recollection of his wife as a kind of whirling dervish in her successive labors of pantry servant, butler, cook, hostess, festival entertainer, and *bon homme* drinking companion authorizes his calling her tasks labor—work so physically strenuous that it reddens her face. Michael Bristol has described the extent to which sheepshearing in Shakespeare's England required a special "coordination of husbandry (man's work) with huswifery (woman's work)."[8] The same apparently holds true for the production of the festivity associated with the shearing. One has the distinct impresssion that homely pastoral labors could refine Perdita's character, as they did that of Imogen. The Old Shepherd's criticism that Perdita appears "retired," as though she were "a feasted one and not/The hostess of the meeting," implies that she, like Imogen, has something to learn about charitably relieving the basic needs of others for such commodities as food and recreation.

By calling his deceased wife's holiday entertainment labor, the Old Shepherd integrates mirth and work. In fact, Shakespeare suggests that festive merrymaking, with its renewed feelings of community, represents a proper use of labor and its wages. By Hallett Smith's calculation, the Old Shepherd and his son are prosperous herders. The son reveals that fifteen-hundred shorn sheep will net the family approximately £143; every eleven shorn animals produces a tod of wool, a rounded £28 worth (IV. iii. 32-34).[9] Part of this projected revenue will pay for the sheepshearing festival:

> Let me see: what am I to buy for our sheep-shearing feast? Three pound of sugar, five pound of currants, rice—what will this sister of mine do with rice? . . . I must have saffron to color the warden pies; mace; dates, none—that's out of my note; nutmegs, seven; a race or two of ginger . . . and as many of raisins o' th' sun.
> (IV. iii. 36-39, 49-50)

The joint labor of everyone will purchase the ingredients of a rejuvenating feast of brotherly good feeling. It will be a reward for the laboring sheep shearers worth as much or more than their wages. Bristol has shown that the feast accompanying Elizabethan and Jacobean sheepshearings was usually regarded as partial recompense for the hirelings' labor. Festivity masked "the open secret of the wage-labor relations that define this activity."[10] Shakespeare suggests that wage labor becomes meaningful for the worker when a context of mirth and good cheer envelops it, investing it with non-utilitarian value. Into this organic relationship Autolycus intrudes, symbolically short-circuiting it. Certainly the money that he steals from the clownish son amounts to a fraction of the total sum that the shearing will bring. Yet by depriving the Clown and, through him, his family and their guests of the funds for buying the ingredients of festivity, Autolycus becomes a kind of killjoy. When the well-meaning Clown reaches for his purse to give some of his money to Autolycus, who has already cut it, the quick-witted rogue grabs his arm, exclaiming, "Offer me no money, I pray you, that kills my heart" (IV. iii. 82-83). The dialogue implies that acts of charity and festive fellowship enliven the hearts of distressed persons and laborers, whereas the cold calculation of financial remuneration kills them. Yet it is that chilling blight that Autolycus portends when he deprives the Clown of the means to obtain the proper reward of labor—holiday fare.

Excited by his easy thievery, Autolycus concludes, "I'll be with you at your sheep-shearing too. If I make not this cheat bring out another, and the shearers prove sheep, let me be unroll'd, and my name put in the book of virtue!" (IV. iii. 119-22). Later, Autolycus boasts that "To have an open ear, a quick eye, and a nimble hand, is necessary for a cutpurse; a good nose is requisite also, to smell out work for th' other senses." . . . "Every lane's end, every shop, church, session, hanging, yields a careful man work" (IV. iv. 670-73, 685-86). Autolycus terms his criminal activity "work." As a rogue and beggar, he automatically labeled himself as slothful in most Jacobean minds. His parasitic attachment to laborers in the ordinary sense of the word cheats them of the fruits of their work. Thus Shakespeare's giving him these particular boasts calls attention to the antithesis of his calling—honest work. Autolycus joins the paid shearers after the shearing, "working" at his trade to strip them of their recently paid wages. As the rustics crowd around him to buy the peddler's trinkets and wares, he cuts several purses, breaking the cycle of traditional work and wages. Autolycus' dishonest "labor" of "shearing" rustic "sheep" acts as a foil to accentuate their customary labor. The song with which he concludes his spoken resolve to shear the country sheep—

> Jog on, jog on, the foot-path way,
>   And merrily hent the stile-a;
> A merry heart goes all the day,
>   Your sad tires in a mile-a.
>   (IV. iii. 123-26)

—suggests, from its position in a sequence, that the "work" of thievery cheers the thief's heart and revitalizes him to the same degree that the actual sheepshearing and its associated mirth does those of the shearers themselves.

In this respect, the parallel operates to undermine the authenticity of the actual shearers' labor by suggesting that it amounts to a kind of easy thievery.[11] By "stealing" the sheeps' coats, the shepherds unscrupuously take advantage of a natural product without compensating the producers. In *As You Like It*, the shepherd Corin tells Touchstone, "Sir, I am a true laborer: I earn that I eat, get that I wear, owe no man hate, envy no man's happiness, glad of other men's good, content with my harm, and the greatest of my pride is to see my ewes graze and my lambs suck" (III. ii. 73-77). Touchstone, however, wittily indicates that the shepherd's "true labor" constitutes an ethically questionable exploitation of nature:

> That is another simple sin in you, to bring the ewes and the rams together, and to offer to get your living by the copulation of cattle; to be bawd to a bell-wether, and to betray a she-lamb of a twelve-month to a crooked-pated old cuckoldly ram, out of all reasonable match. If thou beest not damn'd for this, the devil himself will have no shepherds; I cannot see else how thou shouldst scape.
> (III. ii. 78-85)

While Touchstone's clever rejoinder mainly functions to display the jester's courtly wit and to maintain the celebrated balance between court and country in *As You Like It*, his remark also characterizes the unidyllic activities of the pastoral shepherd, which amount to natural exploitation rather than true labor.[12] By making sheep multiply only for financial gain, the shepherd represented by Corin provokes recollection of a dialogue in *The Merchant of Venice* between Antonio and Shylock, in which the Venetian asserts that the Jew tells the story of Jacob's manipulation of the natural breeding of sheep in order to rationalize the usurer's own handling of money so as to make it "breed" interest (I. ii. 71-97). While Corin is no usurer, Touchstone's claim that the breeding of sheep solely for financial gain cannot be praised as genuine labor gains strength from a piece of weighted dialogue in *The Merchant of Venice*.

The creation in *The Winter's Tale* of a comic analogy suggesting that the shearing for which sheep are bred involves a kind of thievery concludes Shakespeare's criticism of a major pastoral vocation.

While good-natured, festive, and kind, the Old Shepherd makes it clear that money rules his attitude toward his sheep. He and his son find Perdita on the sea coast of Bohemia because they search there for two sheep frightened from the flock by two boiled-brain hunters (III. iii. 59-67). Finding the gold left with the infant, the Old Shepherd states, "This is fairy gold, boy, and 'twill prove so. Up with't, keep it close. Home, home, the next way. We are lucky, boy, and to be so still requires nothing but secrecy. Let my sheep go" (III. iii. 123-26). The Old Shepherd's assertion that the gold has been left by fairies serves as a self-deluding equivocation that makes keeping it ethically acceptable to his conscious mind. He has just said that he believes that Perdita represents the "behind-door-work"—the illegitimate product—of mortals, possibly a man and woman of the court. Granted this opinion, he might logically conclude that they—not fairies—left behind the gold. But so fearful is he of being forced to return the gold that he concocts a supernatural source, exclaiming, "Let my sheep go." The conclusion follows that sheep solely represent monetary profit in his mind, and that when a greater gain comes along they are expendable. In this episode, Shakespeare evokes details of the Parable of the Lost Sheep chiefly in order to depict the Old Shepherd's denial of its meaning.[13] Whereas the Parable maintains that the faithful search for and finding of one lost sheep spiritually outweighs the value of a hundred which never become lost (Luke 15:3-7), the Old Shepherd easily gives up his quest for his two lost sheep when greed and gold displace them. Obviously Shakespeare does not evoke the Parable in order to make playgoers harshly judge the basically charitable Old Shepherd.[14] The allusion exists as an early indicator that the labor of shepherds, an activity usually rendered ideally in Renaissance literary pastorals, is more self-interested and questionable than one might suppose.[15]

Such is not the case with Perdita's pastoral labor. When she takes upon herself the role of "mistress o' th' feast," Flora the goddess of flowers, her rapid, graceful movement as she turns from one guest to another, bestowing her flowers upon them or richly describing those which she lacks but would give if she could, mimics the faultless labor of the Old Shepherd's deceased wife.[16] The wife

> welcom'd all, serv'd all;
> Would sing her song, and dance her turn; now here,
> At upper end o' th' table, now i' th' middle;
> On his shoulder, and his. . . .
> (IV. iv. 57-60)

Like those of her supposed mother, Perdita's graceful, ballet-like movements form a composite image of genuine welcome, a physical poem bewitching its admirers.[17] "What you do," enraptured Florizel proclaims,

> Still betters what is done. When you speak, sweet,
> I'ld have you do it ever; when you sing,
> I'ld have you buy and sell so; so give alms;
> Pray so; and for the ord'ring your affairs,
> To sing them too. When you do dance, I wish you
> A wave o' th' sea, that you might ever do
> Nothing but that; move still, still so,
> And own no other function. Each your doing
> (So singular in each particular)
> Crowns what you are doing in the present deeds,
> That all your acts are queens.[18]
> (IV. iv. 135-46)

Paulina's phrase "still winter/In storm perpetual," spoken during her malediction against Leontes, captured the paradoxical motion and fixity peculiar to the poetry of *The Winter's Tale*. Florizel's request that Perdita be a wave of the sea that would "move still, still so,/And own no other function" is the redemptive counterpart to Paulina's barren utterance. As a moving swell of the sea, dancing Perdita would appear motionless in her unbroken form while moving too, in a third mode of being not easily known in nature. This essentially static image results from Florizel's inspired description of Perdita's activities, her "doings"—her speaking, singing, buying, selling, giving of alms, praying, and dancing. Forever dancing as Flora, Perdita would in her lover's view "move still, still so." The four words themselves form a wave: motion crests with the first "still," suspends itself at the caesural pause, and sweeps downward and onward again with the second "still" and ensuing "so" (a universalizing adverb that stands for renewed motion). The idea, like the poetry forming it and Florizel's exquisite speech in general, teases the listener out of thought. Murray Krieger, in an essay upon the ekphrastic principle in poetry, has extensively described the fused meanings contained in the poetic word "still."[19] Because it can connote at the same time the freezing and unqualified occurrence of an event, the word captures, for Krieger, a major function of poetry—the rendering spatial and permanent the flux of unordered happenings, the chaotic stir which inspires the artist by its vitality and potential, which provides him or her with material, but from which he or she recoils in pain into an artifice of eternity. It is plausible to assume that a similar dynamic of attraction and repulsion motivated Shakespeare to crystallize stasis and movement in perfected poetic passages and ravishing images, in a hypnotic phrase, and finally in the single word "still," with its connotations of "forever-now." Shakespeare's simultaneous and unresolved commitment to physical life, the pleasures and rewards of the passing day, and to eternity, represented by serene images, accounts for his fascination with the merging of opposites.[20]

For Florizel and presumably for playgoers, all this is inspired by Perdita's labor—her work of pastoral hospitality. Paradoxically that labor produces an immensely satisfying rest, the bewitching stasis of Florizel's love lyric. Perdita's labor of hospitality obviously is the counterpart of Hermione's failed, tragic effort to make Polixenes feel welcome in Sicilia. As a labored counterpart, Perdita's welcome contrasts with the aristocratic idleness that (in Leontes' mind at least) drives Hermione to commit adultery and then supposedly flirt with her adulterer before her husband's face. Moreover, Florizel's love lyric invites comparison with another passage from the wintry section of the play. Critics have established a pervasive number symbolism in *The Winter's Tale*, which focuses upon the wide gap of time separating the action (sixteen years) and especially the number twenty three as it relates to Leontes' and Polixenes' specific ages, the ages of humankind, and a frequent date of the autumnal equinox (September 23rd)—"Not yet on summer's death, nor on the birth/Of trembling winter" (IV. iv. 80-81).[21] Granted this extensive symbolism, readers of the received text of *The Winter's Tale* might note that Florizel's lyric, in its versification (IV. iv. 135-46), occupies the same place in its scene that Leontes' rapture on affection's and dream's authorizing the "something" of Hermione's adultery does in its context (I. ii. 135-46). The parallel versification, identical in the numbering of *The Riverside Shakespeare* text, encourages readers to think of Florizel's lyric as rectifying, even redeeming, the destructive effects of Leontes' rapture. In both cases, love and imagination join to create an intangible, which is illusory in Leontes' case but transcendentally real in Florizel's.[22] We saw that Leontes' rapture, the king's unaided creation of Perdita's identity, is the male equivalent of female labor. Florizel's rapture derives from the pastoral labor of that child, now grown into a beautiful young woman. Leontes' labor is illegitimate not only in its misapplication of the enfranchising faculties of the mind but also in its product, the "bastard" Perdita. Perdita's labor legitimizes her being in the strikingly authentic ideas that she prompts in her admirer. One labor has come to supersede and rectify an earlier work.

Viewed through the elevating context provided by Florizel's lyric, dancing Perdita, especially if played by an actress of consummate beauty and training in gesture, can merge motion and stillness for the theater audience. But the spell is broken by the peddler Autolycus, come to shear his own sheep at the festival. Many commentators on *The Winter's Tale* have argued that, in the Servant's account of the hypnotic effect of the rogue's singing of his trinkets and wares upon listening shepherds and shepherdesses, Shakespeare appears to be parodying the paralytic impact of artfully moving Perdita upon her beholders, especially Florizel.[23] For example, the Servant exclaims, "if you did but hear the pedlar at the door, you would never dance after a tabor and pipe; no, the bagpipe could not move you" (IV. iv. 181-83). Florizel's love lyric seems to be specifically parodied in the Servant's description of Autolycus' exaggerated manner of musically itemizing his ribbons, laces, linen and worsted tapes, and fine linen cloth: "Why, he sings 'em over as they were gods or goddesses: you would think a smock were a she-angel, he so chaunts to the sleeve-hand and the work about the square on't" (IV. iv. 207-10). Later, Autolycus describes the immobilizing effect upon the Clown of the song that he has sold the wenches:

> he would not stir his pettitoes till he had both tune and words, which so drew the rest of the herd to me that all their other senses stuck in ears. You might have pinch'd a placket, it was senseless; 'twas nothing to geld a codpiece of a purse; I would have fil'd keys off that hung in chains. No hearing, no feeling, but my sir's song, and admiring the nothing of it. So that in this time of lethargy I pick'd and cut most of their festival purses.[24]
>
> (IV. iv. 606-15)

These passages suggest that the work of art, whether Autolycus' peddler's chant, celebrating the workmanship of a smock; wenches' popular songs; or Florizel's magnificent lyric of love, can rob its appreciator of something valuable—not only money but the critical presence of mind that understands that ethereal effects derive from quite mundane aesthetic properties.[25] The tunes and words of songs sold by Jacobean peddlers could never be mistaken for great art, and the brilliant robe that Perdita as Flora wears is a smock that goes a long way toward making her appear a she-angel in Florizel's eyes. The parody created by the Servant's account of Autolycus' hypnotic effect on his rural audience suggests that Florizel may unknowingly worship the means—the artistry—rather than the subject, Perdita, transformed by it. Florizel may be singing over her garments as Flora as though they were a goddess. The work of art, to use Autolycus' word, may induce a "lethargy" of mind dangerous for its appreciator. The implications of this suggestion for Shakespeare's writing of *The Winter's Tale* will be explored at the end of this chapter.[26] The meaningful stasis that labor works, whether it is thought of as the result of Perdita's labor as hostess, the work of Flora's artistry, or Shakespeare's labor in creating this episode and its transfixing poetry, may in fact be as deleterious as the lethargy wrought by Autolycus' trivial art on those who buy it to perform it.

Art, nevertheless, provides the means for Leontes' earthly salvation. A creative kind of stir made possible by art displaces a psychological stir self-destructive for Leontes. "O my brother," Leontes exclaims upon seeing Florizel, "Good gentleman! the wrongs I have done thee stir/Afresh within me" (V. i. 147-49). Leontes is finally not a tragic character because Paulina preserves Hermione, and because Camillo directs Florizel and Perdita to the Sicilian court, an act which draws Leontes' "brother" Polixenes to him. But he cannot fully rejoice in his rediscovered bonds of family and friendship as long as the inner stir of shame and remorse possesses him. By choosing to pose Hermione as a marvelous sculpture, Paulina urges Leontes and the rest of the court to think of her as a work of art. According to Third Gentleman, the "statue" is "a piece many years in doing and now newly perform'd by that rare Italian master, Julio Romano, who, had he himself eternity and could put breath into his work, would beguile Nature of her custom, so perfectly he is her ape" (V. ii. 95-100). But Julio Romano cannot put breath into his labor, his work of art. Nor does he have eternity to try to do so. In fact, Julio Romano, the sixteenth-century Italian Mannerist artist, judged within the context of Paulina's report, is a sham. His name is evoked simply to give authority to Hermione posing as a statue. This description again calls into question the status of art as a work, e. g., a product whose inherent value and positive effect upon appreciators correspond to the painstaking, special labor that went into its creation. Even as different kinds of artistry in the pastoral scene appear to make possible varieties of theft, so Paulina's report robs the historical Julio Romano of his good name and steals the wish of both characters and playgoers alike that posing Hermione might live again.

In what sense, then, can the statue of Hermione be regarded as a work of art? When *"Paulina draws a curtain, and discovers Hermione standing like a statue"* (*The Riverside Shakespeare* stage direction), wonder transfixes Leontes, Perdita, and the other beholders. In *Cymbeline*, wonder is the antithesis of work; Posthumus rebuked a cowardly aristocrat for wondering at the heroism of battle rather than working heroic deeds. "O royal piece," Leontes addresses the "statue,"

> There's magic in thy majesty, which has
> My evils conjur'd to remembrance, and
> From thy admiring daughter took the spirits,
> Standing like stone with thee.
> (V. iii. 38-42)

The wonder produced in Florizel by his vision of Perdita as Flora so transfixes him that he would freeze her forever as a still-moving wave of the sea, and the wonder instilled in the rustics by Autolycus' songs so paralyze them that they remain ignorant of his rough thievery. The "artistry" of Hermione's so-called statue similarly immobilizes Perdita, stealing her signs of life. Ironically, a work that lacks only breath robs Perdita of her spirit, seemingly her very breathing.

Yet while the statue first provokes Leontes to wonder, it quickly stirs within him the memory of the evil that he has done. "If I had thought the sight of my poor image/Would thus have wrought you," Paulina disingenuously tells Leontes, "I'ld not have show'd it" (V. iii. 57-59). But as her word "wrought" signals, Paulina intends the vision of Hermione as statue to work on Leontes, to work him into a redemptive idea of Hermione and himself as husband and wife. Ironically Leontes is the statue's work—the work of a work of art.[27] In a sense, it can be said to create him, into a new life.

Art does this by becoming a contrary signifier. When Leontes adopts the cliché Renaissance aesthetic attitude that art mocks him with its lifelikeness, his recollection of Hermione corrects this view:

> Chide me, dear stone, that I may say indeed
> Thou art Hermione; or rather, thou art she
> In thy not chiding; for she was as tender
> As infancy and grace.
> (V. iii. 24-27)

"O, thus she stood," Leontes painfully recalls, "Even with such life of majesty (warm life,/As now it coldly stands), when first I woo'd her!" (V. iii. 34-36). In his shame, he believes that the stone reprimands him "For being more stone than it" (V. iii. 37-38). Through a process of contrary definition, Leontes uses art to work—to fashion—the tender, virtuous Hermione of his youth. The creation and delivery of that person in his mind represents a legitimate birth labor, one wrought with the help of "feminine" art, a labor that in its healthy results for him and his family supersedes and lays to rest any traces of perversion lingering from his malign labor of delivering the illegitimate Perdita. Leontes is also in a sense giving birth to himself, a recreated self as Hermione's trusting, loving husband.

Noting that Leontes' mental labor is giving birth to new beings, Paulina realizes that Hermione might begin to stir from her deathly stasis. The stir that Paulina through spoken cues gradually orchestrates in Hermione matches the increasing agitation of Leontes. Having been wrought to the partial recreation of a virtuous wife, Leontes responds to Paulina's subtle suggestion that his fancy might think the statue moves by, for the first time, noticing the almost imperceptible signs of Hermione's breathing, her beating pulse, and faintly flickering eyes (V. iii. 56-68). And when he excitedly wishes to think that the statue lives, Paulina says, "I am sorry, sir, I have thus far stirr'd you; but/I could afflict you farther" (V. iii. 74-75). Her claim to be able to make the statue move, descend from its pedestal, and take Leontes by the hand involves a requirement of stasis on the part of beholders. "All stand still," she commands; "Proceed;/ No foot shall stir" (V. iii. 95-98), Leontes replies. The "art" of Hermione's statue has stirred Leontes into a new life; yet he must become as lifeless and immobile as a statue for that art itself to stir, to become alive physically. Shakespeare at the end of *The Winter's Tale* indicates that the maker and appreciator's mutually cooperative work of art—of art making—imposes restrictions, even a penalty, upon their joint participation. A fully alive or shared life never seems possible for either member of the partnership at any given moment.

Granted this problem, human beneficiaries of works of art like Hermione's statue gain the new life made possible by their enabling response to art when art is sacrificed, when art vanishes. "Music! awake her! strike!" Paulina commands,

> 'Tis time; descend; be stone no more; approach;
> Strike all that look upon with marvel. Come;

> I'll fill your grave up. Stir; nay, come away;
> Bequeath to death your numbness; for from him
> Dear life redeems you. You perceive she stirs.
> (V. iii. 98-103)

Paulina's repetition of the word "stir" stresses the life that Leontes has wrought for Hermione and for himself. The stillness of their tableau-like, silent embrace promises a fulfilled life together by registering the depth of their new-found love. Having wrought this miracle, art is expendable; it disappears as a show, in fact.

Finally speaking to her daughter Perdita, Hermione explains "that I,"

> Knowing by Paulina that the oracle
> Gave hope thou wast in being, have preserv'd
> Myself to see the issue.
> (V. iii. 125-28)

By "issue," Paulina of course means "event." But the word has also referred in the play to "child." In this case, the "issue" is both reunion with Perdita and the reborn child as well. While Leontes figuratively delivers a youthful Hermione and a new self, Perdita's rebirth is Time's labor. Time, the agent of Apollo, has so fashioned events that Perdita's rebirth within the context of her family constitutes his "issue." Shakespeare plays a variation upon the Renaissance iconic motif *Veritas filia temporis*. Truth's sudden appearance from behind the plighted cloth of her father Time signified that truth is born in the course of time. As the play's most truthful character, Perdita qualifies as Time's issue, the fruit of his long labor in *The Winter's Tale*.

By playing a crucial role in the rebirth of a royal family, art compensates for the paralysis or numbing of its consumer's intellectual faculties. Stealing its appreciator's assent can be excused when it helps to bring new beings to life. What does saying that Shakespeare is the playwright of a "birthing" art mean? When Perdita wonders how Florizel's father would "look to see his work, so noble,/ Vildly bound up" (IV. iv. 21-22), she conflates the child with an artifact, a book—specifically a volume of pastoral literature nobly written but cheaply bound.[28] The metaphor realizes the Jacobean patriarchal belief that fathers reproductively print themselves on the pages of female matter. "Your mother was most true to wedlock," Leontes tells Florizel when he first sees him; "For she did print your royal father off,/ Conceiving you" (V. i. 124-26). If as a book *The Winter's Tale* is Shakespeare's issue, his child, he needs the participation of others in its production, if it is to become a true copy.[29] Autonomous male creation brings nothing wholesome to light. Leontes' metaphor of printing off the author points to the typesetter and publisher, while Perdita's earlier conceit focuses on the binder. By working with blank and then printed pages, the typesetter closely associates himself with the female role in creating an issue. It is significant that *The Winter's Tale* apparently never became a quarto during Shakespeare's lifetime; the 1623 Folio text is the only known version of the play. In this respect, Shakespeare almost certainly never saw either a noble or an illegitimate (pirated) copy of himself. Textual critics generally agree that the Folio text of the play "was printed from a transcript made by Ralph Crane, scrivener to the King's Men, and probably specifically prepared for the printer."[30] This judgment of G. Blakemore Evans' serves as a reminder that, as a play acted at the Globe and perhaps at Blackfriars, *The Winter's Tale* could never exist as its author's self-begot child. Its birth as dramatic spectacle depended upon the participation of at least the preparer of the promptbook, whose task involved regularizing the text and adding directions for entrances, exits, and special effects. Evans notes that Crane, in preparing the text of the play for the Folio edition, appears to have "worked directly from Shakespeare's 'foul papers.' Nothing in the text suggests any use of the official prompt-book; indeed, an entry in the *Office Book* of Sir Henry Herbert, Master of the Revels, strongly suggests that the company's prompt-book was lost at the time copy was needed for F1."[31]

The irony here is thick. The basic written text (the dramatist's and promptbook preparer's child) of a play that celebrates the providential finding of what seemed irretrievably lost was found in the playwright's foul papers after the nobler, more legitimate copy was lost. Granted his emphasis on the transformation of an illegitimate child into a legitimate one, Shakespeare most likely would have appreciated Crane's preparation of an unusually clean text out of his foul papers.

That irony, however, the dramatist never lived to enjoy. Dependent upon the participation of another for the birth of his play, Shakespeare saw and heard his issue as the evanescent creature of an afternoon, a child that faded in the eyes and ears of playgoers before becoming dim and forgotten. Without the participation of the typesetter and publisher, Shakespeare joins Leontes as laboring father/mother. Each may play the father imaginatively to passive female matter in his mind to give birth to a new identity, but his work remains illusory, fictional, without the physical participation of another creator. This parallel holds even though Shakespeare's self-begot works, his hundreds of characters, acquire a certain legitimacy in the powerful truth of their resemblance to nature. In other words, Shakespeare in a certain sense lived long enough to come to the likely conclusion that, as regards *The Winter's Tale*, his labor in at least two dimensions of the word was lost.

In the midst of the great pastoral scene, Mopsa naively declares, "I love a ballet in print, a-life, for then we are sure they are true" (IV. iv. 260-61). Foolishly she assumes that the decision to print and the process of printing validate the truth of published matter. In one respect, however, she is right; the physical participation of two begetters in giving birth to an issue is more likely to result in a truer child. Deprived of the correcting and enhancing participation of an accomplice, the solitary begetter, the playwright over his foul papers, suffers from his own myopic, unobjective perspective on his creation. Mopsa's interjection "a-life" is usually glossed "on my life"—a kind of oath. But playgoers generally hear the word as "alive," the notion being that putting a ballad in print makes it alive, gives it life. An issue most fully comes alive when two partners labor together to bring forth a clean, legitimate copy. Birthing labor becomes Shakespeare's focus in Mopsa's talk with Autolycus:

> *Aut.* Here's one to a very doleful tune, how a usurer's wife was brought to bed of twenty money-bags at a

	burthen, and how she long'd to eat adders' heads, and toads carbonado'd.
Mop.	Is it true, think you?
Aut.	Very true, and but a month old.
Dor.	Bless me from marrying a usurer!
Aut.	Here's the midwive's name to't, one Mistress Tale-porter, and five or six honest wives that were present. Why should I carry lies abroad?

(IV. iv. 262-71)

This conversation specifically equates the legitimacy of physical child labor with the truth of the writer's and typesetter/publisher's mutual labor. Even though the "burthen," the issue, may be grotesque (as in the case of the usurer's wife), the child authentically prints off the father—so genuinely in fact that the passive mother delivers moneybags, the exact copy of the maker's avarice! The pun on the midwife's name ("Tail-porter"/"Tale-porter") equates her with the publisher's representative who assists in the author/typesetter's labor to bring forth a "tale" and who, because a witness to the process of birth, can attest to the legitimacy of the work.[32]

Nevertheless, Mopsa's and Autolycus' comic dialogue underscores the fact that the process of printing can make palpable lies legitimate. It cannot make truthful an author's solitary misconceptions, or false conceptions—the works of his laboring brain. If *The Winter's Tale* finally amounts to a misconception of life, no manner of printing can make it legitimate. Leontes' fantastic illusions resemble the fanciful extravagances of Autolycus' ballads, as may also several details of providential plotting and the great pastoral scene. Still, Shakespeare's play has struck generations of spectators and readers alike as true to imaginative life. At Shakespeare's desk, at his elbow, during the writing of *The Winter's Tale* was Robert Greene's *Pandosto*, a printed text that he legitimized by finding in it the germs of truth. In the final analysis, the play may be thought of as the issue of Greene and Shakespeare's mutual labor, or—more properly—as Shakespeare's remaking of the disproportioned, relatively weaker child of another. Shakespeare's creative analogue in the play is not so much Leontes or Autolycus or even Paulina, the stage director who provides cues for bringing something lifeless to life, but the Old Shepherd, the nurturer and transformer of another's orphan. Truthful Perdita and the genuine play containing her represent the finest fruits of pastoral labor.

Notes

1 Leontes' infamous "affection" speech has been analyzed by, among others, Harold C. Goddard, *The Meaning of Shakespeare* (Chicago: U of Chicago P, 1951) 2:264-65; J. V. Cunningham, *Woe or Wonder* (Denver: U of Denver P, 1951) 113-14; Hallett Smith, "Leontes' *Affectio*," *Shakespeare Quarterly* 14 (1963): 163-66; *The Winter's Tale*, ed. J. H. P. Pafford, Arden Shakespeare (London: Methuen, 1965) 165-67; Jonathan Smith, "The Language of Leontes," *Shakespeare Quarterly* 19 (1968): 317-27, esp. 317-18; Marjorie Garber, *Dream in Shakespeare: From Metaphor to Metamorphosis* (New Haven: Yale UP, 1974) 165-66; Carol Thomas Neely, "*The Winter's Tale*: The Triumph of Speech," *Studies in English Literature* 15 (1975): 321-38, esp. 324-27; and David Ward, "Affection, Intention, and Dreams in *The Winter's Tale*," *Modern Language Review* 82 (1987): 545-54.

2 Charles Frey has remarked that, "as king," Leontes "has perhaps some reason to become trapped in divine analogy, but as man, dependent upon woman in order to play his part in creation, he cannot be self-sufficient" (*Shakespeare's Vast Romance: A Study of "The Winter's Tale"* [Columbia: U of Missouri P, 1980] 131).

3 Ernest Schanzer, "The Structural Pattern of *The Winter's Tale*," *Review of English Literature* 5 (1964): 72-82, esp. 79; David Young, *The Heart's Forest: A Study of Shakespeare's Pastoral Plays* (New Haven: Yale UP, 1972) 119, 125, 133-45.

4 On Time's literal and figurative turning of his hourglass, see Frey 142-43.

5 Howard Felperin, in *Shakespearean Romance* (Princeton, NJ: Princeton UP, 1972), has characterized the birth labor of Time in this play: "Perdita and her fortunes will be 'brought forth' as an actress is brought forth onto the stage, but also as a child is brought forth into the world: 'By law and process of great nature' (II. ii. 60)" (231).

6 The fullest explication of this idea is that of Soji Iwasaki, "*Veritas Filia Temporis* and Shakespeare," *English Literary Renaissance* 3 (1973): 249-63, esp. 261-63 (for *The Winter's Tale*). But also see Fritz Saxl, "*Veritas Filia Temporis*," *Philosophy and History: Essays Presented to Ernst Cassirer*, ed. Raymond Klibansky and H. J. Paton (Oxford: Clarendon P, 1936) 197-222; and Erwin Panofsky, *Studies in Iconology* (New York: Oxford UP, 1939) 83-91.

7 Mythili Kaul, in "The Old Shepherd's Speech in *The Winter's Tale*," *The Upstart Crow* 7 (1987): 96-100, explains the relevance of IV. iv. 55-70 for the play as a whole.

8 Michael D. Bristol, "In Search of the Bear: Spatiotemporal Form and the Heterogeneity of Economies in *The Winter's Tale*," *Shakespeare Quarterly* 42 (1991): 145-67, esp. 164. "The sheepshearing is one of the cycle of ploughman's feasts mentioned by Tusser, and it is the huswife's duty to make provision for this observance" (164).

9 *The Riverside Shakespeare* 1587.

10 Bristol, "In Search of the Bear" 164.

11 The comic subplot's ability to function simultaneously as foil and parody is amply demonstrated by Richard Levin, *The Multiple Plot in English Renaissance Drama* (Chicago: U of Chicago P, 1971) 109-47.

12 For a different view of Shakespeare's commentary in *As You Like It* on contemporary social abuses of country labor, see Richard Wilson, "'Like the old Robin Hood': *As You Like It* and the Enclosure Riots," *Shakespeare Quarterly* 43 (1992): 1-19.

13 Roy Battenhouse, in "Theme and Structure in *The Winter's Tale*," *Shakespeare Survey* 33 (1980): 123-38, also finds a religious dimension in this episode: "although this scene is not a Bible-story nativity, it does seem to me analogous to such a pattern from within the limits of a rustic natural piety" (134).

14 Nevertheless, Kirby Farrell, in *Shakespeare's Creation: The Language of Magic and Play* (Amherst: U of Massachusetts P, 1975), thinks that we are meant to do so: the Old Shepherd's "parodic association with Christ the shepherd" makes him "a comically imperfect figure . . . . This shepherd is no saint, given a choice between duty and gold, he knows which to follow" (219).

15 The material economy of Elizabethan sheepowning and shepherding is described by Louis A. Montrose, "Of Gentlemen and Shepherds: The Politics of Elizabethan Pastoral Form," *English Literary History*, 50 (1983): 415-59, esp. 421-33. Montrose argues that, for Shakespeare's age, "the sheep becomes a hierarchy-transcending incorporation of property, a subject of human exploitation uniting or identifying the interests of groups that had profoundly differing proprietary relations to the land itself, to their own labor, and to each other" (423-24).

16 A slightly different connection between Perdita and the wife is suggested by R. S. White, *"Let Wonder Seem Familiar": Endings in Shakespeare's Romance Vision* (London: Athlone, 1985) 151.

17 The richest explication of Perdita's flower poetry (IV. iv. 73-135) is provided by Charles R. Forker, "Perdita's Distribution of Flowers and the

Function of Lyricism in *The Winter's Tale*," *Fancy's Images: Contexts, Settings, and Perspectives in Shakespeare and His Contemporaries* (Carbondale: Southern Illinois UP, 1990) 113-25, esp. 118-25.

18 F. David Hoeniger, in "The Meaning of *The Winter's Tale*," *University of Toronto Quarterly* 20 (1950): 11-26, has judged that "Florizel's praise of Perdita (IV. iv. 135-46) is one of the most moving passages in the whole of Shakespeare" (12)—a conclusion shared by G. Wilson Knight, *The Crown of Life: Essays in Interpretation of Shakespeare's Final Plays* (1947; rpt. New York: Barnes and Noble, 1966) 120.

19 Murray Krieger, "The Ekphrastic Principle and the Still Movement of Poetry; or *Laokoön* Revisited," *The Play and Place of Criticism* (Baltimore: The Johns Hopkins UP, 1967) 105-28.

20 The concept of the merged opposite is defined and applied to *The Winter's Tale* by Jay B. Ludwig, "Shakespearean Decorum: An Essay on *The Winter's Tale*," *Style* 8 (1974): 365-404.

21 For evidence for these claims, see F. W. Bateson, "How Old Was Leontes?" *Essays and Studies* 31 (1978): 65-74; Alastair Fowler, "Leontes' Contrition and the Repair of Nature," *Essays and Studies* 31 (1978): 36-64, esp. 56-64; A. P. Riemer, *Antic Fables: Patterns of Evasion in Shakespeare's Comedies* (New York: St. Martin's Press, 1980) 170-79; and Maurice Hunt, "The Three Seasons of Mankind: Age, Nature, and Art in *The Winter's Tale*," *Iowa State Journal of Research* 58 (1984): 299-309. In *The Winter's Tale*, the sheepshearing festival, which had no prescribed fixed date in the sixteenth-century farmers almanac, occurs at the very end of summer. (See Bristol 164 and Lachlan Mackinnon, *Shakespeare the Aesthete* [New York: St. Martin's Press, 1988] 144). In fact it occurs at or very near the autumn equinox. For September sheepshearings in Shakespeare's England, see John Lyly, "Speeches Delivered to Her Majesty this last Progress," *The Complete Works of John Lyly*, ed. R. Warwick Bond (Oxford: Clarendon Press, 1967) 1:471-90, esp. 477. In his Arden edition of *The Winter's Tale*, Pafford judges that "in the pastoral scene the season approaches winter" (liv, lxix). This evidence counters the claim, made typically by Peter Lindenbaum, in "Time, Sexual Love, and the Uses of Pastoral in *The Winter's Tale*," *Modern Language Quarterly* 33 (1972): 3-22, esp. 15, that the sheepshearing of the play occurs "most likely [in] late June" and that Perdita's lines are simply "an explanation of why Perdita could not give Polixenes and Camillo the late summer flowers that would have been more appropriate for them."

22 The transcendental reality of Florizel's vision of Perdita is defined Neoplatonically by Patricia S. Gourlay, "'O my most sacred lady': Female Metaphor in *The Winter's Tale*," *English Literary Renaissance* 5 (1975): 375-95, esp. 387-88.

23 See, for example, Lee Sheridan Cox, "The Role of Autolycus in *The Winter's Tale*," *Studies in English Literature* 9 (1969): 283-301, esp. 289-90,

300. And cf. David Kaula, "Autolycus' Trumpery," *Studies in English Literature* 26 (1976): 287-303, esp. 294.

24 Northrop Frye, in "Recognition in *The Winter's Tale*," *Essays on Shakespeare and Elizabethan Drama in Honor of Hardin Craig*, ed. Richard Hosley (Columbia: U of Missouri P, 1962) 235-46, calls Autolycus "a kind of rascally Orpheus at the sheep-shearing festival" (245).

25 A similar conclusion is reached by R. A. Foakes, *Shakespeare: The Dark Comedies to the Last Plays—From Satire to Celebration* (Charlottesville: UP of Virginia, 1971) 140.

26 "Drama is not so different from the confidence man's art that Autolycus practices," Joan Hartwig concludes in *Shakespeare's Tragicomic Vision* (Baton Rouge: Louisiana State UP, 1972) 120. Also see S. L. Bethell, *"The Winter's Tale": A Study* (London: Staples Press, 1947) 46.

27 According to Frey, during the course of the statue scene "we become, like Leontes, 'wrought'—anguished with fellow feeling but also wrought into works of art sharing the universal substance of our humanity" (160).

28 In "The Natural Art of *The Winter's Tale*," *Modern Language Quarterly* 30 (1969): 340-55, Mary L. Livingston notes that "Perdita uses a traditional book metaphor to describe Florizel as the noble 'work' of his father the author" (344 n5).

29 A different account of the Renaissance literary artifact as a child delivered by the writer's mind is given by Patricia Fumerton, *Cultural Aesthetics: Renaissance Literature and the Practice of Social Ornament* (Chicago: U of Chicago P, 1991) 55-62. Referring to the Garden of Adonis episode of *The Faerie Queene*, Fumerton claims that "the poet/genius is a kind of Sidnean poet who clothes the 'naked babes' of his mind—his poetic Ideas—with the 'fleshly weedes' . . . of rhetorical ornaments on 'delivering them forth,' as Sidney would say, to an audience" (56).

30 *The Riverside Shakespeare* 1604.

31 *The Riverside Shakespeare* 1604.

32 A different reading of these details is given by Joan Hartwig, "Cloten, Autolycus, and Caliban: Bearers of Parodic Burdens," *Shakespeare's Romances Reconsidered*, ed. Carol McGinnis Kay and Henry E. Jacobs (Lincoln: U of Nebraska P, 1978) 91-103, esp. 100-1; and by Cox 284-85.

Chapter 6

The Tempest

Critics have often considered the opening scene of *The Tempest* to be a paradigm of the perilous state of existence and the range of moral reactions to sudden trial and threatened death.[1] Shakespeare presents timely labor not only as the difference between life and death but also as the means for winnowing courage from cowardice and self-conceit. "Bestir, bestir" are the Master's first words to sailors afflicted by the raging tempest. Desperate noblemen bursting forth from their place below deck interrupt disciplined work, ordered by the Master's whistle and necessary for survival during storm at sea. "You mar our labor," the Master pointedly tells them. "Keep your cabins; you do assist the storm" (I. i. 13-14), he commands. His words focus a dramatic conflict—natural disorder, assisted by passion, versus redemptive work. The first term of this opposition is familiar because it appears in virtually every Shakespeare play. The second term is special to the last plays, representing a principal means by which they avert tragedy and attain the relative harmony of dramatic romance.

At the beginning of *The Tempest*, disorder proves stronger than the sailors' labored attempt to contain it. Admittedly, Prospero's magical storm would defeat the navigational skills of any group of well-trained sailors. Nevertheless, Shakespeare chooses not to stress that fact in this brief episode. Instead, he creates the impression that the aristocrats' physical interference with the carefully disciplined labor of the mariners causes the ship to sink. Furthermore, he suggests that this interference proceeds from the uselessness of the noblemen in a context in which manual work is required. "What cares these roarers for the name of king?" the angry Boatswain asks frightened Alonso and his company; "To cabin! silence! trouble us not" (I. i. 16-

18), he shouts. The storm makes the aristocrats' habit of command a liability. "You are a councillor," the Boatswain reminds Gonzalo; "if you can command these elements to silence, and work the peace of the present, we will not hand a rope more. Use your authority" (I. i. 20-23).[2] Of course aristocratic orders by themselves are ineffectual against the seething sea, and the noblemen return to their place below deck. But their terrified cries soon prompt the laboring Boatswain to swear, "A plague upon this howling! they are louder than the weather, or our office" (I. i. 36-37). By being louder than the sailors' duties, the aristocrats' cries interfere with their performance.

Erupting again from below deck, Sebastian, Antonio, and Gonzalo engage the Boatswain in curses and insults:

> *Enter* Sebastian, Antonio, *and* Gonzalo.
> Boats. Yet again? What do you here? Shall we give o'er and drown? Have you a mind to sink?
> Seb. A pox o' your throat, you bawling, blasphemous, incharitable dog!
> Boats. Work you then.
> Ant. Hang, cur! hang, you whoreson, insolent noisemaker! We are less afraid to be drown'd than thou art.
> Gon. I'll warrant him for drowning, though the ship were no stronger than a nutshell, and as leaky as an unstanch'd wench.
> Boats. Lay her a-hold, a-hold! Set her two courses off to sea again! Lay her off.
> *Enter* Mariners *wet.*
> Mariners. All lost! To prayers, to prayers! All lost!
> (I. i. 38-52)

The Boatswain's challenge "Work you then" underscores an unfortunate reality: aristocratic privilege has exempted the noblemen from manual labor that could save their lives. Sebastian's and Antonio's curses become for them a nervous compensation for their idleness, an admission that in this moment they have no work to perform that could relieve their anxiety. Regarded as speech acts—deeds done in and by speech—their curses constitute the obverse of their customary authoritative and political utterances. Excused from a life of physical work (with warfare the exception), the nobility resorts to different kinds of non-reciprocal speech acts. Shakespeare fashions the dialogue quoted above so as to convey the impression that all is lost because the noblemen's inability to work productively and their compensatory curses overwhelm the Boatswain's commands for saving labor. In the conflict of natural disorder versus redemptive work, the consequences of the nobles' incapacity for useful work give the edge to chaos.

The emblematic opening scene of *The Tempest* thus valorizes physical labor, even though that work fails to achieve its end. Gonzalo's celebrated portrait of a utopian society is the apparent counterpart of this emblematic scene. If he were king on an island like that on which the nobles find themselves stranded, Gonzalo would ban the supposedly corrupting agents of civilization such as business, law courts, and money. Work would be virtually unknown in Gonzalo's paradise. Banished would be any "use of service," "tilth" [tillage], even vineyards—"No use of metal, corn, or wine, or oil;/ No occupation, all men idle, all" (II. i. 152-55). In this utopia, "all things in common nature should produce/ Without sweat or endeavor" (II. i. 160-61):

> nature should bring forth,
> Of it own kind, all foison, all abundance,
> To feed my innocent people.
> (II. i. 163-65)

The sacrilege latent in Gonzalo's utopia materializes in his claim that humanity need not sweat to make nature yield the necessities of life. Physical labor in the sweat of humankind's brow is the inescapable penalty for the original sin of Adam and Eve. The idleness of Gonzalo's utopia mirrors the essential idleness of its aristocratic speaker, a nobleman never required to work hard manually.[3]

Even as Sebastian and Antonio interrupt and ruin the sailors' disciplined labor, so they destroy Gonzalo's utopia. When Gonzalo proclaims "no sovereignty" among the people of his isle, Sebastian jokes, "Yet he would be king on't," and Antonio comments, "The latter end of his commonwealth forgets the beginning" (II. i. 157-59). Gonzalo has forgotten the beginning in a sense unintended by disruptive Antonio—humankind's beginning as recounted in Genesis, where sweat labor is ordained for every man and woman. When Gonzalo suggests that men and women need not wed in paradise, Sebastian mockingly asks, "No marrying 'mong his subjects?"—a question sarcastically answered by Antonio: "None, man, all idle—whores and knaves" (II. i. 166-67). Whereas Antonio's interruptions of the Boatswain in the play's opening scene characterize him as antithetical to redemptive work, his jest in the present instance makes him a critic of idleness. Yet rather than making him a moral spokesman, his shrewd remark functions mainly to highlight his aristocratic bias. Among Jacobeans, the nobles and upper gentry promulgated the belief that prostitution and knavery sprang from the slothfulness of lower social classes. Even when whipped, idle whores and knaves seemed, in aristocrats' opinion, averse to the hard manual labor that supposedly was their preordained lot in life. Antonio's remark registers his fear of idleness in subject classes rather than any conviction that work might possess inherent virtues.

Undaunted by Sebastian's and Antonio's interruptions, Gonzalo, unlike the Boatswain, completes the performance of his "labor," by his own admission a "kind of merry fooling" wherein he makes himself a comic butt through whom others can ease anxieties and reconstitute their sense of courtly self.[4] While such an activity may conform to Gonzalo's idea of the meaningful "work" he performs as a member of a court retinue, his dismissal of his own account of utopia may simply be a face-saving strategy (a lame attempt to practice *sprezzatura*). In this respect, his tale of utopia basically becomes an idle pastime.

After Antonio and Sebastian fracture Gonzalo's utopia and the other members of the court party fall asleep, Shakespeare further qualifies the substance of Gonzalo's vision. In doing so, he answers a question posed concerning Antonio's characteristic form of work. When viciously opportunistic Antonio says that he can teach Sebastian how to "flow" to kingship, how, that is, to act selfishly by murdering his brother Alonso, his dupe jokes, "Do so. To ebb/ Hereditary sloth instructs me" (II. i. 222-23).[5] Self-confessedly, Sebastian is the lazy aristocrat. This image of the unemployed man provides an unexpected perspective upon Gonzalo's utopia. Primitivism and cultural decadence are polar conditions in which idleness flourishes. The realms of innocence and corruption surprisingly are not that dissimilar. Granted Shakespeare's early depiction of Antonio, playgoers assume that aristocratic sloth also taints Prospero's brother. When Antonio caustically replies to Gonzalo's claim that the island provides "every thing advantageous to life" with the quip, "True, save means to live" (II. i. 50-51), he unintentionally discloses his aversion to the physical labor that could make nature yield its fruits.[6] Although brighter and less lecherous than Cloten, Antonio—as an aristocrat—resembles the boor of *Cymbeline* in several respects. In both cases, quarrelsomeness and homicidal plots appear bred out of leisure. Like that of the son of Cymbeline's queen, Antonio's accustomed leisurely way of life addicts him to gambling, a pastime pursued even amidst shipwreck. "Which, of he or Adrian, for a good wager, first begins to crow" (II. i. 28-29), bored Antonio asks Sebastian concerning their silent companions in disaster. Nevertheless, Antonio's greater intelligence manifests itself in his remarkable command of rhetoric, a kind of speech that constitutes Antonio's distinctive labor.

Antonio wants to persuade Sebastian to murder his brother Alonso so that he can free himself from paying the tribute pledged to Alonso (II. i. 292-94). Antonio's yearning for freedom to rule Milan can be measured by the number of dazzling figures of rhetoric that he marshals into an argument. His face reveals that he has significant matter to deliver. "Prithee say on," Sebastian commands,

> The setting of thine eye and cheek proclaim
> A matter from thee; and a birth, indeed,
> Which throes thee much to yield.
> (II. i. 228-31)

Rhetorical persuasion forms politic Antonio's labor. Like Milton's Lucifer, he gives birth to sin. Shakespeare's and Milton's conceit can be traced ultimately to Jove's labor in giving birth to Athena, who sprang fully formed from the god's mind. But whereas wisdom was Jove's brainchild, a cowardly crime is Antonio's issue. The metaphoric motif of birth labor that Shakespeare established in *Pericles* and developed in *The Winter's Tale* extends to *The Tempest*.[7] As it did for Leontes, the unaided, self-determined nature of Antonio's labor and delivery serves to define his cold isolation from the rest of society, his alienation from sources of warmth and mutual creativity. His opposite in the play in this respect is not Prospero—but Miranda.

The frankest kind of undeceiving speech conveys her love for Ferdinand (and his for her). Significantly, images of conception and pregnancy attach themselves to her single foray into purposely opaque speech. Ferdinand asks, "Wherefore weep you," and she replies,

> At mine unworthiness, that dare not offer
> What I desire to give; and much less take
> What I shall die to want. But this is trifling,
> And all the more it seeks to hide itself,
> The bigger bulk it shows. Hence, bashful cunning,
> And prompt me, plain and holy innocence!
> I am your wife, if you will marry me;
> If not, I'll die your maid.
>   (III. i. 76-84)

Miranda's healthy desire to give herself sexually to Ferdinand (and to take him as frankly) fashions thoughts of pregnancy in her, thoughts which substitute the metaphor of pregnancy for the failing labor of indirect, "cunning" speech. She distinguishes herself from Antonio by quickly rejecting deceptive discourse and the effort involved in fabricating it; unlike Prospero's keener-minded brother, Miranda grasps the ultimately self-defeating nature of labored rhetoric. It never, or rarely, achieves its calculated end.

In act II, scene i, Ariel's thwarting Antonio's and Sebastian's fatal deed makes this point. Among the many parallels of *The Tempest* exists the correspondence between Antonio's and Sebastian's murderous conspiracy against Alonso and Stephano's, Trinculo's, and Caliban's plot against Prospero. Temporarily distracted by Ariel's music from killing Prospero, Trinculo remarks, "The sound is going away. Let's follow it, and after do our work" (III. ii. 148-49). Even as Trinculo's and his comrades' vicious "work" never gets performed, so Antonio's reprehensible "labor" fizzles when Ariel wakes sleeping Alonso and his courtiers. Antonio's attempt to get

Sebastian to kill Alonso reflects the failure of rhetoric to secure complete power. Nevertheless, at one time, twelve years earlier in Milan, Antonio was apparently successful in his rhetorical work, recreating—new forming (I. ii. 83)—Prospero's "creatures" into his own servants. These "throes" of persuasion were the means by which Antonio fashioned a new self: the ruler of Milan. Unexpectedly, however, his bondage to Alonso proved irksome, so much so that he presently (as he did not before) risks the personal crime of murder.

Antonio's rhetorical labor contrasts with the work of his brother Prospero. Finding that the practice of policy and devious rhetoric, required of the civil governor, did not suit his temperament, Prospero withdrew into his study, where he labored to perfect himself in the knowledge of the liberal arts and magic. Yet by growing a stranger to his state (I. ii. 76), Prospero paid a high price for his bookish work. By neglecting the art of politics, he bears prime responsibility for the shipwreck of state, the subjugation of Milan to Naples and to Antonio's dark de facto rule. Thus Prospero's being condemned to float aimlessly on a "rotten carcass of a butt, not rigg'd,/ Nor tackle, sail, nor mast" reflects a degree of cruel poetic justice. Having through his abrogation of duty destroyed the ship of state, he and innocent Miranda drift upon its "carcass" (I. ii. 144-48). Brought to the island by, in his own words, "bountiful Fortune" (I. ii. 178), Prospero never abandons the secret studies that once transported him in his library (I. ii. 76-77). Not surprisingly, Shakespeare suggests time and again in *The Tempest* that Prospero's magical activities might be regarded as his characteristic work. "It works" (I. ii. 494), he simply says concerning his magical enchantment of Ferdinand. "Shortly shall all my labors end," he tells his servant Ariel at the conclusion of act IV; and the spirit reminds him at the beginning of act V that he promised that their "work" would cease during the sixth hour of the day (V. i. 4-5).[8] So preoccupied is Prospero with his labor of magic that he imagines that the time during which he must work is itself a laborer. He prefaces his asking Ariel for the time of day, the question that prompts his servant's replying the sixth hour, with the assertion that "Time/ Goes upright with his carriage" (V. i. 2-3). So fixated is Prospero at this moment with freeing himself from the burden of his magical labors that he conceives of time as standing erect, practically free of the load of hours that has bowed him throughout the day. Finally, the language of labor appears even in his promise to abjure irrevocably his rough magic after a last requiring of heavenly music "To work mine end upon their senses that/ This airy charm is for" (V. i. 53-54).

Prospero's initial work of magic in the play is the great tempest that drives the subjects of further intended spells onto his island. Understandably (given the intangible nature of magic and the physical limitations of the stage), playgoers never see Prospero the magical worker. Still, while Ariel works the storm, Prospero remains its source; his ability to perform it derives from his labor of poring over magical books. Such utterances as Miranda's "My father/ Is hard at study" (III. i. 19-20), spoken with reference to Prospero's withdrawal off-stage into his cell, represent his unseen labor. Nevertheless, on-stage images of a work of Prospero's appear early in *The Tempest*, a work allied with his magical practices. When Prospero notes how quickly and completely Miranda and Ferdinand fall "in either's pow'rs," succumb to, that is, the erotic spell that can transform the lover into the beloved's slave, he confides in the audience:

> but this swift business
> I must uneasy make, lest too light winning
> Make the prize light.
> (I. ii. 451-53)

Prospero makes the prize he intends to give Ferdinand weighty—intrinsically valuable—by making the lover earn her through hard physical labor, imposed by the father. This project represents Prospero's task with regard to his daughter and her lover, a task that at one point requires a work of magic. When Prospero, playing the role of the angry father as Simonides did in *Pericles*, commands Ferdinand to follow him, ostensibly to manacling as punishment for imputed betrayal, the young man draws his rapier, and Prospero magically charms him into paralysis. He releases Ferdinand from this charm into the slavery of log bearing, the kind of work performed by abject Caliban.

Considered as an aristocrat, a prince who has lived an easeful life in a hedonistic (because Italian) court, Ferdinand might be infected by the sloth that Sebastian self-confesses. Francisco's vivid account, however, of Ferdinand's likely survival of the shipwreck—

> Sir, he may live.
> I saw him beat the surges under him,
> And ride upon their backs. He trod the water,
> Whose enmity he flung aside, and breasted
> The surge most swoll'n that met him. His bold head
> 'Bove the contentious waves he kept, and oared
> Himself with his good arms in lusty stroke
> To th' shore, that o'er his wave-worn basis bowed,
> As stooping to relieve him.
> (II. i. 114-22)

—testifies early in the play to Ferdinand's active, industrious temperament. He could never be confused for the lazy Sebastian. Still, as a privileged aristocrat, Ferdinand requires a mighty incentive to make him perform hard manual labor.

Bearing logs, Ferdinand learns that work becomes fulfilling when it is done willingly for an ennobling end, the winning of his beloved Miranda.[9] "There be some sports are painful," Ferdinand moralizes at the beginning of act III:

> and their labor
> Delight in them sets off; some kinds of baseness
> Are nobly undergone; and most poor matters
> Point to rich ends. This my mean task
> Would be as heavy to me as odious, but
> The mistress which I serve quickens what's dead,
> And makes my labors pleasures. O, she is
> Ten times more gentle than her father's crabbed;
> And he's compos'd of harshness. I must remove
> Some thousands of these logs, and pile them up,
> Upon a sore injunction. My sweet mistress
> Weeps when she sees me work, and says such baseness
> Had never like executor. I forget;
> But these sweet thoughts do even refresh my labors,
> Most busil'est when I do it.
> (III. i. 1-15)

Ferdinand's labors are "pleasures" in his own estimate because they are performed as a lover's service for his mistress. He thus achieves through freely given work the delightful release that Caliban and Ariel long for.[10] Imagining that his work is a visible symbol of both the depth of his love and his esteem for Miranda, he discovers that his labors refresh him. Such love and conceived work help inoculate Ferdinand against a typically aristocratic vice.

When Miranda out of love would share his burden of logs, he exclaims,

> No, precious creature,
> I had rather crack my sinews, break my back,
> Than you should such dishonor undergo,
> While I sit lazy by.
> (III. i. 25-28)

Still, Ferdinand emphasizes that serving only Miranda justifies the inherent baseness of manual labor (judged so by his princely sense of self). "I am, in my condition,/ A prince," he tells Miranda,

> and would no more endure
> This wooden slavery than to suffer
> The flesh-fly blow my mouth.
> (III. i. 59-63)

Ferdinand's graphic comparison evokes the image of the diseased mouth, a synecdoche for the play's widespread reference to and staging of corrupted speech. Rhetoric in a corrupt cause is Antonio's special labor. There is an aptness in the evocation and juxtaposition of Antonio's easy, vicious labor with Ferdinand's painful, purely undertaken and offered work. Even as Antonio's self-conceit precludes his imagining himself laboring manually for any woman, so Ferdinand's love for Miranda stands in the way of any desire on his part to use his rhetorical skills to take advantage of her. Physical work will be his speech—a silent love poem dedicated to her. "Hear my soul speak," he continues,

> The very instant that I saw you, did
> My heart fly to your service, there resides,
> To make me slave to it, and for your sake
> Am I this patient log-man.
> (III. i. 63-67)

Since Prospero has enforced Ferdinand's labor without hope of wages, it is, removed from the context of its performance, a "wooden slavery." But Ferdinand carefully says he is not a slave. His heart is the slave. It has flown to serve Miranda. By being a slave to his heart, Ferdinand becomes the servant of his lady. Slavery is simply a metaphor for the completeness of his devotion to Miranda. For him, the way to an enfranchising service leads through a labor that would be slavery for any other worker.[11]

For reasons that will soon be explained, Ferdinand's value-creating labor of log bearing appears to be Prospero's most unequivocally successful work involving magic. His other magical labors concern driving Alonso and presumably Antonio to repent their buried or forgotten crimes and presenting the Masque of Ceres to celebrate Ferdinand's and Miranda's handfast. After the harpy Ariel has tempted Alonso and his party with a disappearing banquet and told them in speech that sounds like thunder and crashing waves that they are being tormented on the isle because of their old crime against Prospero, the magician exclaims, "My high charms work,/ And these, mine enemies, are all knit up/ In their distractions" (III. iii. 88-90). Prospero's working charms catalyze a guilt latent in Alonso that, like poison, begins to torture him. As distraught Alonso rushes from the stage and Antonio and Sebastian exit to fight the "fiends" that they have just seen, Gonzalo concludes that

> All three of them are desperate: their great guilt
> (Like poison given to work a great time after)
> Now gins to bite the spirits.
> (III. iii. 104-6)

Alonso would not say, at the end of the play, "Thy dukedom I resign, and do entreat/ Thou pardon me my wrongs" (V. i. 118-19), if Prospero's magical ordeal had not made him penitent. But Sebastian's and especially sullen Antonio's failure to speak similar words suggests that this magical task of Prospero's only partially attains its goal. It seems as though only Alonso has the moral capacity of mind for translating Ariel's thunder into a clearly understood message of sin, damnation, and potential redemption.

Prospero's third magical task, the creation of the Masque of Ceres, is less successful than his attempt to move his former enemies to repentance.[12] The magician's recollection of the imminent danger posed by Caliban's conspiracy forces him to break off his entertainment and dismiss its spirit actors. The problematic image of work in the masque predicts the entertainment's failure. In his vision of an island utopia, Gonzalo contrasts work and spontaneous natural fertility, primarily to offset the latter value. Prospero, however, merges the two values in the Masque of Ceres. At the beginning of this betrothal masque, the goddess Iris in Juno's name calls Ceres to leave her world of agriculture to crown a contract of true love and "some donation freely to estate/ On the bless'd lovers" (IV. i. 85-86). Yet while Iris calls Ceres "bounteous" and mentions her "rich leas/ Of wheat, rye, barley, fetches, oats, and pease" (IV. i. 60-61), the bounty of the goddess of agriculture does not burst forth in Iris' language.[13] Instead, a relative lack of color and life distinguishes her invocation:

> Thy turfy mountains, where live nibbling sheep,
> And flat meads thatch'd with stover, them to keep;
> Thy banks with pioned and twilled brims,
> Which spungy April at thy hest betrims,
> To make cold nymphs chaste crowns; and thy broomgroves,
> Whose shadow the dismissed bachelor loves,
> Being lass-lorn; thy pole-clipt vineyard,
> And thy sea-marge, sterile and rocky-hard,
> Where thou thyself dost air—. . . . .
> (IV. i. 62-70)

Considered by itself, this passage moves from fertility to barrenness.[14] It is immediately preceded by Iris' recreation of Ceres' fruitful meadows—"leas"—thick with food for both humankind and beast. That fertility modulates into "live nibbling sheep" before regressing to "spungy April" and eventually the winter-like "sea-marge, sterile and rocky-hard." In this respect, the passage reverses the overall progression in the masque from barrenness to fertility, from a cold April and relative sterility to the harvest of August near the masque's conclusion.

We can assume that the masque, in every detail, is a projection of Prospero's mind and values. By beginning with an agricultural heartland of life-giving crops and moving outward to grazing lands and the sterile beaches of the sea, Prospero's word picture reflects not his tropical island but Shakespeare's less-fruitful Britain. Prospero's belief in the importance of work for survival surfaces in such small details as the "flat meads thatch'd with stover," with hay for sheep in the winter, and the "pole-clipt vineyard," the vineyard either "with top growth pruned back" or "enclosed by a fence of poles."[15] These details reflect Prospero's conviction that humankind's husbandry, its prudent and calculated labor, is necessary for survival during times of natural barrenness, times that Shakespeare's audience certainly experienced and times that married Ferdinand and Miranda would confront in Italy. Husbandry is the apt term for this kind of work, for these poetic details appear at the beginning of a betrothal masque designed to celebrate the husband Ferdinand and the greater husbandry of man and wife.

Regarded in light of the restraint of the masque's language for the agrarian year, the luxuriant bounty of Ceres' blessing upon the lovers comes as something of a surprise:

> Earth's increase, foison plenty,
> Barns and garners never empty;
> Vines with clust'ring bunches growing,
> Plants with goodly burthen bowing;
> Spring come to you at the farthest
> In the very end of harvest!
> Scarcity and want shall shun you,
> Ceres' blessing so is on you.
> (IV. i. 110-17)

Prospero has never worked at agricultural or pastoral husbandry, neither in Italy nor on his island. Still, he knows that manual labor must play a part in making real Ceres' (and his) blessing of "Spring come to you at the farthest/ In the very end of harvest." Within the betrothal masque, "sunburn'd sicklemen, of August weary" (IV. i. 134) are summoned to dance with April's chaste nymphs. A group of figures, the sicklemen, condense into symbolic personifications the masque's earlier references to and insistence upon agricultural husbandry for both growing and barren seasons. "Weary," they represent the hard manual labor necessary for life (ironically the hard manual labor that Prospero has never performed). Ceres' command that the laborers "encounter" the "fresh nymphs" in "country footing" amounts to a holiday reward for their toil. This reward reprises Prospero's own gift of refreshing Miranda to Ferdinand as "pay" for the toil of log bearing. Joining with the figures of Spring, the sicklemen depict, in terms of Ceres' blessing, "the farthest" of the year, the time of late summer harvest. Merged in a betrothal-masque dance, the nymphs and sicklemen physically enact the marriage benediction of Prospero: an ideal of chaste fertility that knows no want and is endlessly bountiful, lacking as it does the element of winter and barrenness. Work—cultivation—would make possible a utopian blessing.[16] The texts of surviving Jacobean betrothal masques indicate that, by being "taken out," by mingling with symbolic dancers, Ferdinand and Miranda could participate in a Neoplatonic idea of Chaste Fertility, which—given a Renaissance philosophy of the dance—they might know and possess.[17] By dancing, they might mystically incorporate the Idea of Chaste Fertility within themselves and their union as man and wife.

But the dance and incorporation never occur in *The Tempest*. Prospero's memory of Caliban supersedes them. It obliterates the promise, the fruit, of cultivated labor—the work both cultivated and of cultivation—inherent in Prospero's masque. This failure, however, seems appropriate. Prospero himself, both by his own account and by the impression he conveys, has never labored in the physical sense necessary to create one strand, one element, of his endlessly bountiful blessing. That blessing remains a product of magic, work that requires "hard study" but which apparently cannot—or will not—grow corn on the island or drop fruit immediately into Prospero's hand. Spontaneously fertile to a degree that England and Italy cannot attain, the tropical isle has allowed Caliban to survive without having to labor in the sweat of his brow. Ironically, the most depraved character in the play escapes Adam's curse of work; at least he did so before Prospero arrived and colonized him. Picking crab apples and "clust'ring filberts," digging up peanuts, gathering jays' eggs, trapping the "nimble marmazet" (II. ii. 167-72), Caliban is a hunter and gatherer. While modern editors may never identify Caliban's "Young scamels" (are they shell-fish, rock-inhabiting birds, or a bizarre delicacy known only to Caliban?), gathering the creatures from rocks is apparently easy for the island's native.

Caliban directs his lyrical account of the island's natural riches to Stephano and Caliban—not to Prospero. Caliban's hunting and gathering the island's provender is offered gratefully to the "gods" who have "dropp'd from heaven" to bless him with celestial liquor—European sack. Though wrongheaded, Caliban's gratitude is joyous and freely given, qualities that purge any traces of work from the hunting and gathering that he would perform for his new masters.[18] Playgoers never learn what Prospero and Miranda eat on the island, or the foodstuffs that Caliban under magical compulsion produces for them. But because Caliban has grown to hate them, especially Prospero, playgoers conclude that the hunting and gathering of fruit and game that he slavishly performs for them are not as abundantly yielding as what he would do for Stephano.

All this is to say that Prospero's understanding of hunting and gathering and of the island's fertility cannot match Caliban's. Nor could the magician's performance, if he had the understanding. Concerning Caliban's fire making, wood fetching, and serving "in offices/ That profit us," Prospero tells Miranda, "We cannot miss him" (I. ii. 311-13). For some reason, Prospero cannot do the physical work that Caliban performs.[19] Whether as a duke he thinks that manual labor is beneath him, or whether his magic has unstated limits, remains unclear.[20] But by admitting that he cannot do without Caliban's labors, Prospero excludes himself from his own masque, from the value of the sicklemen and labored cultivation and harvest in their several represented images. These limitations within Prospero preclude the successful performance of the magical masque. If Prospero's memory of Caliban aborts the masque, that recollection could just as well be of Caliban the worker as Caliban the conspirator.

Prospero's failure to complete the Masque of Ceres calls into question his ability to perform his chosen work—the practice of magic. In fact, close analysis reveals that the exercise of his magic never, or rarely, seems constructive labor in the sense that the phrase connotes a tangible making of something. During the play, Prospero's art involves either release or paralysis—each the seeming contrary of work. To drive his former enemies to his island, he undoes natural calm. He stupefies the mariners under their ship's hatches only to release them later. Through Ariel, he "allays" (stills) the water's fury and Ferdinand's grief. He undoes Ferdinand's valor, immobilizing him and rendering his sword impotent. To test Alonso's and the courtiers' faiths, he undoes their reason, maddening them. They end up "Confin'd together," paralyzed, in the lime grove weather-fending Prospero's cell, unable to budge until the magician's release from anger (V. i. 7-11). To converse with the dead, Prospero has undone graves, releasing their "sleepers." The interplay between these and other instances of the often violent release of natural forces within the atmosphere and the minds of men and stasis, sleep, and paralysis invites the kind of harmonizing achieved in *The Winter's Tale* in Florizel's vision of Perdita as a dancing wave of the sea. In that play art played a role in reconciling stir and stasis. Prospero's art, however, seems unable to accomplish a magnificent synthesis of this kind.

While Prospero's magical labors cause his subjects to suffer, the practice of his art nevertheless gives its agent pleasure. In poetic language and rhythms reminiscent of Marlowe's *Dr. Faustus*, Ariel, upon his entry in the play, pronounces,

> All hail, great master, grave sir, hail! I come
> To answer thy best pleasure; be't to fly,
> To swim, to dive into the fire, to ride
> On the curl'd clouds. To thy strong bidding, task
> Ariel, and all his quality.
> (I. ii. 189-93)

Ariel assumes that the performance of Prospero's magical tasks answers the mage's best pleasures because it gives the spirit pleasure. The assumption seems partly, if not wholly, justified in Prospero's rejoicing over the handfast brought about by his magic. Still, the counterpoint of Ariel's fluid portrayal of the joy he gets from being Prospero's agent and the relatively pleasureless, stolid phrase "strong bidding, task" creates strong tension in the passage, a tension between play and work.

For Ariel, performing "to point" the tempest has amounted to purely hedonistic sport, partly one assumes because the feat involves the full, exhilarating release for which the spirit yearns. Prospero's magical labor does not feel like work to Ariel:

> I boarded the King's ship; now on the beak,
> Now in the waist, the deck, in every cabin,
> I flam'd amazement. Sometime I'ld divide,
> And burn in many places; on the topmast,
> The yards and boresprit, would I flame distinctly,
> Then meet and join. Jove's lightning, the precursors
> O' th' dreadful thunder-claps, more momentary
> And sight-outrunning were not; the fire and cracks
> Of sulphurous roaring the most mighty Neptune
> Seem to besiege, and make his bold waves tremble,
> Yea, his dread trident shake.
> (I. ii. 196-206)

Ariel maintains the impression that his performance of Prospero's magic feels like pleasurable play in the first half of this narrative. But in the latter part of the passage, the language, poetic rhythms, and tone change, becoming respectively more abstract, polysyllabic, and august. The modulation captures what Ariel's play felt like to its victims. *The Tempest* abounds in similarly divided passages of verse, the most memorable being Prospero's farewell to his art. A brief comparison of Prospero's farewell with Ariel's narration of his role in creating the sea storm further clarifies the respective roles of master and agent in their joint work of magic.

In the first half of his farewell, Prospero conjures elves of woodlands, lakes, and sea beaches, spirits "that on the sands with printless foot/ Do chase the ebbing Neptune, and do fly him/ When he comes back" (V. i. 34-36). Without the mage's direction, left to their own motiveless mischief, the elves would only make such trivial things as mushrooms or such bitter, useless products as "the green sour ringlets . . . Whereof the ewe not bites" (V. i. 37-38). Prospero's epithet for them, "Weak masters," seems justified by their tiny size, marginal activities, and failure to make any momentous impact upon nature. Their feet do not even leave prints in the sand; the flowing tides of Neptune compel them, frightened, to outrun the water. Paradoxically, Prospero is dependent for his magical work on beings seemingly weaker than a child. The phrase "Weak masters," however, is an oxymoron that informs auditors that these slight creatures somehow master nature in ways that humankind cannot.

The oxymoronic phrase "Weak masters" condenses the hybrid quality of Prospero's farewell speech as a whole. Like the corresponding early part of Ariel's narrative of the sea storm (I. ii. 196-201), the first nine verses of Prospero's farewell, those describing and invoking his weak masters, reflect a playful, even quaint, diction; a relatively straightforward syntax and easy rhythm; and a relatively low quotient of energy. But after the pivot-like phrase "Weak masters," the poetic language, rhythms, and energy abruptly change, resembling those of Ariel in the latter part of his speech (I. ii. 201-6). In fact, the content is much the same—a vivid description of storm, thunder, and lightning. By the aid of magical spirits, Prospero has "bedimm'd"

> The noontide sun, call'd forth the mutinous winds,
> And 'twixt the green sea and the azur'd vault
> Set roaring war; to the dread rattling thunder
> Have I given fire, and rifted Jove's stout oak
> With his own bolt; the strong-bas'd promontory
> Have I made shake, and by the spurs pluck'd up
> The pine and cedar.
>   (V. i. 41-48)

The Miltonic weight of this tremendous utterance comes from both its imposing inversions of language, emphasizing the powerful speaker, and its prophetic, almost-biblical, quality. Prospero's specific function, beyond drawing magical circles and conjuring spirits, in performing joint labors of magic lies in supplying the intense energy that animates and gives purpose to weak and playful masters of nature.[21] What may feel at times of release like pleasurable play to them requires a straining on Prospero's part that gets registered in the energized syntax and rhythms of his speech. Whether elf or Ariel, Prospero's magical spirits willingly serve him in large part because he has released them from paralysis or constriction. Originally freed by Prospero from painful imprisonment in a pine tree, Ariel joys in those moments in Prospero's service when his master releases him into the free play of the atmospheric elements. Likewise, one assumes that the elves of nature happily serve Prospero because his magic broadens the scope of their prescribed world. Normally privileged, by their own account, to wander abroad only at night, they rejoice to hear the curfew (V. i. 40). Prospero's art releases elves from a dark world, where they make "midnight mushrumps," to perform in apocalyptic storms like the tempest Ariel creates.

Given the strain involved in energizing his weak spirits, Prospero can be excused for calling "work" what feels like play to Ariel. "Ariel, thy charge/ Exactly is perform'd," he concludes; "but there's more work" (I. ii. 237-38). The tempest that seems from Ariel's perspective to be no more than St. Elmo's fire is an arduous task for Prospero. Yet what proves work for Prospero in one sense is an illusion—something that never exists. While certainly felt by the sailors as a world-ending reality and by Ariel as pleasurable sport, the tempest viewed by Miranda from shore never exists.[22] The ship that she sees sink never sank. Midway between the extreme perspectives is that of the theater audience, which saw and heard the tempest in scene i, but only as the effect of illusory play making.[23] Shakespeare introduces these multiple, even contradictory, perspectives on the product of Prospero's art for several reasons, but primarily to sustain and deepen the ambiguous status of Prospero's labor. Is it real—worthwhile, beneficial—or inconsequential, minimal, even an illusion?

That is not to say that Prospero's imposed tasks never feel like work to Ariel. When Prospero tells him more work must be done that afternoon, Ariel grumbles,

> Is there more toil? Since thou dost give me pains,
> Let me remember thee what thou hast promis'd,
> Which is not yet perform'd me.
> (I. ii. 242-44)

During none of his performances of Prospero's magical designs does Ariel ever indicate that they pain him. Like the euphoria conveyed by his execution of the tempest, his response to Prospero's ordering the Masque of Ceres takes the form of a lighthearted little song promising swift compliance, a dutiful lyric ending in the tender question, "Do you love me, master? no?" (IV. i. 44-48). This query prompts Prospero's genuine reply, "Dearly, my delicate Ariel" (IV. i. 49). In performance, Ariel's tasks are felt like the actor's play, a release of a confined self in the pleasure of protean role playing, whether the script calls for the part of a harpy or the goddess Juno. Only afterward, in retrospect, does that play feel like toil, when a master has not apparently fulfilled his part in a master/apprentice contract.

Barbara Mowat has demonstrated that Prospero and Ariel have compounded for a bond closely resembling a Jacobean multi-year master/apprentice indenture.[24] Usually bound to a master craftsman for seven years, Jacobean apprentices gave up most of their legal rights in exchange for room and board and instruction in the master's craft. Records indicate that they were often beaten and sometimes starved while severely worked, facts that may help to explain their fearful rioting in the streets and in playhouses.[25] Ariel claims that Prospero has broken his promise in not giving him his liberty. Prospero's angry rejoinder, "Before the time be out?" (I. ii. 246), reveals that he and Ariel have opted for a time contract; Ariel's assertion that Prospero promised to reduce the time of his indenture a year for the servant's cheerful, compliant performance of his duties indicates that the contract covers several years. One assumes that Prospero freed Ariel from the pine in which Sycorax had confined him soon after his arrival on the island. Since Prospero and Miranda have lived on the island twelve years, apprentices in the Globe audience must have thought that Ariel had a legitimate gripe.

Ariel's belief that his master is not honoring a mutually agreed upon amendment of their indenture makes the performance of duties called for by that contract feel like work rather than play. Apparently, to use Prospero's phraseology, the time is not yet out, not to the point of the full-year's reduction. By his own admission, Ariel was Sycorax's servant—not her slave.

In that respect, he may have attempted service under another mutually agreed upon contract of indenture. But because he was too delicate, too refined, to perform her "earthy and abhorr'd commands," she imprisoned him, perhaps for breech of agreement. Under English law, Jacobean masters could jail uncompliant apprentices. Prospero does not say that the mutually agreed upon date triggering the abatement of the final year (and thus the end) of Ariel's indenture stands in the future. Instead, he reminds Ariel that the spirit has exchanged a grisly taskmaster for a humane one. His appeal to his servant's sense of gratitude is successful; Ariel begs pardon and promises to be "correspondent to command" (I. ii. 296-98). Impressed by Ariel's obedience and mindful of the conclusive feats of magic to be performed that day, Prospero reduces further the time of Ariel's indenture to only two more days (I. ii. 298-99), a remarkable abridgment that guarantees Ariel's absolutely dutiful performance. Inherent in this staging lies an enlightened message for Jacobean master craftsmen concerning labor relations.[26]

I have explored at length the nature of Prospero's and Ariel's work relations because criticism has revealed that the difference between servitude and slavery is an important issue in *The Tempest*. Service involves mutually agreed upon work of some recompense to the worker. Ariel's report of Prospero's enslavement of him would be true if the magician were dishonestly making him work after the terms of a contract had expired. Then the recompense of liberty for work would have been denied, perhaps forever. But such does not at all appear to be the case; Ariel's performance of his duties is service for a master whose willingness to abridge contracts would have startled Jacobean masters and apprentices. In summary, Shakespeare's presentation of Ariel's and Prospero's working relationship draws attention to the mechanics of Jacobean master/ apprentice bonds, specifically to the question of their fairness to the subjugated worker, their potential for abuse, and the conditions that transform service into the worker's enslavement. In the image of the stern but loving Prospero, willing to amend a worker's bondage as unrequired recompense for good work,

Shakespeare challenged members of his playhouse society to conform their practices to an ideal standard.

As we have seen, however, Prospero's tasking of Caliban essentially resembles slavery. While Caliban's slavish wood gathering and fire making sustain Prospero's and Miranda's lives, his hard labor also serves as punishment for his attempted rape of Miranda. In this sense, Prospero maintains a penal colony. No work contract exists between Caliban and Prospero; no wages or meaningful recompense passes between them.[27] Whatever food Prospero gives Caliban the slave could improve upon were he allowed the freedom of the island. Even though Prospero and Miranda refer to Caliban as a slave no fewer than five times (I. ii. 308, 313, 344, 351, 374), Prospero calls him his servant at one point in his heated dispute with Ariel over their indenture (I. ii. 285-86). This slip is revealing. One could argue that Prospero's passionate insistence that he has made Ariel a servant rather than a slave colors his thinking of Caliban. Prospero's remark nevertheless could function to mask his guilt over his enslavement of Caliban as well as his unadmitted confusion concerning Caliban's place in the magician's program of work. Previous analysis suggested that, unlike Ariel's performances, the slave Caliban's labor catalyzes awareness of certain vulnerabilities and limitations in the character of the slavemaster. Insisting that a genuine slave is in fact a servant helps to dispel this painful awareness.

Obviously Shakespeare's strategy concerns driving into contemporary audiences' consciousness the price for peace of mind that European enslavers of new-world natives pay.[28] The work that slaves are made to do makes the slavemaster painfully cognizant of what he cannot do—of who he in his sophisticated idleness is. The dissolute Trinculo is chosen to make the point. At his first sight of freakish Caliban, Trinculo moralizes,

> Were I in England now (as once I was) and had but this fish painted, not a holiday fool there but would give a piece of silver. There would this monster make a man; any strange beast there makes a man. When they will not give a doit to relieve a lame beggar, they will lay out ten to see a dead Indian.
>
> (II. ii. 27-33)

When Stephano shortly admits his intention of intoxicating and taming Caliban in order to sell him as a curiosity to the highest Neopolitan bidder, the accuracy of Trinculo's moralizing is confirmed. Europeans' unscrupulousness in enslaving American Indians for personal profit touches Prospero. While he is above selling Caliban in the base manner described by Trinculo, Caliban's work nevertheless "makes him"—Prospero—"a man" in the same sense that strange, exhibited Indians provided the means of sustenance for their side-show masters.[29] Clearly Trinculo uses the word "make" in that sense, of providing the means for the master's life. Trinculo's judgment suggests that a monster like Caliban is a man when supposedly civilized men devolve to beasts by immorally enslaving Indians to capitalize upon their seeming outlandishness and insensitive spectators' cruel desire to gawk at them. But Prospero cannot escape the other dimension of the idea of man making, that he must enslave Caliban to be the man he is (an aristocrat unable or unwilling to do the work that preserves his life blood). Made such a man by Caliban, he is even more the basically soft nobleman.

Kindling Stephano to kill Prospero by listing the loot they could acquire by the act, Caliban claims that Prospero has "brave utensils (for so he calls them)/ Which when he has a house, he'll deck withal" (III. ii. 96-97). Hallett Smith glosses the word "utensils" as "furnishings," but Shakespeare wants the sharp connotation of tools for useful work in order to juxtapose it with the overtones of aesthetic uselessness conveyed by the word "deck." In Prospero's home, items useful for work become aristocratic wall hangings. This revelation risks placing Prospero within an idle, courtly context like that affecting Imogen in Cymbeline's hypercultivated palace. Prospero may call the "*glistering apparel*" with which he baits Caliban and his co-conspirators "trumpery," "stale to catch . . . thieves" (IV. i. 186-87), but concluding that these pejorative terms reflect his true estimate of this "showy finery"—Hallett Smith's gloss of "trumpery"—would be a mistake. The rich garments become the subject of Caliban's final labor for Prospero on the island. "Go, sirrah, to my cell," the mage commands at play's end. "Take with you your companions. As you look/ To have my pardon, trim it handsomely" (V i. 292-94). Along with the utensils that deck his cell, this trumpery, a wardrobe for a king according to Trinculo (IV. i. 222-23), evidently pleases Prospero by its courtly handsomeness. He orders it rehung, even though he does not plan to remain on the island for more than a night and a morning (V. i. 301-12).

The tendency to allegorize *The Tempest* has proved difficult to suppress. If we consider Caliban and Prospero as parts of a single organism, we realize the price that the cultivated ego and superego pay for enslaving the baser parts of the being to the physical labor necessary for preservation, a supposedly inferior production that in fact makes possible the person's identity.[30] Shakespeare in *The Tempest* suggests that, among masters and laborers (and even within the individual), creation of flexible contracts of service freely given and accepted prevents the diminishment of not only the worker's but the master's dignity as well. Caliban's ignorance that, in subjugating himself to Stephano, he has merely exchanged one kind of slavery for another is partly Prospero's fault. Caliban can define freedom only by its abhorrent contrary—Prospero's enslavement of his labor. His one song in the play makes this much clear:

> No more dams I'll make for fish,
>   Nor fetch in firing
>   At requiring,
> Nor scrape trenchering, nor wash dish.
>   'Ban, 'Ban, Ca-Caliban
> Has a new master, get a new man.
>   (II. ii. 180-85)

Even though Stephano's liquor enslaves Caliban as effectively as Prospero's magic does, Caliban believes that he tastes freedom, chiefly because his new, "god-like" masters do not exact manual labor. Caliban's attitude toward labor becomes natural once work is not enforced; his previously analyzed, spontaneously fertile speech about his easy gathering of food for his adopted masters testifies to the change.

This analysis suggests that Shakespeare systematically qualifies our image of Prospero the worker. Throughout *The Tempest*, Prospero's magical labors are parodied, a fact which encourages a mildly skeptical view of them. During Adrian and

Gonzalo's dispute over whether Tunis was once ancient Carthage, Antonio sarcastically compares Gonzalo's claim that they were once the same to Amphion's city-creating music: "His word is more than the miraculous harp."

> *Seb.* He hath rais'd the wall, and houses too.
> *Ant.* What impossible matter will he make easy next?
> (II. i. 87-90)

Prospero's magic also ultimately concerns the transporting of one community, the regenerate society forged on the island, to Naples, which occupies the place of Carthage in Adrian and Gonzalo's dispute. Prospero's magical words make this impossible matter seem easy. But he is no Amphion, no founder of humanity's civilization; his new city of the spirit is metaphorical not literal (as Amphion's building of Thebe's walls was). His spiritual city is populated by dangerous incontrovertibles like Antonio and Sebastian, who are immune to his words—magical or otherwise.

Although their natures and the impulses behind their projects are markedly different, both Stephano's and Prospero's labors concern the consolidation of political power. Because they both enslave Caliban, albeit for different reasons, Stephano and Prospero invite comparison of their characters. Both figures arrive on the island on a "butt"—Prospero's "rotten carcass" of a ship and Stephano's barrel of sack (I. ii. 146, II. ii. 121). Like Prospero, Stephano derives his power over Caliban from a "book," his fanciful name for the bottle of liquor that captivates the monster of the island (II. ii. 130). Prospero's magic and Stephano's intoxicating liquor are thus established as the primary terms of an equation. Like Prospero, Stephano keeps the source of his power over Caliban—his butt of sack—in a rocky cell. Like Prospero, Stephano repeatedly finds personal comfort in the "use" of his special "magic." "Well, here's my comfort" (II. ii. 45), he exclaims self-satisfiedly as he takes a swig from his book-bottle. Even as Prospero's magic helps him initially to teach Caliban language, so Stephano sticks his bottle in Caliban's mouth, stating, "Open your mouth; here is that which will give language to you, cat" (II. ii. 82-83). These and other details operate through parody to deflate the essence of Prospero's magic and the solemnity of his control over Caliban. Even as Prospero's enslavement of Caliban finds a place in his grand project of restoring himself to the dukedom of Milan and Ferdinand and Miranda to the rule of Naples, so Stephano's different subjugation of Caliban makes up his "project" of seizing control of the island and crowning himself the king of it. But the temptation of *"glistering apparel"* distracts Stephano, turning him aside from his project. Likewise, Prospero's project, at least as it relates to Ferdinand and Miranda, never gets fully performed. The immediate threat posed by Stephano's murderous project forces him to interrupt the Masque of Ceres, bait the conspirators with trumpery, and then hunt them down with magical hounds. The bright robes constituting the trumpery could in performance easily be the garments worn by the goddesses of the aborted masque, rich apparel taken from the walls of Prospero's cell and later ordered rehung there. This staging option further identifies Prospero with Stephano; the means that Prospero uses to interrupt Stephano's project comes from the magical work that Stephano's project shattered. In each case, work is never completed. From the aborted labor of the mariners at the beginning of the play to the uncompleted Masque of Ceres, interrupted activity, especially that of work, is a hallmark of *The Tempest*.[31] Focusing upon the parody of Prospero's magic created by the analogous action of Stephano's role in the play forces playgoers to wonder whether Prospero's art possesses an inherent virtue sufficient to complete his grand design.

This question is complicated by a conflict within Prospero that critics have widely noted. Intellectually Prospero's goal for his former enemies involves forgiveness of their crimes and reconciliation with them. In this respect, his end differs from Stephano's. However, Prospero's lingering emotional hatred of them for the suffering that they have caused him and Miranda makes him resemble his alter ego, Stephano. Both characters harbor vicious feelings toward the subjects of their projects. This unresolved conflict within Prospero between his head and heart accounts for the strange ambiguity of his stated intentions with regard to the bewitched victims of his art.[32] "Now does my project gather to a head," he says enigmatically at the beginning of act V; "My charms crack not; my spirits obey; and Time/ Goes upright with his carriage" (V. i. 1-3). The intense anger that Prospero feels upon the interruption of his artistic "vanity," the Masque of Ceres, only strengthens the impasse within him.

For the dissolution of this conflict, the timely labor required is mental rather than physical. Labor in *The Tempest* is not always external. Miranda's mind "beats" to know Prospero's reason for raising the tempest. Prospero's passion concerning Caliban's plot "works him strongly" (IV. i. 144). He is "vex'd." His "old brain is troubled," and he withdraws from the lovers to "still" his "beating mind." "Do not infest your mind," he tells Alonso at play's end, "with beating on/ The strangeness of this business" (V. i. 246-47). "Working" is one of Shakespeare's favorite adjectives for describing impassioned states of mind in the late plays. The Prologue of *King Henry VIII* announces,

> I come no more to make you laugh; things now
> That bear a weighty and a serious brow,
> Sad, high, and working, full of state and woe:
> Such noble scenes as draw the eye to flow,
> We now present.
> (Prologue, 1-5)

The term "working" in this context suggests the history play's effect upon its audience: agitation and pity. Similarly, the spectacle of suffering wrought in his paralyzed victims, especially old Gonzalo, works Prospero into feeling compassion for them.

Prospero's mind has been working throughout *The Tempest*, troubled successively by his memory of the wrongs done to him, by Caliban's and Ariel's different insubordinations, by Miranda's quick and slightly defiant love, by the ruination of his masque and the conspiracy against him, and finally by the thought of the apocalyptic fading away of all earthly things.[33] His harsh charm "so strongly works" Alonso and his courtiers, Ariel states, that the magician's affections would become tender if he directly saw their pain and grief. Unlike Ferdinand, Prospero has not clearly been in the service of an ideal cause; consequently, the quality and goal of his work have remained ambiguous.[34] Prospero momentarily finds himself in the service of Ariel and the spirit's empathy when his servant vividly describes aged Gonzalo's tearful face. Deeply moved, Prospero reasons that, if the nonhuman Ariel can feel compassion for men, he should express a greater pity for his human kind. If a creature of air has been touched by mortal afflictions, Prospero believes that he should have a more profound feeling of tenderness, simply because he, unlike Ariel, knows passion as other men do (V. i. 20-32). Shared passion is thus the chief element in a deductive speech upon which the play's resolution depends. The mind's capacity for stir—for passion—helps to make possible personal and general salvation in *The Tempest*.[35] By acknowledging the inevitability and "rightness" of passion, Prospero chooses mercy rather than revenge. His working mind thus completes his grand labor.

Unlike Stephano, Prospero willingly consigns the corresponding tools of his magic, his books, to the sea bottom. Led astray by Ariel's hypnotic music, Stephano loses his "magical" bottle in the stagnant pool of standing water near Prospero's cell. "I will fetch off my bottle," vice-addicted Stephano says, "though I be o'er ears for my labor" (IV. i. 213-14). Prospero parts company with his ignorant alter ego, giving up the tools of his trade, resolving to break his magical wand and drown his book. Prospero realizes that he has found a greater magic that he can work in Italy without their aid. He equates Ariel with art in the conflation of a phrase such as "which art but air" (uttered in the question "Hast thou, which art but air, a touch, a feeling/ Of their afflictions") (V. i. 21-22).[36] Significantly, Ariel's account of Gonzalo's weeping face, the catalyst for Prospero's revolution in attitude, takes the form of a poetic simile: an artistic miniature. Gonzalo's "tears runs down his beard like winter's drops/ From eaves of reeds" (V. i. 16-17). Prospero retains the ability to use inspirational, nonmagical art to work the creation of ennobling sentiments within himself whenever such art is available. From the postulate of art, created by Ariel, Prospero's mind works its regeneration. Ariel's moving simile stands for the multitude of similarly inspirational images inscribed in the classical and Renaissance texts, paintings, and sculptures found in the libraries and palaces of Milan and Naples. Ariel suggests to Prospero the unmagical means to avoid regressing to bitter feelings and attitudes; having found a different kind of magic in the humanizing power of art, Prospero breaks and drowns the tools of his supernatural occupation. Announcing his retirement to Milan, where every third thought will be of his grave (V. i. 311-12), Prospero is through working in the usual sense of the word. In essence, he has come close to attaining on earth that reward for work celebrated in the dirge of *Cymbeline*.

In its operation on the playgoer's emotions, *The Tempest* duplicates the working of Ariel's simile upon Prospero's feelings. Perceived as an inspirational artifact of the highest order, Shakespeare's play reminds audiences of their human*kind*ness, that virtue is preferable to vengeance. The play in its entirety becomes an artistic postulate that encourages its beholders to approximate Prospero's intellectual act of discovery. Creating this catalytic composite of artistic imagery which moves spectators to refined self-discovery represents the end of Shakespeare's labor as playwright. What was play for Ariel must to some degree have been work for him. The playwright's artistic labor integrates and releases the Prospero part of himself. It is Shakespeare's work as artist that allows Prospero to rest, to give up the practice of his magical labors because he has found both a harmonized self and an accessible mode of personal renovation through art.

Still, Shakespeare implies in Prospero's Epilogue that the responsibility and credit for working the marvelous effects of a play like *The Tempest* are not his alone. The actor who has played Prospero reminds his audience that his "project" has involved entertaining them for a few hours (Epilogue, 12-13). Giving pleasure has been the aim of his professional labor during the performance. But the actor explains that his labor will be lost unless the audience indicates by shouts and applause that he has successfully entertained them. In fact, he can only stand frozen on the stage, like Hermione's statue, until the audience's stir releases him from his dependent stasis:

> But release me from my bands
> With the help of your good hands.
> Gentle breath of yours my sails

>   Must fill, or else my project fails,
>   Which was to please.
>
>   (Epilogue, 9-13)

By begging playgoers mercifully to forgive faults of performance, the actor tests for the result of Shakespeare's artistic labor: the audience's readiness to feel and extend compassion. The strong labor of the playwright depends upon something as slight and evanescent as air, the transitory speech spoken by actors. Prospero's phrase "which art but air" reminds us that Shakespeare's art chiefly relies upon air, vocalized breath. The moving poetic images of *The Tempest*, of which Ariel's simile of Gonzalo is an archetype, are essentially and properly only formulated air, the quickly born, rapidly dying products of the actor's breath. Shakespeare in Prospero's Epilogue implies that the playwright's inspiring actors to inspire playgoers depends upon a literally inspirational labor of the audience. By the imagery of "Gentle breath of yours my sails/ Must fill" Shakespeare conveys more than his (and his actor's) desire for the audience's shouts of approval. As early as *A Midsummer Night's Dream*, in Titania's eloquent comparison of the pregnant Indian votaress to a ship's sails full-bellied in the empowering breeze, Shakespeare associates nautical imagery with impregnation and the creation of life. The audience's air—its "Gentle breath"—inspires Shakespeare's art, making it grow in composition until he delivers it in the shape of a newborn play. Playwright and audience work mutually through the medium of actors to inspire one another to future performances, of new plays and virtuous deeds such as forgiveness. All three groups are bound together in their labors by—to use Ulysses' words in *Troilus and Cressida*—"a bond of air strong as the axle-tree/ On which heaven rides" (I. iii. 66-67). In the case of *The Tempest*, by filling the actors' and Shakespeare's sails with their shouts of approval, the audience's breath moves the ship of the play to its destined harbor. This labor completes the aborted work of the sailors of act I, scene i. Shakespeare may have brought Prospero's interrupted project to unexpected fruition, yet only his playgoers' striving can complete his own task.[37]

Notes

1 See, for example, Douglas L. Peterson, *Time, Tide, and Tempest: A Study of Shakespeare's Romances* (San Marino: Huntington Library, 1973) 219-20; and G. Wilson Knight, *The Crown of Life: Essays in Interpretation of Shakespeare's Final Plays* (1947; rpt. New York: Barnes and Noble, 1966) 231.

2 Joseph Summers, in *Dreams of Love and Power: On Shakespeare's Plays* (Oxford: Clarendon Press, 1984) 145-46, compares the Boatswain's work in the first scene of *The Tempest* to the labor of a king who attempts to preserve the ship of state.

3 The relevance of biblical and Patristic texts for Gonzalo's disquisition on labor and idleness is explained by William Rockett, "Labor and Virtue in *The Tempest*," *Shakespeare Quarterly* 24 (1973): 77-84, esp. 78-79.

4 This is the interpretation of Peterson 238-39.

5 Biblical and Burtonian contexts for Sebastian's idleness are described by Maxwell Luria, "Standing Water and Sloth in *The Tempest*," *English Studies* 49 (1968): 328-31.

6 Concerning the stranded court party, Robert M. Adams has remarked, in *Shakespeare: The Four Romances* (New York: Norton, 1989), that the courtiers are "helpless in the absence of experienced and knowledgeable workmen. This point is not made in the text, perhaps because it could by made by costuming. The court costumes of the royal party—unsoiled, unstained, holding their freshness and glosses—can only contribute to a sense of comic inappropriateness in a tropical rain forest" (132-33).

7 Stephen Orgel, in his Oxford Shakespeare edition of *The Tempest* (Oxford: Oxford UP, 1987), notes that "in one extraordinary passage"—I. ii. 155-58—Prospero conceives his suffering as a literal childbirth. . . . He has reconceived himself, as Miranda's only parent, but also as the family's favourite child" (18-19).

8 Regarding Ariel's reminder, Cynthia Marshall, in *Last Things and Last Plays: Shakespearean Eschatology* (Carbondale: Southern Illinois UP, 1991), has judged that "the pattern implicit in this prophesied end to labor mimics that of the biblical creation narrative, in which God rests after six days of creative labor, and that of the Seven Ages scheme, in which God rests after six ages of earthly history" (93).

9 Philip Brockbank, in "*The Tempest*: Conventions of Art and Empire," *Later Shakespeare*, ed. John Russell Brown and Bernard Harris, Stratford-

Upon-Avon Studies 8 (London: Edward Arnold, 1966), 183-201, provides a context for Ferdinand's labor: "The tillers of the earth and the fetchers of wood, runs the argument, are the heirs to God's plenty: 'Dei laboribus omnia vendunt, God sells us all things for our labour, when Adam himself might not live in Paradise without dressing the Garden.' It is this thought that seems to hover mockingly behind the log-bearing labours of Ferdinand. Prospero.... sells Miranda (the richest of the island's bounties) only in return for work" (192).

10 In *Shakespearean Romance* (Princeton: Princeton UP, 1972), Howard Felperin writes "in so far as Ferdinand regards his servitude as the condition of his freedom, however, it begins to resemble Ariel's labor more than Caliban's: that labor which Yeats calls 'blossoming or dancing' and which represents the fulfillment of human nature rather than its curse" (265).

11 A different account of the value of Ferdinand's labor is given by Terence Eagleton, *Shakespeare and Society* (New York: Schocken, 1967) 165-66.

12 Detailed explications of the Masque of Ceres are given by Glynne Wickham, "Masque and Anti-masque in *The Tempest*," *Essays and Studies* 28 (1975): 1-14; Yves Peyré, "Les Masques d'Ariel," *Cahiers Elisabéthains* 19 (1981): 53-71; and Orgel 47-50.

13 See Kevin McNamara, "Golden Worlds at Court: *The Tempest* and Its Masque," *Shakespeare Studies* 19 (1987): 183-202, esp. 193.

14 See Knight 245.

15 *The Riverside Shakespeare* 1629.

16 This point is also made by Theresa Coletti, "Music and Tempest," *Shakespeare's Late Plays: Essays in Honor of Charles Crow*, ed. Richard C. Tobias and Paul G. Zolbrod (Athens: Ohio UP, 1974) 185-99, esp. 196-97. Coletti compares Juno's and Ceres' song to Gonzalo's utopia, noting that cultivation is the essential ingredient missing from the latter. See also Felperin 266-67.

17 See Catherine M. Shaw, "*The Tempest* and *Hymenaei*," *Cahiers Elisabéthains* 26 (1984): 29-39, esp. 33-34. Sir Thomas Elyot explains how classical ideas can be learned from dancing in the *Book Named the Governor* (London: Dent, 1962) 76-88.

18 Loren E. Pennington, in "The Amerindian in English Promotional Literature, 1575-1625," *The Westward Enterprise: English Activities in Ireland, the Atlantic, and America, 1480-1650*, ed. K. R. Andrews, N. P. Canny, and P. E. H. Hair (Liverpool: Liverpool UP, 1978) 175-94, has shown that, in the first decade of the seventeenth century, English travel writers, influenced by the promotional tactics of the Virginia Company of

London, began depicting the Amerindian in highly positive images, among which was the savage happy to provide Europeans with food and game at little or no charge (187-91). It is possible that Shakespeare's characterization of Caliban owes something to a popular promotional image of the New World savage, although one must note that a strong element of satire or criticism informs the playwright's portrait. On the Amerindian Caliban as an Anglo-American sociopolitical construct, see Alden T. Vaughan, "Shakespeare's Indian: The Americanization of Caliban," *Shakespeare Quarterly* 39 (1988): 137-53, esp. 139-53.

19 In this respect, the relationship between Prospero and Caliban reprises that of English gentry and Amerindians in Jamestown and other New World settlements. Edmund S. Morgan, in "The Labor Problem at Jamestown, 1607-18," *The American Historical Review* 76 (1971): 595-611, has demonstrated that the Jamestown settlers included a disproportionate number of gentlemen and captains (perhaps retainers of the 32 present or future earls, 4 countesses, 3 viscounts, and 19 barons in the parent Virginia Company), that Captain John Smith and other authorities repeatedly complained about the settlers' lack of industry in growing and providing their own foodstuffs, and that the general plan was to depend upon the labor and generosity of naive Amerindians for many necessities of life. Jacobean pamphleteers such as Alexander Whitaker, *Good Newes From Virginia* (London: William Welby, 1613), had portrayed Amerindians as "industrious in their labour" (25). The anticipated native labor never materialized, however; and idling settlers generally remained malnourished, threatened on several occasions with starvation.

20 Harry Berger, Jr., in "Miraculous Harp: A Reading of Shakespeare's *Tempest*," *Second World and Green World: Studies in Renaissance Fiction-Making* (Berkeley: U of California P, 1988) 147-85, notes that "the former Duke of Milan has an unhealthy attitude toward labor—toward clean manual work. We hardly expect him, as an aristocrat, to wash his own dishes and light his own fires. But he seems to have an ethical as well as a practical and social aversion to labor: Caliban and Ferdinand do not simply do his chores for him; he makes it clear that they do them as punishment and as an ordeal of degradation" (155). Berger's suggestion that Prospero perhaps derives this aversion from otherworldly Ariel is unconvincing.

21 My analysis thus qualifies the judgment of Berger that "like Plato's poet, Ariel is a winged thing whose art is magically inspired, therefore brought forth without labor" (152).

22 This point is memorably made by D. G. James, *The Dream of Prospero* (Oxford: Clarendon Press, 1967) 27-44.

23 See Robert B. Pierce, "'Very Like a Whale': Scepticism and Seeing in *The Tempest*," *Shakespeare Survey* 38 (1985): 167-73, esp. 168-69.

24 Barbara A. Mowat, "Prospero, Agrippa, and Hocus Pocus," *English Literary Renaissance* 11 (1981): 281-303.

25 See Roger B. Manning, "Apprentices' Riots in London," *Village Revolts: Social Protest and Popular Disturbance in England, 1509-1640* (Oxford: Clarendon Press, 1988) 187-219; and A. L. Beier, *Masterless Men: The Vagrancy Problem in England 1560-1640* (London: Methuen, 1985) 24-25, 44-45. Beier notes that "servants and apprentices were indeed most prone to vagrancy of all London's socio-economic groups, accounting for almost three-quarters of the Londoners whose occupations were listed in Bridewell [prison] records from 1597-1608, thus surpassing even their substantial share of the labour force" (44).

26 Rather than an apprenticeship, Donna B. Hamilton, in *Virgil and "The Tempest": The Politics of Imitation* (Columbus: Ohio State UP, 1990), offers other views of Prospero and Ariel's work contract: "Thus, Ariel's contract with Prospero, whereby Ariel will work for him in return for freedom, is as analogous to the situation of the Irish undertaker seeking a fair schedule of rent payments as to the English Parliament promising James supply in exchange for a proper settlement of their grievances" (64).

27 The irreversibility of Prospero and Caliban's master/slave relationship has been well argued by Thomas Cartelli, "Prospero in Africa: *The Tempest* as Colonialist Text and Pretext," *Shakespeare Reproduced: The Text in History and Ideology*, ed. Jean E. Howard and Marion F. O'Connor (New York: Methuen, 1987) 99-115, esp. 109-11; and by Octave Mannoni, *Prospero and Caliban: The Psychology of Colonization*, trans. Pamela Powesland (New York: Praeger, 1964) 105-8.

28 John D. Cox, *Shakespeare and the Dramaturgy of Power* (Princeton, NJ: Princeton UP, 1989) 3-21.

29 Cf. Harry Levin, "Two Magian Comedies: *The Tempest* and *The Alchemist*," *Shakespeare and the Revolution of the Times* (Oxford: Oxford UP, 1976) 210-31, esp. 213-14.

30 The history of construing "Prospero as ego and Ariel and Caliban as superego and id" is described by Ruth Nevo, *Shakespeare's Other Language* (New York: Methuen, 1987) 137-39.

31 See A. Lynne Magnusson, "Interruption in *The Tempest*," *Shakespeare Quarterly* 37 (1986): 52-65; and Russ McDonald, "Reading *The Tempest*," *Shakespeare Survey* 43 (1990): 15-28, esp. 24-25.

32 Typical descriptions of this conflict are those of F. D. Hoeniger, "Prospero's Storm and Miracle," *Shakespeare Quarterly* 7 (1956): 33-38; Harold C. Goddard, *The Meaning of Shakespeare* (Chicago: U of Chicago P, 1951) 2:282-83; Peterson 228; and Nevo 135.

33 These dramatic facts contradict Melvin Seiden's claim, made in "Utopianism in *The Tempest*," *Modern Language Quarterly* 30 (1970): 3-21, that "Prospero's contemplative life, free from the burdens of labor, leisurely and humane, resembles the existence Gonzalo has in mind when he allows 'all men idle, all' in his commonwealth" (16).

34 At one point, Prospero says that he must court an auspicious star's influence (I. ii. 177-84). This service, however, remains vague. The magician is curiously unattached throughout four acts of *The Tempest*.

35 Detailed analyses of Ariel's and Prospero's transformative dialogue appear in David Horowitz, *Shakespeare: An Existential View* (London: Tavistock, 1965) 87; D'Orsay W. Pearson, "'Unless I Be Reliev'd by Prayer': *The Tempest* in Perspective," *Shakespeare Studies* 7 (1974): 253-82, esp. 271-73; Cosmo Corfield, "Why Does Prospero Abjure His 'Rough Magic'?" *Shakespeare Quarterly* 36 (1985): 31-48, esp. 40-46, 47; and in Maurice Hunt, *Shakespeare's Romance of the Word* (Lewisburg, PA: Bucknell UP, 1990) 136-39.

36 Knight also equates Ariel with art (210-11, 222).

37 Different views of the place of work in *The Tempest* are offered by Rockett 77-84; by Ronald B. Bond, "Labour, Ease, and *The Tempest* as Pastoral Romance," *Journal of English and Germanic Philology* 77 (1978): 330-42; and by Hamilton 98-103. The analyses of these critics differ significantly from mine. Bond judges that "the emphasis the play places on labour is, in fact, a major deviation from the pastoral tradition, which is informed by a contrast between *otium* and *negotium*" (332), while Hamilton compares selected features of *The Tempest* with images of heroic labor in the *Aeneid*.

Chapter 7

King Henry VIII

In the previous chapter, the notion of "working" things "That bear a weighty and serious brow" was taken from the Prologue of *King Henry VIII* and applied to Shakespeare's depiction of Prospero's troubled ("beating") mind in order to characterize its operations within the larger context of the various labors of *The Tempest*. This borrowing suggests the turn that Shakespeare's preoccupation with the portrayal of labor took in writing *King Henry VIII* and his parts of *The Two Noble Kinsmen*. Although they still labor physically, characters in Shakespeare's final plays more often than not work in strenuous, distinctly intellectual or emotional ways. In Shakespeare's final history play,[1] certain fits of mind derive from the arduous work required for achieving and maintaining worldly greatness. Before presenting the intellectual labors of *King Henry VIII*, Shakespeare first defines the nature of the pompous work associated with them. Several early episodes of the play perform this function.

Near the end of his induction, the Prologue elicits a second meaning from his promise that the play contains events "Sad, high, and working" (Prologue, 3):

> Think ye see
> The very persons of our noble story
> As they were living. Think you see them great,
> And follow'd with the general throng and sweat
> Of thousand friends; then, in a moment, see
> How soon this mightiness meets misery.
> (Prologue, 25-30)

The Prologue links greatness with sweat, with the labor of courtiers who would befriend the great man or woman. Shakespeare clarifies this notion in the Duke of Norfolk's description of earthly glory surrounding Henry VIII and Francis I's meeting in June 1520 at the Field of the Cloth of Gold:

> To-day the French,
> All clinquant, all in gold, like heathen gods,
> Shone down the English; and, to-morrow, they
> Made Britain India: every man that stood
> Show'd like a mine. Their dwarfish pages were
> As cherubins, all gilt; the madams too,
> Not us'd to toil, did almost sweat to bear
> The pride upon them, that their very labor
> Was to them as a painting.
> (I. i. 18-26)

By his choice of poetic diction, Shakespeare implicitly criticizes the opulence that Norfolk, a nobleman, ostensibly celebrates.[2] "All in gold," the French are gods but heathen in appearance; the "cherubins" (all "gilt"/"guilt") that pages became were "dwarfish"—reduced in stature. Shakespeare's criticism of the nobles' sloth and aversion to useful work, a note struck repeatedly in previous late plays, informs the image of wealthy noblewomen, soft and out-of-shape ("Not us'd to toil"), loading themselves with so much gold, jewelry, and robes that they perspired under their burden. The folly inherent in such pride is focused by Buckingham's later comment that, to attend the kings' meeting in style, many English nobles "Have broke their backs with laying manors on 'em/ For this great journey" (I. i. 84-85). The work involved in building and sustaining a manor (generally not the lord's personal labor) is lost when its value is translated into the jewelry and finery under which lord and lady toil. In this case, their vain labor is lost when the diplomatic meeting for which they bought the jewels and finery comes to nothing.[3] "The peace between the French and us not values/ The cost that did conclude it" (I. i. 88-89), Norfolk judges, an opinion with which Buckingham agrees:

> Every man,
> After the hideous storm that follow'd, was
> A thing inspir'd, and, not consulting, broke
> Into a general prophecy: that this tempest,
> Dashing the garment of this peace, aboded
> The sudden breach on't.
> (I. i. 89-94)

The natural storm following Henry and Francis' negotiations becomes the familiar Shakespearean tempest, the metaphor for the great stir that tests the mettle of late-play characters. In the present context of *King Henry VIII*, the Shakespearean tempest reveals the vain emptiness of the peculiar labor associated with earthly greatness.[4]

Throughout the play, Shakespeare maintains his portrayal of earthly pomp as a heavy load under which ambitious mortals sweat. The meretricious Old Lady who baits Anne Boleyn with the king's sudden attraction to her asks, "What think you of a duchess? Have you limbs/ To bear that load of title?" (II. iii. 38-39). "If your back/ Cannot vouchsafe this burthen," the Old Lady continues, "'tis too weak/ Ever to get a boy" (II. iii. 42-44). Sleazily the Old Lady connects one kind of work with another; the labor of childbirth that would likely result from Anne's becoming Henry's mistress pays for the jewels, robes, and titles under whose weight she might labor as proudly as other court madams. "I know your back will bear a duchess" (II. iii. 99), the Old Lady concludes with a leer. In *The Tempest*, a character's being bowed or stooped is often part of a process of refinement through arduous trial. Similar imagery in *King Henry VIII*, however, without exception conveys a weight of vanity detrimental to the bearer's physical and especially spiritual health. In the present episode, Shakespeare positively depicts Anne Boleyn, perhaps to counter long-lived Catholic propaganda that she was merely a whore (and Elizabeth I thus a bastard). Anne's unfeigned distaste for the Old Lady's gross innuendoes and her rejection of the idea of complying with Henry's sexual advances solely to sweat under a load of glory distinguish her from a group of noblemen in the play who pridefully burden themselves with the trappings of greatness.[5]

Specifically, Anne Boleyn differs from the Duke of Buckingham and Cardinal Wolsey, who have unscrupulously sought the outward symbols of glory. As a self-fashioned man of the Renaissance, Wolsey is "spider-like," giving beholders note "Out of his self-drawing web" of "the force of his own merit," which "makes his way" (I. i. 62-64). Machiavellian webs of political self-advancement constitute this spider's distinctive work.[6] To make them, he—by his own admission—must continually plot against others; "If we shall stand still," he tells Henry,

> In fear our motion will be mock'd or carp'd at,
> We should take root here where we sit, or sit
> State-statues only.
> (I. ii. 85-88)

Wolsey's selfish striving to make himself great, in Norfolk's opinion, "will work us all/ From princes into pages":

> All men's honors
> Lie like one lump before him, to be fashion'd
> Into what pitch he please.
> (II. ii. 46-49)

Suffolk, however, in his reply to Norfolk alludes to another kind of man-making labor that represents a redemptive alternative to Wolsey's pernicious work:

> For me, my lords,
> I love him not, nor fear him; there's my creed.
> As I am made without him, so I'll stand,
> If the King please; his curses and his blessings
> Touch me alike; th' are breath I not believe in.
> (II. ii. 49-53)

Suffolk's recollection that God worked him from clay into His own image becomes his defense against both Wolsey's threat to remake him or, if he resists the overture, to undo him.

Such retrospect might have once prevented Buckingham in his pursuit of earthly greatness from conspiring treasonably against his king. Brought to the bar, hearing his fatal judgment, he manifests the working mind typical of *King Henry VIII*. In First Gentleman's account,

> he was stirr'd
> With such an agony he sweat extremely,
> And something spoke in choler, ill, and hasty.
> (II. i. 32-34)

This agitated, this fretted state of mind, a spiritual "agony" in its implications the opposite of Christ's, is a final product of Buckingham's Machiavellian efforts to load himself with glory. Nevertheless, in a dramaturgy characteristic of *King Henry VIII*, this profound intellectual stir quickly modulates into a relative calm, a quiescence of mind accentuated by previous turbulence. No sooner did Buckingham speak "in choler, ill, and hasty" than "he fell to himself again, and sweetly/ In all the rest show'd a most noble patience" (II. i. 35-36). The sharp juxtaposition of sweetness and placidity with rough stir that first manifested itself in the late plays in Guiderius' rude interruption of Arviragus' sweet elegy for Fidele appears in *King Henry VIII*. A sweetness of phrase and sentiment; smooth, nonelliptical, unhurried rhythms of speech; a relative simplicity of diction and plainness of metaphor—these traits mark Buckingham's valediction, a farewell in which, to use his own phrase, he makes a "sweet sacrifice" of himself (II. i. 55-134, esp. 77).

The Christian piety and forgiveness finally voiced by Buckingham largely account for the unruffled quality of his utterances. For over one-hundred years, the argument has been made that John Fletcher wrote part of *King Henry VIII*—this despite the fact that Heminge and Condell included the play in the First Folio and that no major irregularities surround or appear in the text. It is usually on the basis of sweet, unenergetic verse like that making up Buckingham's valediction that the argument for Fletcher's share is built. The quality of such poetry generally resembles that of the plays that he authored, either alone or in conjunction with Francis Beaumont.[7] But we have seen that the juxtaposition of limpid, sweet verse with rough, elliptical, often metaphorically opaque poetry was Shakespeare's preoccupation in *Cymbeline* and *The Tempest*. Prospero's farewell to his art—significantly another valediction—breaks into two parts: the first quaint, nonelliptical, even dotted with the "ye's" characteristic of Fletcher's style; the second elliptical, stirred, writhing with energy. The abrupt contrast in *King Henry VIII* between Buckingham's stirred, working mind and his sweet, serene verse signals a dramatic strategy of the late Shakespeare. Stating emphatically that he has shed his greatness, reverting from the identity of the Duke of Buckingham to "poor" Edward Bohun (II. i. 98-103), Buckingham reveals that his untroubled speech proceeds from his casting off the greatness that is both a cause and a result of the fitful, working mind. Unlike its redemptive status in the last acts of *The Tempest*, in which its exercise effects Prospero's revolution of character, the working mind, as dramatized in the figure of Buckingham, exists as a seeming obstacle to the attainment of a more attractive, placid, Christian attitude of forgiveness and self content.

Shakespeare's apparent reversal of his previous weighting of values is also suggested by Anne Boleyn's reaction to the Lord Chamberlain's announcement that Henry has bestowed upon her the title of Marchioness of Pembroke along with its accompanying riches. This event occurs during her conversation with the opportunistic Old Lady. Playgoers' impression of Anne's modesty, created mainly through her correction of the Old Lady's greasy imputations, colors their hearing of her reaction to the Old Lady's crowing over the unlooked-for gift of the aristocratic title. The Chamberlain's news threatens to agitate Anne with the prospect of secular greatness, but she says,

> Good lady,
> Make yourself mirth with your particular fancy,
> And leave me out on't. Would I had no being
> If this salute my blood a jot; it faints me
> To think what follows.
> The Queen is comfortless, and we forgetful
> In our long absence.
> (II. iii. 100-6)

Hallett Smith glosses Anne's word "salute" as "stir"; her commitment to the Christian charity heard in her final utterance here strengthens her resolve to keep her blood—and mind—unstirred by the Chamberlain's news. As depicted by Shakespeare (*pace* historians), she apparently will not suffer the lethal consequences of the working mind.

The sharp division between the working, impassioned mind and sweet patience that distinguishes Buckingham's speech and behavior also marks those qualities in Queen Katherine. Made to undergo a trial concerning the legal status of her marriage, Katherine first speaks to the assembled consistory as a "poor woman," a patient stranger in England, begging for pity (II. iv. 13-57). Laced with pathos, her plea in its smooth rhythms and simple diction testifies to her basically patient, unstirred mind.

But when Wolsey informs her that certain members of the consistory will speak for her, Katherine's mood changes; and her mind and passions begin to work fitfully. "My drops of tears/ I'll turn to sparks of fire" (II. iv. 72-73), she angrily tells Wolsey, reassuming her royal identity. Wolsey's brief admonition, "Be patient yet" (II. iv. 73), cannot divert the torrent of bitter words. His plea identifies the virtue that stinging Katherine temporarily loses. Her charged portrayal of Wolsey's meddling and malice and her haughty, sarcastic account of his false humility and arrogant ambition (II. iv. 74-84, 105-21) correspond to the stirred section of other divided speeches in the play. "You speak not like yourself" (II. iv. 85), a chastened Wolsey at one point says, interrupting her tirade. In the sense that Katherine's speech becomes stirred by the very vices that she imputes to Wolsey, his judgment is unexpectedly accurate. Moreover, by claiming that he has been unjustly accused and that only Henry can "cure" him by removing Katherine's hateful thoughts regarding him (II. iv. 98-102), Wolsey suggests that the working of Katherine's mind is noxious (not only to him but perhaps also to herself). "I do beseech/ You, gracious madam" the Cardinal pleads, "to unthink your speaking" (II. iv. 104).

After Katherine's incensed departure, playgoers learn by Henry's own testimony that Wolsey has strived to preserve the royal marriage and avert the need to call a consistory (II. iv. 144-231).[8] "You ever/ Have wish'd the sleeping of this business," Henry publicly tells Wolsey,

> never desir'd
> It to be stirr'd; but oft have hind'red, oft,
> The passages made toward it.
> (II. iv. 163-66)

Later we learn that Wolsey struggled to allay Henry's efforts to make a trial of his marriage because he feared that, if it were annulled, Henry would make Anne Boleyn queen. In that case, a known Lutheran could oppose his Catholic ambitions.[9] Shakespeare's dramatic method with regard to the characterizations of Katherine and Wolsey thus makes her loss of sweet patience in the fits of a working mind appear especially grievous. Even though dramatic events establish Wolsey's nasty disposition, in the matter of her marriage Katherine has unjustly attacked the Cardinal.

In Katherine's next scene (III. i), Shakespeare objectifies the working mind that exercised Katherine during her trial. The Folio stage direction for the beginning of act III reads, "*Enter* Queen *and her* Women *as at work*." Their work takes the traditional literary form of woman's labor—sewing or weaving.[10] "Take thy lute, wench, my soul grows sad with troubles," Katherine states; "Sing, and disperse 'em if thou canst. Leave working" (III. i. 1-2). Until this moment, the physical working of thread has provided a release for Katherine's anxiety over her marriage.[11] But gloomy thoughts now so work her mind that her soul saddens and she seeks the antidote of music. Through the character of Katherine, Shakespeare suggests that art might alleviate the agitated, working mind; in this respect, he indicates that the remedy that Ariel—a symbol of art—found for Prospero's beating mind might resolve the turmoil of characters in *King Henry VIII*.

The sentiment of the servant's song links it to major values of *The Tempest*:

> Orpheus with his lute made trees,
> And the mountain tops that freeze,
>   Bow themselves when he did sing.
> To his music plants and flowers
> Ever sprung, as sun and showers
>   There had made a lasting spring.
> Every thing that heard him play,
> Even the billows of the sea,
>   Hung their heads, and then lay by.
> In sweet music is such art,
> Killing care and grief of heart
>   Fall asleep, or hearing, die.
>   (III. i. 3-14)

The "lasting spring" that Orpheus' magical music makes resembles the perpetual fertility that Ceres wishes for Ferdinand and Miranda when she sings, "Spring come to you at the farthest/ In the very end of harvest." The first stanza of the song in *King Henry VIII* celebrates the mystical power of art to stir creation to acts of homage and rebirth. The second stanza, conversely, commemorates divine art's ability to soothe, to induce quiet and rest. Shakespeare's late-play preoccupation with counterpointing stir and stasis surfaces in the song's two stanzas. Supernatural music in *The Tempest*, by Ferdinand's admission,

> ... crept by me upon the waters,
> Allaying both their fury and my passion
> With its sweet air.
> (I. ii. 392-94)

This represents a double calming reprised in the final stanza of the song in *King Henry VIII*. At basis, the song implies that music can quiet the very nature that it works, something that the mind cannot always do.[12] Metadramatically, Shakespeare in *The Tempest* likens his theatrical art to Ariel's supernatural art, implying that works like his play can calm troubled minds by inciting their appreciators to prefer virtue to vice. With the midplay song of *King Henry VIII*, he appears to be designing his play to make the same claim.

While the wench's voice and lute could never be confused with those of Orpheus, they produce a sweetness dimly echoing the beatitude of divine art. Sufficient vestiges of Orphic art remain in mortal music for it to work its healing effects. But a gentleman abruptly enters, intruding upon the song's last, fading notes, startling Katherine and thus not only ruining the hope of music's cure but also making impossible the judgment that art can (and will) redemptively relieve the working minds of certain characters of *King Henry VIII*. "How now?" Katherine nervously exclaims, seeing him. "And't please your Grace, the two great Cardinals/ Wait in the presence" (III. i. 15-17), he announces, referring to Wolsey and Campeius. The pattern of interrupted remedial work that distinguishes *The Tempest* extends into *King Henry VIII*. In the history play, however, interruption ruins the kind of artistic solution that is not broken off in the last act of Prospero's play and that makes possible its romance ending.

The two Cardinals come to Katherine's apartment to know "How [she] stand[s] minded in the weighty difference" between Henry and herself (III. i. 57-59). By reminding Katherine of her troubles, the churchmen recreate the symbolic tempest of the late plays, the storm of adversity that periodically shakes characters as a painful condition of living in the fallen world. The turmoil that they introduce into the scene stirs Katherine's mind, which was beginning to relax; and her anxious fear of Wolsey manifests itself again (III. i. 19-23, 67-80, 98-153). Katherine intuits that the Cardinals' troubling of her provokes—in her words—"the last fit of my greatness" (III. i. 78), the final stirring of her royal mind. When Campeius protests, "Your rage mistakes us" (III. i. 101), he specifies the anger that should animate the actress playing Katherine as she lashes out at the prelates who she believes come to entrap her (III. i. 98-153). But as she makes abundantly clear in this episode, Katherine's settled desire involves simply being a "woman," patient and diligent in the duties falling to a wife.

When Katherine says, "Your Graces find me here part of a huswife/ (I would be all) against the worst may happen" (III. i. 24-25), she suggests that her work as a seamstress represents the dutiful service of the good wife. In *Cymbeline*, working as a huswife for Belarius and her two brothers becomes the primary means by which Imogen's marital fidelity is strengthened and reestablished. Katherine utilizes a similar vehicle, formulating its symbolic value for her marriage. Unlike Imogen, however, who "mannishly" fights her weakness in the Welsh mountains, Katherine makes her work as seamstress typify woman's stereotypic debility. "I was set at work/ Among my maids," she complains, "full little, God knows, looking/ Either for such men or such business" (III. i. 74-76). Unlike Imogen's huswifery, Katherine's work plays no effective role in qualifying her as a worthy marriage partner or in dissolving the storm of doubt in Henry's mind—the strong suspicion that God will never give him a male heir because his marriage violates scripture.

Unfortunately, Katherine invokes the cliché of woman's "weak wit" (III. i. 72), fearfully wrapping herself in a debilitating caricature. Katherine's great tempests of anger violate the image of the weak self that she would create, but she recovers that nascent identity at scene's end. When Wolsey reminds her that kings "swell and grow, as terrible as storms" to "stubborn spirits" and that she should reclaim her "gentle, noble temper,/ A soul as even as a calm" (III. i. 163-66), he redefines female nobility for her. Campeius seconds Wolsey's redefinition:

> You wrong your virtues
> With these weak women's fears. A noble spirit
> As yours was put into you, ever casts
> Such doubts, as false coin, from it.
> (III. i. 168-71)

Discovering privately that Henry is determined to cast off Katherine, Wolsey has decided to no longer block a divorce; instead, he opportunistically strives to refashion the Queen into a pliant woman submitting herself to a public trial (where she can more conclusively be disposed of). Katherine's nobility has consisted of sparks of fire, fits of righteous indignation over affronts to royal nature. But Campeius cleverly terms these fits the product of "weak woman's fears." According to the churchman, true female nobility of spirit, even royal female nobility, consists in adopting the stereotypic passivity and obedience—the essentially static emotional role—of woman as wife, endlessly patient. Campeius has slyly capitalized upon the cliché version of the identity that Katherine has informed him that she wants to cultivate in herself.

Calm and dutiful once more, Katherine apologizes:

> If I have us'd myself unmannerly,
> You know I am a woman, lacking wit
> To make a seemly answer to such persons.
> (III. i. 176-78)

These self-impairing words hardly reflect a noble spirit, if for no other reason than that their speaker loses herself in a masculinist cliché that controls her behavior. Such passivity should not be confused with the late-play virtue of patience, which is an active quality (*patiens*) as John F. Danby has shown.[13] It is part of Katherine's personal tragedy that she chooses to adopt this cliché, rather than resisting to the end its attribution to her (as Hermione successfully does).

When we last see Katherine, she is laboring under the weight of sickness and old age. The play's characteristic imagery informs us of that much. In reply to Griffith's question, "How does your Grace?" (IV. ii. 1), she answers,

> O Griffith, sick to death!
> My legs like loaden branches bow to th' earth,

Willing to leave their burthen.
(IV. ii. 1-3)

The poetic imagery earlier used to convey the labor of bearing earthly greatness shifts its tenor to illness in old age, making Katherine's maintenance of her physical life continual, painful work. Although the historical Katherine was forty-three years old when Henry divorced her, Shakespeare's Queen says, "I am old, my lords" (III. i. 120). Advanced in years and mortally ill, she finds that not simply the trappings of greatness but life itself can be a burden. That Katherine desires the virtue of patience is iconographically suggested by the name—Patience—of the gentlewoman helping to guide her feeble steps. Just before her salvific dream vision, she states, "Patience, be near me still, and set me lower;/ I have not long to trouble thee" (IV. ii. 76-77). "Nay, Patience,/ You must not leave me yet" (IV. ii. 165-66), she exclaims as her eyes grow dim. Shakespeare leads his audience to believe that patience plays a major part in Katherine's capacity for the inner peace signified by the staging of her vision.

By holding a garland of bay leaves over sleeping Katherine's head, the white-robed personages of the vision suggest that Katherine has been elected to enjoy a heavenly—if not an earthly—crown.[14] The personages' golden vizards and garland of bay require no labor to wear. As far as the audience is concerned, the vision, unlike the spectacles of *The Tempest*, concludes without interruption. Having held the garland three times over Katherine's head, after which "*she makes (in her sleep) signs of rejoicing, and holdeth up her hands to heaven,*" the spirits vanish. The iconic value of the dream vision appears in Katherine's first question when awake: "Spirits of peace, where are ye?" (IV. ii. 83). The spirits of the vision could bring a peace, a profound calm to a mind troubled with earthly loss, sickness, and age. Awake, Katherine ecstatically speaks of being invited to a celestial banquet by spirits who "promis'd me eternal happiness" (IV. ii. 90). Yet despite the audience's sense of the spectacle's completion, Katherine, like Prospero, experiences a radical interruption of a spectacle of eternity. Significantly, the "*Sad and solemn music*" that lulled Katherine asleep continues to play after the vanishing of the spirits, thus creating the impression that the spectacle is not yet over. Katherine's calling to the departed spirits of peace proceeds from a stirred mind, fretful over having been given a vision of happiness only to have it evaporate. "Are ye all gone?" she asks queruously, "And leave me here in wretchedness behind ye?" (IV. ii. 83-84). Like Ferdinand, Katherine was in effect about to call a place defined by a marvelous vision paradise. Like Prospero, she—admittedly to a lesser degree—feels the pulse of the beating, the working mind that seeks relief. "Bid the music leave," she gloomily commands, "They are harsh and heavy to me" (IV. ii. 94-95).

An entering messenger receives the brunt of a mind in turmoil, fixating again upon earthly greatness:

	Enter a Messenger.
Mess.	And't like your Grace—
Kath.	You are a saucy fellow, Deserve we no more reverence?
Grif.	You are to blame, Knowing she will not lose her wonted greatness, To use so rude behavior. Go to, kneel.
	(IV. ii. 100-3)

When she learns the messenger's purpose (to admit Lord Capuchius, sent by Henry), she waspishly concludes, "Admit him entrance, Griffith; but this fellow/ Let me ne'er see again" (IV. ii. 107-8). While the working mind led Prospero to discover a way of resolving his inner strife between virtue and vengeance, it mars the heavenly calm imposed upon Katherine.[15]

Katherine's last wishes involve the reward of labors—both her own and others. She asks Capuchius to promise that her men will "have their wages duly paid 'em" (IV. ii. 150). As for herself, she commends her daughter, Mary Tudor, in a letter written to the king, an epistle which she begs Capuchius to "deliver" (IV. ii. 129-30). Her word "deliver" recalls what in her estimation has been the greatest labor of her life: the delivery of England's future queen. Now that child is reborn in the image of the letter whose delivery she urges. In the epistle Mary is reborn as "The model of our chaste loves, his young daughter" and rebaptized– "The dews of heaven fall thick in blessings on her!" (IV. ii. 132-

33). Shakespeare's audience's knowledge of the terrible reign of Bloody Mary, her premature death, and her subsequent portrayal as the Whore of Babylon (*Faerie Queene* I. vii) makes Katherine's final written words ironic in their blessing and pathetic in their plea that Henry "give her virtuous breeding":

> She is young, and of a noble modest nature,
> I hope she will deserve well—and a little
> To love her for her mother's sake that lov'd him
> Heaven knows how dearly.
> (IV. ii. 134-38)

Jacobean audiences realized that Katherine's chief labor would be lost; a protestant heaven never blessed the child. Even as she never fully quiets her working mind, Katherine is cheated by providence in the fruit of her work.

Wolsey's passage from the trouble of a working mind to final calm and comfort parallels that of Katherine. His attainment of ultimate rest, a profound stasis of mind and spirit, however, is unalloyed. The empire built by Wolsey's continual business of mind and body almost instantly crumbles when he inadvertently includes a secret inventory of his wealth, unknown to the king, among state papers sent to Henry. The discovery of this error precipitates Wolsey's most intense mental fit. The intellectual agitation is apparent to Norfolk:

> My lord, we have
> Stood here observing him. Some strange commotion
> Is in his brain; he bites his lip, and starts,
> Stops on a sudden, looks upon the ground,
> Then lays his finger on his temple; straight
> Springs out into fast gait, then stops again,
> Strikes his breast hard, and anon he casts
> His eye against the moon. In most strange postures
> We have seen him set himself.
> (III. ii. 111-19)

Norfolk's report of Wolsey's casting his eye upon the moon suggests that the Cardinal's fit of mind is lunacy. Not since Belarius' stories of martial adventures physically exercised Guiderius has Shakespeare depicted a state of mind so compulsively working the thinker's body. Wolsey's mind beats as strongly and as painfully as Prospero's did when his old brain was troubled by the thought of Caliban's rebellion. "It may well be,/ There is a mutiny in's mind" (III. ii. 119-20), Henry knowingly concludes in response to Norfolk's report of Wolsey's strange behavior. The rebellion that Wolsey has in effect been committing against his king finally coalesces in his mind when insurgent passions of fear dethrone royal reason. Wolsey's mind, which has long worked to build his greatness, finally exercises itself in a fit not simply unproductive but self-destructive as well.

Stripped of his worldly goods and thrust out of the king's protection, Wolsey asserts,

> I know myself now, and I feel within me
> A peace above all earthly dignities,
> A still and quiet conscience. The King has cur'd me,
> I humbly thank his Grace; and from these shoulders,
> These ruin'd pillars, out of pity taken
> A load would sink a navy—too much honor.
> O, 'tis a burden, Cromwell, 'tis a burden
> Too heavy for a man that hopes for heaven!
> (III. ii. 378-85)

Like Buckingham and Katherine, Wolsey at last is eased of a burden that has made him labor. Shakespeare juxtaposes the play's signature imagery of laboring under a heavy load, here a weight that would sink a navy, with a "still and quiet" conscience, which becomes the alternative to life's painful work. Bereft, old, "broken with the storms of state," Wolsey seeks final refuge in Leicester abbey, where, in Griffith's report, "He gave his honors to the world again,/ His blessed part to heaven, and slept in peace" (IV. ii. 29-30). A celestial stasis replaces the great stir that was Wolsey's life.

During his anagnorisis, Wolsey suggests that his conscience has been troubling him for some time. The character whose conscience is most stirred, however, is King Henry, whose anxiety over a possibly blasphemous marriage sharply works his mind.[16] Norfolk believes that Wolsey

> ... dives into the King's soul, and there scatters
> Dangers, doubts, wringing of the conscience,
> Fears, and despairs, and all these for his marriage.
> (II. ii. 26-28)

While Norfolk distorts Wolsey's role with regard to Henry's marriage (see note 9), he accurately names the wringing of Henry's conscience as the force that agitates the king's mind. "Let's in," he says, "And with some other business put the King/ From these sad thoughts that work too much upon him" (II. ii. 55-57). Henry acknowledges privately that Wolsey represents a "cure" for his "wounded conscience" (II. ii. 74-75), yet its stirring is so intense that only a tribunal can calm it. Katherine's sudden sickness and death unfortunately quiet Henry's working mind.

The condition of absolute inner quiet does not appear to be a desirable trait for a monarch depicted as naive, manipulated, and seemingly ignorant of the rough techniques necessary for grasping and maintaining political rule. Shakespeare portrays Henry VIII as a gullible king who needs to have his mind stirred, exercised over the manipulation of a Wolsey.[17] When Henry reads Wolsey's miscarried letter to the Pope, wherein his efforts to stay the divorce of Katherine are apparent, Surrey exclaims, "Will this work?" (III. ii. 37). Wolsey's treacherous letter, along with the written inventory of the Cardinal's amassed wealth, stirs Henry's mind against Wolsey in the same scene wherein playgoers learn that Cranmer has finally quieted the king's conscience by satisfying him that his divorce is religiously legal (III. ii. 64-67). Like naive Prospero with regard to Antonio's Machiavellian practices, Henry needs to cultivate the working mind requisite for successful rule of a Renaissance state. Once he realizes that Henry has read the incriminating papers, Wolsey desperately asks himself,

> Is there no way to cure this?
> No new device to beat this from his brains?
> I know 'twill stir him strongly. . . .
> (III. ii. 216-18)

Stir Henry strongly the discovered inventory and letter to the Pope do indeed; the king's mind beats on the betrayal in an episode analogous to that in which Caliban's treachery disturbs Prospero's mind. The comparison makes one wonder whether Henry's stirred mind can produce a harmonious resolution like that which the magician's working mind effects in act V of *The Tempest*.

The answer to this question partly involves Anne Boleyn's effect on Henry's mind and passions. In one of the most poetically remarkable passages in the late plays, Shakespeare depicts the almost mystical frenzy that the newly crowned Queen Anne creates in her beholders. At her coronation, Anne Boleyn's beauty causes a stir similar to a sea storm:

> The rich stream
> Of lords and ladies, having brought the Queen
> To a prepar'd place in the choir, fell off
> A distance from her; while her Grace sate down
> To rest a while, some half an hour or so,
> In a rich chair of state, opposing freely
> The beauty of her person to the people.
> Believe me, sir, she is the goodliest woman
> That ever lay by man—which when the people
> Had the full view of, such a noise arose
> As the shrouds make at sea in a stiff tempest,
> As loud and to as many tunes. Hats, cloaks
> (Doublets, I think) flew up, and had their faces
> Been loose, this day they had been lost. Such joy
> I never saw before. Great-bellied women,
> That had not half a week to go, like rams
> In the old time of war, would shake the press
> And make 'em reel before 'em. No man living
> Could say, "This is my wife" there, all were woven
> So strangely in one piece.
> (IV. i. 62-81)

Like a tempest, Anne's beauty in its creation of homage threatens to destroy clothing and obliterate faces—the marks of identity itself. She resembles a fertility goddess in the chthonic power of her beauty. How else can her agitation of pregnant women be explained?[18] One assumes that this was the irresistible force sexually stirring Henry upon first seeing her. As depicted, Anne Boleyn is the *Venus Genetrix* who aggressively recreates society.[19] As the last three verses of Third Gentleman's inspired report reveal, Anne's presence can weave her beholders into a charged, unified group: the prototype of the English nation. Katherine wove to relieve her sorrows; Anne, without effort, performs a royal version of woman's traditional work, weaving diverse threads into a national garment of one piece. Heard in the theater rather than read in the study, the homonymic pun latent in the word "piece"/"peace" predicts the social harmony that Jacobeans nostalgic for Elizabeth's rule liked to imagine was Anne Boleyn's daughter's greatest legacy.

Paradoxically the great stir created by Anne results in a peace, a social calm. This wrought peace is predicted by the bird of peace, "*the rod of silver with the dove*," that the Earl of Surrey carries in her investment progress. It becomes an icon associated with her—and then with her daughter, who would direct its flight into the hearts of English men and women by ending the strife of Bloody Mary and making the Word once more available to the people. As queen, Anne Boleyn has the opportunity to do what the morally transformed Wolsey wishes as a final blessing upon his servant Cromwell: "Still in thy right hand carry gentle peace/ To silence envious tongues" (III. ii. 445-46). While Anne neither living nor dead would be able to silence tongues slanderous of her married fidelity, her virtually supernatural capacity to initiate what was ultimately judged a social peace makes her—not Cromwell—the true recipient of Wolsey's blessing. In this process, Henry is the unwitting agent for something much larger than himself. Regarded from a providential viewpoint, Anne's beauty stirs Henry so that, decades later, a marvelous peace descends upon the English nation.

Laboring in childbirth, Anne Boleyn joins Thaisa and Hermione, other late-play queens, in performing the work upon which their dramatic world's resolution depends. Marina, Perdita, Elizabeth—all three girls grow into women who rectify disasters past and reestablish a joyous community. In *King Henry VIII*, the announcement of the onset of Anne's labor appears in the midst of Gardiner's and Sir Thomas Lovell's talk about the threat posed to the Catholic commonwealth by three protestants—Anne and the king's new favorites, Cranmer and Thomas Cromwell. At one o'clock in the morning, Gardiner invites Lovell to explain his late walking by moralizing:

> Affairs that walk
> (As they say spirits do) at midnight, have

> In them a wilder nature than the business
> That seeks dispatch by day.
> 							(V. i. 13-16)

As Gardiner soon makes clear, the business that he seeks to dispatch by day concerns the thwarting of Archbishop Cranmer by incensing the lords of the Privy Council against him (V. i. 26-54). Lovell responds to Gardiner's invitation to divulge his business by comparing the queen's labor with Gardiner's so-called work:

> 					My lord, I love you;
> And durst commend a secret to your ear
> Much weightier than this work. The Queen's in labor,
> They say in great extremity, and fear'd
> She'll with the labor end.
> 							(V. i. 16-20)

Even as Gardiner works to destroy Cranmer, wishing him, Anne, and Cromwell in their graves (V. i. 31-32), so the labor of childbirth, according to Lovell, threatens the queen's life. Throughout the play, Shakespeare has implied that labor can be a destroyer, sinking the bearers of progressively heavier greatness under a staggering load. In its political repercussions, the child whom Anne labors to deliver represents a burden "weightier" than the day work of politics that Gardiner performs (and bears) in his burdensome plot against Cranmer. Unlike Buckingham, Wolsey, and Katherine, Anne is not relieved by death from the burden of her greatness, her pregnancy. Instead, nature brings forth her "fruit" (V. i. 20), Elizabeth, the word connoting the transformation of a burden into an efflorescence, into something life-giving. Ironically, Catholic Gardiner, not knowing that the child Elizabeth would adopt her mother's protestantism, calls her "fruit," at the same time wishing that the "stock," Anne, might be "grubb'd up" (V. i. 20-23).

What Elizabeth's birth unleashes is depicted in the penultimate scene of the play (V. iii). In a scene of Elizabeth's christening, Anne's labor and delivery are comically recollected in the figure of the Porter at the gate. "Tail-porter" is a pun appearing elsewhere in the canon. Shakespeare conceives this episode so that the infant who would grow into the Virgin Queen is the source of a particular kind of work among her subjects. Like a magnet attracting metal, the babe to be christened profoundly stirs the populace, drawing them to her so that large crowds press against the doors, threatening to break them open. According to the Porter's Man,

> 'tis as much impossible,
> Unless we sweep 'em from the door with cannons,
> To scatter 'em, as 'tis to make 'em sleep
> On May-day morning.
> (V. iii. 12-15)

Strangely, the crowd and its attraction to the infant are portrayed chiefly in terms of sexual desire. The Porter's Man describes those he has hit with his cudgel as "He or she, cuckold or cuckold-maker" (V. iii. 25). And the Porter himself wonders, "Is this Moorfields to muster in? Or have we some strange Indian with the great tool come to court, the women so besiege us? Bless me, what a fry of fornication is at door! On my Christian conscience, this one christening will beget a thousand, here will be father, godfather, and all together" (V. iii. 33-38).

In the magnetic stir that she creates, the babe Elizabeth reveals that she is Anne's daughter. Anne's beauty created a tempest among her common beholders, causing "Great-bellied women . . . [to] shake the press/ And make 'em reel before 'em" (IV. i. 76-79). As her mother did, Elizabeth stirs the sexuality of her future subjects. By Shakespeare's account, Anne Boleyn's physical beauty coexists with a modest, "saint-like" temperament, devoutly religious (IV. i. 82-85). Similarly, the innocent babe Elizabeth is linked to raw desire, especially in its bawdiest and most illegitimate forms. This association, however, discredits neither child nor mother. Clearly the infant's sexual provocation of commoners is symbolic. The key to the compliment lies in the Porter's remark that the present christening will beget a thousand later ones. Out of the source of near-mystical chastity, Shakespeare suggests, comes a national fertility, the incitement of English subjects to engage in the work of procreation. While the rapidly multiplying population of Shakespeare's lifetime created severe economic and social problems everywhere in England, it also provided the strength of numbers able to confront and withstand the Spanish and to explore, populate, and import the New World. Paradoxically the chaste Elizabeth would incite English men and women to the basic labor of making a nation, a provocation foretold in the great sexual stir accompanying her christening.

Anne's momentous labor in producing Elizabeth is offset by Henry's idle recreation. While she suffers the throes of childbirth, he plays the card game primero with the Duke of Suffolk. Moreover, it is at this time that playgoers learn that he will soon have to deal with the political consequences of Gardiner's having slyly incensed the lords of the Privy Council against Henry's new, highly competent deputy, Cranmer. Henry immediately reveals that anxiety over the queen's labor troubles his mind: "Now, Lovell, from the Queen what is the news?" (V. i. 61). Learning that Anne's labor is so severe that his written inquiry of her condition could not be delivered to her and that her "suff'rance made/ Almost each pang a death" (V. i. 68-69), Henry becomes sufficiently alarmed to break off the card game, urging Suffolk to retire for the night and pray for the queen's preservation. Henry, however, apparently does not have the leisure for prayers. He must in the night-time hours develop a plan for thwarting on the morrow the attack by Gardiner and the Privy Councillors upon the Archbishop who has become his political "hand and tongue" (V. i. 38). In addition to its ability to relieve his anxiety over Anne's welfare (a male outlet comparable to the stereotypic female activity of sewing), Henry's card playing also amounts to a pastime while Cranmer is summoned and brought to him. When Henry tells Suffolk—

> Leave me alone,
> For I must think of that which company
> Would not be friendly to
>
> (V. i. 74-76)

—auditors assume that he intends to brood further on Anne's labor. But Sir Anthony Denny's immediate entrance with the news that Cranmer is at hand indicates that the king refers to another matter that works his mind, the fabrication of court intrigue. It is this business that keeps Henry from the prayers that he recommends to Suffolk. From being a foil to Anne's labor, Henry has become a co-worker, a mental rather than physical laborer who simultaneously complements her task of delivering the agent of England's future peace by striving to calm a present turmoil in his court.

His experience of Wolsey has taught Henry to trust policy rather than providence in affairs of state. When Cranmer naively believes that his honesty, without any effort on his own or the king's part, will prevail over his enemies' plot, Henry asks,

> Know you not
> How your state stands i' th' world, with the whole world?
> Your enemies are many, and not small; their practices
> Must bear the same proportion, and not ever
> The justice and the truth o' th' question carries
> The due o' th' verdict with it.
> (V. i. 126-31)

Like the ruling gods of other late plays, Henry puts Cranmer, who would remain calm and passive, into a situation wherein he must bestir himself to prove his virtue. If his enemies propose committing him to the Tower, Cranmer should

> The best persuasions to the contrary
> Fail not to use, and with what vehemency
> Th' occasion shall instruct you.
> (V. i. 147-49)

If these protestations do not move auditors, Henry directs Cranmer to produce the ring he gives him, a talisman bailing him so that he can make his appeal directly to the king. Henry's stratagem thus involves creating the conditions for the utmost testing of his Privy Councillors. He will work them to discover the mettle of which they are made.

During his trial, Cranmer follows Henry's direction that he spiritually and eloquently defend himself (V. ii. 67-83). The actor playing the Archbishop's part should energetically deliver Cranmer's central speech of self-defense to illustrate Henry's cue for vehemency. Significantly, this vigorous plea focuses upon Cranmer's capacity for labor and virtuous stirring:

> My good lords: hitherto, in all the progress
> Both of my life and office, I have labor'd,

> And with no little study, that my teaching
> And the strong course of my authority
> Might go one way, and safely; and the end
> Was ever to do well; nor is there living
> (I speak it with a single heart, my lords)
> A man that more detests, more stirs against,
> Both in his private conscience and his place,
> Defacers of a public peace than I do.
> (V. ii. 67-76)

Cranmer's honest tears of gratitude have earlier signified to Henry that his speech is absolutely authentic. Here he reprises earlier labors in distinctly strenuous language. Gardiner's judgment that Cranmer has grown "strangely troublesome" signals the Archbishop's compliance with Henry's command (V. ii. 129).

Nevertheless Cranmer's innate piety restrains him from fully unleashing his speech, from fully stirring himself and working in his own cause. That unleashing is performed by Cromwell, who bitterly speaks a "bold language" against Gardiner's cruelty to Cranmer (V. ii. 119). Even as characters' labors on their own behalf were inadequate in other late plays, requiring the supernatural intervention of an Ariel for example, so Cranmer's vigorous speech fails to move the lords, necessitating his production of Henry's ring and the royal magical power inherent in it. Henry's testing of his councillors' mettle has failed to demonstrate its hoped-for proof, and the king must descend to rectify injustice and harmonize warring factions of state.

Nevertheless, the threat against Cranmer and the trial have exercised the minds of the king and his two loyal servants, manifesting an intellectual capacity for political rule. Henry's rebuke of Gardiner shows he will not fall to flattery again. The king trusts the Lord Chancellor's words that Cranmer's proposed imprisonment was "meant for his trial/ And fair purgation to the world than malice" (V. ii. 186-87). The Chancellor's words may not be completely true, but Henry takes them for what they profess. His acceptance should not be confused with self-deception, however. He now knows the weakness, even viciousness his councillors are capable of in their flesh. But he also knows that the work of monarchy involves the knitting together of the commonwealth's diverse strands into a single piece/peace. This weaving divests the commonplace idea of woman's work—sewing—of its stereotypic encrustations, cleansing a cliché for use in Henry's political world. Henry commands accusers and accused to embrace mutually. "My Lord of Winchester, I charge you,/ Embrace and love this man [Cranmer]" (V. ii. 204-5), Henry orders. Gardiner's reply, "With a true heart/ And brother-love I do it" (V. ii. 205-6), is too sudden, too absolute a conversion, to be wholly believable. Gardiner's remark functions dramatically like Antonio's silence does at the end of *The Tempest*. Both phenomena indicate a resistance to complete assimilation into the harmonious design that Prospero and King Henry strive to create.

Still, the likely residue of malice does not seriously taint Prospero's or Henry's work. "I long/ To have this young one made a Christian," Henry concludes with reference to the infant Elizabeth's baptism; "As I have made ye one, lords, one remain:/ So I grow stronger, you more honor gain" (V. ii. 212-15). Henry compares the work of baptism, of the initial making of a Christian, to the completion of his political labor in making men into Christians in their mutual forgiveness and forbearance. Inviting comparison with Prospero's noble work, Henry's labor was not destined to persist; his courtiers soon fell to bickering and bloody connivance again. In such acts as his beheading of Anne, Henry himself would promote disorder. But for a moment, Shakespeare's King Henry attains the end of a political task. In begetting Elizabeth, one might say (in the language of *Cymbeline*) that Henry, judged through the hindsight of Jacobean providential history, performed his worldly task, might go, and take his wages.[20]

Fulfilled labor must await the golden reign of Elizabeth. That is the message of Cranmer's play-ending oracle. Unlike the flattering, duplicitous speech that constitutes much of the play's dialogue, Cranmer's language is divinely inspired.[21] "Let me speak, sir," he entreats his king, "For heaven now bids me" (V. iv. 14-15). Concerning the future Virgin Queen, Cranmer prophesies that

> In her days every man shall eat in safety
> Under his own vine what he plants, and sing

> The merry songs of peace to all his neighbors.
> (V. iv. 33-35)

In other words, Elizabeth's reign will be a time of happy, personally satisfying labor and peace. This life-giving work displaces the hard labor of sweating under the glittering load of earthly greatness that Shakespeare has repeatedly represented in the play. The irony of course is that during the Virgin Queen's rule land enclosures and rapidly rising food prices made the lives of agrarian workers and their dependents miserable and usually short. Deciding whether the irony is calculated or accidental is not easy. English unhappiness with James I's spendthrift, publicly indifferent rule had reached such proportions by 1612, the date usually assigned for the writing of *King Henry VIII*, that a wave of nostalgia for Elizabeth swept London and the country.[22] Resentment over the Scottish king's coarse temperament and corrupt government had grown so strong that life under Elizabeth was remembered as edenic by comparison. (Concerning James' unpopularity and Elizabethan hard times, see Chapter 1, 10-18).

The difficulty of assessing Cranmer's image of fulfilled Elizabethan labor is compounded by his subsequent panegyric to James, who likened himself to the Phoenix rising from his predecessor's ashes. Cranmer articulates a popular mythology of the first Stuart king (V. iv. 45-47), paying tribute to James' role as a nation maker (V. iv. 52). Shakespeare refers to James' insistence that Parliament ratify his proposed union of England, Scotland, and Wales into Britain—a new nation. Cranmer celebrates the making of that country as James' chief work. But the construct existed only on paper in 1612. Members of Parliament, resentful of Scots and thwarted by the near-impossible task of integrating Scottish and English law, would not actually create the nation until many years later, after James' death. Again, the possibility looms of a calculated irony on Shakespeare's part concerning fulfilled labor.

If irony disturbs Cranmer's predictions,[23] Henry, hearing them, remains deaf to it. For him, Cranmer's speech is an "oracle of comfort" (V. iv. 66):

> O Lord Archbishop,
> Thou hast made me now a man! never, before
> This happy child, did I get any thing.
> (V. iv. 63-65)

The oracle causes Henry to realize that his greatest work has been not the knitting together of his Privy Councillors (that work will unravel) but the begetting of Elizabeth.[24] Procreation has been consistently portrayed as work in the late plays, especially *Cymbeline*. In other late plays, *Pericles* and *The Winter's Tale*, Shakespeare depicts the adult protagonist's rebirth, his daughter's "delivery" of him into a new life. In *King Henry VIII*, Cranmer assumes the daughter's role in this process; his oracle delivers Henry. By the king's account, it has "made" him a "man." This rebirth of the man Henry VIII amounts to Cranmer's historic labor. Unlike other cases, however, Cranmer's religious piety, his status as Archbishop, and the oracular nature of his speech invite comparison of his man-making with the creation of God who, according to John, made the world, including humankind, with his Word.

The notion that Cranmer's words have recreated Henry echoes in the king's wish

> That when I am in heaven I shall desire
> To see what this child does, and praise my Maker.
> (V. iv. 67-68)

Cranmer's oracle has spiritually remade (or made again) what God made. Henry extends his joy to his subjects. "This day, no man think/ H'as business at his house," the king commands; "for all shall stay:/ This little one shall make it Holy-day" (V. iv. 74-76). Herschel Baker glosses Henry's word "stay" as "cease work."[25] The king commemorates his grand work, Elizabeth, by releasing his subjects from their daily toil into festivity, a holiday with sanctified overtones. In effect, for one day, his subjects shall know the life of ease and song that Cranmer predicts that Elizabethans will enjoy, eating in safety under their own vines. Afterwards, courtiers and the king himself will sweat under the load of greatness; Anne Boleyn will be accused of adultery and executed; and Mary Tudor will steep the land in blood. But for one day English men and women will enjoy a respite from the curse of work to help the king crown the labor of his life—the begetting of Elizabeth. "He that of greatest works is finisher/ Oft does them by the weakest minister" (II. i. 136-37), Helena declares in *All's Well That Ends Well*. In *King Henry VIII*, it is "this little one," a babe, who "make[s] it Holy-day."

Considered as Shakespeare's words rather than Cranmer's, the oracle—and the play as a whole—can "make" the members of its audience in the sense that the drama molds their idea of themselves as English men and women, the products of Tudor historical process. Like Cranmer's oracle, Shakespeare's words also have the power to construct something special. They make up the playwright's creative labor: his distinctive work in the genre of dramatic history. As was the case at the end of *The Tempest*, this authorial labor requires the audience's participation. The Epilogue of *King Henry VIII* implies as much. The speaker of the Epilogue fears that

> All the expected good w'are like to hear
> For this play at this time, is only in
> The merciful construction of good women,
> For such a one we show'd 'em.
> (Epilogue, 8-11)

By the phrase "merciful construction of good women," the speaker asserts that only the generous interpretation of the play by praiseworthy women will rescue it from other (mostly male) spectators' bad reviews. The construction, the making of a play, depends upon the cooperation of the playwright's creative and the audience's empathetic labors. The greater inclination of women than men mercifully to construct the play *King Henry VIII* stems chiefly from the image of the good woman present in it. The "one" good woman that the play has depicted for women in the audience may be understood as a composite dramatic construction, Anne Boleyn and her babe Elizabeth.[26] This reading reminds female members of the audience of their roles as the primary makers and deliverers of life. Shakespeare invites the women in his audience to translate their life-making power into vitality animating his play, giving it longer stage life.

For some spectators (again perhaps mostly male), playgoing amounts to nothing more than a respite from labor, a reprieve during which they can catch up on their sleep. "Some come to take their ease," the speaker of the Epilogue admits, "And sleep an act or two":

> but those, we fear,
> W'have frighted with our trumpets; so 'tis clear,
> They'll say 'tis naught. . . .
> (Epilogue, 2-5)

Not understanding the kind of work a play can be, or the cooperative labor that gleaning its significance requires, certain, perhaps overworked playgoers regard it merely as an occasion for a personal holiday. But the play itself does not coincide with the twenty-four-hour "Holy-day" that King Henry declares. It requires an alert, relatively strenuous "construction" on the Jacobean playgoer's part, who afterward understands (if he or she chooses to understand) why his or her advantageous place in a century of historical process gives cause for merrymaking on the morrow, that is, if work allows and employers are gracious.

Notes

1 In this chapter, I follow the lead of recent critics of *King Henry VIII* in attributing the play to Shakespeare rather than to Shakespeare and Fletcher. G. Wilson Knight, *The Crown of Life: Essays in Interpretation of Shakespeare's Final Plays* (1947; rpt. New York: Barnes & Noble, 1966) 250-336, esp. 258-72; and Lee Bliss, "The Wheel of Fortune and the Maiden Phoenix of Shakespeare's *King Henry the Eighth*," *Journal of English Literary History* 42 (1975): 1-25, esp. 1, typically establish this precedent. For a review of the Shakespeare/Fletcher/*King Henry VIII* controversy, see *Evidence for Authorship*, ed. David V. Erdman and Ephrim G. Fogel (Ithaca, NY: Cornell UP, 1966) 457-78.

2 In *"Henry VIII* and the Dynamics of Spectacle," *Shakespeare Studies* 12 (1979): 229-46, Edward I. Berry concludes that Norfolk's narrated vision of the splendor of the Field of the Cloth of Gold "is an empty show, a kind of antimasque" (232).

3 John D. Cox, in *"Henry VIII* and the Masque," *Journal of English Literary History* 45 (1978): 390-409, asserts that "Norfolk's precious diction as he describes the Field of the Cloth of Gold is a rhetorical counterpart to the glittering show that Wolsey devised as a concealment of the flimsy peace between Henry and Francis I" (398).

4 The presence of the tempest imagery of the late romances in *Henry VIII* has been established by Robert Uphaus, *Beyond Tragedy: Structure and Experience in Shakespeare's Romances* (Lexington: UP of Kentucky, 1981) 125-27.

5 Linda McJ. Micheli, in "'Sit By Us': Visual Imagery and the Two Queens in *Henry VIII*," *Shakespeare Quarterly* 38 (1987): 452-66, notes that "the Old Lady functions in this scene much as the Nurse does in relation to Juliet, or Emilia in relation to Desdemona: her earthiness points up the youth and innocence of her companion" (460).

6 See Tom McBride, *"Henry VIII* as Machiavellian Romance," *Journal of English and Germanic Philology* 76 (1977): 26-39, esp. 30-31.

7 See Cyrus Hoy, "The Language of Fletcherian Tragicomedy," *Mirror Up to Shakespeare: Essays in Honour of G. R. Hibbard*, ed. J. C. Gray (Toronto: U of Toronto P, 1984) 99-113.

8 G. Wilson Knight judges that "Wolsey's attitude to the King's matrimonial adventures is left vague" (279)—an opinion echoed by S. C. Sen Gupta, *Shakespeare's Historical Plays* (Oxford: Oxford UP, 1964) 157; and by Eckhard Auberlen, "*King Henry VIII*: Shakespeare's Break with the 'Bluff-King-Harry' Tradition," *Anglia* 98 (1980): 319-47, esp. 337.

9 In "*Henry VIII* and the Ideal England," *Shakespeare Survey* 38 (1985): 131-43, Alexander Leggatt argues that Wolsey "encourages the King's divorce and then delays it" (135). Also holding this opinion are H. M. Richmond, "Shakespeare's *Henry VIII*: Romance Redeemed by History," *Shakespeare Studies* 4 (1968): 334-49, esp. 343; and Camille Slights, "The Politics of Conscience in *All is True* (or *Henry VIII*)," *Shakespeare Survey* 43 (1990): 59-68, esp. 59, 62.

10 The implications of literary womanhood's traditional task of weaving have been explored by Geoffrey Hartman, "The Voice of the Shuttle: Language from the Point of View of Literature," *Beyond Formalism: Literary Essays 1958-1970* (New Haven: Yale UP, 1970) 337-55.

11 Concerning the scene of Anne Boleyn's and the Old Lady's dialogue (II. iii), Muriel St. Clare Byrne, in "A Stratford Production: *Henry VIII*," *Shakespeare Survey* 3 (1950): 120-29, comments upon Tyrone Guthrie's staging: "Anne Bullen and the Old Lady entered upstage, and came down to the forestage left, where they sat and wound wool as they talked" (124). Such a conception offers an ironic counterpoint to Katherine's later weaving as a diversion for her troubled mind.

12 But cf. Northrop Frye, who claims in *A Natural Perspective: The Development of Shakespearean Comedy and Romance* (New York: Harcourt, Brace & World, 1965), that the song about Orpheus is "a reminder of the greater cycle that [Katherine] enters into in the vision at her death" (147-48).

13 John F. Danby, *Poets on Fortune's Hill: Studies in Sidney, Shakespeare, Beaumont and Fletcher* (1952; rpt. Port Washington, NY: Kennikat P, 1966) 80-82, 92-96.

14 A. Robin Bowers, in "'The Merciful Construction of Good Women': Katherine of Aragon and Pity in Shakespeare's *King Henry VIII*," *Christianity and Literature* 37 (1988): 29-51, esp. 40-41, has identified the presence of "religious art associated with the Assumption," especially as rendered by Titian and his imitators, in Queen Katherine's dream vision.

15 Concerning Katherine's final peevishness, Berry has astutely remarked that "as long as they remain on the stage of this world, it seems, the tragic figures of this play can be no more than 'half in heaven'" (241).

16 See especially the analysis of Alan R. Young, "Shakespeare's *Henry VIII* and the Theme of Conscience," *English Studies in Canada* 7 (1981): 38-53.

17 The argument that King Henry develops from a dependent monarch to a strong ruler in the course of Shakespeare's play was first advanced by Paul Bertram, "*Henry VIII*: The Conscience of the King," *In Defense of Reading*, ed. Reuben Brower and Richard Poirier (New York: Dutton, 1963) 153-73. It was developed by R. A. Foakes in his Arden *King Henry*

VIII (London: Methuen, 1964) lxi-lxii; and by Howard Felperin, *Shakespearean Romance* (Princeton: NJ: Princeton UP, 1972) 204-5.

18 The germ of this interpretation lies in *Pericles*. Boult claims that thunder will not awaken "beds of eels" as promptly as his proclamation of Marina's physical beauty will stir "the lewdly inclin'd" (*Per.* IV. ii. 142-44).

19 Anne Boleyn is described as a *Venus Genetrix* in this episode by Ronald Berman, "*King Henry the Eighth*: History and Romance," *English Studies* 48 (1967): 112-21, esp. 119.

20 Northrop Frye concludes that an "omnipotent and ruthless providence . . . is ready to tear the whole social and religious structure of England to pieces in order to get Queen Elizabeth born" (89-90).

21 The divine status of Cranmer's oracle has been established by Knight 330-36; Howard Felperin, "Shakespeare's *Henry VIII*: History as Myth," *Studies in English Literature* 6 (1966): 225-46, esp. 242-43; Uphaus 136-39; and by Leggatt 131-43.

22 In this respect, see William M. Baillie, "*Henry VIII*: A Jacobean History," *Shakespeare Studies* 12 (1979): 247-66, esp. 255-59.

23 Critics who regard Cranmer's oracle ironically, as a final example of unreliable speech in the play, include Frank V. Cespedes, "'We are one in fortunes': The Sense of History in *Henry VIII*," *English Literary Renaissance* 10 (1980): 413-38, esp. 416; and Peter L. Rudnytsky, "*Henry VIII* and the Deconstruction of History," *Shakespeare Survey* 43 (1990): 43-57, esp. 55-57.

24 In *The Theatre of Praise: The Panegyric Tradition in Seventeenth-Century English Drama* (Newark: U of Delaware P, 1986), Joanne Altieri concludes that, "whether we take him as Machiavellian or Platonic model, the last scene seems to require that we somehow see Henry VIII as the source of England's current greatness, the progenitor of the monarchical line that climaxes in James I, and therefore as the creator of a now-realized future" (60-61).

25 *The Riverside Shakespeare* 1016.

26 The "good woman" of the Epilogue is sometimes taken to refer to Queen Katherine. See, for example, Baillie 261; Clifford Leech, "The Structure of the Last Plays," *Shakespeare Survey* 11 (1958): 19-30, esp. 29; Frank Kermode, "What is *Henry VIII* About?" *Shakespeare the Histories: A Collection of Critical Essays*, ed. Eugene Waith (Englewood Cliffs, NJ: Prentice-Hall, 1965) 168-79, esp. 178-79; and Hugh M. Richmond, "The Feminism of Shakespeare's *Henry VIII*," *Essays in Literature* 6 (1979): 11-20, esp. 12.

Chapter 8

The Two Noble Kinsmen

At the beginning of *The Two Noble Kinsmen*, an undeniable call to perform the work of war produces in Theseus the troubled mind associated with Prospero and King Henry VIII. Even as Theseus and Hippolyta are in progress to their wedding, three mourning queens, their husbands killed by Creon and the bones left unburied, interrupt the ceremony, imploring the duke to punish Creon and inter their husbands' remains. The sequence of events at the beginning of *The Two Noble Kinsmen* resembles the pattern established early in act IV of *The Tempest*. Even as the memory of Caliban causes Prospero to abandon the Masque of Ceres, producing in him a troubled mind that leads to the apocalyptic vision of the revels speech, so the death and discord personified by the three queens blight the pageantry of Theseus' wedding, prompting his gloomy reflections on grief and time—the thoughts of a darkly stirred mind. Theseus recognizes one of the queens as the widow of King Capaneus. "The day/ That he should marry you," Theseus tells her,

> at such a season
> As now it is with me, I met your groom
> By Mars's altar. You were that time fair;
> Not Juno's mantle fairer than your tresses,
> Nor in more bounty spread her. Your wheaten wreath
> Was then nor thresh'd nor blasted; Fortune at you
> Dimpled her cheek with smiles.
> (I. i. 59-66)

"O grief and time,/ Fearful consumers, you will all devour!" (I. i. 69-70), Theseus concludes.

Fearing that Theseus has lost consideration of their specific plea in broad moralizing, First Queen kneels again, hoping that a god will powerfully infuse Theseus' manhood, making him her undertaker (I. i. 71-74). "O, no knees, none, widow!" Theseus exclaims,

> Unto the helmeted Bellona use them,
> And pray for me your soldier.
> Troubled I am.
> (I. i. 74-77)

In both *The Tempest* and *The Two Noble Kinsmen*, the rich ceremony associated with a wedding is displaced by the celebrant's melancholy thought that he too will one day fade away. In both cases, the spectacle interrupted contains special poetry banishing discord from the marriage pageant. Just as Iris in the Masque tells Ceres that Venus and Cupid, agents of carnal love, are removed from Prospero's spectacle, so in *The Two Noble Kinsmen* the singer in the final stanza of his epithalamion—traditionally attributed to Fletcher—banishes the birds of discord from the bride's house (I. i. 19-24).[1] Yet discord returns to blast the pageants in the forms of Caliban and the three troublesome queens. Here, however, Shakespeare reverses the dramaturgy of *The Tempest*. The thoughts of vengeance that the memory of Caliban stirs are transformed into virtuous convictions with Ariel's aid. Theseus' nuptial mindset, on the contrary, becomes, under the queens' prodding, one dedicated to vengeance. In *The Two Noble Kinsmen*, no counterpart of Ariel intervenes to clear Theseus' troubled mind and rededicate him to virtue and mercy.

Begged by the women present, including his bride Hippolyta and her sister Emilia, to revenge the wrongs done to the queens, Theseus resolves to replace one kind of work with another type of labor. "I will give you comfort/ To give your dead lords graves," he promises the widows; "the which to do/ Must make some work with Creon" (I. i. 148-50). In the responses of the three queens to this remark, Shakespeare resurrects the idea of war as work:

> *1. Queen.* And that work presents itself to th' doing:
> Now 'twill take form, the heats are gone to-morrow.
> Then, bootless toil must recompense itself
> With its own sweat; now he's secure,
> Not dreams we stand before your puissance

| | Wrinching our holy begging in our eyes
To make petition clear. |
| --- | --- |
| 2. *Queen.* | Now you may take him
Drunk with his victory. |
| 3. *Queen.* | And his army full
Of bread and sloth. |
| | (I. i. 151-59) |

The preoccupation of war work, such as seizing the militarily opportune moment to avoid wasted toil, focuses Theseus' troubled thoughts, giving them outlet and relief. The queens' dialogue counterpoints war work and sloth. And yet sloth is not Theseus' alternative to the queens' plea. Shakespeare in other late plays portrays sexual intercourse and the begetting of children as a special kind of work. This is the task that the queens' plea interrupts and supersedes. "Prorogue this business we are going about," Hippolyta begs the groom, "and hang/ Your shield afore your heart" (I. i. 196-97). The "business" to which Hippolyta refers is not simply the ceremony of marriage; her word also covers the activity of the wedding night, a business that (in literature at least) results in the creation of new life. That Shakespeare contrasts one kind of labor with another type of work in the scene is evident in the two senses of "business" upon which he plays. "Meet us with/ The forces you can raise," Theseus commands his captain Artesius,

> where we shall find
> The moi'ty of a number for a business
> More bigger-look'd.
> (I. i. 212-15)

The stirring, the troubling of Theseus' mind on his marriage day, which issues in his promise to perform the work of war, supplants what the play's Prologue has called "first night's stir" (Prologue, 6)—the work of love making and child begetting.

So committed are Shakespeare and Fletcher to the counterpointing of two kinds of work in their play that they build it into the tension between the vehicles and tenors of their metaphors. For example, in a part of the play usually attributed to Fletcher, a Messenger describes one of the warriors of Theseus' tourney in these terms:

> his arms are brawny,
> Lin'd with strong sinews; to the shoulder-piece
> Gently they swell, like women new conceiv'd,
> Which speaks him prone to labor, never fainting
> Under the weight of arms.
> (IV. ii. 126-30)

The warrior's capacity for war work is expressed in terms of the labor of childbirth, the tension or incongruity between tenor and vehicle indicative of the difference between destructive and creative work.[2]

The playwright—Shakespeare again—keeps his focus on work in the second scene of the play, which shifts to Thebes and Palamon's and Arcite's complaints over their enforced idleness. First, Arcite counsels that they leave the city and its temptations, which "sully" the "gloss of youth" (I. ii. 5). Abstinence is as shameful as incontinence in his opinion, "and to follow/ The common stream,"

> 'twould bring us to an eddy
> Where we should turn or drown; if labor through,
> Our gain but life and weakness.
> (I. ii. 9-12)

For Arcite, engaging in the pastimes of the "common stream" of Thebans would involve debilitating labor. Palamon then explains that performing the work of the soldier would likewise prove unrewarding.

Like the veterans become beggars that were a common dismal sight in Elizabeth's and James' London, mutilated soldiers, cheated of the spoils of war, populate Thebes. "What strange ruins," Palamon asserts, "Since first we went to school,"

> may we perceive
> Walking in Thebes! scars and bare weeds
> The gain o' th' martialist, who did propound
> To his bold ends honor and golden ingots,
> Which though he won, he had not; and now flurted
> By peace, for whom he fought, who then shall offer
> To Mars's so scorn'd altar?
> (I. ii. 13-20)

Palamon's depressing analysis of the barren toil of war, a truism for many of Shakespeare's contemporaries, graphically illustrates First Queen's earlier claim that the worker of war must recompense himself with his own sweat if he fails to capitalize upon the opportune military moment.[3] Palamon's word picture of Theban streets suggests that the soldier's personally fruitless labor is more the rule than the exception. The recollection of the Queen's remark provoked by Palamon's moralizing creates dramatic suspense by suggesting the odds against Theseus' campaign, at least as regards his soldiers' welfare. Implicitly the life-creating work that he has abandoned for war appears more precious.

In light of his negative view of war's effects, Palamon's remedy for the social injustice that pains him—renewed warfare—comes as something of a surprise. "I do bleed/ When such [neglected, maimed soldiers] I meet," he exclaims,

> and wish great Juno would
> Resume her ancient fit of jealousy
> To get the soldier work, that peace might purge
> For her repletion, and retain anew
> Her charitable heart, now hard, and harsher
> Than strife or war could be.[4]
> (I. ii. 20-26)

In the previous scene, First Queen described her wish that a god might incline Theseus to wage war by putting mercy—pity for the Queens and their lords' bones—into his manhood (I. i. 71-74). Conversely Palamon believes that new wars, more bloodshed, would soften Theban hearts, paradoxically grown hard during a long peace. In Shakespeare's conception, the bloodletting of warfare represents a way of curing a body politic made sick by the luxuries and corruptions of a long peace. And yet Palamon's remedy remains doubtful, especially for the soldier. In the blood required by his renewed performance of war work, he becomes the member sacrificed for his community's spiritual health.

Arcite seeks to return to a broader view, asking Palamon whether the unrewarded soldier is the only figure of decay encountered in Thebes. "Perceive you none that do arouse your pity/ But th'unconsider'd soldier?" he inquires (I. ii. 30-31). "Yes, I pity/ Decays where e'er I find them," Palamon replies,

>   but such most
> That sweating in an honorable toil
> Are paid with ice to cool 'em.
>   (I. ii. 31-34)

That Palamon should later pray to Venus rather than Mars for success in the fight for Emilia reflects his earlier doubt about the value of the warrior's work. It is Arcite, who shows no signs of Palamon's skepticism, who prays to Mars and whose labors in the combat go unrewarded. While he wins the combat, he never gets to enjoy the fruit of his toil—Emilia.

For the moment, noting that Palamon casts a dark pall over the soldier's work is enough. That work is further questioned when Palamon and Arcite fight with Creon's troops against Theseus' army. The kinsmen have just agreed to leave Thebes, not only because of their hatred of their tyrant uncle Creon but also because the city offers them no uncorrupted employment (I. ii. 34-42), when Valerius informs them of Theseus' sudden assault and the enraged king's calling for his nephews. When Arcite complains that the immorality of the uncle they are asked to defend saps his strength, Palamon replies, "Our services stand now for Thebes, not Creon" (I. ii. 99). Arcite, however, has depicted Thebes as a cesspool of vice, a city similar to Cleon's Tharsus in *Pericles*.[5] The weakness of their attempts to rationalize fighting against Theseus is apparent from Palamon's concluding despair (I. ii. 111-13). Their moral quandry and their subsequent reckless committing of themselves to "chance" and the "event" (I. ii. 113-16) illustrate the corrosion surrounding the soldier's work. Palamon wished that "great Juno would/ Resume her ancient fit of jealousy/ To get the soldier work." Ironically, he almost immediately gets his wish, but not in any positive way that he could have imagined. He thought that war might purge (through bloodletting) a sick peace; now he is reduced to claiming that

>   the blood we venture
> Should be as for our health, which were not spent,
> Rather laid out for purchase.
>   (I. ii. 109-11)

The purchase implied is of honor, but for Arcite the war begins a chain of events in which he buys death rather than his beloved Emilia. The honor that Arcite's lion-like war deeds buy him in Theseus' opinion saves his life, yet this preservation contains his love torment, his quarrel with his kinsman, and his death empty-handed of his prize.

Not surprisingly, Palamon's and Arcite's brief war work does not dispel the feelings of uselessness that afflicted them in Thebes. Imprisoned by the victor Theseus (his dubious "purchase" of war), they have no worldly task. Unlike captive Ferdinand, they have no assigned work by which they might refine and prove their virtues. "All valiant uses," Palamon laments, "In us two here shall perish" (II. ii. 51-53). "Shall we make worthy uses of this place/ That all men hate so much?" (II. ii. 69-70), Arcite questions. Palamon's solution recalls the mental labors of Shakespeare's Richard II:[6]

> What worthy blessing
> Can be, but our imaginations
> May make it ours? And here being thus together,
> We are an endless mine to one another;
> We are one another's wife, ever begetting
> New births of love; we are father, friends, acquaintance;
> We are, in one another, families:
> I am your heir, and you are mine; this place
> Is our inheritance.
> (II. ii. 76-84)

Lonely, uncomforted in Pomfret castle, Richard II attempts to make his brain the female to his masculine soul in order to beget "A generation of still-breeding thoughts" that might "people this little world" (V. v. 5-10). Yet this imaginative work, the intellectual equivalent of the labor of child getting and childbirth, merely deepens the distressed king's confusion. Because "no thought is contented" (V. v. 11), the divine and ambitious "people" that Richard hammers out self destruct, and the king and beggar within him—envious of each other—futilely transform themselves back and forth into their opposite (V. v. 1-38). Instead of using their masculine souls and female brains to beget consoling companions, Palamon proposes that the kinsmen imaginatively make themselves "one another's wife, ever begetting/ New births of love." This imaginative labor will be their task in prison. By shifting into the several complementary roles of the family, Palamon and Arcite could occupy themselves by begetting the several virtues associated with family pairings such as husband and wife and father and son.

The appearance of Emilia gathering flowers outside their cell's window soon leads the kinsmen to quarrel over her, putting an end to Palamon's scheme. That the sight of Emilia should preclude its implementation is fitting. As an attractive woman, she is the natural complement to the kinsmen who represents in herself the literal, more satisfying, labors of sexual begetting and childbirth. Arcite later recalls Palamon's notion of the way by which the kinsmen might regeneratively occupy themselves in their cell when he says, just before the climactic tourney,

> I am in labor
> To push your name, your ancient love, our kindred,
> Out of my memory; and i' th' self-same place
> To seat something I would confound.
> (V. i. 25-28)

The image of childbirth labor recurs, with the faculty of memory taking the place of the womb; but in this case Arcite works to decreate—to erase love and obliterate the ties of kindred (rather than creating them as Palamon in prison proposes). This last-act retrieval of Palamon's birthlabor conceit amounts to a reversal of its value, signaling the depth of Arcite's loss of affection for his friend.[7]

The uses to which the kinsmen put their vision of Emilia differ. Palamon and Arcite reprise the relationship of Arviragus and Guiderius—and, more faintly, that of Lysander and Demetrius. More insightful and ratiocinative than Arcite, Palamon corresponds to poetic Arviragus vis-à-vis rough Guiderius. Arcite and Guiderius resemble each other in their greater inclination to fight and rush headlong into battle.[8] In keeping with his more refined character, Palamon worships Emilia as a goddess (II. ii. 133-35). Sexual use does not appear to be part of his vision of her; idolizing her ethereal beauty will be his task. On the contrary, "I will not, as you do—to worship her/ As she is heavenly and a blessed goddess," Arcite protests; "I love her as a woman, to enjoy her" (II. ii. 162-64). Arcite would use Emilia in the familiar Jacobean sense of sexual intercourse, a sense articulated later in the play by the mad Jailer's Daughter when she says, concerning her beloved Palamon,

> Let him do
> What he will with me, so he use me kindly,
> For use me so he shall, or I'll proclaim him,
> And to his face, no man.
> (II. vi. 28-31)

Arcite never gets to use Emilia in the fashion he desires; death precludes his sexual task.

Like warfare, love between the sexes in *The Two Noble Kinsmen* bears a negative relationship to work. Fletcher's characterization of the Jailer's Daughter develops the notion that sexual love is a madness that renders the lover unfit for daily work. "All's char'd"—all chores (tasks) are ended—"when he is gone" (III. ii. 21), she complains of Palamon. Made near-suicidal by passion, she concludes that "All offices [tasks] are done/ Save what I fail in" (III. ii. 36-37). Later, roaming the countryside, deserted by the beloved kinsman whom she has freed, she hallucinates:

> Where am I now?
> Yonder's the sea, and there's a ship. How't tumbles!
> And there's a rock lies watching under water;
> Now, now, it beats upon it—now, now, now!
> There's a leak sprung, a sound one. How they cry!
> Open her before the wind! you'll lose all else.
> Up with a course or two, and tack about, boys!
> Good night, good night, y'are gone.
> (III. iv. 4-11)

The Daughter evokes a nautical image of labor lost consistent with her previous sentiments. It recalls the portrait of the sailors' futile work in the opening scene of *The Tempest,* an analogue to which Shakespeare may have directed Fletcher's attention. By invoking the symbol of the sea tempest, the preeminently Shakespearean cynosure of romance, Fletcher imports archetypal stir into *The Two Noble Kinsmen,* where it becomes a metaphor for the radical affliction of sexual desire. So dislocating is this affliction that it disqualifies the passionate lover from worldly tasks, making any labor attempted lost. The trajectory of the Daughter's character in the play predicts Arcite's ultimately fruitless toil of love.

Without a task, the Jailer's Daughter, her reason undone, undergoes a pastoral hypostasis. The Wooer at length describes the fixation of her passion in her protracted flower gathering and singing of sad love songs. Without an earthly use, the Daughter's passion hypostatizes her into a kind of pastoral goddess. According to the Wooer,

> The place
> Was knee-deep where she sat; her careless tresses
> A wreath of bulrush rounded; about her stuck
> Thousand fresh water-flowers of several colors,
> That methought she appear'd like the fair nymph
> That feeds the lake with waters, or as Iris
> Newly dropp'd down from heaven.
> (IV. i. 82-88)

Thus removed from a world of flux and frenzy, the static Daughter is the "innocent" of the Wooer's vision (IV. i. 41). But it is not long before her sight of the distasteful suitor drives her into deeper water, from which he rescues her. The Daughter's mad reevocation of a ship at sea concludes this episode. For once her father, brother, and friends flatter her madness by recreating the shouts and commands of sailors at work, attempting to sail a bark to safe harbor (IV. i. 142-52). The recreation of tempestuous stir contrasts sharply with the hypostatized pastoral image of the innocent maiden. The Daughter's and relatives' verbal portrayal of life-preserving work throws into relief the maiden's idle, unproductive flower gathering, a symptom of her madness.

If act IV of *The Two Noble Kinsmen* is mostly (or even wholly) by Fletcher, the peculiar dramaturgy under discussion reveals a firm grasp of Shakespeare's late-play interests and techniques. The counterpointing of stir and stasis recurs in the following scene involving the Jailer's Daughter (IV. iii). Distractedly imagining a voyage to the underworld, she evokes an image of idleness: "we shall come there, and do nothing all day long but pick flowers with Proserpine" (IV. iii. 24-25), she exclaims. Immediately afterward, she gives voice to a turbulent hell, violently stirred by pain:

> Alas, 'tis a sore life they have i' th' tother place, such burning, frying, boiling, hissing, howling, chatt'ring, cursing! O, they have shrowd measure! take heed: if one be mad, or hang or drown themselves, thither they go—Jupiter bless us!—and there shall we be put in a cauldron of lead and usurers' grease, amongst a whole million of cutpurses, and there boil like a gammon of bacon that will never be enough.
> (IV. iii. 31-39)

This frantic vision suggests the Daughter's motive for hypostatizing herself; the process amounts to insulation from the suffering dealt by passion, an adjunct of the recurring tempest called life. "What pushes are we wenches driven to/ When fifteen once has found us" (II. iv. 6-7), the Daughter cries upon first feeling passion for Palamon. Unfortunately the passion of love attracts her to a man who tends to idealize and worship women, who shows no desire to put the Daughter to the sexual use she craves. Ironically, driven mad by her frustration, she transforms herself into an idealized figure, a pastoral goddess, whom he might under different circumstances be able to love.

As a hypostatized pastoral goddess, an innocent, the Daughter represents the counterpart of the prepubescent girls that Emilia depicts. In Emilia's words, she and her friend Flavina as eleven year olds "were things innocent,"

> What she lik'd
> Was then of me approv'd, what not, condemn'd,
> No more arraignment. The flow'r that I would pluck
> And put between my breasts (O then but beginning
> To swell about the blossom), she would long
> Till she had such another, and commit it
> To the like innocent cradle, where phoenix-like
> They died in perfume.
> (I. iii. 64-71)

Paradoxically this innocent hypostasis occurs at two extremes—prior to love (in its absence) and at its most frenzied pitch. In each case, the hypostasis precludes the performance of tasks by which the doer might develop his or her character. Until Flavina's premature death, she and Emilia mime one another's idle sports and recreations. The Daughter, we have seen, appears caught in an endless round of wreath making. Strictly speaking, one could say that these generalizations apply only to the play's women. For male lovers such as Palamon and Arcite, the work of warfare provides an outlet from this impasse, creating a diversion for love (albeit an undesirable one).

The counterpointing of stir and stasis in *The Two Noble Kinsmen* climaxes in Arcite's, Palamon's, and Emilia's prayers before the altars respectively of Mars, Venus, and Diana. That Arcite's invocation of Mars is meant to represent a call to bloody work, the contrary of pastoral hypostasis, is made clear by his wish that he and his men not be "snails"—emblems of sloth—and by his belief that "force and great feat/ Must put my garland on, where she sticks/ The queen of flowers" (V. i. 43-45). The great stir of warfare can be sensibly apprehended in Arcite's stirred (and stirring) vision of the god Mars:

> Thou mighty one, that with thy power hast turn'd
> Green Neptune into purple,
> Comets prewarn, whose havoc in vast field
> Unearthed skulls proclaim, whose breath blows down
> The teeming Ceres' foison, who dost pluck
> With hand armipotent from forth blue clouds
> The mason'd turrets, that both mak'st and break'st
> The stony girths of cities. . . .
> (V. i. 49-56)

A powerful energy even more obviously infuses Palamon's prayer to Venus, whom he makes clear he has always served chastely (V. i. 97-107). For Palamon, Venus symbolizes a carnal passion that "choke[s] Mars' drum" and makes "the king/ To be his subject's vassal" (V. i. 80, 83-84). Palamon labors under a load, the debilitating legacy of Venus:

> Take to thy grace
> Me thy vow'd soldier, who do bear thy yoke
> As 'twere a wreath of roses, yet is heavier
> Than lead itself, stings more than nettles.
> (V. i. 94-97)

In his opinion, Venus can compel her sometimes violently twisted human subjects to the generation of new life:[9]

> I knew a man
> Of eighty winters—this I told them—who
> A lass of fourteen brided. 'Twas thy power
> To put life into dust: the aged cramp
> Had screw'd his square foot round,
> The gout had knit his fingers into knots,
> Torturing convulsions from his globy eyes
> Had almost drawn their spheres, that what was life
> In him seem'd torture. This anatomy
> Had by his young fair fere a boy, and I
> Believ'd it was his, for she swore it was,
> And who would not believe her?
> (V. i. 107-18)

Palamon describes Venus' regenerative spirit rather than the misuse of her gifts in wasted acts of lust. Venus can unknot, momentarily at least, muscles and bones grotesquely deformed by old age, a feat of undoing by doing. Still, there is something grotesque in the vision of an eighty-year-old man, knotted and convulsed by age, making love to a fourteen-year-old girl.[10] Venus' rule could easily feel like tyranny to a girl so positioned.

Respectively destructive and regenerative, the work of Mars and Venus involves stirring, often strenuous effort. The contrariety is not neatly divided by the two gods but occurs in the regular course of their operation. Mars, for example, "both mak'st and break'st/ The stony girths of cities" (V. i. 55-56). The fear of Mars that drives citizens to construct great walls converts to the rage of attackers bent on leveling them. Mars initiates a distinctly unproductive, self-defeating round of activities, a martial spinning of wheels. This impression is congruent with Shakespeare's generally negative portrayal of the work of war in the play. While the work of Venus does not so clearly involve such cancellation (although Palamon implies that the flames of lust can be self-consuming, i. e., through venereal disease), her devotee complains that serving her involves sweating under a heavy load—bearing a wreath of roses "heavier/ Than lead itself." Palamon's startling conceit makes Venus' service unpleasant toil. Erotic lovemaking feels like work to the idealistic kinsman. In the weighted diction of Palamon's verbal portrait of a seventy-year-old man abusing young lays of love, Venus' breaking of decorum, her role as disorderer, becomes apparent (as it does in the grotesque January and May union of an eighty year old with a fourteen year old).

Coming after the tainted praise of Mars' and Venus' work, Emilia's prayer to Diana appears attractive, mainly because chastity is depicted as a hypostatized virtue; at least it appears so in comparison to previously defined divine traits. As the goddess of stasis, of the still, white moment, Diana offers chaste contemplation rather than work of the martial or venereal kind to her devotees. Removed, abstracted from the world of flux, Diana is the goddess of refined meditation rather than stirred action. "O sacred, shadowy, cold, and constant queen," Emilia begins,

> Abandoner of revels, mute, contemplative,
> Sweet, solitary, white as chaste, and pure
> As wind-fann'd snow. . . .
>
> (V. i. 137-40)

Unlike the cameos of Mars and Venus, Emilia's prayer to Diana contains no description of either the goddess' influence upon mortals or their stirrings under her influence. Diana remains primarily a deity of absence, of nondoing—the "Abandoner of revels." As represented, her deity poses the attractive alternative to the work of Mars and Venus.

This tipping of the scales toward chastity, away from love and war, has major implications for Shakespeare's and Fletcher's view of themselves as workers of plays, especially as a single worker made up of two parts in collaboration. *The Two Noble Kinsmen* is no exception to the rule that Shakespeare metadramatically explores his relation to his craft in his late plays. In the play's Prologue, attributed to Fletcher, Chaucer is characterized as a "noble breeder and a pure," not only the begetter of *The Knight's Tale*, a Canterbury story "constant to eternity" (Prologue 10, 14) but also the father of Shakespeare's and Fletcher's play. Once again play making is likened to child getting. The extent of exact reproduction becomes the dramatic question. In this case, Shakespeare and Fletcher have not strived to imitate exactly Chaucer's work. "For to say truth," the Prologue admits,

> it were an endless thing,
> And too ambitious, to aspire to him,
> Weak as we are, and almost breathless swim
> In this deep water.
>
> (Prologue, 22-25)

During their dialogue on the difficulty of living in a vicious city, Palamon responds to Arcite's fear that false fashions corrupt manners by proclaiming,

> What need I
> Affect another's gait, which is not catching
> Where there is faith? or to be fond upon
> Another's way of speech, when by mine own
> I may be reasonably conceiv'd; sav'd too,
> Speaking it truly? Why am I bound
> By any generous bond to follow him
> Follows his tailor, haply so long until
> The follow'd make pursuit?
>
> (I. ii. 44-52)

Palamon's attractive speech against imitation is one of several in the play that strengthens Shakespeare's and Fletcher's portrayal of themselves as breeders of a child related to but substantially different from Chaucer's honored offspring (bred in conjunction with Boccaccio).

By claiming that their play has a "noble breeder," father Chaucer, Fletcher casts himself and Shakespeare as a single organism into the role of the passive, germinating female. The result of this intercourse is a male offspring paradoxically likened to a chaste maiden. Concerning this play/child, "You shall hear/ Scenes," the Prologue claims, "though below his [Chaucer's] art, may yet appear/ Worth two hours' travail" (Prologue, 27-29). By the word "travail," the speaker mainly refers to the audience's work of apprehension and interpretation. Nevertheless, the word's customary meaning concerns birth labor, the implication being that Chaucer and Fletcher/Shakespeare labored a short time to deliver their burden: a chaste child, likened to a girl with her maidenhead intact.

By focusing on the play/child's yet unblemished purity, Fletcher associates his and Shakespeare's work with Diana, whose virtue of chastity appears poetically preferred in the multiple prayer scene of the play. Their chaste dramatic work, however, is about to be violated:

> New plays and maidenheads are near akin—
> Much follow'd both, for both much money gi'n,
> If they stand sound and well; and a good play
> (Whose modest scenes blush on his marriage-day,
> And shake to lose his honor) is like her
> That after holy tie and first night's stir,
> Yet still is modesty, and still retains
> More of the maid to sight than husband's pains.
> We pray our play may be so.
> (Prologue, 1-9)

Playwrights and actors, considered corporately, and their audiences engage in an imaginative intercourse that replicates the creative intercourse between a breeder like Chaucer and passive, "female" matter—Shakespeare and Fletcher. The playwrights create something like an undefiled maiden for the sensual enjoyment of paying customers, who will initiate a "first night's stir." A play's opening performance is likened to its "marriage-day" (Prologue, 4); it is then that the audience/groom figuratively copulates with it, the aforementioned "two hours' travail" amounting to the "husband's pains" (Prologue, 8). Both the form and content of Palamon's prayer to Venus stress the venereal stir; in act V, the still whiteness of chastity appears to be preferred over such stir, which possesses negative, painful overtones. A certain cynicism attaches to the notion of playwrights making chaste plays in order to earn money from their gross violation; such a conception risks turning Shakespeare and Fletcher into pimps, versions of the Pander and Bawd of *Pericles*—men tolerant of the hypocrisy inherent in an often violated and degraded play that *outwardly* appears pure. Such a tolerance may spring from the need to believe that the artist's child, his work, has not been sullied by the contemptible (but necessary because paying) crowd. So depicted, such an art-child scarcely does credit to Chaucer, even if it is not hissed, or to his original, eternal progeny—*The Knight's Tale*. The speaker of the Prologue fears that Chaucer will cry out from underground:

> "O, fan
> From me the witless chaff of such a writer
> That blasts my bays and my fam'd works makes lighter
> Than Robin Hood!"
> (Prologue, 18-21)

In short, the Prologue of *The Two Noble Kinsmen* calculatingly devalues Shakespeare's and Fletcher's artistic labor.[11]

The reason for the devaluation may lie in the collaborators' skeptical appraisal of the artistic merit of collaborated works. As many commentators have noted, the play abounds in images of collaboration and competition. For example, Emilia portrays Pirithous' preoccupation with his beloved Theseus in terms of unsynchronized coordination:

> How his longing
> Follows his friend: since his depart, his sports,
> Though craving seriousness and skill, pass'd slightly
> His careless execution, where nor gain
> Made him regard, or loss consider, but
> Playing o'er business in his hand, another
> Directing in his head, his mind nurse equal
> To these so diff'ring twins. Have you observ'd him
> Since our great lord departed?
> (I. iii. 26-34)

Pirithous' mind may be "nurse equal" to his head and hand; nevertheless, his great worry makes them "diff'ring twins"—unsynchronized members of a single organism. The speaker of the Prologue has portrayed the authors of *The Two Noble Kinsmen* as a corporate playwright, the mate of breeding Chaucer. The implication follows that only the most intense, pure love of two male friends for one another can assure the coordination of the head and hand necessary in the case of collaborating writers for the successful execution of the details of dramatic design over the span of five acts.

Late in the play, in a scene ascribed to Shakespeare, Theseus describes the kinsmen's competition for Emilia in terms of a traditional artistic metaphor:

> I have heard
> Two emulous Philomels beat the ear o' th' night
> With their contentious throats, now one the higher,
> Anon the other, then again the first,

> And by and by out-breasted, that the sense
> Could not be judge between 'em. So it far'd
> Good space between these kinsmen; till heavens did
> Make hardly one the winner.
>
> (V. iii. 123-30)

One commentator on the play has gone so far as to argue that this passage reveals that the collaboration of an unknown dramatist (Nathan Field?) and Fletcher issued from an artistic challenge and competition, with a prize awarded by unknown judges to the playwright most successful as "Shakespeare" in implementing his part of an agreed-upon, overall design.[12] The claim lacks proof and remains doubtful. Still, auditors are tempted to hear the nightingale metaphor metadramatically, as Shakespeare's comment on his collaboration with Fletcher in writing the play. Rather than coordination, the image is of artistic competition nevertheless so friendly and intimate that two voices blend in a single musical utterance, resistant to analysis of its separate parts.[13] The examination of the play conducted thus far in this chapter has demonstrated a remarkable familiarity on Fletcher's part with the details and leitmotifs of Shakespeare's last plays.[14] Nevertheless, it is doubtful that Shakespeare and Fletcher loved one another to the degree necessary for perfectly synchronizing a corporate author's head and hand in the production of a play. Fletcher's friendship with Beaumont may have led to their rooming together, even to the sharing of a wench; but it remains doubtful that his acquaintance with Shakespeare reached this pitch of intimacy. No record or apocryphal story exists of Shakespeare's and Fletcher's relationship. By 1613, Shakespeare most likely had retired to Stratford and to his wife, grown daughters, and their families. Possibly one of the collaborators traveled to a distant city to participate in the composing of *The Two Noble Kinsmen*.

Certain inconsistencies in characterization in *The Two Noble Kinsmen* support the notion of a less-than-intimate collaboration between Shakespeare and Fletcher. While a remarkable carry over of poetic imagery, diction, and thematic content appears in the two established authorial shares of the play, certain scenes—almost all of them purportedly Fletcher's—show signs of a lapse of artistic control. The most noteworthy of these slippages occurs in act III, scene iii, the episode in which the nobleness of Arcite is shown in his bringing food and a file for the chains of the kinsman he plans to fight afterwards for the love of Emilia. The dialogue of this scene possesses an unShakespearean ring, resembling instead the flaccid talk of gallants that Fletcher was later to popularize. Shakespeare had taken pains to distinguish Palamon's ideal worship of woman from Arcite's sensual desire, but in this scene Palamon proposes a toast to the wenches (evidently quite a few!) that he and Arcite have sexually known.[15] What follows is the bawdy conversation of two gallants familiar with the ways of the town (III. iii. 28-42). Fletcher's image of two wenching gallants contradicts Shakespeare's portrayal of Palamon's and Arcite's unbesmirched virtue in Thebes, whose corruption they seek to flee in order to keep themselves morally clean.[16] This artistic lapse—along with others—challenges Shakespeare's image of ideal artistic competition, validating instead Fletcher's midplay metaphor for dramatic collaboration.

Gerrold's labor, his entertainment for Theseus, amounts to a collaborated work—one made by the joint efforts of the schoolmaster and the morris dancers. During his part of the entertainment, the "oration," Gerrold asks Theseus to look "right and straight"

> Upon this mighty *Morr*—of mickle weight—
> *Is*—now comes in, which being glu'd together
> Makes *Morris*, and the cause that we came hither.
> (III. v. 117-20)

While this utterance mainly illustrates a-la-Holofernes the philological pedantry of Gerrold, it secondarily presents an image of unideal collaboration, of an artifact not organically unified but made of parts figuratively "glu'd together." Significantly, that part of the entertainment not of Gerrold's making threatens to ruin the whole. "Have my rudiments/ Been labor'd so long with ye" (III. v. 3-4), Gerrold asks, dissatisfied with his performers' rehearsal. When he learns that the dancer Cicely, who is essential to the morris dance, has disappeared, he exclaims, "We have been *fatuus* [foolish], and labored vainly" (III. v. 41).[17] Ironically, the lesser artist Fletcher may have been the partner harboring doubts about the quality of a collaborated play. The devalued images of playmaking in the Prologue attributed to Fletcher strengthen the assumption of doubts on his part. So too does the fact that Gerrold's entertainment is essentially derived from the second antimasque of Beaumont's *Inner Temple and Gray's Inn Mask* (1613). The importation of Beaumont's material in a sense makes this part of the scene a collaboration between Beaumont and Fletcher. Fittingly, Gerrold's remark about a "glu'd together" artifact is made in the context of a pre-existing entertainment somewhat roughly affixed to Shakespeare's and Fletcher's play.

Fletcher thus, perhaps in contrast to Shakespeare, qualifies the value of both the labor that goes into collaborating on the writing of a play as well as the produced work itself. His implied attitude mirrors the systematic depiction in the play of the lost labors of love and war. In fact, Gerrold's work operates to underscore the notion of lost labor. By indulging in the bombastic verse and comically excessive alliteration reminiscent of Bottom and his crew's performance of *Pyramus and Thisbe,* Gerrold (and Fletcher) make the entertainment bad art, art so hackneyed that it invites Theseus' sarcastic response. Theseus answers Gerrold's "All hail, sweet ladies!" with the pun "This is a cold beginning" (III. v. 100-1); and he replies, after hearing the blown oration, to Gerrold's invitation that he observe the morris dance with the quip, best laced by the actor with thick irony or a knowing wink, "Ay, ay, by any means, dear domine" (III. v. 135). As far as the intentions of the entertainment's maker are concerned, the labor fails to move Theseus to feel aesthetic pleasure or admiration for the craftsman. Additionally, the turbulence of sexuality threatens the artist's labor, the work he has made. The Bavian, the ape who performs as a stock character in the morris dance, signifies raw sexuality with his "long tool" (III. v. 132), a giant penis. Gerrold specifically mentions this obscene property of the Bavian. During the performance of the morris dance, the Bavian's disruptive behavior threatens the formal design of the work. In the morris dance, this threatening is a calculated part of an aesthetic pattern; in fact, it constitutes a microcosm of other instances in the play of sexuality's pressure against labored attempts to contain it.

Theseus' ceremony for settling the rival claims on Emilia, whereby each kinsman and his supporters strive by combat to force their adversaries to touch a pyramid, reflects his effort to regulate the chaos unleashed by sexual desire. His calling the kinsmen's performance of his ceremony a "noble work" (V. i. 6) indicates that he at least regards his task as creating the conditions by which they might labor civilly, even religiously, to resolve their quarrel. His stipulation, however, that the loser and all his friends shall lose their heads makes this Theseus different from his namesake in *A Midsummer Night's Dream*. That Theseus gave evidence of his reputation as antiquity's man of reason by translating the Athenian law against Hermia from death to seclusion in a nunnery. By pronouncing such a ghastly penalty for losing Emilia (why should all of the losing kinsman's knights die?), the Theseus of Shakespeare's and Fletcher's play irrationally implants fatalism in the very ceremony designed to control it, supposedly in a civilized way.[18] Theseus' project avoids two deaths (Palamon's and Arcite's) by producing many on the losing side. Despite the disorder latent in his ceremony, Theseus commands Pirithous to "order" the field of tourney (IV. ii. 150). The Messenger's lengthy verse portraits of the magnificent knights who cast their lots with Palamon and Arcite exist to accentuate the waste inherent in Theseus' ceremony. Emilia's pathetic question, "Must these men die too?" (IV. ii. 112), makes us question the justice of the scheme.

The playwright—Fletcher presumably—through analogous action directs the audience's judgment against the "cure" Theseus has ordained. Like Theseus, the Doctor attempts to cure a subject maddened by love. His cure involves the standard Jacobean therapy for melancholy of flattering the patient's delusion by pretending that it is real. If the Daughter's former suitor, the Wooer, can persuade the Daughter he is Palamon, even going so far as to lie with her, her fixation on the kinsman may disappear. Naturally the Jailer objects to this extreme measure, but he is overruled. "But, doctor," he exclaims as he exits to fetch the Daughter, "Methinks you are i' th' wrong still" (V. ii. 26-27). The laughter provoked by this comic scene should not detract from its serious purpose: that of suggesting that Theseus' complementary remedy may be morally wrong (in the deaths of knights untouched by love madness).

One could argue that Theseus' work, the ceremonious contest, is a success. Arcite forces Palamon to touch the pyramid and so wins Emilia. But the disorder that the tourney was designed to control persists, personified in the black horse that Emilia gave Arcite. Paradoxically fatal disorder proceeds from—issues out of—a figure symbolic of chastity and relative stillness. As described, the black horse represents the disordering sexual desire aroused by Emilia in Arcite.[19] The symbolic process of Arcite's downfall makes this much clear:

> And he thus went counting
> The flinty pavement, dancing as 'twere to th' music
> His own hoofs made (for as they say from iron
> Came music's origin), what envious flint,
> Cold as old Saturn, and like him possess'd
> With fire malevolent, darted a spark,
> Or what fierce sulphur else, to this end made,
> I comment not—the hot horse, hot as fire,
> Took toy at this, and fell to what disorder
> His power could give his will, bounds, comes on end,
> Forgets school-doing. . . .
> (V. iv. 58-68)

Lethal stir emerges from hypostatized virginity; Emilia gave this "gift" to Arcite. So portrayed, the black horse mimics the mad act of falling in love, from the first sparks of passion to raging disorder, through the unseating of the lover's reason, to death. In heavily weighted language, Arcite struggles to keep "him 'tween his legs" (V. iv. 76) but cannot prevent the world-upside-down disorder of sexual love from overwhelming him:

> . . . on end he stands,
> That Arcite's legs, being higher than his head,
> Seem'd with strange art to hang.
> (V. iv. 77-79)

With Arcite's death and Palamon's unlooked-for gaining of Emilia, Theseus moralizes that "the gods my justice/ Take from my hand, and they themselves become/ The executioners" (V. iv. 120-22). Theseus can arrive at this neat conclusion because he has just told Palamon that "the powerful Venus well hath grac'd her altar,/ And given you your love":

> Our master Mars
> Hath vouch'd his oracle, and to Arcite gave
> The grace of the contention.
> (V. iv. 105-8)

Certain tensions within Theseus' self-comforting interpretation of final events suggest that it may be a mistaken construction of the wills of gods who remain enigmatic. The elaborate symbolism of the black horse suggests that Arcite died for Venus—not Mars. The falseness latent in Theseus' cure of love madness appears in these tensions. In fact, reexamination of Palamon's prayer to Venus shows him no more asking for the prize Emilia than Arcite does in his prayer to Mars. Theseus' pat moralizing at the end of the play resembles his ceremonious contest; neither satisfactorily contains the profoundly disruptive stir of sexuality. While satisfying himself and other characters on stage, his fabrications, which represent his labors in the play, remain as problematic as the war work does by which the kinsmen would win love.

When Arcite wins Theseus' contest and the duke condemns Palamon and his followers to death, stunned Emilia questions, "Is this winning?" (V. iii. 138). The rhetorical ring of her query—this is not winning—suggests that Palamon's unexpected triumph is also no victory. It, too, comes at the price of a death. More so than any of the late plays previously analyzed, *The Two Noble Kinsmen* presents images of labor either lost or qualified so strongly that its value seems doubtful.[20] The judgment applies to the work of Shakespeare and Fletcher themselves. Their romance has never been the object of either wide popular applause or high critical esteem. In this respect, Fletcher's view of the collaborated work as a "glu'd together" artifact may be more accurate than Shakespeare's vision of two Philomels marvelously blending their voices. In other Shakespearean late plays, a ruling god or powerful magician either contrives or directs the labor of elect morals so that work educates or refines them. If Mars and Venus have ruled Arcite's and Palamon's lives, they have done so in such an obscure and cruel fashion that educational benefits are not apparent.[21]

"O you heavenly charmers," a newly and sadly meditative Theseus concludes at play's end:

> What things you make of us! For what we lack
> We laugh, for what we have are sorry, still
> Are children in some kind.
> (V. iv. 131-34)

Reducing humanity to "things," keeping them "children," chasing men and women like hunters after herds of game, the gods and goddesses of *The Two Noble Kinsmen* reduce rather than elevate their subjects. "Charmers," casters of spells, these deities manifest themselves to humankind in obscure magic, such as the suddenly ascending rose tree on Venus' altar. Prospero in god-like fashion likewise uses magic to express his purposes to his subjects, but in his case labor is also part of his redemptive plan for them. Jupiter's tablet left on Posthumus' breast is as cryptic as Venus' rose bush with its single falling rose, but Welsh work forms part of the god's redemptive program for Imogen. The "heavenly charmers" of *The Two Noble Kinsmen*, however, never make labor a crucial element in a salvatory design. They remain—to use a Jonsonian phrase—far-removed mysteries.[22] The wages that the characters of this troubling last play by Shakespeare eventually take to their final home are never clearly defined or counted.

Notes

1 The critical consensus as regards Shakespeare's and Fletcher's shares of *The Two Noble Kinsmen* has taken this form: I. i-II. i Shakespeare (but I. iv, v uncertain); II. ii-vi Fletcher; III. i Shakespeare; III. ii-V. i. 33 Fletcher (but IV. ii uncertain); V. i. 34-173 Shakespeare; V. ii Fletcher; V. iii, iv Shakespeare; Prologue, Epilogue, epithalamion I. i. 19-24 Fletcher. (*The Riverside Shakespeare* 1640). However, Eugene Waith, in the Oxford Shakespeare edition of the play (Oxford: Oxford UP, 1989), 22-23, has challenged this traditional division, awarding III. ii, IV. iii, and all of V. i to Shakespeare. Waith admits uncertainty about the assignation of II. i, IV. iii, and V. i. 1-33. In this chapter, I follow the traditional scheme of collaboration outlined in *The Riverside Shakespeare*.

2 Such metaphors, however, do not appear in the play's opening scene. Lacking the increased charge that comes from condensation in metaphor, the juxtaposition of two kinds of work there is looser, more diffuse, less electric. Nevertheless, its presence in the opening scene reveals the kinship of this final romance to the late plays of Shakespeare, must notably *Cymbeline*.

3 The questionable value of labor in Palamon's and Arcite's Theban meditations provides a rationale for their dialogue that counters Theodore Spencer's claim, made in "*The Two Noble Kinsmen*," *Modern Philology* 36 (1939): 255-76, that "Palamon and Arcite look back in disgust at Thebes before we have been given any satisfactory reason for their disgust" (268).

4 That this sentiment was an Elizabethan commonplace is shown by Kenneth Muir, *Shakespeare as Collaborator* (London: Methuen, 1960) 138.

5 The contradiction between the kinsmen's beliefs and actions as regards Thebes has been analyzed by Mary Beth Rose, *The Expense of Spirit: Love and Sexuality in English Renaissance Drama* (Ithaca, NY: Cornell UP, 1988) 218.

6 This similarity is also noted by Madelon Lief and Nicholas F. Radel, "Linguistic Subversion and the Artifice of Rhetoric in *The Two Noble Kinsmen*," *Shakespeare Quarterly* 38 (1987): 405-25, esp. 411.

7 Paula S. Berggren, in "'For what we lack,/ We laugh': Incompletion and *The Two Noble Kinsmen*," *Modern Language Studies* 14.4 (1984): 3-17, judges that "one of the most disturbing elements of the final movement of the play is a sequence of childbirth images that reverse the hopeful sense of organic continuity through which the late romances transmute tragic pain" (9).

8 The differences in Palamon's and Arcite's characterizations have been described by Jeanne Addison Roberts, "Crises of Male Self-Definition in *The Two Noble Kinsmen*," *Shakespeare, Fletcher, and "The Two Noble Kinsmen*," ed. Charles H. Frey (Columbia: U of Missouri P, 1989) 133-144, esp. 139-40; and by Paul Bertram, *Shakespeare and "The Two Noble Kinsmen"* (New Brunswick, NJ: Rutgers UP, 1965) 281-82.

9 In a catalogue of sexual allusions in the Shakespeare canon, cited by Norman N. Holland in *Psychoanalysis and Shakespeare* (1964; rpt. New York: Octagon Books, 1976) 123, violent action is the most common metaphoric vehicle for the sexual act.

10 The grotesquerie of Palamon's prayer to Venus was first described by Philip Edwards, "On the Design of *The Two Noble Kinsmen*," *Review of English Literature* 5.4 (1964): 89-105, esp. 91-93.

11 For an alternative analysis of the metatheatrical functions of the labor of breeding and delivery as described by the Prologue of *The Two Noble Kinsmen*, see Charles H. Frey, "Collaborating with Shakespeare: After the Final Play," *Shakespeare, Fletcher, and "The Two Noble Kinsmen"* 31-44, esp. 32-36.

12 This is the argument of Donald K. Hedrick, "'Be Rough With Me': The Collaborative Arenas of *The Two Noble Kinsmen*" (Frey 45-77). Eugene Waith essentially rejects Hedrick's argument in the Oxford Shakespeare edition of the play (18 n3).

13 The fine integration of dramatic elements in *The Two Noble Kinsmen* leads Paul Bertram to conclude—mistakenly, I believe—that Shakespeare alone wrote the play (244-82). "The play is better unified than is often granted," Eugene Waith argues in "Shakespeare and Fletcher on Love and Friendship," *Shakespeare Studies* 18 (1986): 235-50, esp. 237. Waith reprints this article in *Patterns and Perspectives in English Renaissance Drama* (Newark: U of Delaware P, 1988) 289-303.

14 Madelon Lief and Nicholas F. Radel also find the method and content of scenes generally assigned to Fletcher integrated with those of the Shakespearean portions of the play (405-25), as does Eugene M. Waith, "Shakespeare and Fletcher on Love and Friendship" 237.

15 Waith also notices this contradiction in "Shakespeare and Fletcher on Love and Friendship" 248.

16 This inconsistency is described by Waith, *The Two Noble Kinsmen* 20.

17 But when the mad Jailer's Daughter stumbles into the scene and is conscripted to become the dancer, Gerrold joyfully (but pedantically) utters, "*Et opus exegi, quod nec Jovis ira, nec ignis*" (III. v. 88)—"And I have built a work which neither the wrath of Jove nor fire [will destroy]." As a version of *Metamorphoses* xv. 871, the schoolmaster's solemn declaration that his ephemeral entertainment amounts to an enduring work

comparable to Ovid's masterpiece invites mocking laughter. Gerrold's grandiose claim serves to accentuate the deficiencies of a collaborated work.

18 On this aspect of Theseus' characterization, see Rose 219; and E. Talbot Donaldson, *The Swan at the Well* (New Haven: Yale UP, 1985) 67-68.

19 For an extensive analysis of Arcite's black horse as sexual symbol, see Richard Abrams, "*The Two Noble Kinsmen* as Bourgeois Drama" (Frey 145-62, esp. 158-59).

20 Berggren argues that "the entire play seems mired in the impossibility of moving freely from intention to achievement, from the birth of an idea to its fulfillment" (3). A similar thesis is developed by Richard Hillman, "Shakespeare's Romantic Innocents and the Misappropriation of the Romance Past: The Case of *The Two Noble Kinsmen*," *Shakespeare Survey* 43 (1990): 69-79, esp. 70-71.

21 Donaldson 53-54.

22 Such is the judgment of James R. Andreas, "Remythologizing *The Knight's Tale*: *A Midsummer Night's Dream* and *The Two Noble Kinsmen*," *Shakespeare Yearbook* 2 (1991): 49-67, esp. 49-51, 56-58, 60-63.

Chapter 9

Shakespeare's Labored Art

We have seen that Shakespeare, beginning with *Coriolanus* and *Timon of Athens* (but especially with *Pericles*), incorporated numerous multivalent images of labor into his work. This dramatic representation encompasses physical labor of several kinds, including warfare; literal and figurative birth labor; and intense mental and spiritual work, usually on the protagonist's part. In *Pericles* and *Cymbeline*, the work performed in the play is chiefly physical; directed by a ruling deity, it proves redemptive for afflicted characters such as Pericles and Imogen. During the course of this renovation, Shakespeare satirizes the sloth of certain (upper) Jacobean social classes and allied character types (such as the boor Cloten). In *The Winter's Tale*, labor is mainly an inner activity; in this romance spiritual birth labor becomes Leontes' means for recovering Hermione and delivering himself to a new life. The working mind continues to take precedence over physical labor in *The Tempest* and *King Henry VIII*, functioning in Prospero's and Henry's cases as the instrument for resolving an impasse of character and achieving a relatively integrated self. One senses that in the accomplishments of Prospero and King Henry, Shakespeare personally attained somewhat satisfying closure to his exploration of the manifold use and abuse of labor. The portrayal of labor in *The Two Noble Kinsmen* marks a loss of this resolution and synthesis. As is the case in this collaborated play with other motifs that Shakespeare had previously employed brilliantly, the imagery of labor in *The Two Noble Kinsmen* seems generally cold, negative, dispirited. The reason for this lapse will undoubtedly remain a mystery. For our purposes, however, the falling off neatly accentuates the triumph of labor in *King Henry VIII* and especially *The Tempest*.

In this final chapter, Shakespeare's labored art will be considered from several perspectives in order to facilitate understanding it as both a cultural and personal phenomenon. Certainly the perceived idleness and decadence of King James' court and the social injustices involving labor that were described in Chapter 1 provide a context for grasping the significance of Shakespeare's decision to depict various corruptions of labor and its essential, often primitively regenerative value. Contemporary protestant belief in the inherent virtue of work made Shakespeare's decision timely and culturally acceptable. Throughout this study, Shakespeare's labored art has been understood in two related senses—as dramatic art that is about labor, and as dramatic art that is labored. At optimum moments, the labored (highly wrought/ overwrought) quality of Shakespeare's art conveys either an insight into or a truth about the nature of work, whether it be that of the warrior or playwright. Cyrus Hoy, in an analysis of several Jacobean plays (including *Antony and Cleopatra*), has labeled this highly worked style Mannerist.[1] Since art historians have defined Mannerism by its relationship to both idleness and work, this complex of aesthetic traits can help us to differentiate major strands of Shakespeare's labored art.

Despite recent efforts at synthesis, art historians remain divided over the definition and features of Mannerist art. On the one hand, one group of art critics, represented by John Shearman, reserve the term Mannerist for those Renaissance (mainly sixteenth-century) artists who developed *maniera*, a highly elegant, urbane style of expression. According to Shearman, Mannerism meant "savoir-faire, effortless accomplishment and sophistication; it was inimical to revealed passion, evident effort and rude naiveté."[2] *Sprezzatura* thus is a literary equivalent of painterly Mannerism. These overtones, however, soon acquired a negative charge as the sixteenth century progressed. Mannerism became a pejorative tag for precious art—enervated, perhaps overdecorated art which makes affected beauty rather than moral content its real subject. The term shifted meaning chiefly because "an insulated society, self-sufficient in its amusements and in conversation elaborately stylized," promoted it.[3] In other words, superficially decorative and lifeless qualities of certain Mannerist artifacts reflect the idle, hypercultivated Renaissance aristocracy for whom it was produced. This aspect of Mannerism can account for the consciously "pretty" artifacts and manner of speaking associated with aristocratic Imogen, cloistered in the "Renaissance" court of her pagan father until providentially forced to work and rectify the flaws of idleness.

Shearman's brand of Mannerism constitutes a sharp reaction to what had become the primary description of Mannerism. Established by Arnold Hauser, this account of Mannerism stresses the disturbance, the fracturing, of the formal classical harmonies of earlier Renaissance art into decentered, often violently energized works.[4] The twisting, serpentine figures of Parmigianino and the electrified forms and restricted, chromatic coloring of El Greco illustrate this version of Mannerism, which Hauser claims operates across centuries whenever societies are especially anxious and unstable. The disjunctive energy, inorganicism, and troubled aesthetic forms of Mannerism register the radical instability, even the break up, of a way of life. The present study reveals the appropriateness of understanding Shakespeare's final six plays as Mannerist creations in the Hauserian sense of the term (which is the sense that Hoy adopts in his analysis).[5] The social turmoil that many Jacobeans attested to could be considered the cultural ground of Shakespeare's preference for disturbingly stirred poetic and dramatic forms in the late romances and *King Henry VIII*.[6] Certainly the violent contrast between King James' irenic predisposition and his coarse, quarrelsome habits befits a Mannerist age. One can regard the pronounced juxtaposition of Shakespeare's images of stir and stasis as a Mannerist disjunction, or discontinuity. (These juxtapositions ironically condense and represent chief elements of the two main varieties of Mannerism—Hauser's stir and Shearman's stasis).

Hauserian Mannerism—strenuous, strained, tortuous—can account for much in Shakespeare's labored art. What cannot be accounted for is the emphasis upon work, especially physical labor, as a refiner of character. Mannerism, whether of the Shearman or Hauser variety, evolved out of privileged, aristocratic settings, social contexts of leisure wherein work was what servants and the lower classes did. David Evett, in his analysis of literature and the visual arts in sixteenth-century England, contrasts Mannerism with Tudor Demotic art, which "not only indicates but actually imitates items from the realm of common experience."[7] Itemization of the world of common experience is a trademark of Elizabethan and Jacobean playwrights. According to Evett, a principal feature of the Tudor Demotic voice "is a sense of the necessity, even value, of work—an idea, after all, that posits a world in which things are not tied into static and inescapable patterns"—as the aristocratic group giving birth to Mannerism would have it—"but rather one where something can be accomplished, that is, brought toward an end. Thus Wyatt: 'I must goo worke, I se, by craft and art,/ For truth and faith in her is laide apart.'"[8] Evett concludes that the demotic emphasis upon the value of work resulted from "the Shakespeares and Caravaggios of the world stepping outside [Mannerist] conventions altogether . . . in obedience to their sense of the common people around them."[9]

If one admits the validity of Evett's portrayal of demotic art, one must shift focus in Shakespeare's case from the Tudor period to the Jacobean years 1606-13, especially 1609-10 to 1613; for that is the time during which labor in its many images became prominent in his work. Throughout the present study, but especially in Chapters 1 and 2, reasons for this late interest of Shakespeare's in labor have been sought in the milieu of Jacobean society, most notably that of James I's court. Nevertheless Evett implies that practitioners of demotic art who highlight the phenomenon of work usually feel some sympathy for the working class, especially the hardships and injustices that it suffers.

Recently Gary Taylor has argued that Shakespeare had no interest in depicting the English laborer of his day, or the social inequities he endured:

> The absence of prostitutes from *Measure for Measure* . . . originates in the social and institutional conditions of Elizabethan theatre and in Shakespeare's own ambivalences about prostitution, about acting, about women. But it also belongs to a more general pattern of attitudes toward the working class. Of the twenty-one specified adult characters in *Measure*

> *for Measure*, only four belong to the vast majority of the population beneath the rank of gentlemen: Mistress Overdone the bawd, Pompey the pimp, Elbow the constable, and Abhorson the executioner—criminals and clowns. These characters in combination speak less than 11 percent of the text. It would be absurd to demand some sort of quota system, by which the characters in each play are proportioned demographically along lines of gender and class; but what happens in *Measure for Measure* happens in the other plays too. Like women, the lower and middle classes are systematically under-represented in Shakespeare. They are also, as the sample from *Measure for Measure* makes clear, misrepresented. They are all, like Shakespeare's prostitutes, seen from above.[10]

Taylor cites Shakespeare's cursory treatment of the whores in *Pericles* as evidence of the playwright's lack of feeling for oppressed London classes, especially the multitude of working women.[11] Readers may feel inclined to take issue with several of Taylor's categorical assertions (such as that concerning the under-representation of women in Shakespeare's plays); but before they do so, they should note that Taylor summons no less a presence than Leo Tolstoy to bolster his claim that Shakespeare ignored the lower, poorer classes. In *Shakespeare and the Drama* (1906), the author of *War and Peace* maintains that Shakespeare wrote in the service of a philosophy that "'despises' the working class."[12]

Annabel Patterson has claimed that Shakespeare "must have regarded himself, certainly when he began his career as actor and playwright, as one of the largest of all possible groupings in England at that time—those below the rank of the landed aristocracy or gentry"—a group that included "yeomen or merchants, wage laborers, apprentices, or, at the bottom of the scale, the rural poor."[13] Ben Jonson was the stepson of a common laborer—a brickmaker. His efforts to distance himself from his origin are well-documented. "It is a represented fact, as far as Jonson is concerned, about his ignorance of manual laborers: their access to the sacred well of Helicon does them no good but only incites them to profane the mysteries they cannot comprehend."[14] Can the charge of ingratitude be made to stick against Shakespeare (as it apparently can be made to do against Jonson)?

The evidence that can be drawn from the pages of this book suggests otherwise. The happy tradesmen undisturbed by the impostume Coriolanus, the labor that the good steward Flavius attempts to do on bankrupt Timon's behalf, the redemptive industry of the poor fishermen in *Pericles*, the refining Welsh labors of Imogen as humble servant, the courageous and loyal work of the sailors to preserve their ship in *The Tempest*—these and other positive images of common work in Shakespeare's late plays contradict Taylor's distorted portrait of the playwright.[15] They bar the accusation that can be brought against Jonson from being made against him. If these proofs appear insufficient, others can be found in Patterson's *Shakespeare and the Popular Voice*, a book that establishes Shakespeare's positive "attitude to the ordinary working people inside and outside his plays."[16]

Intimately involved with the question of Shakespeare's depiction of the working class is his probable attitude toward himself as the maker of plays. Did he regard their making as a craft or an art? Did he primarily consider himself a playwright, a worker in a craft, or a poetic artist? The question actually became a contentious issue during Shakespeare's career. Admittedly, the word "playwright" never appears in the Shakespeare canon.[17] The earliest entries for the term cited in the *Oxford English Dictionary* date from the 1670s and 1680s. David Willbern, among others, has based a critical argument partly on the absence of the concept "playwright" in the language of Shakespeare's contemporaries.[18] But David Riggs has cited the twice-repeated use of the word "playwright" in Jonson's *Epicoene*, in which it appears as a term of abuse.[19] In his admirable *Ben Jonson: A Life*, Riggs presents the most thorough and illuminating analysis to date of the workman status of public dramatists in Shakespeare's age.

According to Riggs, "A professional entertainer who earned his living by turning out scripts in response to the demands of the marketplace still wore the appearance of a skilled artisan. His place in the social hierarchy was akin to that of a craftsman . . . or of a tradesman who dealt in speeches and plots; but a lettered poet who improved the moral condition of his times by holding popular errors up to ridicule could claim that he was practicing a liberal art. His status was akin to that of a schoolmaster, a university don, or a counselor to the commonwealth at large."[20] Riggs points out that the Elizabethan schoolmaster Richard Mulcaster's division of the English people into gentlemen and the commonality—"'marchants and manuaries'"—would have placed the crafter of playscripts among manual laborers.[21] Since they were generally actors who also made scripts, and since their nongentle births precluded university education, one is first inclined to believe that many of Shakespeare's and Jonson's fellow dramatists thought of their occupation as a craft, the "wrighting"—working—of plays rather than wood or brick. Shakespeare's and Jonson's contemporaries may have distinguished such playwrights from university men who now and then made money by selling scripts to theater troupes. In theory, university-educated public dramatists could be regarded as gentlemen who practiced a liberal art. "But such distinctions," Riggs notes, "quickly dissolved in the fluid ambiance of the playhouse. Robert Greene, a Cambridge graduate, felt that he had compromised his status as gentleman by entering the employ of his social inferiors."[22]

No gentleman-born, Shakespeare in the late 1580s or early 1590s began life in London almost certainly at a low rung of the social ladder, that of wage earner, an actor in a repertory company—a base hireling.[23] In Chapter 1, we saw in what low esteem working for wages was held during Shakespeare's lifetime. In 1579, Stephen Gosson, in *The School of Abuse*, castigated public actors as hirelings, "and in 1615 one of the worst things that could be said against an actor was that 'his wages and dependence prove him to be a servant of the people.'"[24] This jaundiced view of hireling actors partly stemmed from the fact that they were not freemen; they neither owned land nor had rights of property in the product of their labor. An actor who wrote and sold scripts to his acting company remained an unenfranchised hireling. But by becoming a shareholder of the Lord Chamberlain's Men, Shakespeare retained a property interest in the product of his labor and could at that moment be considered a freeman.

Shakespeare, like Jonson, represents an interesting example of the Marxist writer/capitalist, whose labor process makes him a wage earner or hireling, part of the downcast working class, but whose labor product gradually brings him not only esteem but also the opportunity to buy into a higher class of gentlemen. First ridiculed by the "gentleman" Robert Greene as a base hireling actor, an upstart crow who stole from the work of university-educated writers, Shakespeare eventually had the financial wherewithal to begin acquiring land and property in Stratford. He purchased for his father—and through him for himself—a coat of arms and the right to be called a gentleman. He retired to one of the two most impressive houses in his boyhood town. At some point in the later 1590s or early 1600s, certainly several years before the writing of the plays that are the subject of this book, Shakespeare had earned the social right to reject any accusation that he was a worker, allied to wage earners and artisans. (Viewed from this perspective, his late, positively charged portrayal of humble industry is especially noteworthy).

Whether the Shakespeare of changed circumstances thought of himself and what he did as entities different from worker and work we have no way of knowing. Some clues exist, however, as to what his attitude may have been. In 1616, the year of Shakespeare's death, Ben Jonson carefully saw his plays through the press and into eternity, bound handsomely in a folio edition titled *Works*. Jonson's and Shakespeare's contemporaries must have noted the following social irony: classical poets like Virgil, whom they would have considered a gentleman, gave the title *Opera*—*Works*—to their collected verse, including the noble epic. Work, after all, was something that Jacobeans imagined that gentlemen and epic poets did not do. Nevertheless, they overlooked this irony by imitating the ancients in reserving the title *Works* for the dignified writings of educated men such as sermons and heroic poems. Thus Jonson's audacity in calling a group of collected plays *Works* was striking, a legitimate butt of satire. In most cases, public plays were thought scarcely worth preserving or printing. Shortly after *The Works of Benjamin Jonson* appeared, "a wag posed the famous question, 'Pray tell me, Ben, where doth the mystery lurk,/ What others call a play you call a work.'"[25] Thomas Heywood, who claimed to have had "either an entire hand, or at least a main finger" in the composition of two-hundred-and-twenty Elizabethan and Stuart plays, almost certainly had Jonson in mind when in 1633 . . . he wrote, "'True it is that my plays are not exposed unto the world in volumes to bear the title of *Works*—as others.'"[26] Jonson's notorious title ought not to have shocked Jacobeans as intensely as it did; his careful preparation and heavy annotation of plays previously printed as quartos, plays such as *Every Man Out of His Humour* (1600) and *Sejanus* (1606), reveal his inclination to treat a playscript as though it were a classical literary text.

Shakespeare, however, never appears to have thought of his plays in this way. Approximately half of Shakespeare's plays were published in one or more quarto editions during his lifetime. "Yet in not one of his plays published in his lifetime," Stanley Wells remarks, "is there anything to dignify it as a work of literature—no dedication, no epistle, no commendatory poem. The only partial exception is *Troilus and Cressida*, the 1609 edition of which has a printer's epistle."[27] The authorial care that went into preparing the texts of Shakespeare's two narrative poems, *Venus and Adonis* and *The Rape of Lucrece*, is absent in the generally mangled quartos of his plays. He does not appear to have thought of plays as works—deserving inductions and annotation—in the sense that Jonson did. In terms of our subject, there is an irony here. Even though he had risen from a brickmaker's stepson through the occupation of public actor and dramatist to become court poet, the writer of royal masques and "Master of Arts in both ye Universities by yr favour, not his studie,"[28] Ben Jonson reveals, both in his life and art, that he never overcame a nagging sense of his own inferiority, of his impoverished and humble origin and his mainly self-administered education. To title his classically prepared playtexts *Works* was to tell a doubtful part of himself that he had arrived. The title separated Jonson forever from the working class and the manual labor that he as a bricklayer had hated. Shakespeare, likewise rising out of relatively modest origins, seems to have never felt the need to transform his playscripts into literary works. Rising to the rank of the gentry, he could perhaps with little anxiety regard them as the products of a playwright. (The use of the term in *Epicoene* gives us the precedent for supposing that he might have used the word in thought or conversation).

Without the example of Jonson's thousand-page folio, Heminge and Condell might never have gathered and published their beloved colleague's plays. Nevertheless, they and their printer Jaggard avoid Jonson's kind of title. In the 1623 Folio, Shakespeare's plays are not called *Works* but rather *Mr. William Shakespeare's Comedies, Histories, and Tragedies*. It is not likely that Shakespeare, dying in the year of Jonson's folio and dead for seven years, personally dictated the title of the volume containing his collected plays. And yet by not bearing the title *Works*, a mark of aristocratic literary privilege, but a more neutral title, one descriptive of the dramatic genres in which he wrote, the 1623 Folio does not contradict or detract from the endorsement of often humble labor and laborers found inscribed in the plays, especially those written late in Shakespeare's career. There is little to change one's impression that Shakespeare thought of himself as a playwright, as a worker of plays which paid for the social elevation he achieved, rather than as a poet writing drama. Poets and even a painter appear on Shakespeare's stage, but a professional playwright never does. The play within *Titus Andronicus* was written by Titus himself, an amateur like Holofernes and Gerrold. The two plays within *Hamlet*, the one caviar for the common playgoer and the other an example of choice Italian, are the works of invisible, nameless creators. They are thus works in the most modest sense, the anti-Jonsonian sense, the sense truest to our analysis of Shakespeare's labored art.

C. L. Barber and Richard Wheeler have written that Shakespeare's "works, in one aspect, are a titanic work of knowing his age. In a complementary aspect, what we see in Shakespeare's development is his work of knowing himself as his works."[29] The judgment is suggestive, implying that Shakespeare may have recognized that the degree of self-understanding that composing a play brought him was proportional to the labor that went into its creation. According to Erik Erikson, "the ideological polarization of the Western world which has made Freud the century's theorist of sex, and Marx that of work, has, until quite recently, left a whole area of man's mind uncharted in psychoanalysis. I refer to man's *love for his works and ideas as well as for his children,* and the necessary self-verification which adult man's ego receives, and must receive, from his labor's challenge."[30] Many—perhaps most—Elizabethan and Jacobean plays in the texts that have come down to us appear longer than the standard two-hour afternoon time-frame for acting in the London theaters, when natural light begins failing in autumn and winter as early as three-thirty or four o'clock. But the texts of Shakespeare's plays appear excessively—and unnecessarily (from a money-making perspective)—overwritten. *Hamlet,* which uncut takes between four and five hours to perform, is the classic example, but *Cymbeline* makes the point just as well. Most likely Shakespeare himself participated in the process of cutting his texts for performance. How else can one explain his penchant for commercially unproductive overwriting but by suggesting that drama early became for him a compelling vehicle for self discovery? Self-knowledge chiefly gained retrospectively from seeing and knowing one's deeds is almost always given negative overtones by Shakespeare. It is the method of Macbeth, whose mind has been corrupted by crime, and of Coriolanus, who lives in a pagan world deprived of Christian epistemology. But the fact that the process and product of labor shape and define the worker must have held personal meaning for Shakespeare. His probable use of drama as a vehicle for self discovery was tied, at least in part, to its commercial value. If Shakespeare saw that his work could shape him into the desired image of a material man, he also saw that this progressively prosperous theatrical entrepreneur could consolidate his fortunes by creating works appealing to shifting tastes and the widest variety of paying customers.

But the material Shakespeare is not the Shakespeare we finally care about. We want to know how his work and his inner spiritual life reciprocally shaped and developed each other. In Chapter 2, we saw that Shakespeare in *Timon of Athens* included a Poet and Painter so that he could imply that effective creative artists must be persons of integrity, uncorrupted by the sole wish to make large sums of money by flattering the vanity and darker character traits of their consumers. The art of the Poet and Painter in *Timon* fails to make an impact—Timon, for example, ignores the Poet's warning against Fortune's fickleness—because it is created primarily to make money rather than to convey moral or ethical truth. One assumes that Shakespeare imagined that these generalizations apply to the playwright. If work defines the man, including the playwright, the works of Shakespeare's final phase in particular are the products of an ethically good man (one whom many years of writing moral, compassionate art had helped to make so). Shakespeare's last plays breathe the spirit of labor by which they were made. Reinforcing this impression are the many images of beneficial or redemptive industry that appear in these plays. By including the morally refining labor of the poor fishermen of *Pericles* and that of the powerful Duke of Milan, Prospero, these images span humanity, indicating Shakespeare's extension of the strenuous mode that shaped him into the man he was to the different classes and members of his audience.

Doubtlessly, my reader, mindful of the evidence of Shakespeare's modesty and skeptical bent of thought, has become uncomfortable with the idealistic overtones of the previous paragraphs. I would simply remind him or her that they describe theoretically the logical implications of the representation of the creative artist in *Timon of Athens* for the work following it. Nevertheless, my claims certainly require explanation. Shakespeare's preoccupation with the positive depiction of different kinds of work in his late plays invites comparison with the interest of certain Elizabethan and Jacobean godly protestants in the ability of work, especially physical labor, to regulate daily life morally and refine Christian faith. Almost instinctively, a reader familiar with Shakespeare's plays hesitates to link the playwright with godly protestants. If Shakespeare was a Christian (as he probably was), Hookerian (liberal) protestant or even Catholic would be a candidate for a descriptive label for him before the phrase godly protestant would command attention. Certain traits in Malvolio's characterization, after all, were designed to evoke the caricature of the laughable stage puritan.[31] Still, the association of protestantism with images of work in the late plays warrants examination.

Certain speeches in *King Henry VIII* appear to have been designed to depict the birth of protestantism in England. The incorporation of work, what has become rightly or wrongly a hallmark of the denomination, into a play containing "protestant" episodes and speeches is appropriate. Moreover, the possibility that Shakespeare's audience, especially the groundlings, could have found in the late plays images of redemptive industry may have defused certain complaints of godly protestants against the London public theaters—that they were places of idleness where nothing worthwhile was learned, that they distracted patrons from worship and work (two main activities of life).[32] Michel Foucault, in accounting for the historical coincidence of early capitalism and the widespread institutionalized repression of the sexual drive, has concluded that "a principle of explanation emerges after the fact: if sex is so rigorously repressed, this is because it is incompatible with a general and intensive work imperative. At a time when labor capacity was being systematically exploited, how could this capacity be allowed to dissipate itself in pleasurable pursuits, except in those—reduced to a minimum—that enabled it to reproduce itself?"[33] Certainly protestantism, especially godly protestantism, was ideally suited to wed the work imperative to nascent capitalism. When sexual repression is figured into this union, the final equation permits Foucault's kind of interpretation. Foucault describes the effect of Prospero's imposed work on Ferdinand's sexual drive, channeled by refining labor away from promiscuity into the institutional mode of marriage and family. This does not exactly make Shakespeare a protestant dramatist, but it does suggest the relevance of Elizabethan protestantism for understanding fully the importance of work in the late plays.

Nevertheless, in the final analysis, Shakespeare's preoccupation late in his career with representing various forms of labor strikes one as a highly personal rather than doctrinal event. By personal, I mean issuing from the psychology or temperament of the playwright, a Jacobean male in his mid- to late forties. In the first place, one should recognize the significant labor that Shakespeare spent in creating these plays resonant of work. Stephen Greenblatt has asserted that, "to an envious contemporary like Robert Greene, Shakespeare seems a kind of greenroom Iago, appropriating for himself the labors of others....

Still, at the least we must grant Robert Greene that it would have seemed fatal to be imitated by Shakespeare. He possessed a limitless talent for entering into the consciousness of another, perceiving its deepest structures as a manipulable fiction, reinscribing it into his narrative form."[34] Appropriating the labors of other imaginative writers, Greenblatt's Shakespeare appears temperamentally disinclined to the hard work of playwrighting. In fact, he resembles a male witch, or succubus—a spirit stealer like those drawn from Renaissance history and Shakespeare's own plays and defined and analyzed in Greenblatt's later criticism. Such a portrait of an indolent, slightly malevolent Shakespeare, however, is at odds with the image of an industrious playwright projected by the high seriousness, pronounced length, and rich complexity of plays such as *Antony and Cleopatra*, *Cymbeline*, *The Winter's Tale*, and *King Henry VIII*. In this respect, an irony of *The Tempest* is that a short play of remarkable lyrical ease should be so focused on industry. The symmetrical craftsmanship of the play and, most notably, its apparently sourceless status belie Greenblatt's portrait of an opportunistic Shakespeare stealing the labor of others. Shakespeare may have rarely blotted a line, but considerable effort went into mentally formulating and writing the verses and the dramatic structures in which they are embedded. Actor; director; writer of thirty-eight known plays, two long narrative poems and 154 sonnets in a roughly twenty-four-year period; theatrical entrepreneur; Stratford land and property owner; husband and father—Shakespeare gives the impression of a man who experienced first-hand the rigors of work and knew its benefits.

Still, one also has the distinct impression that Shakespeare's biological age figured into his representation of work in the plays that we have examined. Psychoanalytic criticism of Shakespeare's plays has generally centered upon a basic division within the man. In the words of Bernard Paris, "historically, it has been between an aggressive, vindictive, power-hungry masculine side, which generates 'images of ... violent actions' ... and a gentle, submissive, idealistic feminine side, which dislikes cruelty and is given to loving-kindness and Christian charity."[35] Stressing the psychological importance for Shakespeare of the birth order in John Shakespeare's family and the future playwright's enjoyment of his mother's undivided attention during the first years of his life (until Gilbert's birth, in October 1566), C. L. Barber and Richard Wheeler endorse the idea of a radical conflict within the playwright and argue that the feminine, maternal side of Shakespeare's personality was dominant and that oedipal confrontation with his father was extremely delayed (as evidenced by its eruption during his thirties in the writing of *Hamlet*).[36] Absorbed within the normal oedipal dynamics of adulthood, the aggressive/vindictive masculine side of Shakespeare's personality in his late plays continued to create not only images of violent action—witness the battle scenes of *Coriolanus* and *Cymbeline*—but an especially stirred poetic style as well. The irenic or static moments and verse of the late plays that are juxtaposed to stirred dramatic elements can be taken to reflect the dominant maternal, feminine side of Shakespeare's personality. The oedipal conflict that convulsed *Hamlet* is present in the late plays, informing the relationships of Posthumus and Cymbeline, Leontes and Polixenes and Polixenes and Florizel, Prospero and Antonio/Alonso, and King Henry and Wolsey;[37] but Shakespeare—as he had never wholly done—at the close of his career accommodated it to the maternal/feminine side of himself. The images of calm and stasis in Florizel's vision of dancing Perdita supersede those of oedipal conflict between himself and his father Polixenes. To the extent that stir proceeds from working minds and bodies (including the playwright's), Shakespeare successfully in the late plays integrates labor within experience that culminates in the irenic harmonies of reconciled families, diffused with maternal love.

Nevertheless, conspicuously stirred verse and imagery in the late plays sometimes create unpleasant feelings within either the theater audience or characters onstage, who voice their misgivings. Buckingham's and the playgoer's negative reaction to Norfolk's writhing narrative of the Field of the Cloth of Gold and Palamon's agitated tribute to the venereal power contorting mortals illustrate two occasions when we sense that something may be a bit wrong. The stirred nature of Norfolk's speech in *King Henry VIII* may be construed as a compensatory reaction to the dead spiritual core of Jacobean society, especially that of the court, where men and women could be perceived to behave—to use Bacon's phrasing—"as if they were dead images, and engines moved only by the wheels of custom."[38] Read this way, the compensatory reaction is mainly Shakespeare's. Palamon's fretted account of the contortions into which Venus throws humankind may represent something else, however. David Brailow and William Kerrigan have shown that *The Tempest* can be read as a play of old age, Prospero's old age and the troubles and penalties that old age inflicts on youth.[39] The physical stooping that old age enforces is mentioned in the play (I. ii. 258-59), and it figures in the graphic hooping and bending that Prospero literally and figuratively inflicts upon Ferdinand and other characters on his island. At the time he wrote *The Tempest*, Shakespeare was probably forty-seven-years old, apparently too young to be regarded as Prospero's alter ego in this respect. Yet the valedictory nature of certain of Prospero's speeches, and of *The Tempest* as a whole, has encouraged generations of playgoers and readers to suspect that at moments Shakespeare saw himself in Prospero—a gifted but aged man. Elizabeth Bieman describes a psychological trajectory through the late romances to this ultimate figure. This critic has identified and analyzed Shakespeare's character Pericles as the Jungian *puer aeternus*, the "boy" fixated at an early stage of development within the individual.[40] Described in this way, Pericles resembles the boy eternal that Leontes and Polixenes nostalgically, dangerously wish to resurrect in themselves. Bieman points out that "several post-Jungian analysts . . . have followed an ancient and medieval convention in associating the archetype of the puer with that of the *senex* or old man" (78). "The *puer*-driven man who does not come to know the anima within, his internal principle of love, life, inspiration, will come," Bieman argues, "under the *senex* years before his time" (79). Bieman demonstrates that Leontes illustrates this pattern, becoming the wise *senex* only when he can acknowledge his mature identity and the losses naturally brought by aging and transcend the frightened *puer* within him. Shakespeare's representation of this Jungian pattern and final integration in *The Winter's Tale* implies that, as aging playwright, he was able to achieve personally a similar integration (which then made possible his creations of the pattern and its transcendence in the characters Leontes and Prospero). In one sense, Shakespeare's late creative work fashioned a self with whom he could live.

Shakespeare's interest in his late plays in redemptive work may have grown out of the aging playwright's desire to cram as much as possible within his last creative years. His industry takes the form of a fascination with itself, the creation of a labored art—an art recommending the virtues of work of all kinds, from physical labor to the work of the mind. Whatever puritanical strain we detect in this recommendation (as in Prospero's setting of tasks for Ferdinand) results not so much from a turn toward godly protestantism in his last years—though for all we know that may have happened—but from an earnestness to endorse a value coincidental with life, usually in its most vital forms.[41] As death's pressure is felt by the aging artist, he often strives to make the last years of artistic life as or more productive than those of his or her prime. Criticism has finally recognized that the last plays of Shakespeare represent no artistic lapse of powers but, in many ways, the fulfillment of creative promise. Shakespeare's last plays will never enjoy the reputation of the great tragedies. Still, they show no slackening of creative effort, simply a rechanneling of it. Whether Shakespeare's sense of himself as aging artist—or his art as aged—drove him to occupy himself with dramatic portrayals of stir and work, we can never surely know. Yet this motive—or something like it—must have fueled Shakespeare's labored art.

Notes

1 Cyrus Hoy, "Jacobean Tragedy and the Mannerist Style," *Shakespeare Survey* 26 (1973): 49-67.

2 John Shearman, *Mannerism* (London: Penguin, 1967) 17.

3 Shearman 41.

4 Arnold Hauser, *Mannerism: The Crisis of The Renaissance and the Origin of Modern Art*, trans. Eric Mosbacher (New York: Knopf, 1965) 2 vols.

5 This has been partly done by John Greenwood, *Shifting Perspectives and the Stylish Style: Mannerism in Shakespeare and His Jacobean Contemporaries* (Toronto: U of Toronto P, 1988) esp. 40-42, 45-52, 103-11, 142-49, 173-89; and by Jeffrey R. Myers, *Shakespeare's Mannerist Canon: "Ut Pictura Poemata"* (New York: Peter Lang, 1989) esp. 81-110, 199-219.

6 This connection is made by Greenwood 3, 33-37, 185-86.

7 David Evett, *Literature and the Visual Arts in Tudor England* (Athens: U of Georgia P, 1990) 242-68, esp. 265.

8 Evett 267.

9 Evett 268.

10 Gary Taylor, *Reinventing Shakespeare: A Cultural History from the Restoration to the Present* (1989; rpt. Oxford: Oxford UP, 1991) 394-95.

11 "The working women who do appear in his plays are accused of murdering their customers outright (Doll Tearsheet, in *Henry IV, Part 2*) or of murdering them piecemeal, with disease (Phrynia and Timandra, in *Timon of Athens*), in both cases without compunction or compulsion" (Taylor 391).

12 Taylor 398-99.

13 Annabel Patterson, *Shakespeare and the Popular Voice* (Oxford: Basil Blackwell, 1989) 2.

14 John D. Cox, *Shakespeare and the Dramaturgy of Power* (Princeton, NJ: Princeton UP, 1989) 196-97.

15 Recently, William C. Carroll, in "Language, Politics, and Poverty in Shakespearian Drama," *Shakespeare Survey* 44 (1991): 17-24, has demon-

strated by many quotations from the plays that Shakespeare was responsive to the crushing poverty of his age.

16 Patterson 1.

17 Gary Schmidgall, *Shakespeare and the Poet's Life* (Lexington: UP of Kentucky, 1990) 99.

18 David Willbern, "What is Shakespeare?" *Shakespeare's Personality*, ed. Norman N. Holland, Sidney Homan, and Bernard J. Paris (Berkeley: U of California P, 1989) 226-43, esp. 230.

19 David Riggs, *Ben Jonson: A Life* (Cambridge, MA: Harvard UP, 1989) 25.

20 Riggs 25.

21 Riggs 25.

22 Riggs 25.

23 In *The Place of the Stage: License, Play, and Power in Renaissance England* (Chicago: U of Chicago P, 1988), Steven Mullaney concludes that, in Shakespeare's age, "companies of players organized themselves along the lines of corporate guilds, but to the city such imitation hardly represented social respectability. It registered instead as a bold mockery of civic hierarchies. Drama earned its living by a theatrical sleight of hand, translating work into play. 'Outraged by their profits,' as Muriel Bradbrook aptly notes, 'the City saw the players as a horrible parody of a guild'" (47).

24 Cited by Christopher Hill, "Pottage for Freeborn Englishmen: Attitudes to Wage Labour," *Change and Continuity in Seventeenth-Century England* (Cambridge, MA: Harvard UP, 1975) 219-38, esp. 224-25.

25 Irvin Matus, "The Case for Shakespeare," *The Atlantic* 268.4 (October 1991) 71.

26 Cited by Stanley Wells, *Literature and Drama* (London: Routledge & Kegan Paul, 1970) 40.

27 Wells 39.

28 Ben Jonson, *Conversations with William Drummond of Hawthorndon*, ed. G. B. Harrison, Elizabethan and Jacobean Quartos (New York: Barnes & Noble, 1966) 11.

29 C. L. Barber and Richard Wheeler, *The Whole Journey: Shakespeare's Power of Development* (Berkeley: U of California P, 1986) 2.

30 Erik Erikson, *Insight and Responsibility: Lectures on the Ethical Implications of Psychoanalytical Insight* (New York: Norton, 1964) 131.

31 See J. L. Simmons, "A Source for Shakespeare's Malvolio: The Elizabethan Controversy with the Puritans," *Huntington Library Quarterly* 36 (1972-73): 181-201; and Paul N. Siegel, "Malvolio: Comic Puritan Automaton," *Shakespearean Comedy*, ed. Maurice Charney (New York: New York Literary Forum, 1980) 217-30.

32 A representative sampling of godly protestants' portrayal of the public theater as a place wherein people are "engaged in neither work nor worship," practicing "'ydlenes'" instead, appears in Paul Yachnin, "The Powerless Theater," *English Literary Renaissance* 21 (1991): 49-74, esp. 49-50.

33 Michel Foucault, *The History of Sexuality*, trans. Robert Hurley (1976; rpt. New York: Pantheon, 1978) 5-6. "All this garrulous attention which has us in a stew over sexuality, is it not motivated by one basic concern: to ensure population, to reproduce labor capacity, to perpetuate the form of social relations: in short, to constitute a sexuality that is economically useful and politically conservative?" (36-37).

34 Stephen Greenblatt, *Renaissance Self-Fashioning: From More to Shakespeare* (Chicago: U of Chicago P, 1980) 252.

35 Bernard J. Paris, "*The Tempest*: Shakespeare's Ideal Solution," *Shakespeare's Personality* 206-25, esp. 206.

36 Barber and Wheeler 1-67, esp. 1-38.

37 For the presence of the oedipal conflict in *The Tempest*, see Norman N. Holland, *Psychoanalysis and Shakespeare* (1964; rpt. New York: Octagon Books, 1976) 287-88; and H. Peter Hildebrand, "The Other Side of the Wall: A Psychoanalytic Study of Creativity in Later Life," *International Review of Psycho-Analysis* 15 (1988): 353-63, esp. 357-61.

38 Sir Francis Bacon, "Of Custom and Education," *Selected Writings of Sir Francis Bacon* (New York: Random House, 1955) 103-4, esp. 103.

39 David Brailow, "Prospero's 'Old Brain': The Old Man as Metaphor in *The Tempest*," *Shakespeare Studies* 14 (1981): 285-303; William Kerrigan, "Life's Iamb: The Scansion of Late Creativity in the Culture of the Renaissance," *Aging-Literature-Psychoanalysis*, ed. Kathleen Woodward and Murray M. Schwartz (Bloomington: Indiana UP, 1986) 168-91, esp. 172-80.

40 Elizabeth Bieman, *William Shakespeare: The Romances* (Boston: Twayne, 1990) 32.

41 See Kerrigan's speculations on the source of Milton's late creativity (180-85).

Works Cited

Abrams, Richard. "*The Two Noble Kinsmen* as Bourgeois Drama." *Shakespeare, Fletcher, and "The Two Noble Kinsmen."* Ed. Charles H. Frey. Columbia: U of Missouri P, 1989. 145-62.

Adams, Robert M. *Shakespeare: The Four Romances.* New York: Norton, 1989.

Adelman, Janet. *The Common Liar: An Essay on "Antony and Cleopatra."* New Haven: Yale UP, 1973.

Akrigg, G. P. V. *Jacobean Pageant, or the Court of King James I.* 1962. N.p.: Atheneum, 1974.

Altieri, Joanne. *The Theatre of Praise: The Panegyric Tradition in Seventeenth-Century English Drama.* Newark: U of Delaware P, 1986.

Amussen, Susan D. *An Ordered Society: Gender and Class in Early Modern England.* Oxford: Basil Blackwell, 1988.

Andreas, James R. "Remythologizing *The Knight's Tale*: *A Midsummer Night's Dream* and *The Two Noble Kinsmen.*" *Shakespeare Yearbook* 2 (1991): 49-67.

Arthos, John. "*Pericles, Prince of Tyre:* A Study in the Dramatic Use of Romantic Narrative." *Shakespeare Quarterly* 4 (1953): 257-70.

Ashton, Robert, ed. *James I by His Contemporaries.* London: Hutchinson, 1969.

Auberlen, Eckhard. "*King Henry VIII*: Shakespeare's Break with the 'Bluff-King-Harry' Tradition." *Anglia* 98 (1980): 319-47.

Bacon, Francis. *The Advancement of Learning, Book I.* Ed. William A. Armstrong. London: Athlone, 1975.

———. "Of Custom and Education." *Selected Writings of Sir Francis Bacon.* New York: Random House, 1955. 103-4.

———. *The New Organon. The Works of Francis Bacon.* Ed. James Spedding, Robert L. Ellis, and Douglas D. Heath. Vol. 8. Boston: Taggard and Thompson, 1863. 15 vols.

Baillie, William M. "*Henry VIII*: A Jacobean History." *Shakespeare Studies* 12 (1979): 247-66.

Barber, C. L. "'Thou That Beget'st Him That Did Thee Beget': Transformation in *Pericles* and *The Winter's Tale*." *Shakespeare Survey* 22 (1969): 59-67.

———, and Richard Wheeler. *The Whole Journey: Shakespeare's Power of Development.* Berkeley: U of California P, 1986.

Barkin, Leonard. *Nature's Work of Art: The Human Body as Image.* New Haven: Yale UP, 1975.

Barroll, J. Leeds. *Shakespearean Tragedy: Genre, Tradition, and Change in "Antony and Cleopatra."* Washington: Folger Books, 1984.

Bateson, F. W. "How Old Was Leontes?" *Essays and Studies* 31 (1978): 65-74.

Battenhouse, Roy. "Theme and Structure in *The Winter's Tale*." *Shakespeare Survey* 33 (1980): 123-38.

Beier, A. L. *Masterless Men: The Vagrancy Problem in England 1560-1640.* London: Methuen, 1985.

Berger, Harry, Jr. "Miraculous Harp: A Reading of Shakespeare's *Tempest*." *Second World and Green World: Studies in Renaissance Fiction-Making.* Berkeley: U of California P, 1988. 147-85.

Bergeron, David M. *Shakespeare's Romances and the Royal Family.* Lawrence: U of Kansas P, 1985.

Berggren, Paula S. "'For what we lack,/ We laugh': Incompletion and *The Two Noble Kinsmen*." *Modern Language Studies* 14.4 (1984): 3-17.

Berman, Ronald. "*King Henry the Eighth*: History and Romance." *English Studies* 48 (1967): 112-21.

Berry, Edward I. "*Henry VIII* and the Dynamics of Spectacle." *Shakespeare Studies* 12 (1979): 229-46.

Bertram, Paul. "*Henry VIII*: The Conscience of the King." *In Defense of Reading.* Ed. Reuben Brower and Richard Poirier. New York: Dutton, 1963. 153-73.

———. *Shakespeare and "The Two Noble Kinsmen."* New Brunswick: Rutgers UP, 1965.

Bethell, S. L. *"The Winter's Tale": A Study.* London: Staples Press, 1947.

Bieman, Elizabeth. *William Shakespeare: The Romances.* Boston: Twayne, 1990.

Bliss, Lee. "The Wheel of Fortune and the Maiden Phoenix of Shakespeare's *King Henry the Eighth*." *Journal of English Literary History* 42 (1975): 1-25.

Bloom, Harold, ed. *William Shakespeare's "Coriolanus."* New York: Chelsea House, 1988.

Bond, Ronald B. "Labour, Ease, and *The Tempest* as Pastoral Romance." *Journal of English and Germanic Philology* 77 (1978): 330-42.

Boose, Lynda E. "Othello's Handkerchief: 'The Recognizance and Pledge of Love.'" *English Literary Renaissance* 5 (1975): 360-74.

Booth, Stephen. "Speculations on Doubling in Shakespeare's Plays." *Shakespeare: The Theatrical Dimension.* Ed. Philip C. McGuire and David A. Samuelson. New York: AMS Press, 1979. 103-31.

Bowers, A. Robin. "'The Merciful Construction of Good Women': Katherine of Aragon and Pity in Shakespeare's *King Henry VIII*." *Christianity and Literature* 37 (1988): 29-51.

Brailow, David. "Prospero's 'Old Brain': The Old Man as Metaphor in *The Tempest*." *Shakespeare Studies* 14 (1981): 285-303.

Bristol, Michael D. "In Search of the Bear: Spatiotemporal Form and the Heterogeneity of Economies in *The Winter's Tale*." *Shakespeare Quarterly* 42 (1991): 145-67.

———. "Lenten Butchery: Legitimation Crisis in *Coriolanus*." *Shakespeare Reproduced: The Text in History and Ideology*. Ed. Jean E. Howard and Marion F. O'Connor. New York: Methuen, 1987. 207-24.

Brockbank, Philip. "*The Tempest*: Conventions of Art and Empire." *Later Shakespeare*. Ed. John Russell Brown and Bernard Harris. Stratford-Upon-Avon Studies 8. London: Edward Arnold, 1966. 183-201.

Brownlow, Frank W. *Two Shakespearean Sequences: "Henry VI" to "Richard II" and "Pericles" to "Timon of Athens."* Pittsburgh: U of Pittsburgh P, 1977.

Burke, Kenneth. "*Coriolanus*—and the Delights of Faction." *Hudson Review* 19 (1966): 185-202.

———. "*Timon of Athens* and Misanthropic Gold." *Language as Symbolic Action*. Berkeley: U of California P, 1966. 115-24.

Burton, Robert. *The Anatomy of Melancholy*. Ed. Thomas C. Faulkner, Nicholas K. Kiessling, and Rhonda L. Blair. Vol. 1. Oxford: Clarendon Press, 1989- .

Byrne, Muriel St. Clare. "A Stratford Production: *Henry VIII*." *Shakespeare Survey* 3 (1950): 120-29.

Carroll, William C. "'The Base Shall Top Th'Legitimate': The Bedlam Beggar and the Role of Edgar in *King Lear*." *Shakespeare Quarterly* 38 (1987): 426-41.

———. "Language, Politics, and Poverty in Shakespearian Drama." *Shakespeare Survey* 44 (1991): 17-24.

Cartelli, Thomas. "Prospero in Africa: *The Tempest* as Colonialist Text and Pretext." *Shakespeare Reproduced: The Text in History and Ideology*. Ed. Jean E. Howard and Marion F. O'Connor. New York: Methuen, 1987. 99-115.

Cavell, Stanley. "'Who Does the Wolf Love?': *Coriolanus* and the Interpretations of Politics." *Shakespeare and the Question of Theory*. Ed. Patricia Parker and Geoffrey Hartman. New York: Methuen, 1985. 245-72.

Cespedes, Frank V. "'We are one in fortunes': The Sense of History in *Henry VIII*." *English Literary Renaissance* 10 (1980): 413-38.

Chamberlain, John. *The Letters of John Chamberlain*. Ed. Norman E. McClure. Vol. 1. Philadelphia: American Philosophical Society, 1939. 2 vols.

Clark, Peter and Paul Slack. *English Towns in Transition 1500-1700*. London: Oxford UP, 1976.

Coletti, Theresa. "Music and Tempest." *Shakespeare's Late Plays: Essays in Honor of Charles Crow*. Ed. Richard C. Tobias and Paul G. Zolbrod. Athens: Ohio UP, 1974. 185-99.

Colie, Rosalie L. "Reason and Need: *King Lear* and the 'Crisis' of the Aristocracy." *Some Facets of "King Lear": Essays in Prismatic Criticism*. Ed. Rosalie L. Colie and F. T. Flahiff. Toronto: U of Toronto P, 1974. 185-219.

———. *Shakespeare's Living Art*. Princeton: Princeton UP, 1974.

Colman, D. C. "Labour in the English Economy of the Seventeenth Century." *The Economic History Review* 8 (1956): 280-95.

Corfield, Cosmo. "Why Does Prospero Abjure His 'Rough Magic'?" *Shakespeare Quarterly* 36 (1985): 31-48.

Cox, John D. "*Henry VIII* and the Masque." *Journal of English Literary History* 45 (1978): 390-409.

———. *Shakespeare and the Dramaturgy of Power*. Princeton: Princeton UP, 1989.

Cox, Lee Sheridan. "The Role of Autolycus in *The Winter's Tale*." *Studies in English Literature* 9 (1969): 283-301.

Cunningham, J. V. *Woe or Wonder*. Denver: U of Denver P, 1951.

Curtis, Mark. "The Alienated Intellectuals of Early Stuart England." *Past and Present* 23 (1962): 25-43.

Danby, John F. *Poets on Fortune's Hill: Studies in Sidney, Shakespeare, Beaumont and Fletcher*. 1952. Port Washington: Kennikat Press, 1966.

The Dartmouth Bible. Ed. Roy B. Chamberlin and Herman Feldman. Boston: Houghton Mifflin, 1961.

Davies, Margaret G. *The Enforcement of English Apprenticeship, 1563-1642*. Harvard Economic Studies 97. Cambridge: Harvard UP, 1956.

Davies, Stevie. *The Idea of Woman in Renaissance Literature: The Feminine Reclaimed*. Brighton: Harvester Press, 1986.

Dickey, Stephen. "Language and Role in *Pericles*." *English Literary Renaissance* 16 (1986): 550-66.

Dollimore, Jonathan. *Radical Tragedy: Religion, Ideology and Power in the Drama of Shakespeare and His Contemporaries*. Chicago: U of Chicago P, 1984.

Donaldson, E. Talbot. *The Swan at the Well*. New Haven: Yale UP, 1985.

Donne, John. *The Poems of John Donne*. Ed. Herbert Grierson. London: Oxford UP, 1964.

Eagleton, Terence. *Shakespeare and Society*. New York: Schocken, 1967.

Edwards, Philip. "On the Design of *The Two Noble Kinsmen*." *Review of English Literature* 5.4 (1964): 89-105.

Ellis-Fermor, Una. "*Timon of Athens*: An Unfinished Play." *Review of English Studies* 18 (1942): 270-83.

Elyot, Thomas. *The Book Named the Governor*. London: Dent, 1962.

Erdman, David V. and Ephrim G. Fogel, eds. *Evidence for Authorship*. Ithaca: Cornell UP, 1966.

Erikson, Erik. *Insight and Responsibility: Lectures on the Ethical Implications of Psychoanalytical Insight*. New York: Norton, 1964.

Evett, David. *Literature and the Visual Arts in Tudor England*. Athens: U of Georgia P, 1990.

Farnham, Willard. *Shakespeare's Tragic Frontier*. 1950. Berkeley: U of California P, 1963.

Farrell, Kirby. *Shakespeare's Creation: The Language of Magic and Play*. Amherst: U of Massachusetts P, 1975.

Felperin, Howard. "Shakespeare's *Henry VIII*: History as Myth." *Studies in English Literature* 6 (1966): 225-46.

——. *Shakespearean Romance*. Princeton: Princeton UP, 1972.

Flower, Annette C. "Disguise and Identity in *Pericles, Prince of Tyre*." *Shakespeare Quarterly* 26 (1975): 30-41.

Fly, Richard. "The Unmediated World of *Timon of Athens*." *Shakespeare's Mediated World*. Amherst: U of Massachusetts P, 1976. 119-42.

Foakes, R. A. Introduction. *King Henry VIII*. By William Shakespeare. London: Methuen, 1964. xv-lxvii.

———. *Shakespeare: The Dark Comedies to the Last Plays–From Satire to Celebration.* Charlottesville: UP of Virginia, 1971.

Forker, Charles R. "Perdita's Distribution of Flowers and the Function of Lyricism in *The Winter's Tale.*" *Fancy's Images: Contexts, Settings, and Perspectives in Shakespeare and His Contemporaries.* Carbondale: Southern Illinois UP, 1990. 113-25.

Foucault, Michel. *The History of Sexuality.* Trans. Robert Hurley. 1976. New York: Pantheon, 1978.

Fowler, Alastair. "Leontes' Contrition and the Repair of Nature." *Essays and Studies* 31 (1978): 36-64.

Fraser, Russell. *Young Shakespeare.* New York: Columbia UP, 1988.

Freer, Coburn. *The Poetics of Jacobean Drama.* Baltimore: The Johns Hopkins UP, 1981.

Frey, Charles H. "Collaborating with Shakespeare: After the Final Play." *Shakespeare, Fletcher, and "The Two Noble Kinsmen."* Ed. Charles H. Frey. Columbia: U of Missouri P, 1989. 31-44.

———. *Shakespeare's Vast Romance: A Study of "The Winter's Tale."* Columbia: U of Missouri P, 1980.

Frost, David L. "'Mouldy Tales': The Context of Shakespeare's *Cymbeline.*" *Essays and Studies* 39 (1986): 19-38.

Frye, Northrop. *A Natural Perspective: The Development of Shakespearean Comedy and Romance.* New York: Harcourt, Brace & World, 1965.

———. "Recognition in *The Winter's Tale.*" *Essays on Shakespeare and Elizabethan Drama in Honor of Hardin Craig.* Ed. Richard Hosley. Columbia: U of Missouri P, 1962. 235-46.

Fuller, Thomas. *The History of the Worthies of England.* Vol. 3. 1840. New York: AMS Press, 1965. 3 vols.

Fumerton, Patricia. *Cultural Aesthetics: Renaissance Literature and the Practice of Social Ornament*. Chicago: U of Chicago P, 1991.

Garber, Marjorie. *Dream in Shakespeare: From Metaphor to Metamorphosis*. New Haven: Yale UP, 1974.

Gardiner, Samuel R. *History of England from the Accession of James I to the Outbreak of the Civil War*. Vol. 1. 1883-84. New York: AMS Press, 1965. 10 vols.

Geller, Lila. "*Cymbeline* and the Imagery of Covenant Theology." *Studies in English Literature* 20 (1980): 241-55.

George, Charles H. and Katherine George. *The Protestant Mind of the English Reformation, 1570-1640*. Princeton: Princeton UP, 1961.

Goddard, Harold C. *The Meaning of Shakespeare*. Vol. 2. Chicago: U of Chicago P, 1951. 2 vols.

Goldberg, Jonathan. "Hamlet's Hand." *Shakespeare Quarterly* 39 (1988): 307-27.

Gorfain, Phyllis. "Puzzle and Artifice: The Riddle as Metapoetry in *Pericles*." *Shakespeare Survey* 29 (1976): 11-20.

Gourlay, Patricia S. "'O my most sacred lady': Female Metaphor in *The Winter's Tale*." *English Literary Renaissance* 5 (1975): 375-95.

Greenblatt, Stephen. *Renaissance Self-Fashioning: From More to Shakespeare*. Chicago: U of Chicago P, 1980.

Greenfield, Thelma N. "A Re-Examination of the 'Patient' Pericles." *Shakespeare Studies* 3 (1967): 51-61.

Greenwood, John. *Shifting Perspectives and the Stylish Style: Mannerism in Shakespeare and His Jacobean Contemporaries*. Toronto: U of Toronto P, 1988.

Greville, Fulke. *The Prose Works of Fulke Greville, Lord Brooke*. Ed. John Gouws. Oxford: Clarendon P, 1986.

Grudin, Robert. *Mighty Opposites: Shakespeare and Renaissance Contrariety*. Berkeley: U of California P, 1979.

Gupta, S. C. Sen. *Shakespeare's Historical Plays*. Oxford: Oxford UP, 1964.

Hamilton, Donna B. *Virgil and "The Tempest": The Politics of Imitation*. Columbus: Ohio State UP, 1990.

Harris, Bernard. "'What's past is prologue': *Cymbeline* and *Henry VIII*." *Later Shakespeare*. Ed. John Russell Brown and Bernard Harris. Stratford-Upon-Avon Studies 8. London: Edward Arnold, 1966. 203-33.

Harris, Victor. *All Coherence Gone*. Chicago: U of Chicago P, 1949.

Harrison, William. *The Description of England*. Ed. Georges Edelen. Ithaca: Cornell UP, 1968.

Hartman, Geoffrey. "The Voice of the Shuttle: Language from the Point of View of Literature." *Beyond Formalism: Literary Essays 1958-1970*. New Haven: Yale UP, 1970. 337-55.

Hartwig, Joan. "Cloten, Autolycus, and Caliban: Bearers of Parodic Burdens." *Shakespeare's Romances Reconsidered*. Ed. Carol McGinnis Kay and Henry E. Jacobs. Lincoln: U of Nebraska P, 1978. 91-103.

———. "Cloten and Caliban: Parodic Villains." *Shakespeare's Analogical Scene*. Lincoln: U of Nebraska P, 1983. 171-90.

———. *Shakespeare's Tragicomic Vision*. Baton Rouge: Louisiana State UP, 1972.

Hauser, Arnold. *Mannerism: The Crisis of The Renaissance and the Origin of Modern Art*. Trans. Eric Mosbacher. 2 vols. New York: Knopf, 1965.

Hedrick, Donald K. "'Be Rough With Me': The Collaborative Arenas of *The Two Noble Kinsmen*." *Shakespeare, Fletcher,* and *"The Two Noble Kinsmen."* Ed. Charles H. Frey. Columbia: U of Missouri P, 1989. 45-77.

Heinemann, Margot. *Puritanism and the Theatre: Thomas Middleton and Opposition Drama under the Early Stuarts.* Cambridge: Cambridge UP, 1980.

Helms, Lorraine. "The Saint in the Brothel: Or, Eloquence Rewarded." *Shakespeare Quarterly* 41 (1990): 319-32.

Hexter, J. H. "Storm Over the Gentry." *Reappraisals in History.* Evanston: Northwestern UP, 1962. 117-62.

Hildebrand, H. Peter. "The Other Side of the Wall: A Psychoanalytic Study of Creativity in Later Life." *International Review of Psycho-Analysis* 15 (1988): 353-63.

Hill, Christopher. "Pottage for Freeborn Englishmen: Attitudes to Wage-Labour." *Change and Continuity in Seventeenth-Century England.* Cambridge: Harvard UP, 1975. 219-38.

———. "Protestantism and the Rise of Capitalism." *Change and Continuity in Seventeenth-Century England.* Cambridge: Harvard UP, 1975. 81-102.

———. *The World Turned Upside Down.* New York: Viking, 1972.

Hillman, Richard. "Shakespeare's Gower and Gower's Shakespeare: The Larger Debt of *Pericles*." *Shakespeare Quarterly* 36 (1985): 427-37.

———. "Shakespeare's Romantic Innocents and the Misappropriation of the Romance Past: The Case of *The Two Noble Kinsmen.*" *Shakespeare Survey* 43 (1990): 69-79.

Hoeniger, F. D. Introduction. *Pericles.* By William Shakespeare. London: Methuen, 1963. xiii-xci.

———. "The Meaning of *The Winter's Tale.*" *University of Toronto Quarterly* 20 (1950): 11-26.

———. "Prospero's Storm and Miracle." *Shakespeare Quarterly* 7 (1956): 33-38.

Holland, Norman N. *Psychoanalysis and Shakespeare*. 1964. New York: Octagon Books, 1976.

Holloway, John. *The Story of the Night: Studies in Shakespeare's Major Tragedies*. 1961. Lincoln: U of Nebraska P, 1963.

Holstun, James. "Tragic Superfluity in *Coriolanus*." *Journal of English Literary History* 50 (1983): 485-507.

Horowitz, David. *Shakespeare: An Existential View*. London: Tavistock, 1965.

Hoy, Cyrus. "Jacobean Tragedy and the Mannerist Style." *Shakespeare Survey* 26 (1973): 49-67.

———. "The Language of Fletcherian Tragicomedy." *Mirror Up to Shakespeare: Essays in Honour of G. R. Hibbard*. Ed. J. C. Gray. Toronto: U of Toronto P, 1984. 99-113.

Hunt, John Dixon. "Shakespeare and the Paragone: A Reading of *Timon of Athens*." *Images of Shakespeare*. Ed. Werner Habicht, D. J. Palmer, and Roger Pringle. Newark: U of Delaware P, 1988. 47-63.

Hunt, Maurice. "Pericles and the Emblematic Imagination." *Studies in the Humanities* 17 (1990): 1-20.

———. "Perspectivism in *King Lear* and *Cymbeline*." *Studies in the Humanities* 14 (1987): 18-29.

———. *Shakespeare's Romance of the Word*. Lewisburg, PA: Bucknell UP, 1990.

———. "'Stir' and Work in Shakespeare's Last Plays." *Studies in English Literature* 22 (1982): 285-304.

———. "The Three Seasons of Mankind: Age, Nature, and Art in *The Winter's Tale*." *Iowa State Journal of Research* 58 (1984): 299-309.

Hunter, G. K. *John Lyly: The Humanist as Courtier*. London: Routledge & Kegan Paul, 1962.

Iwasaki, Soji. "*Veritas Filia Temporis* and Shakespeare." *English Literary Renaissance* 3 (1973): 249-63.

Jagendorf, Zvi. "*Coriolanus*: Body Politic and Private Parts." *Shakespeare Quarterly* 41 (1990): 455-69.

James, D. G. *The Dream of Prospero*. Oxford: Clarendon Press, 1967.

Johnson, Samuel. *The Yale Edition of the Works of Samuel Johnson*. Ed. Arthur Sherbo, et al. 16 vols. New Haven: Yale UP, 1958-.

Jones, Emyrs. "Stuart *Cymbeline*." *Essays in Criticism* 11 (1961): 84-99.

Jonson, Ben. *Conversations with William Drummond of Hawthorndon*. Ed. G. B. Harrison. Elizabethan and Jacobean Quartos. New York: Barnes & Noble, 1966.

Jorgensen, Paul A. *Shakespeare's Military World*. Berkeley: U of California P, 1956.

Kahn, Coppélia. "'Magic of bounty': *Timon of Athens*, Jacobean Patronage, and Maternal Power." *Shakespeare Quarterly* 38 (1987): 34-57.

Kaul, Mythili. "The Old Shepherd's Speech in *The Winter's Tale*." *The Upstart Crow* 7 (1987): 96-100.

Kaula, David. "Autolycus' Trumpery." *Studies in English Literature* 26 (1976): 287-303.

Kermode, Frank. "What is *Henry VIII* About?" *Shakespeare the Histories: A Collection of Critical Essays*. Ed. Eugene Waith. Englewood Cliffs: Prentice-Hall, 1965. 168-79.

Kerrigan, William. "Life's Iamb: The Scansion of Late Creativity in the Culture of the Renaissance." *Aging-Literature-Psychoanalysis*. Ed. Kathleen Woodward and Murray M. Schwartz. Bloomington: Indiana UP, 1986. 168-91.

Knight, G. Wilson. *The Crown of Life: Essays in Interpretation of Shakespeare's Final Plays.* 1947. New York: Barnes & Noble, 1966.

——. *The Imperial Theme.* 1931. London: Methuen, 1965.

Knights, L. C. *Some Shakespearean Themes and An Approach to "Hamlet."* 1960, 1961. Stanford: Stanford UP, 1966.

Knowles, Richard P. "'Wishes Fall Out as They're Will'd': Artist, Audience, and *Pericles's* Gower." *English Studies in Canada* 9 (1983): 14-24.

Krieger, Elliot. *A Marxist Study of Shakespeare's Comedies.* London: Macmillan, 1979.

Krieger, Murray. "The Ekphrastic Principle and the Still Movement of Poetry; or *Laokoön* Revisited." *The Play and Place of Criticism.* Baltimore: The Johns Hopkins UP, 1967. 105-28.

Laslett, Peter. *The World We Have Lost: England Before the Industrial Age.* New York: Scribner's, 1971.

Lawrence, Judiana. "Natural Bonds and Artistic Coherence in the Ending of *Cymbeline.*" *Shakespeare Quarterly* 35 (1984): 440-60.

Le Goff, Jacques. *Time, Work and Culture in the Middle Ages.* Trans. Arthur Goldhammer. Chicago: U of Chicago P, 1980.

Leavis, F. R. "The Criticism of Shakespeare's Late Plays." *The Common Pursuit.* London: Chatto & Windus, 1958. 173-81.

Lee, Maurice, Jr., ed. *Dudley Carleton to John Chamberlain 1603-1624: Jacobean Letters.* New Brunswick: Rutgers UP, 1972.

Leech, Clifford. "The Structure of the Last Plays." *Shakespeare Survey* 11 (1958): 19-30.

Leggatt, Alexander. "*Henry VIII* and the Ideal England." *Shakespeare Survey* 38 (1985): 131-43.

———. "*Macbeth* and the Last Plays." *Mirror Up to Shakespeare: Essays in Honour of G. R. Hibbard.* Ed. J. C. Gray. Toronto: U of Toronto P, 1984. 189-207.

Levin, Harry. "Two Magian Comedies: *The Tempest* and *The Alchemist.*" *Shakespeare and the Revolution of the Times.* Oxford: Oxford UP, 1976. 210-31.

Levin, Richard. *The Multiple Plot in English Renaissance Drama.* Chicago: U of Chicago P, 1971.

Lewalski, Barbara K. *Protestant Poetics and the Seventeenth-Century Religious Lyric.* Princeton: Princeton UP, 1979.

Lewis, Anthony J. "'I feed on Mother's Flesh': Incest and Eating in *Pericles.*" *Essays in Literature* 15 (1988): 147-63.

Lewis, Cynthia. "'With Simular Proof Enough': Modes of Misperception in *Cymbeline.*" *Studies in English Literature* 31 (1991): 341-64.

Lief, Madelon and Nicholas F. Radel. "Linguistic Subversion and the Artifice of Rhetoric in *The Two Noble Kinsmen.*" *Shakespeare Quarterly* 38 (1987): 405-25.

Lindenbaum, Peter. *Changing Landscapes: Anti-Pastoral Sentiment in the English Renaissance.* Athens: U of Georgia P, 1986.

———. "Time, Sexual Love, and the Uses of Pastoral in *The Winter's Tale.*" *Modern Language Quarterly* 33 (1972): 3-22.

Lis, Catharina and Hugo Soly. *Poverty and Capitalism in Pre-Industrial Europe.* Trans. James Coonan. Atlantic Highlands: Humanities P, 1979.

Livingston, Mary L. "The Natural Art of *The Winter's Tale.*" *Modern Language Quarterly* 30 (1969): 340-55.

Lockyer, Roger. *The Early Stuarts: A Political History of England, 1603-1642.* London: Longman, 1989.

Luckyj, Christina. "Volumnia's Silence." *Studies in English Literature* 31 (1991): 327-42.

Ludwig, Jay B. "Shakespearean Decorum: An Essay on *The Winter's Tale*." *Style* 8 (1974): 365-404.

Luria, Maxwell. "Standing Water and Sloth in *The Tempest*." *English Studies* 49 (1968): 328-31.

Lyly, John. "Speeches Delivered to Her Majesty this last Progress." *The Complete Works of John Lyly*. Ed. R. Warwick Bond. Vol. 1. Oxford: Clarendon Press, 1967. 471-90. 3 vols.

Mackinnon, Lachlan. *Shakespeare the Aesthete*. New York: St. Martin's Press, 1988.

Magnusson, A. Lynne. "Interruption in *The Tempest*." *Shakespeare Quarterly* 37 (1986): 52-65.

Manning, Roger B. *Village Revolts: Social Protest and Popular Disturbances, 1509-1640*. Oxford: Clarendon P, 1988.

Mannoni, Octave. *Prospero and Caliban: The Psychology of Colonization*. Trans. Pamela Powesland. New York: Praeger, 1964.

Marcus, Leah S. *The Politics of Mirth: Herrick, Milton, Marvell, and the Defense of Old Holiday Pastimes*. Chicago: U of Chicago P, 1986.

Markels, Julian. *The Pillar of the World: "Antony and Cleopatra" in Shakespeare's Development*. Columbus: Ohio State UP, 1968.

Marsh, Derick R. C. *The Recurring Miracle: A Study of "Cymbeline" and the Last Plays*. Pietrmaritzburg: U of Natal P, 1962.

Marshall, Cynthia. *Last Things and Last Plays: Shakespearean Eschatology*. Carbondale: Southern Illinois UP, 1991.

Matus, Irvin. "The Case for Shakespeare." *The Atlantic* (October 1991): 64-72.

McBride, Tom. "*Henry VIII* as Machiavellian Romance." *Journal of English and Germanic Philology* 76 (1977): 26-39.

McCanles, Michael. "The Dialectic of Transcendence in Shakespeare's *Coriolanus*." *PMLA* 82 (1967): 44-53.

McDonald, Russ. "Reading *The Tempest*." *Shakespeare Survey* 43 (1990): 15-28.

McIlwain, Charles H., ed. *The Political Works of James I*. Cambridge: Harvard UP, 1918.

McKenzie, Stanley D. "'Unshout the noise that banish'd Martius': Structural Paradox and Dissembling in *Coriolanus*." *Shakespeare Studies* 18 (1986): 189-204.

McNamara, Kevin. "Golden Worlds at Court: *The Tempest* and Its Masque." *Shakespeare Studies* 19 (1987): 183-202.

Merchant, W. M. "*Timon* and the Conceit of Art." *Shakespeare Quarterly* 6 (1955): 249-57.

Micheli, Linda McJ. "'Sit By Us': Visual Imagery and the Two Queens in *Henry VIII*." *Shakespeare Quarterly* 38 (1987): 452-66.

Moffet, Robin. "*Cymbeline* and the Nativity." *Shakespeare Quarterly* 13 (1962): 207-18.

Montaigne, Michel de. *Essays*. Trans. John Florio. Vol. 3. 1910. London: Dent, 1965. 3 vols.

Montrose, Louis A. "Of Gentlemen and Shepherds: The Politics of Elizabethan Pastoral Form." *Journal of English Literary History* 50 (1983): 415-59.

Morgan, Edmund S. "The Labor Problem at Jamestown, 1607-18." *The American Historical Review* 76 (1971): 595-611.

Mowat, Barbara A. *The Dramaturgy of Shakespeare's Romances*. Athens: U of Georgia P, 1976.

———. "Prospero, Agrippa, and Hocus Pocus." *English Literary Renaissance* 11 (1981): 281-303.

Muir, Kenneth. *Shakespeare as Collaborator*. London: Methuen, 1960.

Mullaney, Steven. *The Place of the Stage: License, Play, and Power in Renaissance England*. Chicago: U of Chicago P, 1988.

Myers, Jeffrey R. *Shakespeare's Mannerist Canon: "Ut Pictura Poemata."* New York: Peter Lang, 1989.

Neely, Carol Thomas. "*The Winter's Tale*: The Triumph of Speech." *Studies in English Literature* 15 (1975): 321-38.

Nevo, Ruth. *Shakespeare's Other Language*. New York: Methuen, 1987.

Nuttall, Anthony D. "*Timon of Athens*." Twayne's New Critical Introductions to Shakespeare. Boston: Twayne, 1989.

Orgel, Stephen. Introduction. *The Tempest*. By William Shakespeare. Oxford: Oxford UP, 1987. 1-87.

Ornstein, Robert. "The Ethic of the Imagination: Love and Art in *Antony and Cleopatra*." *Later Shakespeare*. Ed. John Russell Brown and Bernard Harris. Stratford-Upon-Avon Studies 8. London: Edward Arnold, 1966. 31-46.

Pafford, J. H. P. Introduction. *The Winter's Tale*. By William Shakespeare. London: Methuen, 1965. xv-lxxxix.

Panofsky, Erwin. *Studies in Iconology*. New York: Oxford UP, 1939.

Paris, Bernard J. "*The Tempest*: Shakespeare's Ideal Solution." *Shakespeare's Personality*. Ed. Norman Holland, Sidney Homan and Bernard J. Paris. Berkeley: U of California P, 1989. 206-25.

Patterson, Annabel. *Shakespeare and the Popular Voice*. Oxford: Basil Blackwell, 1989.

Pearson, D'Orsay W. "'Unless I Be Reliev'd by Prayer': *The Tempest* in Perspective." *Shakespeare Studies* 7 (1974): 253-82.

Pennington, Loren E. "The Amerindian in English Promotional Literature, 1575-1625." *The Westward Enterprise: English Activities in Ireland, the Atlantic, and America, 1480-1650*. Ed. K. R. Andrews, N. P. Canny, and P. E. H. Hair. Liverpool: Liverpool UP, 1978. 175-94.

Peterson, Douglas L. *Time, Tide, and Tempest: A Study of Shakespeare's Romances*. San Marino: Huntington Library, 1972.

Pettet, E. C. "*Coriolanus* and the Midlands Insurrection of 1607." *Shakespeare Survey* 3 (1950): 34-42.

Peyré, Yves. "Les Masques d'Ariel." *Cahiers Elisabéthains* 19 (1981): 53-71.

Pierce, Robert B. "'Very Like a Whale': Scepticism and Seeing in *The Tempest*." *Shakespeare Survey* 38 (1985): 167-73.

Pitcher, John. "The Poet and the Taboo: The Riddle of Shakespeare's *Pericles*." *Essays and Studies* 35 (1982): 14-29.

Proser, Matthew N. *The Heroic Image in Five Shakespearean Tragedies*. Princeton: Princeton UP, 1967.

Puttenham, George. *The Arte of English Poesie*. Ed. Edward Arber. 1906. Kent: Kent State UP, 1970.

Rabkin, Norman. *Shakespeare and the Common Understanding*. New York: Macmillan, 1967.

Rackin, Phyllis. "Coriolanus: Shakespeare's Anatomy of *Virtus*." *Modern Language Studies* 13.2 (1983): 68-79.

Ralegh, Walter. *The Works of Sir Walter Ralegh*. Ed. William Oldys and Thomas Birch. Vol. 8. Oxford: Oxford UP, 1829. 8 vols.

Richmond, Hugh M. "The Feminism of Shakespeare's *Henry VIII*." *Essays in Literature* 6 (1979): 11-20.

———. "Shakespeare's *Henry VIII*: Romance Redeemed by History." *Shakespeare Studies* 4 (1968): 334-49.

Ridley, Jasper. *Elizabeth I: The Shrewdness of Virtue*. New York: Viking, 1988.

Riemer, A. P. *Antic Fables: Patterns of Evasion in Shakespeare's Comedies*. Sydney: Sydney UP, 1968.

———. *A Reading of Shakespeare's "Antony and Cleopatra."* New York: St. Martin's Press, 1980.

Riggs, David. *Ben Jonson: A Life*. Cambridge: Harvard UP, 1989.

Roberts, Jeanne Addison. "Crises of Male Self-Definition in *The Two Noble Kinsmen*." *Shakespeare, Fletcher, and "The Two Noble Kinsmen."* Ed. Charles H. Frey. Columbia: U of Missouri P, 1989. 133-144.

Rockett, William. "Labor and Virtue in *The Tempest*." *Shakespeare Quarterly* 24 (1973): 77-84.

Rose, Mary Beth. *The Expense of Spirit: Love and Sexuality in English Renaissance Drama*. Ithaca: Cornell UP, 1988.

Rozett, Martha T. *The Doctrine of Election and the Emergence of Elizabethan Tragedy*. Princeton: Princeton UP, 1984.

Rudnytsky, Peter L. "*Henry VIII* and the Deconstruction of History." *Shakespeare Survey* 43 (1990): 43-57.

Sacks, Elizabeth. *Shakespeare's Images of Pregnancy*. New York: St. Martin's P, 1980.

Saxl, Fritz. "*Veritas Filia Temporis*." *Philosophy and History: Essays Presented to Ernst Cassirer*. Ed. Raymond Klibansky and H. J. Paton. Oxford: Clarendon P, 1936. 197-222.

Schanzer, Ernest. *The Problem Plays of Shakespeare: A Study of "Julius Caesar," "Measure for Measure," and "Antony and Cleopatra."* 1963. New York: Schocken, 1965.

———. "The Structural Pattern of *The Winter's Tale*." *Review of English Literature* 5 (1964): 72-82.

Schmidgall, Gary. *Shakespeare and the Poet's Life*. Lexington: UP of Kentucky, 1990.

Seiden, Melvin. "Utopianism in *The Tempest*." *Modern Language Quarterly* 30 (1970): 3-21.

Selden, Raman. "King Lear and True Need." *Shakespeare Studies* 19 (1987): 143-69.

Shakespeare, William. *The Riverside Shakespeare*. Ed. G. Blakemore Evans, et al. Boston: Houghton Mifflin, 1974.

Shaw, Catherine M. "*The Tempest* and *Hymenaei*." *Cahiers Elisabéthains* 26 (1984): 29-39.

Shearman, John. *Mannerism*. London: Penguin, 1967.

Siegel, Paul N. "Malvolio: Comic Puritan Automaton." *Shakespearean Comedy*. Ed. Maurice Charney. New York: New York Literary Forum, 1980. 217-30.

———. *Shakespeare's English and Roman History Plays: A Marxist Approach*. Rutherford: Fairleigh Dickinson UP, 1986.

Simmons, J. L. *Shakespeare's Pagan World: The Roman Tragedies*. Charlottesville: UP of Virginia, 1973.

———. "A Source for Shakespeare's Malvolio: The Elizabethan Controversy with the Puritans." *Huntington Library Quarterly* 36 (1972-73): 181-201.

Simonds, Peggy Muñoz. "The Iconography of Primitivism in *Cymbeline*." *Renaissance Drama* 16 (1985): 95-120.

———. "The Marriage Topos in *Cymbeline*: Shakespeare's Variations on a Classical Theme." *English Literary Renaissance* 19 (1989): 94-117.

———. "'No More . . . Offend Our Hearing': Aural Imagery in *Cymbeline*." *Texas Studies in Literature and Language* 24 (1982): 137-54.

Skura, Meredith. "Interpreting Posthumus' Dream from Above and Below." *Representing Shakespeare: New Psychoanalytic Essays*. Ed. Murray Schwartz and Coppélia Kahn. Baltimore: The Johns Hopkins UP, 1980. 203-16.

Slights, Camille. "The Politics of Conscience in *All is True* (or *Henry VIII*)." *Shakespeare Survey* 43 (1990): 59-68.

Smith, Hallett. "Leontes' *Affectio*." *Shakespeare Quarterly* 14 (1963): 163-66.

———. *Shakespeare's Romances: A Study of Some Ways of the Imagination*. San Marino: Huntington Library, 1972.

Smith, Jonathan. "The Language of Leontes." *Shakespeare Quarterly* 19 (1968): 317-27.

Soellner, Rolf. *"Timon of Athens": Shakespeare's Pessimistic Tragedy*. Columbus: Ohio State UP, 1979.

Sommerville, J. P. *Politics and Ideology in England, 1603-1640*. London: Longman, 1986.

Sorge, Thomas. "The Failure of Orthodoxy in *Coriolanus*." *Shakespeare Reproduced: The Text in History and Ideology*. Ed. Jean E. Howard and Marion F. O'Connor. New York: Methuen, 1987. 225-41.

Spencer, Theodore. "*The Two Noble Kinsmen*." *Modern Philology* 36 (1939): 255-76.

States, Bert O. *"Hamlet" and the Concept of Character*. Baltimore: The Johns Hopkins UP, 1992.

Stone, Lawrence. *The Crisis of the Aristocracy 1558-1641*. Oxford: Clarendon Press, 1965.

———. *Social Change and Revolution in England 1540-1640*. New York: Barnes & Noble, 1965.

Summers, Joseph. *Dreams of Love and Power: On Shakespeare's Plays*. Oxford: Clarendon Press, 1984.

Sutherland, James. "The Language of the Last Plays." *More Talking of Shakespeare*. Ed. John Garrett. New York: Theatre Arts Books, 1959. 144-51.

Tawney, R. H. and Eileen Power, eds. *Tudor Economic Documents*. Vol. 1. London: Longmans, Green and Co., 1924. 3 vols.

Taylor, Gary. *Reinventing Shakespeare: A Cultural History from the Restoration to the Present*. 1989. Oxford: Oxford UP, 1991.

Taylor, Michael. "'Here is a thing too young for such a place': Innocence in *Pericles*." *Ariel* 13.3 (1982): 3-19.

———. "The Pastoral Reckoning of *Cymbeline*." *Shakespeare Survey* 36 (1983): 97-106.

Taylor, Thomas. *Works*. London: J. Bartlet, 1653.

Thirsk, Joan. "Enclosing and Engrossing." *The Agrarian History of England and Wales, Vol. IV, 1500-1700*. Ed. Joan Thirsk. Cambridge: Cambridge UP, 1967. 200-55.

Thorne, W. B. "*Pericles* and the Incest-Fertility Opposition." *Shakespeare Quarterly* 22 (1971): 43-56.

Thompson, Ann and John O. Thompson. "The Syntax of Metaphor in *Cymbeline*." *Images of Shakespeare*. Ed. Werner Habicht, D. J. Palmer, and Roger Pringle. Newark: U of Delaware P, 1988. 80-97.

Traversi, Derek A. *Shakespeare: The Last Phase*. 1954. Stanford: Stanford UP, 1965.

Tricomi, Albert H. *Anticourt Drama in England, 1603-1642*. Charlottesville: U of Virginia P, 1989.

Uphaus, Robert. *Beyond Tragedy: Structure and Experience in Shakespeare's Romances*. Lexington: UP of Kentucky, 1981.

Vaughan, Alden T. "Shakespeare's Indian: The Americanization of Caliban." *Shakespeare Quarterly* 39 (1988): 137-53.

Waith, Eugene M. *The Herculean Hero in Marlowe, Chapman, Shakespeare, and Dryden.* New York: Columbia UP, 1962.

———. Introduction. *The Two Noble Kinsmen.* By William Shakespeare. Oxford: Oxford UP, 1989. 1-66.

———. "Shakespeare and Fletcher on Love and Friendship." *Shakespeare Studies* 18 (1986): 235-50. Rpt. in *Patterns and Perspectives in English Renaissance Drama.* Newark: U of Delaware P, 1988. 289-303.

Walzer, Michael. *The Revolution of the Saints: A Study in the Origins of Radical Politics.* Cambridge: Harvard UP, 1965.

Ward, David. "Affection, Intention, and Dreams in *The Winter's Tale.*" *Modern Language Review* 82 (1987): 545-54.

Wells, Stanley. *Literature and Drama.* London: Routledge & Kegan Paul, 1970.

———, and Gary Taylor. *William Shakespeare: A Textual Companion.* Oxford: Clarendon Press, 1987.

Whitaker, Alexander. *Good Newes From Virginia.* London: William Welby, 1613.

White, R. S. *"Let Wonder Seem Familiar": Endings in Shakespeare's Romance Vision.* London: Athlone, 1985.

Wickham, Glynne. "Masque and Anti-masque in *The Tempest.*" *Essays and Studies* 28 (1975): 1-14.

Willbern, David. "What is Shakespeare?" *Shakespeare's Personality.* Ed. Norman N. Holland, Sidney Homan, and Bernard J. Paris. Berkeley: U of California P, 1989. 226-43.

Wilson, Richard. "Against the Grain: Representing the Market in *Coriolanus.*" *The Seventeenth Century* 6 (1991): 111-48.

———. "'Like the old Robin Hood': *As You Like It* and the Enclosure Riots." *Shakespeare Quarterly* 43 (1992): 1-19.

Wrightson, Keith. *English Society 1580-1680*. New Brunswick: Rutgers UP, 1982.

Yachnin, Paul. "The Powerless Theater." *English Literary Renaissance* 21 (1991): 49-74.

Young, Alan R. "Shakespeare's *Henry VIII* and the Theme of Conscience." *English Studies in Canada* 7 (1981): 38-53.

Young, David. *The Heart's Forest: A Study of Shakespeare's Pastoral Plays*. New Haven: Yale UP, 1972.

Index

Abercrombie, Lascelles, 92
Abrams, Richard, 257
Adams, Robert M., 92, 93, 193
Adams, Thomas, 5
Adelman, Janet, 64, 65
Advancement of Learning, The, 6-7
Akrigg, G. P. V., 11, 24, 35
All's Well That Ends Well, 225
Altieri, Joanne, 229
Ambrose, Saint, 6
Amussen, Susan, 16, 23, 65
Anatomy of Melancholy, The, 12-13
Andreas, James R., 257
Anne, Queen, 20, 57
Anniversary, The First, 8
Antony and Cleopatra, 36-41, 64-65, 260, 272
Aquinas, Saint Thomas, 5
Arte of English Poesie, The, 55
Arthos, John, 91-92
As You Like It, 27, 60, 145
Ashton, Robert, 24
Auberlen, Eckhard, 227
Augustine, Saint, 2, 6

Bacon, Francis, 6, 8, 9-10, 18, 26, 274, 278
Baillie, William M., 229
Baker, Herschel, 224
Banquet of Sense, The, 56
Baptism, 141, 222
Barber, C. L., 93, 268, 273, 277, 278
Barkin, Leonard, 66
Barroll, J. Leeds, 64
Basilikon Doron, The, 13
Bateson, F. W., 161
Battenhouse, Roy, 160
Beaumont, Francis, 203, 248, 250
Beier, A. L., 25, 26
Ben Jonson: A Life, 264

Berger, Harry, Jr., 195
Bergeron, David M., 24
Berggren, Paula S., 255, 257
Berman, Ronald, 229
Berry, Edward I., 227, 228
Bertram, Paul, 228, 256
Bethell, S. L., 162
Bible, The, 1, 2, 5, 6, 9, 44, 110-11, 114, 128, 146, 165, 224
Bieman, Elizabeth, 274, 278
Black Book, The, 12
Bliss, Lee, 227
Bloom, Harold, 67
Boccaccio, Giovanni, 245
Bond, Ronald B., 197
Boose, Lynda E., 30, 63
Booth, Stephen, 131
Bowers, A. Robin, 228
Brailow, David, 274, 278
Bristol, Michael D., 66, 142, 143, 159, 161
Brockbank, Philip, 193-94
Brownlow, Frank W., 69
Burke, Kenneth, 67, 69
Burton, Robert, 12-13, 19-20, 25

Calvin, John, 123
Calvinism, 4, 112, 123
Canterbury Tales, The, 2
Caravaggio, Michelangelo da, 262
Carroll, William C., 63, 276-77
Cartelli, Thomas, 196
Cavell, Stanley, 67
Cecil, Robert, 11
Cespedes, Frank V., 229
Chamberlain, John, 11
Chamberlayne, Edward, 12
Chapman, George, 11, 13, 141
Chaucer, Geoffrey, 2, 244-47
Christianity, 1-2, 3-7, 8-9, 34, 44, 50, 66, 83, 88, 89, 93, 110-

11, 112-13, 114, 122-23,
    126-27, 128, 146, 193, 202,
    203, 204, 222-24, 269, 270
Clark, Peter, 25
Coletti, Theresa, 194
Colie, Rosalie L., 63, 131
Colman, D. C., 25
Condell, Henry, 203, 268
Corfield, Cosmo, 197
Coriolanus, 36, 41-53, 62, 115, 259,
    264, 269, 273
Cox, John D., 196, 227, 276
Cox, Lee Sheridan, 161, 162
Crane, Ralph, 155, 156
Cunningham, J. V., 159
Curtis, Mark, 13, 25
Cymbeline, 13, 20, 36, 95-133, 135,
    141, 151, 167, 191, 203,
    208, 212, 222, 224, 238,
    254, 259, 261, 264, 269,
    272, 273

Danby, John F., 88, 92, 93, 209,
    228
Dance, 147-49, 176, 178, 194, 249
Davies, Margaret G., 25
Davies, Stevie, 88, 92, 93
Day, John, 11
Devereux, Robert, 50-51
Dickey, Stephen, 91, 93
Discorsi, 52
Dollimore, Jonathan, 8, 23
Donaldson, E. Talbot, 257
Donatus, 52
Donne, John, 8, 103
Doubling, Role, 130-31
Doctor Faustus, The Tragedy of, 178
Dream Vision, 121-24, 210-11
Dumb Show, 90

Eagleton, Terence, 194
Eastward Ho, 11
Edwards, Philip, 256
Elizabeth I, Queen, 10, 12, 51,
    107, 201, 216-18, 222-26,
    229
Ellis-Fermor, Una, 69
Elyot, Sir Thomas, 194

Emblem, 78-79, 88, 105, 210, 216,
    242
Epicoene, 264, 267
Erdman, David V., 227
Erikson, Erik, 268-69, 277
Evans, G. Blakemore, 155
Everyman Out of His Humour, 267
Evett, David, 262, 276

Faerie Queene, The, 58, 74, 113,
    212
Farnham, Willard, 57, 69
Farrell, Kirby, 94, 160
Father Hubbard's Tales, 12
Felperin, Howard, 91, 133, 159,
    194, 229
Field, Nathan, 248
Field of the Cloth of Gold, The,
    200
Fletcher, John, 203, 233, 239, 240,
    244-50, 251, 253
Flower, Annette C., 91
Fly, Richard, 69
Foakes, R. A., 131, 162, 228-29
Fogel, Ephrim G., 227
Forker, Charles R., 160
Foucault, Michel, 271, 278
Fowler, Alastair, 161
Francis I, King, 200
Fraser, Russell, 27, 63
Freer, Coburn, 130, 131, 132
Frey, Charles, 159, 162, 256
Frost, David, 118, 132
Frye, Northrop, 162, 228, 229
Fuller, Thomas, 132
Fumerton, Patricia, 162

Garber, Marjorie, 159
Gardiner, Samuel R., 24
Geller, Lila, 132
George, Charles, 5, 23
George, Katherine, 5, 23
Goddard, Harold C., 159, 196
Goldberg, Jonathan, 63
Good Newes From Virginia, 195
Gorfain, Phyllis, 91
Gosson, Stephen, 265
Gourlay, Patricia S., 161

Greco, El, 261
Greenblatt, Stephen, 7-8, 23, 271-72, 278
Greene, Robert, 157, 265, 266
Greenfield, Thelma N., 92
Greenwood, John, 276
Greville, Fulke, 51, 68, 114
Grierson, Herbert, 23
Grudin, Robert, 65

Hakewill, George, 8
Hamilton, Donna B., 196, 197
Hamlet, 8, 21, 27-30, 41, 268, 269, 273
Harris, Bernard, 133
Harris, Victor, 23
Harrison, William, 2-3, 22
Hartman, Geoffrey, 228
Hartwig, Joan, 92, 130, 162
Hauser, Arnold, 261, 276
Hedrick, Donald K., 256
Heinemann, Margot, 12, 24
Helms, Lorraine, 93
Heminge, John, 203, 268
Henry IV, Part One, 27
Henry IV, Part Two, 43
Henry VIII, King, 19, 20, 36, 189, 199-229, 259, 261, 270, 272, 273
Henry Stuart, Prince, 13
Herbert, George, 4
Herbert, Sir Henry, 155
Hercules, 27, 39, 63-64, 71
Hexter, J. H., 51, 68
Heywood, Thomas, 266
Hieron, Samuel, 6
Hildebrand, H. Peter, 278
Hill, Christopher, 3-4, 17, 22, 23, 25, 26, 277
Hillman, Richard, 93-94, 257
Hoeniger, F. David, 92, 94, 161
Holland, Norman N., 256, 278
Holloway, John, 67
Holstun, James, 67
Homeopathy, 83-84
Horowitz, David, 197
House Of Commons, The, 18
Howard, Lady Mary, 107
Hoy, Cyrus, 227, 260, 261, 276

Hunt, John Dixon, 69
Hunt, Maurice, 91, 92, 131, 161, 197
Hunter, G. K., 13, 25

Idleness (*see* Sloth)
Incest, 71-76, 89
Ingram, Sir Arthur, 17
Inner Temple and Gray's Inn Mask, 250
Isle of Gulls, The, 11
Iwasaki, Soji, 159

Jagendorf, Zvi, 66
Jaggard, William, 268
James, D. G., 195
James I, King, 3, 10-11, 12, 13, 14, 17, 18, 20, 24, 43, 50, 51, 57, 66, 196, 223, 260, 261, 262
Jameson, Fredric, 93
Jewell, Bishop John, 4
Jones, Emyrs, 133
Jonson, Ben, 11, 12, 254, 263, 264, 265, 266-68, 277
Jorgensen, Paul, 52, 68

Kahn, Coppélia, 69
Katherine of Aragon, Queen, 210
Kaul, Mythili, 160
Kaula, David, 162
Kermode, Frank, 229
Kerrigan, William, 274, 278
King Lear, 29, 30, 32-35, 39, 41, 80, 85
Knight, G. Wilson, 64, 91, 92, 131, 132, 161, 193, 194, 197, 227, 229
Knights, L. C., 68
Knight's Tale, The, 244, 246
Knowles, Richard P., 94
Krieger, Elliot, 27, 63, 161
Krieger, Murray, 148

Labor: and agrarian husbandry, 2, 3, 10, 15-16, 18, 44-46,

48-49, 52, 142-46, 161, 174-76; and apprenticeship, 14, 15, 25, 182-84, 196; and aristocrats, 1, 3, 7, 10, 12-14, 16, 18, 50-51, 78, 83, 98-99, 141-42, 163-67, 185-86, 195, 200, 265-67; and art, relationship of, 19, 53-56, 57, 59-61, 79, 87-88, 89-90, 99-103, 109-10, 116-21, 124, 125, 127, 129, 147-54, 190-92, 206-7, 250, 260-68, 269-70; as birth labor, 18-19, 47-48, 71, 73, 80, 88, 92-93, 99-100, 121-22, 127, 135-40, 140-41, 153, 154, 156-57, 167-68, 201, 211, 216-17, 234, 237, 238, 255-56; and capitalism, 85-87, 265-66, 271; and Catholicism, 1-3, 4, 5, 123, 201, 205, 216-17, 270; and deeds vs. faith, 3-4, 122-23; and farmers and yeomen, 15-16, 17, 112-13; and forests, relationship of, 17-18; and greatness, 201-8, 210, 211, 213, 217, 223; and healing, 35-36, 62, 82-84, 235, 251-52; and hunting, 104-5, 109, 177; and magic, relationship of, 9, 163, 169-70, 173-76, 178-82, 186-88, 190, 254; manual, 1-2, 3, 4-5, 6, 12, 15-18, 31, 76-78, 130, 163-65, 170-72, 175-76, 262-64; and melancholy, 12-13, 29, 74, 79, 189, 206, 211, 232, 251; as metaphor for life, 109-10; and the middle ages, 1-2, 12; and the mind, 6-7, 19, 71-74, 81-82, 104, 117, 119, 136-38, 153, 189-91, 199, 202, 204-8, 210-11, 212-15, 219-21, 231-33, 237, 238; and monarchy, 32, 35-36, 193, 221-22; and pastoral, relationship of, 18, 45, 46, 52, 57, 104-8, 131, 140, 142-49, 240-41, 242; and patience, 88, 209, 210; and playwrighting, 60-61, 69, 89-90, 128-29, 154-58, 191, 207, 225-26, 244-50, 253, 264-70, 272; and predestination, 4, 82, 111-13, 114, 122-25; and Protestantism, 3-7, 10, 13, 20, 111-13, 114, 122-25, 205, 216-17, 260, 270-71, 278; and redemption, 34-35, 36, 44, 50, 62, 76-78, 82-84, 87-89, 100, 106-8, 110-14, 122-28, 149, 151-54, 163, 171-74, 189-92, 222-26, 270; and scientific method, 8, 9-10, 95, 97; and service, 32-35, 58, 61, 69, 96, 105, 107-8, 114, 173, 182-85, 186, 189-90, 196, 208; and the seventeenth century, 8-9, 10-14, 15-18, 41, 50-52, 77, 85, 112-14, 143, 166, 182-85, 194-95, 223; and sexuality, 31, 34, 38-39, 71, 85-86, 96-97, 98, 103, 126, 136, 154-55, 217-18, 224, 233, 238-43, 245-47, 250-51, 252-53, 271, 278; and the sixteenth century, 2-7, 10-12, 15-16, 65, 218-19, 222-26; and slavery, 7, 14, 15, 66-67, 108-9, 170, 173, 182-85, 186, 196; and social abuses, 1-4, 7, 10-11, 12, 13-14, 15-18, 34, 41-43, 65, 77, 85-87, 105-6, 112-13, 114, 182-86, 223, 262-64; and society, 1, 2-3, 7, 10-13, 15-18, 22, 41-43, 61-62, 86-87, 106-7, 165-66, 169, 215-16, 218-19, 265; and the spiritual, 1-2, 3-7, 8, 34, 44, 77, 110-11, 126 (*see* also Christianity); and tempests, 30-31, 80-81, 89, 137, 140, 181, 201, 234; as

vocation, 1, 5, 85; and wages, relationship of, 15, 16, 17, 18, 25, 28, 34, 43, 66-67, 109-10, 143, 265; and warfare, relationship of, 1, 3, 12, 37-38, 39-40, 43-50, 51-53, 68, 99-100, 105, 115-16, 231, 232-37, 242, 244
Lawrence, Judiana, 133
Leavis, F. R., 132
Lee, Maurice, Jr., 66
Leech, Clifford, 229
Leggatt, Alexander, 63, 228, 229
Le Goff, Jacques, 1-2, 22
Levin, Harry, 196
Levin, Richard, 160
Lewalski, Barbara K., 22
Lewis, Anthony J., 91
Lewis, Cynthia, 130
Lief, Madelon, 255, 256
Lindenbaum, Peter, 23, 68, 161
Lis, Catharina, 25, 26
Livingston, Mary L., 162
Lockyer, Roger, 66, 67
Luckyj, Christina, 67
Ludwig, Jay, 161
Luria, Maxwell, 193
Luther, Martin, 3, 4-5, 123
Lyly, John, 161

Macbeth, 29, 35-36, 269
Machiavelli, Niccolò, 52
Mackinnon, Lachlan, 161
Magnusson, A. Lynne, 196
Mannerism, 102, 151, 260-62
Manning, Roger B., 25, 26, 196
Mannoni, Octave, 196
Marcus, Leah, 11, 24, 51, 68
Markels, Julian, 63, 65
Marlowe, Christopher, 178
Marsh, Derick R. C., 132
Marshall, Cynthia, 91, 193
Marston, John, 11
Mary Tudor, 211-12, 224
Masque, 56-57, 173-76, 188, 210-11, 231, 249-50
Matus, Irvin, 277
McBride, Tom, 227

McCanles, Michael, 67
McClure, Norman E., 24
McDonald, Russ, 196
McKenzie, Stanley D., 66
McNamara, Kevin, 194
Measure for Measure, 28, 32, 39
Merchant of Venice, The, 145
Merchant, W. M., 69
Metamorphoses, 256
Micheli, Linda McJ., 227
Midlands Revolt, The, 41
Midsummer Night's Dream, The, 10, 27, 192, 238, 250, 251
Milton, John, 6, 7, 23, 167, 278
Moffet, Robin, 133
Montaigne, Michel de, 19, 26
Montrose, Louis A., 23, 160
More, Sir Thomas, 53
Morgan, Edmund S., 195
Mowat, Barbara A., 130, 182, 196
Muir, Kenneth, 255
Mulcaster, Richard, 265
Mullaney, Steven, 93, 277
Mutability, 29, 41, 104, 131
Myers, Jeffrey R., 276

Nash, Thomas, 8
Neely, Carol T., 159
Neoplatonism, 161, 176
Nevo, Ruth, 91, 92, 196
New Organon, The, 9
Numerology, 148-49
Nuttall, Anthony J., 68

Orgel, Stephen, 193, 194
Ornstein, Robert, 63
Orpheus, 206-7, 228
Othello, 19, 29-32
Ovid, 57, 256-57

Pandosto, 157
Panofsky, Erwin, 159
Parables, Biblical, 2, 5, 44, 110-11, 114, 146
Paris, Bernard, 272, 278
Parliament, 14, 196, 223
Parmigianino, 261

Patterson, Annabel, 10, 24, 263, 276, 277
Paul, Saint, 1, 3
Pearson, D'Orsay W., 197
Pennington, Loren E., 194
Pericles, 20, 21, 36, 57, 60, 62, 64, 71-94, 104, 137, 167, 170, 224, 229, 236, 246, 259, 263, 264, 270, 274
Perkins, William, 7
Peterson, Douglas L., 92, 94, 193, 196
Pettet, E. C., 65
Peyré, Yves, 194
Pierce, Robert B., 195
Pilgrimage to Parnassus, The, 25
Pitcher, John, 91
Plato, 20
Printing, 154-58, 266-68
Proser, Matthew N., 66
Puttenham, George, 55, 68

Rabkin, Norman, 92
Rackin, Phyllis, 67
Radel, Nicholas F., 255, 256
Ralegh, Sir Walter, 50, 51, 52, 68
Rape of Lucrece, The, 267
Return to Parnassus, The, 25
Rhetoric, 167-69, 172
Richard II, 136, 237
Richmond, Hugh M., 228, 229
Riddle, 71-74, 138
Ridley, Jasper, 131
Riemer, A. P., 65, 161
Riggs, David, 264-65, 277
Roberts, Jeanne Addison, 256
Rockett, William, 193
Romano, Julio, 151
Rose, Mary Beth, 255, 257
Rozett, Martha, 4, 22
Rudnytsky, Peter L., 229

Sacks, Elizabeth, 18-19, 26
St. Clare Byrne, Muriel, 228
St. John, Oliver, 14
Saxl, Fritz, 159
Schanzer, Ernest, 64, 140, 159
Schmidgall, Gary, 53, 54, 68, 277

School of Abuse, The, 265
Seiden, Marvin, 197
Selden, Raman, 63
Sejanus, 267
Sen Gupta, S. C., 227
Shakespeare and the Drama, 263
Shakespeare and the Popular Voice, 264
Shakespeare, John, 272
Shakespeare, Richard, 22
Shakespeare, William, 10, 20-21, 22, 53-54, 60, 65, 89-90, 154-58, 191, 207, 225-26, 239, 244-50, 253, 255, 259, 262-75
Shaw, Catherine M., 194
Shearman, John, 260, 261, 276
Sherbo, Arthur, 133
Siegel, Paul N., 25, 63, 278
Simmons, J. L., 66, 67, 278
Simonds, Peggy Muñoz, 128, 131, 133
Skura, Meredith, 132
Slack, Paul, 25
Slights, Camille, 228
Sloth, 6, 7, 8, 10-13, 14, 18, 19-20, 24, 27-29, 32, 34, 36-38, 40, 43, 48, 51, 53-54, 56, 58-59, 74, 75-76, 82-83, 100, 105, 113, 119, 144, 165-67, 171, 200, 233, 242, 260-61, 271
Smith, Hallett, 132, 143, 159, 185, 204
Smith, Jonathan, 159
Socrates, 20
Soellner, Rolf, 68, 69
Soly, Hugo, 25, 26
Sommerville, J. P., 14, 25
Sorge, Thomas, 65
Southampton, Earl of, 54
Speech Act, 73, 165
Spencer, Theodore, 255
Spenser, Edmund, 74, 113
States, Bert O., 63
Stasis, 19-20, 31, 36, 41, 58, 64-65, 81, 86, 119-20, 139-40, 147-48, 150, 153-54, 178, 191, 203-7, 212, 213, 215-16, 240-44, 252, 261, 273
Statute of Artificers (1563), 15

Statute of Laborers (1495), 15
Stir, 20, 29, 30, 31, 38, 64-65, 74, 76-78, 79, 81, 83-84, 86, 88-89, 104, 116-17, 119, 139-40, 147-48, 151, 153-54, 190, 191, 201, 203-8, 213, 215-16, 220-21, 239-44, 246, 252, 261, 273-74
Stoicism, 88
Stone, Lawrence, 12, 24, 51, 67, 68
Summer's Last Will and Testament, 8
Summers, Joseph, 193
Sutherland, James, 133
Swinburne, Algernon Charles, 118

Taylor, Gary, 92, 262-63, 264, 276
Taylor, Michael, 92, 133
Taylor, Thomas, 4, 22, 111
Tempest, The, 9, 14, 19, 20, 36, 107, 163-97, 199, 203, 204, 206, 207, 210, 211, 212-13, 214-15, 222, 225, 231, 232, 239, 254, 259, 264, 271, 272, 274
Thirsk, Joan, 26
Thompson, Ann, 130
Thompson, John O., 130
Thorne, W. B., 91
Time, 140-41, 159, 169-70
Timon of Athens, 36, 53-62, 259, 264, 269-70
Titus Andronicus, 123, 268
Tolstoy, Leo, 263
Tourneur, Cyril, 13, 141
Troilus and Cressida, 115, 132, 192, 267
Traversi, Derek A., 92, 93, 130, 133
Treatise of the Vocations, The, 7
Treaty of London, The, 50
Tricomi, Albert, 11, 24, 25
Twelfth Night, 270
Two Noble Kinsmen, The, 20, 199, 231-57, 259, 274

Uphaus, Robert, 227, 229
Utopia, 165-66, 174, 176

Vagrancy Act, The (1572), 15
Vaughan, Alden T., 195
Venus and Adonis, 53-54, 267
Virgil, 52, 142, 266
Vision of Delight, The, 12

Waith, Eugene M., 64, 255, 256
Walzer, Michael, 5-6, 23
War and Peace, 263
Ward, David, 159
Webster, John, 13
Wells, Stanley, 92, 267, 277
Wentworth, Thomas, 14
Wheeler, Richard, 93, 268, 273, 277, 278
Whitaker, Alexander, 195
White, R. S., 93, 160
Wickham, Glynne, 194
Willbern, David, 264, 277
William Shakespeare's Comedies, Histories, and Tragedies, 268
Winwood, Ralph, 11
Wilson, Richard, 24, 65, 67, 114, 132, 160
Wilson, Sir Thomas, 3, 51, 52
Winter's Tale, The, 19, 20, 64, 120, 135-62, 167, 178, 224, 259, 272, 274
Work (*see* Labor)
Works of Benjamin Jonson, The, 266
Wrightson, Keith, 16, 17, 22, 24, 65
Wyatt, Sir Thomas, 262

Yachnin, Paul, 278
Yeats, William Butler, 140
Young, Alan R., 228
Young, David, 140